"Browse any bookstore and you'll find dozens of books about these personages, but no historian has linked them into a coherent narrative as splendidly as Brandon."

—David Bowman, *Bookforum*

"[Brandon's] research is impeccable, and the connections she makes are deft and unexpected."

—A. S. Hamrah, *The Boston Book Review*

"[Ruth Brandon] lands with insouciant ease on many fertile connections, rather like a Surrealist inspired by the magic dictates of the subconscious."—Frances Spalding, *Daily Telegraph*

"Swift and punchy to a fault . . . This account of the flawed and ambitious group of Surrealists is enthralling, for despite their many failures, the questions the Surrealists sought to raise are more relevant today than ever."—*Publishers Weekly*

"Deliciously gossipy . . . By concentrating on personal chemistries, Brandon . . . shows how a volatile dialectic bound the two halves of Europe together."—Lawrence Osborne, *Salon*

"An interesting and acute book."

—Martin Gayford, *The Sunday Telegraph* (London)

"Fresh . . . witty and vivacious . . . an entertaining read."

—*Booklist* (starred review)

"Engaging . . . well told . . . An unusually coherent and readable map of the Surrealist movement."—*The Washington Times*

"A fascinating look at an art movement . . . Brandon chronicles events that often seem to come from the pages of a novel."
—David B. Hinton, *Bookpage*

"Witty . . . engaging . . . a suggestive and instructive book."
—Peter Ackroyd, *The Times* (London)

"Brandon . . . explores the aesthetics, politics, and psychology of Surrealism by unraveling the complex personal histories of the movement's key players . . . marvelous."—*Kirkus Reviews*

"Riveting."—Marina Benjamin, *The Sunday Express* (London)

SURREAL
LIVES

RUTH BRANDON

SURREAL LIVES

THE SURREALISTS

1917–1945

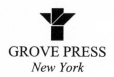

GROVE PRESS
New York

First published by Macmillan, an imprint of Macmillan Publishers Ltd., in
London in 1999

Published simultaneously in Canada
Printed in the United States of America

FIRST GROVE PRESS PAPERBACK EDITION

Library of Congress Cataloging-in-Publication Data

Brandon, Ruth.
    Surreal lives : the surrealists, 1917–1945 / Ruth Brandon.
      p.   cm.
    Includes bibliographical references and index.
    ISBN 0-8021-3727-X (pbk.)
    1. Surrealism. 2. Arts, Modern—20th century. I. Title.
NX456.5.S8B745   1999
709'.04'063—dc21   99-25492
                                         CIP

Grove Press
841 Broadway
New York, NY 10003

00 01 02 03 10 9 8 7 6 5 4 3 2 1

In memoriam
Alison Fairlie
Odette de Mourgues

ACKNOWLEDGEMENTS

I have received help from a great many people during the preparation of this book. I should like to thank the Leverhulme Trust for their timely support. I am also extremely grateful to Stephen Bann, Nick Bullock, Carole Callow, Marc Dachy, David and Judy Gascoyne, Richard Hearne, Nick and Ayla Humphrey, Caradoc King, Jan Marsh, Mark Polizzotti, Anthony Rudolf, Marc and Sylvie Sator, Elaine Showalter, Philip Steadman, Tanya Stobbs, Frank Whitford, Ann Simpson of the Scottish National Gallery of Modern Art, and the staff of the library of the Museum of Modern Art, New York.

CONTENTS

LIST OF ILLUSTRATIONS

1. *Les Mamelles de Tirésias* (Bibliothèque nationale)
2. André Breton and Louis Aragon, WWI (archive Sylvie Sator)
3. Jacques Vaché
4. Tristan Tzara
5. Hugo Ball and Emmy Hennings
6. Hans Arp, Tristan Tzara and Hans Richter
7. R. Mutt's *Fountain* (Alfried Stieglitz: Philadelphia Museum of Art, The Louise and Walter Arensberg Collection)
8. Duchamp's Large Glass (Philadelphia Museum of Art, Bequest of Katherine S. Dreier)
9. *Raising Dust* (Man Ray, 1920: ©Man Ray Trust/ADAGP, Paris and DACS, London 1998)
10. Francis Picabia
11. Arthur Cravan
12. *Américaine* (Francis Picabia, © ADAGP, Paris and DACS, London 1998)
13. Rrose Sélavy (Man Ray, 1921: Philadelphia Museum of Art: the Samuel S. White 3d and Vera White Collection. © Man Ray Trust/ADAGP, Paris and DACS, London 1998.)
14. Man Ray and Marcel Duchamp (British Film Institute)
15. Erik Satie and Francis Picabia (British Film Institute)
16. L.H.O.O.Q. (Francis Picabia, © ADAGP, Paris, and DACS, London 1998)
17. Tzara, Simone Breton, André Breton (archive Sylvie Sator)

PREFACE

MENTION THE WORD 'surrealism' today, and certain visual images spring immediately to mind. Man Ray's glass tears, Magritte's rain of bowler-hatted men, are common cultural currency, gracing a thousand neckties, umbrellas, coffee cups and keyrings. Salvador Dalí's waxed moustaches and soft watches are familiar to millions who have never seen his paintings. And images such as these inevitably lead to certain assumptions about Surrealism: that it was primarily concerned with the visual arts; that it was about jokes; that it was designed with a beady eye to the market.

Nothing could be further from the truth. Surrealism began among poets whose aim was to create a revolution, both political and artistic, combining the visions of Freud, Marx, Sade and Lautréamont. Jokes always formed part of the mix, but the movement's leader, André Breton, was a man of the utmost gravity – indeed, almost totally without humour – to whom commercialism was anathema. And although the group always included some painters, and concerned itself with paint-ing, it was not until fairly late that the visual arts came to occupy a dominant place in the Surrealist canon. *Surreal Lives* is, in part, the story of this shift, both in the movement itself and in public perception of it.

It is about a group of people rather than a movement – the *ists* rather than the *ism*. But they can hardly be separated. Each revolutionary model, including Surrealism, has its iron rules, which take on a quality of inevitability. However, despite their patina of impersonality these rules are in fact thought up by particular people for particular reasons. In the case of Surreal-ism the theorist was André Breton, and the movement closely reflected the peculiarities of his own life. Thus, black humour and willed outrageousness were touted as Surrealist qualities

3

par excellence, though neither came naturally to Breton. Why? Because they had characterized his beloved friend Jacques Vaché; and Surrealism was, among other things, Breton's search for a new Vaché after the latter's early death. Other Surrealist rules reflected Breton's own character – his asceticism, his discomfort with any but the outsider's role, his reliance upon external forms and rituals to impose meaning upon life's shapelessness.

Of course Breton was not the only strong character among the Surrealists – far from it. Marcel Duchamp, Man Ray, Louis Aragon, Paul Eluard, Salvador Dalí, Tristan Tzara, Francis Picabia – it would be hard to name more outsize a collection of individualities. Yet all except Duchamp at some point accepted Breton's leadership, and only left the movement at the cost of great personal trauma. What was his secret?

The nature of charisma is always elusive, and in Breton's case particularly so. His charm was legendary. Even those who deeply disagreed with him hesitated to risk exclusion from his company. Yet his qualities, on the face of it, were not particularly attractive: he was rigid, bullying, humourless and unforgiving. Perhaps the attraction lay in his irresistible urge to shape and frame. The creation of a revolutionary movement demands an unusual capacity to take the historical view and impose a form on events. The charismatic embraces us within this life view; so comforting and consoling is the fact of that embrace that we accept it, even with reservations. Within lies certainty; outside, all is chaos.

Such, in politics, is the stuff of totalitarianism: the subordination of life to dogma. Breton, so passionate about freedom, both personal and artistic, was totalitarian in his impulses, a dictator in the age of dictators. Can these two impulses – to freedom and to total control – possibly be reconciled? This is the clash at the heart of the Surrealists' story.

Anglophones generally tend to pragmatism: when the

demands of life conflict with those of dogma, life wins and dogma is rearranged to fit. *Surreal Lives* examines the opposite extreme, the shoehorning of life into an almost impossible theoretical framework. In the end the trick proved too hard: the erstwhile Surrealists spun off in their different orbits leaving Breton in the brooding isolation of his uncompromised integrity. But by then Surrealism had given us a new way of looking at the world.

CHAPTER ONE

A BAS GUILLAUME

THE WORD 'SURREALISM' first appeared in Paris during the summer of 1917. It was coined by the poet Guillaume Apollinaire. That summer saw the first performance of his play *Les Mamelles de Tirésias*, staged under the auspices of the review *SIC* (Sons, Idées, Couleurs).

The performance was announced for Sunday, 24 June, at the tiny Salle Maubel in Montmartre. André Breton, a young poet then serving as a medical auxiliary at the Val de Grâce hospital near the Sorbonne, urged his friend Jacques Vaché, who was due for some leave, to meet him there. Vaché agreed; he would try to arrive in time for the show, 'which I suspect will begin a little late perhaps'.[1]

So it did. By the time the curtain rose the audience had been sitting in the tiny theatre for more than two hours, with nothing to watch except a curtain of a blue so brilliant as to be almost offensive. Their impatience was becoming deafening. Madame Rachilde, self-styled queen of literary Paris, and no friend of Apollinaire, yelled above the hubbub: 'Enough of that blue!' Finally, however, the moment came. The curtain rose, a fat woman entered and unbuttoned her blouse to reveal her breasts: two gas-filled balloons. She pulled them out and flung them into the audience. The first Surrealist drama was under way.

In fact the term *Surrealism* had first appeared six weeks earlier, on 18 May, in Apollinaire's programme note for the ballet *Parade*: scenario by Cocteau, choreography by Massine, décor by Picasso and music by Erik Satie (scored for typewriters, sirens, airplane propellers, Morse tickers, lottery wheels and two pianos). This new alliance of all the arts, Apollinaire announced, had 'given rise, in *Parade*, to a kind of Surrealism. In my view this is just the first of many manifestations of the New Spirit now abroad.' He added characteristically, 'We may expect it to bring about profound changes in our arts and manners through universal joyfulness.'[2]

Joyfulness, alas, was far from universal. In the embattled atmosphere of wartime France, Apollinaire's quenchless appetite for the new was not widely shared. Xenophobia reigned. Modernism, Cubism and their ilk were perceived as some kind of suspicious German-Jewish conspiracy. *Parade* was tarred with a traitorous, dreyfusard brush, and consigned to oblivion.

Apollinaire, however, pleased with his new coining, was unwilling to abandon it. He took the opportunity of his own play to air it once more. The piece, as he freely admitted, though as yet unstaged, was not new. It had been written (all but the prologue and the last scene of the second act) as long ago as 1903. Nevertheless, the new adjective was pressed into service to define 'an artistic tendency which, if it is no more new than anything else under the sun, has nevertheless not been used to describe any artistic or literary credo or affirmation'. He went on to define this tendency by means of an example: 'When man wanted to imitate walking, he invented the wheel, which does not look like a leg. Without knowing it, he was a Surrealist.'[3]

'The décor', Apollinaire instructed his designer, Serge Férat, 'will be the air in the theatre. If you like, on the night before, it could be given a Zanzibarian appearance by a strip of paper to look like roofs.'[4] The author announced that his drama would discuss 'a vital question ... the problem of repopulation' – a subject offering ample opportunity for buffoonery. The opening joke was one he had long wished to stage. The jettisoned balloons transformed the leading lady from Thérèse (who won't let her husband have his way because 'I am a feminist and I don't recognise man's authority') into Tirésias, a member of the very gender whose authority she doesn't recognize. Great play was made with these eponymous accessories, which doubled as nipples, contraceptives or rubber teats. When a (real) baby began to cry, a wit in the gallery urged Tirésias to 'Pass it the tits! It wants some milk!'[5]

Unfortunately, though full of wit, the play was entirely devoid of structure. Soon the theatre was in uproar once more – so much so that nobody seemed to notice the young officer in English uniform who entered the stalls at the end of the first act, pulled out his revolver, and prepared to discharge it into the audience. In the nick of time another young man, a studious-looking fellow with thick auburn hair, dashed up and dissuaded his friend (for evidently they were acquainted) from his murderous intentions. This tangential irruption was to become part of Surrealism's legend. Whether or not the play was surreal, it was thus an occasion for Surrealism, the movement which was to take its name from Apollinaire's coining.

Did the incident really occur? Perhaps it was a purely imagined act. No one except André Breton, the auburn-haired young man, remembered this episode; the other participant, the 'officer' (who was Jacques Vaché and not English at all) never gave his side of the story. The only certainty is that, years later, Breton defined 'the simplest Surrealist act' as 'going into the street, revolver in hand, and shooting at random into the crowd'.[6] Not that he himself would ever have done any such thing. But Vaché might – or so Breton liked to think; and – perhaps – Vaché really had.

*

Apollinaire at this time was the undisputed leader of the avant-garde. His collection *Alcoöls*, published in 1913, had established him as a gifted and original poet, but this was not the only talent of this complex and ambiguous man. Perhaps even more remarkable was his faultless taste. He followed his rather long nose, and (for reasons he could not always articulate) it led him to the truffles. He was, said Max Jacob, who knew everyone – who had known Picasso since his first arrival in Paris in 1901 – 'an improviser'.[7]

It was true; but few have improvised to greater effect. He and his friend Alfred Jarry had been the earliest promoters of the naïve painter Henri Rousseau, whom Apollinaire immediately nicknamed *le douanier* (he was in fact an employee of the municipal toll service). Rousseau had been exhibiting for years, but Apollinaire was the first to sense that something extraordinary might be lurking behind the old man's naïvetés. And Rousseau was but one of many such discoveries. Apollinaire was Picasso's earliest champion in the art world. He, almost alone, welcomed the manifesto of the Italian Futurists; he supported Derain, Picabia, Duchamp, Chagall and Chirico. Painting (he noted after a dinner in Picasso's studio) was 'a wonderful language that no literature can describe, for words are made in advance, alas!'[8] What was this New Spirit he now so eagerly proposed? No one, not even Apollinaire, could be sure. But he would know it when he saw it. He was, in a friend's wonderful phrase, 'situated at the centre of his time like a spider at the centre of its web'.[9]

He was universally loved. The sight of his tall, rotund yet nimble figure, his large, smiling face with its small features and close-set eyes, was a pleasure in itself. Fernande Olivier, Picasso's mistress at the time when the two were intimate friends, remembered his 'little mouth, which he often seemed to make deliberately smaller when he spoke, as though to give more bite to what he was saying'.[10] As if by osmosis, his admirers picked up certain habits and gestures, so that long after his death a particular mannerism or phrase could be traced back to him. Thus, a certain slightly affected way he had of laughing behind his hand as he spoke became fashionable during the glory days of the Boeuf sur le Toit nightclub, whose habitués attributed it to Jean Cocteau. His authoritative way of closing all discussion by pronouncing: '*C'est une chose forte belle*', given weight by the slight prolongation of the final double l, was passed to the Surrealists by way of André Breton.[11] Immortality takes many forms, and Apollinaire remained as various after his death as he had been in life. 'How delightful he was!' remembered his friend André Billy. 'Whenever I saw him I wanted to rush up to him and laugh. Life was suddenly wonderful. It was so difficult for his friends – every one of them wanted Apollinaire all to himself.'[12]

And Apollinaire wanted them all.

Je souhaite dans ma maison
Une femme ayant sa raison
Un chat passant parmi les livres
Des amis en toute saison
Sans lesquels je ne peux pas vivre.[13]

In my house I hope to find
A woman of sound mind
Among the books a cat
Friends of every kind
What's life without all that?

Among these friends was the young man, André Breton, who had been involved in the disturbance (and possibly prevented a massacre of the audience) at the performance of *Les Mamelles de Tirésias*. Breton had helped with the play's preface, and it was he who had thought of the line about walking and the wheel.

Breton and Apollinaire had at this time known each other for two years. In 1915 Breton, then a conscript in the artillery, had written to Apollinaire, enclosing some of his own poems. He was nineteen years old, and officially a medical student, though inevitably his studies were in abeyance for the duration of the war. His father, after a variety of jobs (gendarme, commercial traveller) was now assistant manager of a small glassworks in Pantin on the outskirts of Paris, and it was intended that André should complete the family's rise to the ranks of the comfortable bourgeoisie. But medicine never really interested him, any more than did material prospects. Since the momentous day a teacher at his lycée had read to the class a poem by Mallarmé, poetry had filled his thoughts. To be a poet was all he wanted.

Replying to Breton's first letter, Apollinaire wrote: 'I'm obviously in excellent company in your circle, and I'm grateful to you for thinking of me. Your lines show a remarkable talent.'[14] Over the next three months, the two maintained a copious correspondence. 'I'm delighted to write to you,' Apollinaire assured his new young friend, whom he addressed as *Mon cher poète*. 'Ask me whatever questions you want, and my letters will be the replies.'

Breton took him at his word. He wanted to know about Apollinaire's taste in books (he liked catalogues, medical journals, fairy tales, grammars, fragments of poets and travel-books, American westerns and detective stories, but 'I don't spend much time reading, especially not new books'), about his painter friends ('Picasso is working in Paris, progressing in his art. Matisse, in my view, is standing still, though enormously talented. As for Derain, he's a soldier like me, he drives a tractor in a heavy battery, and the guns have made his wonderful spirit even purer, if that were possible . . .'), about his own poetry. Its uneven form, Apollinaire explained, was an attempt to reflect the unexpectedness of life itself.

Yet the notice pinned to Apollinaire's front door read: PLEASE DON'T WASTE MY TIME. Everyone may want to know you, but time is finite: you can't encompass the world. How was it, then, that he was immediately prepared to spend so much of this precious commodity on a young man he had never met?

This was not Breton's first such conquest. The previous

year he had struck up a similar friendship with Paul Valéry, the grand old man of French poetry. Breton passionately identified with M. Teste, the ultra-cerebral protagonist of Valéry's *An Evening with M. Teste*. That had appeared fifteen years earlier, and Valéry had published nothing since – a fact which only added to his glamour in the young man's eyes: the abrupt, unexplained decision to renounce one's gift (as Rimbaud had done, as Marcel Duchamp was to do) engendered a mythic gloss he would always find irresistible. When, in 1921, Valéry began to write once more, the effect was instant and fatal: the spell broke; Breton lost interest. But that was still far in the future, inconceivable. For the young André, the unbelievable immediate fact was this: Valéry – Valéry himself and no one else – opened the door, showed him up the stairs, welcomed him to the house in the Rue Villejust where wonderful Impressionist canvases fought for space on the walls and overlapped the mirrors.[15]

And so the pattern was established which would persist until he died. André Breton was someone people wanted to know. His friendship, his good opinion, were important to them.

He was a striking and already somewhat intimidating figure. He had thick, wavy hair brushed back from his forehead, heavy, handsome features, a full-lipped mouth with an unusually prominent lower lip, and jade-green eyes. 'Breton didn't smile, but he sometimes laughed,' observed Adrienne Monnier, proprietor of the bookshop Aux amis des livres in the Rue de l'Odéon, the rendezvous of all the younger poets and writers. His laugh was 'short and sardonic . . . It welled up when he spoke without disturbing the features of his face, like a woman who's careful of her beauty.'[16] Occasionally he wore spectacles with heavy tortoiseshell rims, but lenses (an acquaintance realized) of clear glass. Why? 'If I told you, you wouldn't believe me,' he confessed. 'It's in memory of a grammatical example: "noses were made to hold glasses." So I wear glasses.'[17] He spoke slowly, some thought affectedly; 'words fell from his lips like drops of syrup'.[18] He was unnervingly self-possessed, certain of his own opinions and devastatingly unmoved by what others thought of them. Mlle Monnier often argued with Breton about poetry: they invariably disagreed, even about poets they both liked. 'He had very particular views which disconcerted me. He was much more "advanced" than me. I felt very reactionary.'[19] She remembered him leaning against the wall with a 'fixed, panic-stricken stare . . . awaiting his orders from the black god, the Invisible One'.[20]

It was a potent observation. Breton would spend his life under orders; his constant struggle would be their decipherment. His black god, the source of these commandments, was no less than the problem of life itself. '*Il faut changer la vie,*' said Breton's poetic hero, Arthur Rimbaud. 'We must change life', and Breton agreed with him.

In 1912, the year before Adrienne Monnier observed Breton at the Rue de l'Odéon, an extraordinary letter by Rimbaud was published in the *Nouvelle Revue Française*, the leading Paris literary magazine. When he wrote it, in 1871, Rimbaud was not quite seventeen – the same age as Breton when he read it. The true poet, said Rimbaud, must be a *seer*. And how was this to be achieved? 'By the unchaining of all the senses.' ('*Le dérèglement de tous les sens.*') 'Every form of love, suffering and madness . . . He needs all his faith, all his superhuman strength, to become the greatest invalid, the greatest criminal, the greatest unfortunate – the supreme Savant!'[21]

Three years later, Rimbaud abandoned poetry and France for gun-running in Africa. His words, however, remained; and in 1912, when this now-famous letter was published, it was easy to fall under their spell. Art might change life. Why not? A century and a half of French history underpinned this belief. As Sartre was to point out (somewhat smugly, but nonetheless

16

truly),[22] the French intellectual occupies a position quite different from his lonely counterpart in Britain or America, condemned to isolated struggle and individualism. He is part of a recognized group, a power in the land. It was, after all, intellectuals who set the revolution upon its way; and a little later, in 1830, a group of poets, the young Romantics, precipitated yet another revolution, unseating yet another monarch. As a result (noted Sartre), 'the class in power ... still does us the honour of fearing us a little (a very little); it treats us tactfully'.

Change was certainly in the air. In Russia the Bolsheviks plotted revolution, in Britain the trades unions organized and suffragettes threw themselves in front of racehorses, in Italy the Futurists trumpeted the coming machine age, in Germany the Kaiser grappled with Bismarck's militaristic heritage. And in France? In France the Commune had come – and gone: hence Rimbaud's despair. Politics was no longer interesting. All the energies that elsewhere went into politics, in France were concentrated on the arts. Paris, as Gertrude Stein remarked, was where the twentieth century was happening – in painting, in writing, in music, and (with the arrival in 1913 of Diaghilev's Ballets Russes) with the triumphant amalgam of all these. It was therefore natural that, being who he was, where he was, at this extraordinary moment in this extraordinary place, Breton should see the answer to his question in poetry. Poets, in Paris, were figures seriously to be reckoned with. He would change life, and poetry would be his weapon.

The unrelenting struggle this entailed would occupy the rest of Breton's life. Both the life and the man possessed a sense of clarity and purpose at once intimidating and (while the current swept you along) exhilarating. Friends either shared this dream, or ceased being friends. A few endured. Most were shed along the way, found wanting and forever abandoned. Georges Ribemont-Dessaignes, one of this larger group, remarked on Breton's 'strange integrity which enabled him to distinguish different levels of humanity and gave ideas, as it were, a solid existence'. Twenty years and a war after their falling-out, Ribemont-Dessaignes tried to contact Breton in order to make a radio programme. He did so with difficulty; finally they met, the ice was broken, the programme arranged. 'I had hardly got back home when a telegraph-boy rang the bell. *"Certainly not! You said this here, you said that there, you wrote that article..."*[23] The goal was so clear, the prize so immeasurable. What could compare with it? Never mere friendship. Breton ploughed on, his erstwhile companions churned in his wake. The struggle took precedence, always.

*

In August 1914, poetry was abandoned. All the young men of Europe prepared themselves to kill or be killed.

Breton, predictably, loathed the army. He was called up in February 1915, and sent to an artillery training camp in Brittany. Awkward, aloof, unremittingly intellectual, he hated most of all the mindlessness of his new life. 'Thought fights a losing battle on the parade-ground,' he observed[24] – hardly surprising, the parade-ground's function being, precisely, to stamp thought out. Fortunately this posting did not last long. He was sent to Nantes as a medical auxiliary, which meant he would not come under fire nor be subject to drilling. Even so, the army was hell. The correspondence with Apollinaire, which he now began, was part of an effort to spend as much time as possible away from it, if only inside his head.

Apollinaire, who was by then at the front and under fire, did not share Breton's gloomy view of army life. Quite the contrary. 'Imagine my pleasure at going back to Nice in uniform,' he wrote soon after he had enlisted. 'I opened the eyes of a good many people and here I am again, dead-beat after my leave . . . I am very well and think soldiering is my true profession. I like it very much.'[25]

Apollinaire? Enlisted? Once again, this extraordinary man had astonished all his friends. Not only was he in his mid-thirties when war broke out, he was not even a French national. Born Wilhelm Apollinaris de Kostrowitzky in Rome, he was the son of a disreputable Polish aristocrat and (he liked to hint) a cardinal (though more probably the scion of a prominent Swiss Catholic family). What, then, was he doing trying to enlist in the French army?

But birth, though of some administrative importance, is but a fleeting moment, done with as soon as experienced. Apollinaire's home, the place where he had been educated and lived all his life, was France. And there was the rub; for this kingpin of French culture lived in constant terror of rejection by his adopted country.

> Je suis Guillaume Apollinaire
> Dit d'un nom slave par vrai nom
> Ma vie est triste toute entière
> Un écho répond toujours non
> Lorsque je dis un prière

> I am Guillaume Apollinaire
> But my real name is Slav
> My life is a sad thing
> No says the echo
> Whenever I pray

Apollinaire's fear of rejection was not entirely irrational. It had first become acute in 1909, on the occasion of the theft of the Mona Lisa from the Louvre. The poet had a ne'er-do-well friend who, some time previously, actually had stolen various Iberian and Phoenician statuettes from the Louvre, two of which had been bought by Apollinaire's friend Picasso. This man, who occasionally worked as Apollinaire's secretary, now took the opportunity to sell his story to the press in return for anonymity. The obvious implication was that the same group had committed this new and greater crime. Apollinaire and Picasso, terrified, spent a fruitless evening wandering round Paris with a suitcase containing the statuettes, vainly seeking an opportunity to fling them into the Seine unobserved. They failed, and furtively abandoned their booty at a newspaper office. Shortly after this, Apollinaire, suspect by association, was arrested and thrown into prison. The police seemed determined to convict him, though he knew nothing whatever about the Mona Lisa. '[They] did everything they could to justify their action; they cross-examined my concierge, the neighbours, asked if I brought in young girls, or little boys, and I don't know what else.'[26] Terrified that he might be deported, he called upon Picasso to attest his innocence. But to Apollinaire's horror, his friend, who was also an alien and also afraid of expulsion, refused to help. Confronted with Apollinaire, he would not even admit he knew him.

Eventually other friends procured the poet's release and got the charge dismissed; but the terror of that time – his arrest, the police search of his apartment, his days in the grim Santé prison – would never be forgotten. When war was declared, and Picasso retired discreetly to the Midi, Apollinaire's one aim was to be granted French nationality so that he might prove himself the most patriotic possible Frenchman: a desire reinforced, in the view of one friend, by a hankering after those certainties of objective form and classical formula which he himself had done so much to break, 'the expression, in another sphere, of all the traditions and instincts he had suppressed in life and in literary form'.[27]

Friends tried to dissuade him. They invited him to join them in Switzerland or Spain for the duration; even if he stayed in France, there was no need to fight. Nationality apart, he was already past the age of conscription. Finally, however, an unhappy love affair spurred him to action. On holiday in Nice at the end of 1914 he fell hopelessly and entirely under the spell of Louise de Coligny-Chatillon, an accomplished flirt and tease, whose behaviour finally drove him to take the plunge. He went before a recruiting board, which accepted him. 'My dearest Lou,' he wrote. 'Tomorrow I leave for the 38th regiment of field artillery at Nîmes, where I shall write to you. My application to the recruiting board was rash. I had to join up yesterday. That is why I was so terribly sad today and why you felt that something unusual had happened.'[28]

But he was not sad long, despite his Lou's continued heartless behaviour; for army life suited him wonderfully. He tremendously enjoyed living with the other men and feeling himself 'one of the boys'. From Nîmes some time later he wrote to his friend Paul Léautaud:

> I am not getting any thinner here in spite of the violent exercise, in fact it has been decided that my constitution is 'very good'. I am in the instruction squad for corporals, which means that I work three times harder than other soldiers. Every day polishing galore, theory more than galore, manoeuvres on foot, sabre, musket, revolver, horse management, riding, gymnastics, and a reasoned, practical and thorough study of the 75, which is a beautiful weapon, as beautiful, strong and sweet, I think, as one of my poems.[29]

Even arrival at the front was not enough to shatter this rosy vision, despite the conditions.

> The woods are nothing but a swamp, we live like Crusoe on his island . . . We've begun well. We eat outside and the men have made a tiny garden, with pansies and daisies and inscriptions . . . I don't have a blanket. They didn't give me one at Nîmes and I haven't found one to buy. If I survive

this damp, with only my footwarmer, I shall be amazingly healthy . . . Our captain is very bright, he's a professor at the Polytechnique, so he knows what he's doing . . .[30]

Bombardment found him resolutely upbeat: 'It's Obus-Roi here,' he reported (referring, of course, to *Ubu-Roi*, the play by his old friend Alfred Jarry).[31] He maintained a vigorous correspondence, trying as far as possible to keep his career going, and even finding time to write a book of poems, *Case d'armons*, which he published in an edition of twenty-five produced in purple ink on his battery's mimeograph machine. His powers of invention, his delight in novelty and fun, had evidently not deserted him. He was now experimenting with *calligrammes*, in which the words are arranged to form a picture that is part of the poem. Even under fire, the New Spirit was unquenched.

The pleasures of being at the front, however, carried with them certain occupational hazards. In March 1916, a piece of shrapnel buried itself in Apollinaire's head. One moment he was leaning against a tree trunk reading the *Mercure de France*, the next, though he had felt hardly a thing, the page in front of him was covered in blood. His army career was over.

At first the wound, though severe, did not appear to have caused any permanent damage. The shrapnel, or most of it, was removed, and the poet seemed to be recovering. But then an increasing paralysis set in, and it was decided he would have to be trepanned in order to relieve pressure on his brain. 'Come and see me,' he wrote Breton, who was just then in Paris on leave. Breton did so on 10 May, the day after the operation. It was the first time he had met Apollinaire in the flesh. The invalid appeared 'sad and feeble', reported Breton. He tried to impress his young visitor by chatting about poetry. 'It was very touching. He still can't write.'[32]

He was indeed much changed. The day before the operation, despite his paralysis, he had been his usual genial self, laughing and joking. But afterwards was another story. He became gloomy and irascible. His large face, crowned by its bandage and deprived of its jovial wit, seemed unprecedentedly heavy; his figure, always pleasantly stout, ran to fat; he shunned company. 'Please don't come and see me, I couldn't stand the upset,' he implored his fiancée, Madeleine Pagès, who had succeeded Lou in his affections – he for whom visitors had always been an unfailing source of delight and interest. 'And don't send anyone, people I don't know are too much for me.'[33] His latest book, the fantastical semi-autobiography *Le Poète assassiné*, had just appeared. The title seemed only too apposite.

But he was not dead yet, and some months later appeared somewhat recovered. With the help of friends he found a job in (of all places!) the censor's office, which would provide a salary without taking up too much time and energy. Even the abuse aroused by *Parade* and *Tirésias* did not dampen his spirits. 'All these literary storms leave me cold – I've seen too much of real death for that,' he told a friend. 'My only worry is that the fuss will come to the attention of my boss . . . who doesn't like scandal, and I don't relish the prospect of being sent to my regiment in Béziers as an instructor.'[34]

Fortunately this did not happen; and newly married (not to Madeleine, but red-haired Jacqueline, the subject of his last wonderful poem *La Jolie Rousse*) and installed in his old apartment at 202 Boulevard Saint-Germain, his busy and sociable life resumed where it had been set down before the war so rudely interrupted it. 'I am at your disposal any time,' he assured his *cher poète* in April 1917. 'I think I've already told you that I'm home to friends around 5 o'clock.'[35]

Breton, who had now been posted to the Val de Grâce hospital in Paris following a stint among shell-shock victims at Saint-Dizier, needed little urging. Almost every day until

Apollinaire's death eighteen months later he visited his mentor, either at his apartment or at the Café de Flore just opposite, where Apollinaire held court on Tuesdays, just as he always had.

*

The André Breton who became Apollinaire's close companion in Paris in the spring of 1916 was a very different person from the young man who first wrote to him a year earlier. The intervening months had been momentous, setting Breton on a path which was to colour the rest of his life – the path which led to Surrealism.

The first important event was his meeting with Jacques Vaché, the young officer with the revolver at *Les Mamelles de Tirésias*. This encounter was to transform Breton's life. Not long after Vaché's early death he wrote: 'In literature, I fell successively under the spell of Rimbaud, Jarry, Apollinaire, Nouveau, Lautréamont, but it is to Jacques Vaché that I owe the most.'[36]

Yet Vaché's literary legacy hardly exists. Whatever he might have become, the fact remains: he did not live to become it. As Breton himself once said, Vaché's good fortune was to have produced nothing. His life's work amounted to a couple of sketches, a handful of letters. And even these, divorced from the halo of legend surrounding them and read in the cold light of day, seem unexceptional. A thousand very young men might write such letters. But, for Breton, Jacques Vaché was as far as possible from being one of a thousand young men. 'The time I spent with him at Nantes in 1916 seemed almost enchanted,' he wrote. 'I shall never forget it, and although I still meet people I am drawn to, I know I shall never abandon myself to anyone in quite that way again.'[37]

In short, Vaché was the love of Breton's life. As to whether or not this love was sexual, it is impossible to say. If so it triggered only guilt and defensiveness. Breton had a horror of homosexuality – the more bizarre considering the uninhibited circles in which he lived, and the cult of sexual frankness he initiated. This distaste, and its irrational nature, are clear from his contributions to the investigations of sex held among the Surrealists during 1928 and 1932:

MAN RAY: I don't see any great physical distinction between the love of a man for a woman and homosexuality. It is the emotional ideas of homosexuals which have always separated me from them: emotional relations between men have always seemed to me worse than between men and women.

QUENEAU: I find these emotional relations equally acceptable in both cases.

BRETON: Are you a homosexual, Queneau?

QUENEAU: No. Can we hear Aragon's view of homosexuality?

ARAGON: Homosexuality seems to me to be a sexual inclination like any other . . .

BRETON: I am absolutely opposed to continuing the discussion of this subject. If this promotion of homosexuality carries on, I will leave this meeting forthwith . . .[38]

But whatever the nature of the love between Breton and Vaché, its existence is undeniable, at least on Breton's side. The emotion glows through the extraordinary introduction he wrote for the first edition of Vaché's *Lettres de guerre*, in 1924. 'I have seen him covered by a breastplate, covered is not the word, he was the clear sky. He shone with a jewelled waterfall at his neck, I think it was the Amazon, which still waters Peru . . .'[39] To the end of his life, Breton remained enchanted. In an essay entitled 'Trente ans après' ('Thirty Years Later'), introducing a new edition of the *Lettres*, he describes a wonderful recurring dream. In it, he realizes that, in spite of all that has happened, 'Jacques Vaché is not dead ... He is suddenly beside me, I don't know how, giving me his news, I recognise him in a doorway, I use some unknown, all-powerful password which instantly removes all doubt as to his identity. And once again we freely share that sombre gaiety of his, which marked me so strongly. He disposes of my questions before I can formulate them; they seem so *naïve*. Obviously I am the only one moved by all this (or at least, only I fail to hide it) . . .'[40] Elsewhere Breton tells how, in the most unlikely places – in a heap of sand by a canal, in a bar in the Nevada desert – he becomes suddenly certain that his friend is just around the corner, waiting to step into the scene.

The two met in Nantes, Vaché's home town, in February 1916. Breton, then just twenty, was a medical auxiliary, serving in the neurological centre there; Vaché, a year older, was hospitalized with a calf wound. In civilian life he had been an art student. He passed the time in hospital drawing little postcards and sketches, marking time till he could get out and plunge back into life.

The impression given by Breton is that he was always too occupied with the inner life to be much concerned with the outer shell. Vaché was just the opposite. His life was a series of roles, or perhaps out-takes – for like many of his generation, he was enchanted by the cinema, then so new and exciting. He was part-Irish and liked to be taken for English; he sported a monocle, wore exaggeratedly English-style clothes, and sometimes even spoke with an English accent. (His job in the army was to act as interpreter between the French and English forces: this was how he had come by his British uniform.) He would sign himself variously *Harry James* or *J.T.H.* (for Jacques Tristan Hilar) or *Jean-Michel Strogoff*. In the street he might acknowledge you or not; he might dress as an airman, a lieutenant of hussars, a doctor. He shared a room with a girl who was introduced only by her first name: Louise. Although he liked to call her 'my mistress', he denied any sexual relations between them, affirming that they simply slept side by side. When Breton visited, Louise sat silently in a corner. At five she served tea, and Vaché kissed her hand. From the front (a foxhole in a ruined village) he wrote: 'My dream just now is to wear a red shirt, a red cravat and high boots – and to belong to a pointless Chinese secret society in Australia.'[41] 'What a film I'm going to star in! . . . I shall be a trapper, or thief, or explorer, or hunter, or miner, or caver – Bar de l'Arizona (*Whisky – gin and Mixed?*) and great forests to exploit, and you know those wonderful riding-breeches with a machine pistol, and being very clean-shaven, and beautiful hands with a solitaire ring. It all ends with a fire, or in a salon, having made one's fortune. – *Well.*'[42]

If ever anyone fulfilled Baudelaire's celebrated definition of a dandy – 'the pleasure of surprising, and the arrogant satisfaction of never being surprised' – it was this bitterly light-hearted poseur. He teased Breton, referring to him as the 'pohète'; he mocked Breton's enthusiasms. At the time they met, Breton was in the throes of his passion for Rimbaud. 'Walking the streets of Nantes, I was entirely possessed by Rimbaud: what he saw, in some quite other place, interfered with what I saw, sometimes even substituted itself. Never since has he possessed me to this extent . . .'[43] But Vaché had no time for Rimbaud, and not much more for Apollinaire. 'Are you sure that Apollinaire is still alive or that Rimbaud even existed? Personally, I don't think so – I see only Jarry.'[44]

Indeed, Jarry seems to have pervaded every aspect of Vaché's life. His letters are set in the world of *Ubu-Roi*, Jarry's terrifying creation with his toilet-brush sceptre, whose mad, prophetic visions of anarchy and destruction were being realized daily all around. The war is referred to, in Jarry's

27

phrase, as a 'debraining machine' (*'machine à décerveler'*); Breton's friend Theodore Fraenkel, with whom Vaché also corresponded, is *le peuple polonais*, another protagonist of Jarry's play. He talks about his 'stableful of TANKS – a truly UBIQUE animal, though joyless'.

This furious, flaming nihilism calls to mind not only Jarry, who by then had been dead ten years, but Tristan Tzara and his friends, the Dadaists of the Cabaret Voltaire in Zurich, then in full throat. Breton always insisted that Vaché knew nothing of Dada, though there is some argument about this. But it hardly matters. Dada did not spring fully-formed from nowhere; Dada was in the air. Vaché was a Dadaist whether he knew it or not.

Vaché was everything Breton was not, and everything he yearned to be: confident, cynical, stylish, where Breton was awkward, earnest, enthusiastic. Vaché said, 'A man who believes is a curiosity',[45] but this did not prevent Breton from believing fervently in Vaché. Vaché had humour – the black humour he christened *umour*; Breton had none. In his letters, Vaché tried to capture the essence of this fleeting quality for his friend. For instance, explaining some particularly opaque conceit Breton had failed to understand:

> And then you ask me to define Umour for you – just like that!
> IT IS IN THE ESSENCE OF SYMBOLS TO BE SYMBOLIC
> Example: You know the horrible life of the alarm clock –
> it's a monster that has always frightened me because of the
> number of things its eyes project, and the way in which it
> stares at me like an honest man whenever I enter a room –
> why does he have so much Umour, why? Well: that's just
> the way it is – There is a lot of wonderful UBIQUE in
> Umour also – as you will see – but – of course, this isn't
> definitive and Umour derives too much from a sensation – I
> was going to say SENSE – also – of the theatrical (and
> joyless) futility of everything.[46]

Did Breton get it? If so, only intellectually. Humour, even the darkest, was not part of his makeup. In 1940, engulfed by yet another war, he paid touching tribute to his friend by editing, in Vaché's memory, an anthology of *Humour noir*. Introducing this, he conjures him up, 'walking the course of the "last" war on eggs with his body facing forward and his face cast in profile ... His red hair, "flame-dead" eyes and glacial butterfly monocle supply the continually desired dissonance and isolation ... Instead of desertion to the exterior during wartime, which he would only see as a "weak link", Vaché opposes another form of insubordination which could be called: desertion to the interior ... of himself.'[47]

For Breton, the episode at *Les Mamelles de Tirésias* was an epiphany. The play, though far from perfect, was 'a jolly piece where one could enjoy the release of laughing without a second thought'.[48] But 'the sight of Vaché hurling his defiance at that blasé audience, which was in a way tainted by too much of just this sort of thing, was revelatory. Two ways of thinking were set up in opposition, and within three or four years the break would be achieved.'[49]

Breton's attempt to force himself into the straitjacket of being Vaché informed the rest of his life. Philippe Soupault, whom he was soon to meet and who would be his inseparable companion during Surrealism's early years, observed that his friend, naturally so polite, so punctilious, was 'keenly aware of the importance and necessity of scandal. [He] never forgot this necessity. In spite of his respectable upbringing, in spite of a certain undeniable shyness, he never omitted to be insolent. It was a sort of dandyism.'[50] In this sense, Breton was speaking the literal truth when he said, years later, 'Jacques Vaché is the Surrealist in me.'[51]

*

Vaché and Breton met in February; in May they parted. Vaché returned to his interpreting job at the front, Breton was posted to a psychiatric hospital in Saint-Dizier, where he made his first acquaintance with the writings of Freud, then not generally available in France – yet another vital encounter for the future. The two were to meet again only five or six more times, alone or in company; for Breton, when he finally returned to Paris as an intern at the Val de Grâce military hospital, eagerly introduced Vaché to the companions with whom he now began to map out a new life in the capital.

Philippe Soupault was the first of these, a year younger than Breton, also a poet. Invalided out of the army, he, too, had sent Apollinaire one of his poems. To his astonishment, he was invited to call upon the great man at 202 Boulevard Saint-Germain, where Apollinaire lived at the very top of the building in a small but rambling apartment known to friends as his *pigeonnier*. Visitors had to pick their way between shelves and tables piled with books, African and Oceanic masks and fetishes, canvases by his friends – a blue period Picasso, a Chirico, some Derains, a work by the Russian 'rayonniste' Larionov – until finally, up a narrow staircase, they arrived at the little room where the poet worked.

Soupault, not knowing what to expect, found himself confronted by a big, smiling man, a leather cap covering the scar where he had been trepanned. Apollinaire agreed to read a poem for a concert Soupault was arranging, and in front of his astonished visitor sat down and wrote one on the spot. He offered his young friend a poem by Blaise Cendrars to read, then another by André Breton. Next he gave him a copy of *Alcoöls*, inscribing it: '*To the poet Philippe Soupault, in great anticipation.*' (This, said Soupault, definitively decided him to be a poet and nothing else.) When they parted, Apollinaire invited his new young friend to come and join his circle at the

Café de Flore one Tuesday at six. That was his 'day', when he welcomed his friends with a smile – 'a smile', said Soupault, 'which I have never forgotten'.[52]

Soupault took him at his word. But among Apollinaire's friends Soupault felt intimidated, ill at ease: too young. 'It was another generation. They talked about their past, which interested them but didn't interest me.'[53]

Apollinaire noticed his unease, and guessed its cause. When the gathering broke up, he invited the young man to bring his poems to the *pigeonnier* next day: 'There's someone I want you to meet.' The someone turned out to be André Breton. They at once became inseparable companions.

With Soupault there was none of the alien glamour Breton had experienced with Jacques Vaché. On the contrary, their upbringing, their education, their tastes, were almost identical, though Soupault was rich – his family were industrialists related to the Renaults – which was something Breton would never be. Soupault, in Breton's eyes, was 'joy personified, the poetry of the fleeting moment, prodigiously tactful, a beautiful space that slips away, the letters VINS EN GROS stencilled in blue on the café window, disobedient childhood, gossip, graffiti, the lyre-bird, the empty envelope'.[54]

Thus Apollinaire, with his nose for the New Spirit, brought together two of Surrealism's Three Musketeers. And, more indirectly, he also linked Breton and the remaining member of this trio, Louis Aragon.

Aragon, like Breton, was a medical student, mobilized in the Val de Grâce hospital near the Sorbonne. One evening in early September the class of 1916 was engaged in an initiation ceremony, attacking the dormitories of the newly arrived 1917 class who, naturally, resisted the invasion. Aragon had climbed onto the shelving above the beds to avoid the fracas and, gazing through the panes of glass which gave onto the corridor, he met the glance of a fellow-student similarly stowed across the way. Beneath them the mob surged up and down: marooned, they stared at each other.

The face seemed vaguely familiar, but Aragon couldn't place it. Next morning, however, when he ran into its owner, all was explained. They had been introduced some time before at Adrienne Monnier's bookshop, where Aragon had been reading Apollinaire's periodical, the *Soirées de Paris*. And when it turned out that Breton knew Apollinaire himself, not to speak of Derain, Marie Laurencin, Max Jacob . . . Fifty years later, Aragon remembered the 'exalted colour of that magic moment, an echo of our endless conversation as we paced the boulevard, up and down, up and down. We both very soon realised, as can happen when you're twenty, that this was a meeting of decisive importance. I can't now recall the exact course of our conversation, but it . . . opened perspectives of a shared passion, revealing the singular and wonderful fact: henceforth, neither of us was alone.'[55] They reminisced about *Les Mamelles de Tirésias*, whose performance, it transpired, they had both attended. But that was old news now. Breton talked of Rimbaud, of Jarry, offered to lend numbers of *Soirées de Paris* which his new friend had missed. As soon as possible, he introduced Aragon to Apollinaire. 'Thank you for the introduction,' wrote the poet. 'He's charming. I enjoy his talent and the subtlety of his intelligence.' He promised that his next two poems would be dedicated, one to Breton, the other to Aragon.[56]

'[Aragon] was the sweetest, most sensitive boy anyone could imagine, not to say the most intelligent,' remembered Adrienne Monnier. 'He loved poetry, though nothing too out of the way. He carried copies of Verlaine and Laforgue in his pockets, and was shocked at the language of his colleagues at the hospital. I remember that in one of our first conversations he told me that the stupidity and obscenity of the conversation in the operating theatre almost brought tears to his eyes.'[57]

This effortless charm became a joke among Aragon's friends. In 1920, Soupault published a number of verse portraits of their circle. Aragon's ran:

> Tes petites amies font une ronde
> Elles t'ont tressé des couronnes
> Avec tes petites mensonges
> Je t'ai apporté du papier
> Et une très bonne plume
> Tu feras des poèmes pendant l'éternité
> Ton ange gardien te console
> Il noue ta cravate lavallière
> Et t'apprend à sourire
>
> Tu m'as déjà oublié
>
> Your girlfriends dance in a circle
> They've woven you wreaths
> Made of your little fibs
> I've brought you some paper
> And an excellent pen
> You'll spend eternity writing poems
> Your guardian angel consoles you
> He artistically knots your cravat
> And teaches you how to smile
>
> You've already forgotten me

So Apollinaire united the Three Musketeers who would evolve Surrealism, the new movement which defined intellectual life between the wars. And also (by a further, if tenuous, link in the chain) the poet who would become the fourth member of their circle, Paul Eluard. Another Apollinaire play, *Le Couleur du temps*, was given a performance two weeks after his death. During the interval Breton was chatting with Picasso when a young soldier came rushing up, only to retreat, stammering that he had mistaken Breton for someone else – a friend whom he had believed killed at the front. Soon afterwards Breton and Eluard began to correspond; on Eluard's next leave they arranged to meet – and Breton recognized his interlocutor from *Le Couleur du temps*. At the time Breton could not believe this was a real mistake – he thought it a ruse of Eluard's to strike up acquaintance. Later, when the Surrealist doctrine of 'objective chance' had evolved, he regretted his failure to note a significant coincidence.

Many of Surrealism's icons and techniques were originally Apollinaire's. Its pantheon of Sade, Baudelaire, Rimbaud, Jarry (though Lautréamont, the remaining member of this firmament, was their own discovery), its interest in dreams and chance, its abandonment of 'artistic' subjects in favour of the everyday, its iconoclasm, its inclusion under one net of both written and visual arts – all these were inherited from him. But as time went on, to their embarrassment, the three friends found themselves less and less comfortable with their mentor. They often visited him, but preferred to do so singly. For their life in common was increasingly at odds with what Apollinaire now represented.

Partly this was a generation gap. Apollinaire, too, was feeling it – from the other side. In a letter to Soupault he referred to 'this younger generation for whom I am already an ancestor'.[58] And it was at this time that he wrote the famous lines,

> Voici que vient l'été, la saison violente
> Et ma jeunesse est morte ainsi que le printemps
>
> Summer is coming, the violent season
> and my youth died with the spring

But more than age separated him from his young friends.

Like them, Apollinaire had been a soldier; unlike them he had been wounded, the literal victim of Jarry's 'debraining machine'. But where their experiences had convinced them that war was unspeakable, patriotism futile and the State corrupt, Apollinaire did not seem to have drawn these conclusions. Breton and his friends regarded decorations and honours as worthless baubles; Apollinaire was angry and embittered not to have been awarded the *Légion d'honneur* for his services to France in war and peace. Had not his friend Braque, who also suffered a head-wound, received not just the *Légion d'honneur* but the *Croix de guerre* as well? Apollinaire felt, probably correctly, that the Mona Lisa affair was still held against him.

Worse: he still, after all that had happened, seemed dazzled by the rugged romance of warfare. He spoke of the 'masculine simplicity' of some of the books produced by soldiers. 'What could be more beautiful than to sing of heroes and your country's greatness, to inspire noble feelings in future gener-ations?'[59] Where Vaché saw aeroplanes as 'horrible birds' sowing death, Apollinaire wrote wistful lyrics about gas masks.

Many of the poems in *Calligrammes* reflect this romantic view of war. Philippe Soupault, visiting Apollinaire at home, glanced at some proofs over his shoulder and was deeply shocked to read:

> Ah Dieu que la guerre est jolie
> Avec ses chants ses longs loisirs
>
> God how pretty war is
> With its songs its long emptinesses

How could he think it, much less write it?

'We neither like ART nor artists (down with Apollinaire). AND how right TOGRATH IS TO ASSASSINATE THE

35

POET!' wrote Vaché brutally (referring to Apollinaire's novel *Le Poète assassiné*, which he had recently read).[60] But neither Soupault nor (especially) Breton felt able to go quite so far in scornful dismissiveness. Perhaps Apollinaire's wound had enfeebled him, thought Breton, unwilling to relinquish the affection and respect he still felt for this great figure. In 1917, he observed apropos his friend's war poetry that 'The greatest poets can always find a shining straw somewhere in the stable.'[61] Nevertheless, the absolute inadequacy of these poems was only too plain. Something quite different, Breton knew, would be needed from now on. Even so, for him Apollinaire would always remain 'a very great personage – certainly I've never met anyone like him since … Lyricism personified. Orpheus' procession followed in his steps.'[62]

Perhaps Apollinaire would eventually have toppled from this pedestal; perhaps his post-war career would have marked a sad decline. Once again, we shall never know. In October 1918, he complained to his friend André Billy that he couldn't stop coughing. Billy thought he must be suffering from a kind of asthma; in fact it was the first symptom of influenza, a great epidemic of which was then sweeping through Europe. The flu rapidly developed into pneumonia. Weakened by his wound and his operations, Apollinaire was in no condition to resist. 'Save me, doctor!' he pleaded. 'I want to live! I still have so many things to say!'[63]

His last words echoed his last poem. *La Jolie Rousse* ends on the same poignant note:

> For there are so many things I don't dare tell you
> So many things you won't let me tell you
> Pity me.

But pity is of no avail against pneumonia. On 9 November 1918, at six in the evening, Guillaume Apollinaire died.

Two days later the armistice was signed, and the crowds surged into the centre of Paris. In the Boulevard Saint-Germain, below the window of the room where the body lay, they chanted the Kaiser's downfall: *A bas Guillaume! A bas Guillaume!* It was a scene that could hardly have been invented, even by the dead fabulist himself.

Louis Aragon, still mobilized in Alsace, received a letter from André Breton in Paris. Breton liked to make collages of these letters, gluing in innumerable cuttings and comments. On the reverse of one such scrap he had scrawled, in faint pencil: 'Guillaume Apollinaire is dangerously ill.' But Aragon only noticed that later. For just before posting, Breton had slipped into the envelope a small square of paper inscribed, in the centre:

> mais Guillaume
> Apollinaire
> vient de
> mourir[64]

There was also a letter from Jacques Vaché, who said: 'I told you that poor old G. Apollinaire was writing, at the end, for the *Baïonnette* [the official paper for the troops] ... He was a trepanned lieutenant, wasn't he, and decorated – *Well.*' He added loftily: 'Perhaps we'll let him keep the title of precursor – we won't disagree with that.'[65]

*

Less than two months later, on 7 January 1919, *Le Télégramme des Provinces de l'Ouest* reported, under the headline 'Two Youths Dabble With Drugs', 'a regrettable incident ... that brings tragedy to two of the most respected families in Nantes. Two youths, in their early twenties and currently members of the armed forces, died from an overdose of opium ...'

The story seemed, on the face of it, a simple and tragic case of misadventure. On the preceding Monday evening, an American soldier named Woynow had rushed from a second-floor room at Nantes' Hotel de France and demanded to speak to the manager. He reported that two young men, friends of his, had died in the room. The manager called a doctor, who verified that one of the bodies was cold, while the other was still warm. It seemed clear to him that both had taken an overdose of opium. He tried, but failed, to revive the still-warm body, then turned his attention to Woynow, who had also become ill. The police found a small container in the room containing opium.

The young men were identified as Jacques V. and Paul B., and the paper reported that they belonged to 'a group of young French and American "thrill-seekers" who frequented places of amusement. There, the idea came to them to experiment with opium – perhaps in hopes of finding in it the "high" that this horrible drug brings – as it also brings death.'[66]

The clear implication was that these rash and inexperienced young men had been killed by an accidental overdose. But Breton never accepted this view. In the essay 'La Confession dédaigneuse', which served as a preface to the 1924 edition of his friend's wartime letters, he states unequivocally that Vaché committed suicide. 'The admirable thing about his death', Breton says, 'was that it could be viewed as accidental. He took, I believe, forty grammes of opium, though he was not an inexperienced smoker. However, it is quite possible that his unfortunate companions were not acquainted with the drug, and that, when he killed himself, he couldn't resist playing this last little trick on them.'

Certainly Vaché's own letters to Breton hint at such a possibility. 'Remember', he wrote, 'that I like you a lot (and you must believe this) and that I would kill you moreover – (without scruples, perhaps) – after first having rifled you of unlikely possibilities . . .'[67] And according to a schoolfriend, Vaché, a few hours before he died, said, 'I'll die when I want to . . . But, I'll die with someone else. To die alone is boring.'[68]

Impossible, at this distance, to know for sure what happened. Circumstances certainly seem to point to the suicide/murder theory. It is clear from his letters that Vaché habitually took opium when he was bored or depressed. And even the end of the war, since it found him still in uniform with no prospect of imminent demobilization, had done nothing to lift his spirits. 'How am I ever going to get through these last months in uniform? – (I hear the war's over) – I really can't bear it any longer . . . and THEY are suspicious . . . THEY suspect something – Just so long as they don't debrain me while THEY'VE got me in their power?'[69] wails his penultimate letter. The next, his last, seems more cheerful, anticipating a future meeting in Paris. But it is clear he was in a volatile state.

The interesting question, though, concerns not Vaché, but Breton. Why was he so very insistent upon the suicide scenario – and, by extension, that of murder? He dismissed all other possibilities. Yet Vaché was Breton's friend. Why would anyone seek to honour a friend by imputing a vicious crime to his memory?

Vaché's death devastated Breton, both personally and intellectually. Much of his life can be seen as a search for another such friend. 'I still see him from time to time,' he wrote not long after Vaché's death. 'In the tram a traveller tells his provincial relatives "Boulevard Saint-Michel: the student quarter"; the windows wink in recognition.'[70]

A pattern soon established itself. A figure would appear, seemingly invested with all the right qualities. For a while, Breton would throw himself deliriously into this new relationship. Then disillusion would set in, leaving him once more bereft. Only memory – his friend's perennial memory – never let him down. For the rest of his life, Vaché would be Breton's touchstone, a demonstration of Surrealism as it ought to be: revolutionary, amoral, outrageous.

The episode with the pistol at the *Mamelles de Tirésias* had been one example of this instinctive Surrealism. Unfortunately, only Breton had been aware of it. Vaché's death, however, was a gesture visible to all. How could it be allowed to pass as accidental? 'I don't want to die in wartime,' his friend had said, and it is clear why not: a wartime death is banal, unnoticed, run of the mill – wasted, senseless. Jacques Vaché's death was either the crowning gesture of his life, or as stupid, as senseless, as the war itself.

Suicide, moreover, possessed a number of positive and desirable attributes. There was the manner of death itself – that 'wonderful moment of letting-go'[71] articulated longingly by Antonin Artaud (and, eventually, though much later, found by him). There was, too, the fact that suicide alone enables a person to decide the manner and moment of this death. For as both Apollinaire and Vaché had demonstrated, it is important to die at the right time. Achievement curtailed acquires, *ipso facto*, a certain legendary status – if only because it eliminates the risk of subsequent anticlimactic decline. This was true not only of Vaché but of many other Surrealist icons: Isidore Ducasse, aka the Comte de Lautréamont, the movement's great poetic hero, who died in poverty aged twenty-three; Alfred Jarry, who died of drink aged thirty-four; Arthur Cravan, Oscar Wilde's nephew, who lived a wild life in pre-war Paris, fought a prizefight against Jack Johnson, produced a few mediocre poems and paintings and a little magazine conspicuous principally for its relentless iconoclasm – and who sailed into the Gulf of Mexico in 1918 never to be seen again. It need not even be fatal: Duchamp and Rimbaud abruptly cut off their work, but not their lives.

So suicide it was; and, perhaps not coincidentally, suicide became distinctly fashionable among Surrealists, the subject of questionnaires ('Is suicide a solution?' inquired the first number of *Littérature*, the magazine Breton was to start with Soupault and Aragon), articles, and at least two enactments – Jacques Rigaut and René Crevel, both of whose deaths filled Breton, rightly or wrongly but undoubtedly ironically, with guilty anguish.

But suicide is one thing, murder quite another. And here the scenario of Vaché's death raises a different question – a question that would echo through the Surrealist years. What should be the relation between art and life? How far should life model itself upon art's absolutes? And conversely, should art be constrained by the moral imperatives life imposes?

One of Apollinaire's heroes, as both thinker and sexual sage, was the Marquis de Sade. It is clear from his letters that the poet shared some of Sade's tastes: whips played an important part in his life.[72] They also fill his pornography – yet another of the many trades plied by this multifarious fellow. But Apollinaire's pornography, at its best, is (as one might expect) something more than a mere record of assorted couplings. As Roger Shattuck has pointed out, he stands firmly in the line of the great French moralists, beginning with Montaigne and continuing through La Rochefoucauld and Sade. For him as for them, pragmatism is all and morals as the nineteenth century knew them, irrelevant. In the best-known of these books, *Les Onze mille verges* (*verge* means rod: this is a book in which virgins are few, and soon penetrated), his hero, Mony, who has been sentenced to death, deflowers a twelve-year-old girl who offers herself to him – and then, having nothing more to fear from justice, gouges out her eyes and strangles her. The point of this horrible action is not its cruel nature, but its complete absence of motive. As Roger

41

Shattuck observes, 'Only a man already facing death is free to act unswayed by any human motives of right and wrong, gain and loss, pleasure and pain.'[73]

Apollinaire's interest in such philosophical matters was shared by his contemporary André Gide, who wrote a novel devoted to them – *Les Caves du Vatican*, in which the hero, Lafcadio, commits a series of these *actes gratuits*. This was a seminal work for Breton's generation, whose extreme ambivalence regarding Gide himself stemmed largely from his absolute failure to fulfil in person the hopes he had raised by creating such a hero. There was nothing of Lafcadio in the too-solidly bourgeois Gide, with his town house, his country house, his ambitions for the Académie; and for this Breton and (especially) Aragon never forgave him. 'One could only guess at the lucky chance that had given birth to the hero of the *Caves*,' Aragon wrote. 'His creator had nothing interesting to tell me about Lafcadio.'[74]

For Aragon, Vaché was the living model of Lafcadio. Did he consciously model himself upon Gide's creation? He had certainly read *Les Caves du Vatican*. A letter of June 1917, thanks Breton for sending a copy, along with Apollinaire's novel *Le Poète assassiné*. His immediate reaction was that 'I find Gide truly cold.'[75] Two months later he comments: 'I grant LAFCADIO a little umour – because he doesn't read and he produces only through amusing experiences – such as the murder.'

And now – thrilling thought! – art had become life. Vaché had committed his very own *acte gratuit*. It was something neither Breton nor Apollinaire (nor Gide) could ever have brought himself to do, however much they might enjoy playing with the idea. They thought: Vaché acted. In every way it was a fitting end. It ensured his immortality.

CHAPTER TWO

THE DEATH
OF ART

Jacques Vaché's story, like that of so many of his contemporaries, is a tale of might-have-been. His gifts, had he lived, might – or might not – have lived up to their promise. But until the war was over they could not display themselves. Quite apart from the distractions and demands of army life, what people like Vaché wanted to say was treasonable. For example, a good many French intellectuals found themselves in the Renseignements aux Familles, where they were employed writing letters to break the news of deaths. They circulated a handwritten journal in ubuesque mode. But it was strictly private. Had it been discovered, they would have been at risk of court-martial.[1]

Not everyone languished at the front, however. Some fled to avoid conscription in a war they abhorred. Others found themselves at liberty through no fault of their own. Their fate might have been Vaché's, or Apollinaire's: chance spared them to work out their theories. So Marcel Duchamp found himself in New York because of a heart murmur; and conceptual art was born.

Once more we are at the theatre with Apollinaire. But this time he is spectator rather than author. In June 1912, Raymond Roussel's play *Impressions d'Afrique* was presented at the Théâtre Antoine. Reviewers dismissed it as absurd, and at first audiences were sparse. But word soon got around that this was something out of the ordinary. Apollinaire saw it towards the end of its two-week run. He was accompanied by three friends: Francis Picabia the painter, his wife Gabrielle, and another young painter, Marcel Duchamp, whose first meeting with Apollinaire this was. It was an important day for the future of art. Duchamp would go on to change that future; and this was the day when he began to realize the form these changes might take.

Duchamp, born in 1887, was a notary's son from Blainville, near Rouen, in Normandy. Of the six children in the family, the four eldest were artists. First came Jacques Villon (né Gaston Duchamp), a painter, and Raymond Duchamp-Villon, a sculptor. Eleven years later Marcel arrived, and two years after that Suzanne, the sibling to whom he was closest and who also became a painter. Finally there were two much younger sisters, Yvonne and Magdeleine. Throughout their lives their father uncomplainingly subsidized his offspring; making clear to them, however, that anything they received during his lifetime would be noted down and deducted from their inheritance when he died. Marcel in particular valued the freedom this allowed him, and took care always to live within his means. This was no problem since his tastes were ascetic to the point where the smallest allowance permitted him to live without worry. Or maybe it was the other way round, and he developed his monastically simple lifestyle in order to permit himself the greatest possible latitude. At any rate, he clung to it neurotically – to the point where he would refuse to make money even when he might easily have done so. Baggage of any sort was anathema to him. In the roman-à-cléf *Victor*, written by his close friend Henri-Pierre Roché, the eponymous hero, who is Duchamp, sets out the choice: 'Either liberty and risk. Or the so-called straight path, also a risk, and children.'[2] For Duchamp the choice made itself: liberty, always.

In 1904, aged seventeen, Marcel left home for Paris, where he lodged in Montmartre with his brother Gaston. Later, both Gaston and Raymond left Paris for the (then) leafy suburb of Puteaux, where they formed the nucleus of an artists' colony. Not long afterwards, Marcel followed them out to nearby Neuilly. He described this period of his life as his 'eight years of swimming lessons',[3] in which he tried to evolve a painting style which would suit him. In 1912, these lessons came abruptly to an end. Duchamp the painter put down his brushes; Duchamp the iconoclast, the reverberations of whose innovations are still being felt, began to emerge from his shell.

The great development in painting at this time was Cubism, then being feverishly worked out and evolved by Picasso and Braque. A number of other intellectually-minded painters thereupon declared themselves Cubists too, though Picasso and Braque, egged on by their dealer, refused to recognize them or accept them as followers. Among these were the Duchamp brothers, including, briefly, Marcel. This Puteaux group of Cubists decided to organize a show of their work in the 1912 Salon des Indépendants, which opened on 20 March. Marcel submitted a painting called *Nude Descending a Staircase*.

The *Nude Descending a Staircase* is now one of the most celebrated milestones of modern art, but when the show's organizers saw it, far from being dazzled, they were horrified. Their view of what Cubism was, or ought to be, centred increasingly narrowly upon the mathematics of the Golden Section. Marcel's *Nude* owed nothing to this. In fact it was clearly influenced as much by the Futurists as the Cubists. The Futurists were concerned with speed, noise, movement; their works had been exhibited the previous month at Bernheim Jeune's gallery, an exhibition which Duchamp visited several times. He was at this time concerned not with pure form, but with the problem of describing movement on a static canvas: he said later that the idea for his picture had come from Marey's serial photographs of people and animals in movement, and described its geometry as 'a sort of distortion other than Cubism'.[4] The Puteaux Cubists found all this unacceptable. They also very much disliked the picture's title, which they thought must be some sort of joke at their expense. They rejected it.

The two elder Duchamps were deputed to convey the bad news. They did so the day before the salon's official opening, dressed in black suits 'as if for a funeral'. Their tone was diffident. They begged Marcel at least to change the title. 'They thought it was too much of a literary title, in a bad sense – in a caricatural way ... Even their little revolutionary temple couldn't understand that a nude could be *descending* the stairs. Anyway, the general idea was to have me change something to make it possible to show it, because they didn't want to reject it completely ... So I said nothing. I said all right, all right, and I took a taxi to the show and got my painting and took it away.'[5]

As Duchamp tells it, nothing could have been more matter-of-fact. Drama played no part in his life, then or ever. If there were internal storms, his impassive exterior never hinted at them. But the drama was there nevertheless. His years of uncertainty were over. Rejection had liberated him from his past. He was on his own and would never again form part of any group. Then and there he turned his back upon the notion of 'being an artist'. He would sooner get a proper job.

This, then, was his state of mind when, at the age of twenty-five, he came to see *Impressions d'Afrique*.

Raymond Roussel was one of literature's more bizarre figures. He was to become surprisingly influential in the years following World War II, as the inspiration behind the OULIPO group (OULIPO: *Ouvroir pour une Littérature Potentielle*) which included Raymond Queneau, Italo Calvino, Michel Leiris (whose father had been the Roussel family lawyer), Duchamp himself, and Georges Perec, whose novel *La Disparition*, in which the letter 'e' does not appear, is perhaps OULIPO's most extreme production. Born into a wealthy family, Roussel exhibited great musical gifts (as well as being a champion chess player and pistol shot), and was sent to study the piano under Alfred Cortot. But at the age of nineteen he gave all that up and turned to literature. He began with a book of poems and then moved on to prose. *Impressions d'Afrique* was first published as a novel (Roussel's third), and was serialized in weekly instalments in the ultra-respectable *Gaulois du Dimanche*, where it passed unremarked, possibly unread, almost certainly misunderstood. For Roussel's writings were like no others, and his *Impressions* had little to do with Africa.

The book, however, had one influential fan – Edmond Rostand, the playwright whose verse epics *l'Aiglon* and *La Princesse lointaine* had been the triumphs of Sarah Bernhardt's later years. Roussel had sent him a copy of the book; he liked it so much that he would read extracts aloud to his friends. 'There's an extraordinary play to be made out of this,' he said. Roussel, tired of public indifference and incomprehension, took him at his word. Perhaps a play would succeed where a book could not. And Rostand's judgement was borne out. *Impressions d'Afrique*, though commercially a failure, proved far more significant than any of its more immediately successful contemporaries.

Some years later, in a booklet entitled *Comme j'ai écrit certains de mes livres*, Roussel explained his methods. He would select, in the first place, two almost identical words: for example, *billard* (a billiard table) and *pillard* (an African chieftain). Having lighted upon these near-homonyms, he then constructed two sentences made up of the same words but in which all the meanings were different:

1: Les lettres du blanc sur les bandes du vieux billard . . .
2: Les lettres du blanc sur les bandes du vieux pillard . . .

Roussel goes on to explicate these sentences. In the first, *'lettres'* meant typographical signs, *'blanc'*, white chalk, and *'bandes'*, edges; so that the sentence read, 'The white letters chalked along the edges of the old billiard table.' In the second, *'lettres'* meant missives, *'blanc'* was a white man, and *'bandes'*

49

were hordes – as in warrior hordes. So that *this* sentence read, 'The white man's letters about the old chieftain's armies.' 'Having found the two phrases,' continues Roussel, 'the task was to write a story beginning with the first and ending with the second.'⁶ This was the basis of the medley of bizarre rituals, acrobatics, art, sex, science and machines which form *Impressions d'Afrique*, whose action begins with 'a stormy night in equatorial Africa' and ends with 'the fête given by the members of the Club des Incomparables, with its sideshows: the wind clock from the Land of Cockayne, Monsieur Bex's thermo-mechanical orchestra, the earthworm which plays the zither . . .'

All this – the wordplay, the punning (the play's title can be read as *à fric* – at his own expense: Roussel paid for the publication of all his books), but also the man himself, with his reclusive life, his rejection of society's norms, his obsession with chess – were calculated to appeal to Duchamp, whose own obsessions and inclinations were not dissimilar. Roussel's explanatory booklet would not be published for some years, nor had Duchamp yet evolved into the punster he would become. Nevertheless, he instantly recognized a kindred soul. 'It was tremendous,' he remembered. 'On the stage there was a model and a snake that moved slightly – it was absolutely the madness of the unexpected. I don't remember much of the text. One didn't really listen . . . Afterward, I read the text and could associate the two.'⁷

Duchamp gives two contradictory versions of this event. In one, he attended the performance in the company of the Picabias and Apollinaire. In the other, he says he did not meet Apollinaire until the following October. By then Apollinaire had published his book on the Cubist painters, including the prescient sentence: 'It will perhaps be reserved for an artist as disengaged from aesthetic preoccupations, as occupied with energy as Marcel Duchamp, to reconcile Art and the People.'

Duchamp's response to this was typical: 'I told you, he would say anything!'[8] Nevertheless, Apollinaire, as so often, had sensed the potential hidden in this strange young man. And if Duchamp liked to place his first meeting with Apollinaire at the performance of *Impressions d'Afrique*, perhaps this was because it *should* have taken place there, whether or not it really did so. For as painting now interested him less, so words and what could be done with them were beginning to interest him more. And both Apollinaire and Roussel not only occupied the world of words, but were concerned with pushing them to extremes. Apollinaire's conversations were firework displays, full of puns, quotations, mysterious allusions, helpless laughter. Marcel listened and admired.

Picabia (whose wife's account supports the theatre party contention) was the connecting link: he already knew both Duchamp and Apollinaire. He and Apollinaire had met the previous year, and immediately become companions in voracity, for food, drink, fun and intellectual pyrotechnics.

It is impossible to imagine anyone more different from the diffident, ascetic Duchamp than Francis Picabia. In every way they were polar opposites. Duchamp, the provincial notary's son, knew no one; Picabia, the only son of a wealthy, well-connected Cuban and his equally wealthy and well-connected French wife, knew everyone. Duchamp was tall, thin, red-haired, reserved; Picabia, dark, short, square, powerfully built, explosive; he had 'a Goya head set directly on his shoulders with no intervening neck'.[9] Duchamp was inclined to asceticism, Picabia addicted to excess of every sort – fast cars, drink, opium, women and anything else that might come his way. Where Picabia, as his wife observed, 'abandoned himself to chance and to his exceptional imaginative faculties, Duchamp ... by a discipline that was almost Jansenist and mystical, suppressed every impulse, every desire to create, suppressed all joy in creating, and to avert the danger of a routine reminiscence or reflex, forced himself to a rule of conduct directly counter to the natural'.[10]

But despite these differences of style and also of age (Picabia, born in 1879, was eight years older and already a well-known painter), they became friends from the moment they met. Duchamp, then still very much under the influence of his two elder brothers, immediately grasped what Picabia was trying to do. He found the mental climate Picabia generated much more sympathetic to his own rapidly developing iconoclasm than that of Puteaux. Though their chosen routes seemed so utterly different, they led in the same direction: away from the concepts of 'art' and 'beauty'.

'Fundamentally,' says Duchamp, 'I had a mania for change, like Picabia. One does something for six months, a year, and one goes on to something else. That's what Picabia did all his life.'[11] Indeed, though Picabia was then only thirty-three, he had already run through a variety of different styles. Starting out as a sort of Sisleyite late-Impressionist, in which guise (at the age of sixteen) he met with enormous and immediate success, he had moved on to fauvism, and at the time Duchamp met him was painting in the brightly-coloured geometric style which Apollinaire christened 'simultaneist' or 'orphic'. He was, said his friend Georges Ribemont-Dessaignes, 'terrified of repetition. Repetition meant boredom, nothingness, the void, the pit . . . He spent his whole life giving this emptiness a new face, but his novelty stung. It left weals, like a whiplash across the face of the conformist.'[12] He applied this pitiless standard as much to himself as everyone and everything else; and, in Duchamp, found one of the rare spirits who could keep up with his terrifying and exhilarating race through life's possibilities.

Picabia operated on a far larger stage than anything the notary's son from the provinces had ever encountered: as Duchamp himself put it, 'He had entry into a world I knew nothing of.'[13] Several worlds, indeed. Picabia moved freely between the diplomatic and intellectual high society into which he had been born, the art world, the musical world inhabited by his gifted wife, the circle of avant-garde poets and writers of which Apollinaire was the hub, and the opium dens and bars where he indulged his taste for drink and drugs. With the lofty contempt available to those possessing a private income, he scoffed at the Puteaux Cubists. They were 'professional painters' leading 'artistic lives'. He could offer other, better and more exciting alternatives.

Soon after the Roussel performance, however, Duchamp left the excitements of Paris and travelled alone to Munich. It was his first trip out of France, and it was to last four months. He arrived in Bavaria on 21 June, and stayed until October.

Why Munich, and what did he do there? It seems safe to assume that he felt deeply in need of a pause for digestion: all these new events and impressions had constituted a rich and compressed diet of change. And Munich, as a centre of new thought, had, on the face of it, much to offer. In particular it was the home of Wassily Kandinsky, who was then evolving his theory of the mystico-musico-visual *Gesamtkunstwerk*. For Hugo Ball, who four years later was to begin the Cabaret Voltaire in Zurich, and who was also in Munich at this time, Kandinsky 'by his mere presence, placed this city far above all other German cities in its modernity'.[14] Did Duchamp know of this? If so, he never admitted it. All he would ever say was, 'I had met a cow painter in Paris, I mean a German who painted cows, the very best cows of course, an admirer of Lovis Corinth and all those people, and when this cow painter said "Go to Munich," I got up and went there and lived for months in a little furnished room . . . Munich had a lot of style in those days. I never met a soul and had a great time.'[15] Was he elaborating his new philosophy of life and art, equipping

53

himself with a set of excellent German paints, mapping out future projects? Any or all of these. As far as Duchamp was concerned, one answer was as good as another. He thought the viewer's perception a legitimate part of any picture: valid, whatever it might be.

The only acquaintance to see him during these months was Gabrielle Picabia, with whom he had fallen desperately in love – perhaps another reason for his sudden flight: for Duchamp was a correct and bashful young man. He telephoned her before his departure to confess his feelings, and she told him he could write to her in Kent, where she was to spend part of July with her two children. She received 'two very beautiful letters' from him there, including one comparing them to the lovers in a novel by (inevitably) Gide, *La Porte étroite* (*Strait is the Gate*), who determine to behave so selflessly that they deny themselves a life together. She said, 'I remember being astonished by this letter. These clandestine things greatly troubled me, but at the same time I was very moved by his friendly attitude toward me. He said he wanted so badly to see me alone.'

They met later that summer. Gabrielle and the children were now staying with her mother at Etival in the Jura. She told Marcel she was making a brief excursion to Paris: he could meet her at the rail station of Andelot, where the branch from Etival joined the main line: she had to wait there for an hour or so between trains. It seemed a meagre reward for so long a journey; but somewhat to her astonishment there he was, waiting on the platform when she arrived. They spent several hours together in the little waiting room, not touching, though it was clear Marcel was consumed with desire.

There was only the main train which went by at about two in the morning, and another later. And I stayed: instead of taking the first, I took the second. We remained in

54

the station on a wooden bench. We spent the night, and I left before him. Even now I find it really astonishing and very moving, very young, too. It was a kind of madness, idiocy, to travel from Munich to the Jura to pass a few hours of the night with me ... Above all, I thought, I must be very careful with everything I say to him because he understands things in quite an alarming way, in an absolute way.[16]

But this episode, touching and revealing though it is, still tells us nothing about what Marcel was doing in Munich.

One thing he undoubtedly did do was draw and paint – he produced several of his most important works during this brief but intensely productive period. But he was nevertheless adamant that he no longer wanted to be an *artiste-peintre*. He liked to quote the French saying *'Bête comme un peintre'* (As stupid as a painter). This was what Marcel Duchamp was *not* going to be. Since the Renaissance, the assumption had been that an artist was both craftsman *and* intellectual. By the time Duchamp returned from Munich, he had separated out these strands. The debacle of his rejection had confirmed his growing distaste for the actual process of putting paint on canvas. He had never, he declared later, enjoyed this in itself.[17] Craftsmanship no longer interested him. What concerned him now was what went on in the mind, 'intellectual expression rather than animal expression'.[18] For the rest of his life, making would be less important to him than thinking.

He returned from Munich in October to find an American friend, Walter Pach, in Paris collecting works for a big show of modern art to be held at the 69th Regiment Armory in New York the following February. Would Marcel contribute? Why not? He agreed to enter four paintings, including the infamous *Nude*, and thought no more about it.

*

Picabia also entered four paintings for the Armory Show, and perhaps because his recent work had been very badly received at the 1912 Salon d'Automne, decided to leave Paris and accompany them. He would personally represent the avant-garde in New York. In January 1913, he and Gabrielle crossed the Atlantic. They were immediately bewitched. Picabia adored New York's garish, buzzing vitality, its teeming streets and bridges, its neon signs and skyscrapers, its girls, its booze, its breezy informality. He and Gabrielle had intended to stay two weeks, but in fact did not leave until the end of April, four months later.

New York, then as now, loved celebrities; Picabia instantly became one. The Armory Show was the talk of the town, and Picabia's and Duchamp's paintings its main sensation. Not that everybody appreciated them – on the contrary. One visitor, speaking for thousands, opined that they 'would be more appropriately placed in the lecture room of a professor of psychology than in an art gallery'. One of Picabia's works was described as 'a chipped block of maple sugar', and Duchamp's *Nude* as 'an explosion in a shingle factory'. But if the tradition-alists hated them, the modernists loved them. For them, the Armory Show represented much more than an art exhibition. It was, rather, a window onto a whole new way of thinking which affected practitioners of all the arts. 'There had been a break somewhere,' wrote the poet William Carlos Williams, 'we were streaming through, each thinking his own thoughts, doing his own designs – towards his self's objectives.'[19] As a result, Picabia immediately found himself at the centre of two of the most interesting groups in the city: Mabel Dodge's eclectic left-leaning salon in Greenwich Village, starring her lover John Reed, where one might meet anyone from Emma Goldman the anarchist to Margaret Sanger the birth-control advocate or Big Bill Haywood of the International Workers of the World; and the group surrounding Alfred Stieglitz's Little Gallery at 291, Fifth Avenue.

Since 1907, Stieglitz had been spreading the gospel of modern art in New York from this small, three-room space. He had studied photography at the Technische Hochschule in Berlin, where he had learned to treat it as something more than mere representation. Part of his aim, on his return, was to spread this word in America. But he was also deeply interested in painting, cultivating and showing a group of American artists including Marsden Hartley, John Marin and Joseph Stella, as well as promoting the European avant-garde, of whose great importance he was absolutely convinced. His first exhibition had been of Rodin's drawings, followed swiftly by those of Matisse, Cézanne – and now Picabia. Two days after the Armory Show closed Stieglitz opened a one-man show devoted to this new sensation. Picabia became one of the small group helping to produce Stieglitz' magazine *291*, in whose large and luxurious pages he would work out his next style: machine painting. Its first number could not have been more Paris-oriented, carrying Apollinaire's calligramme *Voyage* along with caricatures (by Stieglitz' associate Marius de Zayas) of Apollinaire, Picabia, and the Paris art dealer Ambroise Vollard. Indeed, it contained, throughout its run, at least as much French as English – which may go some way to account for its distressingly low New York sales. The Picabias became Stieglitz' bridge to Paris. As the weeks passed their hotel room became a studio, the walls covered with enormous abstract watercolours inspired by the city, which Stieglitz exhibited before the Picabias left at the end of April.

All his life Picabia remembered New York with longing, though after 1917 he would never see the city again. But the children were in Europe, and Gabrielle was pregnant again. Reluctantly they left the fascinating city, and returned to

France. There Picabia painted like a man possessed, ordering canvases three metres square and covering them with feverish rapidity, painting night and day, forgetting even to eat: the resulting works, which he called *Udnie* and *Edtaonisl*, were wonderful, perhaps the best paintings he ever made. Gabrielle recounts that 'we phoned him the news that I had just given birth to a little girl (our third child) ... When he came back that evening he had forgotten all about it and was astonished to find me in bed. "Not just bed, child-bed,"' quipped the ever-tolerant Gaby.[20]

*

Duchamp knew nothing of the sensation he had made, though he was of course aware that all the pictures he had sent to New York had been sold. But although the money was welcome, the news did not excite him. He was no longer an artist but a librarian. Picabia's uncle, Henri Davanne, who was in charge of the Bibliothèque Ste Geneviève, near the Panthéon, had agreed to give him a job. It suited Duchamp perfectly. There was plenty of spare time, and even when he was on duty he could read. Delighted with it, he even took a course in librarianship.

He took a room in the Rue Ste Hippolyte where he surrounded himself with items, found or bought, which (for no particular reason) had caught his eye: a bicycle-wheel standing on its fork, which he liked to turn gently as he lay in bed; a 'hedgehog' bottle-rack which he found in the hardware department of the Bazar de l'Hotel de Ville. Thus congenially surrounded, he began to assemble plans and elements, sketches and scribbled notes, for a large, indeed heroic, project: his Large Glass, *The Bride Stripped Bare by Her Bachelors, Even (La Mariée mise a nu par ses célibataires, même)*, the enormous work whose making would occupy eight years of his life, from 1915 to 1923. The subject was taken from fairground stalls, which at that time 'used to display dolls in the sideshows that frequently represented the partners of a marriage. The spectators threw the balls at them, and if they hit the mark, they beheaded them and won a prize.'[21] This scenario provides the cast for the Glass: the doll Bride, the Bachelors throwing balls at her, the Oculist Witnesses, the watching public, the scoreboard at the top. But the work's conception – the treatment, the materials used – was, Duchamp said, primarily inspired by Roussel – who indeed described something very like it in his second play, *Locus Solus*: 'This transparent construction, in which the straight line ruled supreme, was entirely composed of immense planes of glass supported by a rigid though delicate iron framework . . .'[22]

'The reason I admired Roussel', Duchamp said, 'was because he produced something I had never seen. That is the only thing that brings admiration from my innermost being . . . I saw immediately that he might influence me. I thought that, as a painter, I would do better to be influenced by a writer than another painter.'[23]

Roussel's verbal influence was also important, for the Glass is far more than a construction alone. As he worked, Duchamp collected the odd scraps of paper on which were noted down the thoughts, calculations and sketches which accompanied its development. These scraps were later collected together into a box which in turn became an object of exegesis. 'The *Large Glass* is a design for a piece of machinery and the *Green Box* is therefore . . . like one of those sets of instructions that tell us how to put machines together and how they work'.[24] The Box contains a supporting web of theory, idiosyncratic mathematics, cod science in the tradition of Jarry, obscure and complex wordplays deriving partly from Roussel but (since Duchamp did not yet know Roussel's writing method) perhaps owing more to Mallarmé and Jarry, erotic allusions and *double-entendre*:

Malic castings

By eros matrix we understand the set of hollow uniforms or liveries designed for the lighting gas which takes 8 malic forms (constable, dragoon &c.)

The gas castings thus obtained would hear the litanies sung by the trolley, the refrain of the whole celibate machine, but they will never be able to pass beyond the Mask. – They would have been as if enveloped all along their regrets by a mirror reflecting back to them their own complexity . . .[25]

The reflected complexity was doubtless Duchamp's own.

These many appendages and layers of meaning have provoked countless theses, monographs and commentaries – all, in Duchamp's eyes, valid. Thus (to cite two prominent examples), the austerely intellectual Octavio Paz, referring to part of the work's title – 'a delay in glass' ('It was the poetic aspect of the words that I liked,' Duchamp said. 'I wanted to give "delay" a poetic sense that I couldn't even explain. It was to avoid saying, "a glass painting," "a glass drawing," "a thing drawn on glass," you understand?')[26] – writes that Duchamp 'set up a vertigo of delay in opposition to the [Futurist] vertigo of acceleration'.[27] On another track altogether, Arturo Schwarz, a Freudian, sees Duchamp's (supposed) incestuous or quasi-incestuous relationship with his sister Suzanne as the key to all his work, so that clearly, for Schwarz, the ever-unattainable Bride is Suzanne and the endlessly supplicating Bachelors are Marcel . . .

At this early stage, Duchamp was concerned with planning out the work and developing some of its details. Even the outbreak of war did not distract him. Both his brothers were called up almost at once, but Duchamp, having completed his one year's military service, was temporarily exempt. Since the war would (everyone thought) be over within six months, he would with any luck miss the fighting altogether.

However, it was soon clear that no such swift end was in

sight, and in January 1915, he was called before a draft board – only to be turned down on account of a heart murmur. 'I have been condemned to remain a civilian for the duration,' he wrote his friend Walter Pach in New York. 'They found me too *sick* to be a soldier. I am not too sad about this decision.'[28]

But his position, though enviable, was (often for that very reason) by no means easy. Paris was dark and tense, the streets unlit, the shops closing early. 'One's friends [were] all away at the front. Or else they [had] been already killed . . . I roamed about alone. Everywhere the talk turned upon war . . . In such an atmosphere, especially for one who holds war to be an abomination, it may readily be conceived existence was heavy and dull.'[29] There were other drawbacks, too. Duchamp had not tried to escape the army: it had rejected him. But he could hardly wear a notice to this effect. Meanwhile he was an apparently fit young man walking around a Paris denuded of young men. Sometimes people spat at him in the street. Even his sister-in-law, Raymond's wife Yvonne Duchamp-Villon, scolded him for remaining behind the lines.[30]

In these circumstances he preferred to leave; and New York, where he had sold several pictures and was in the process of shipping out more, was an obvious possibility. 'I have absolutely decided to leave Paris,' he wrote Pach.

> As I had told you last November, I would willingly live in New York. But only on the condition that I could earn my living there. 1st. Do you think that I could easily find a job as a librarian or something analogous that would leave me great freedom to work (Some information about me: I do not speak English, I graduated with my Baccalaureate in literature (don't laugh!!), I worked for two years at the Bibliothèque Ste. Geneviève as an intern. – 2nd. I will leave here at the end of May at the earliest. Do you think this is a good time or should I rather wait until September. I have told no-one about this plan. Thus I ask you to answer me

on this topic on a separate sheet in your letter so that my brothers do not know anything before my resolution is completely made.

In reply to an incredulous letter from Pach, he wrote: 'You miss Paris, yes, I understand this very well because here you were living the free life of an artist with all the joys and all the hard times that one likes to remember – My stay in New York is a very different matter.' He added: '*I do not go to New York I leave Paris. It is altogether different.*'[31]

Duchamp asked Pach to keep his decision from his family because he knew they would be sad to see him go. But he had made up his mind, and booked his passage on the SS *Rochambeau*. He took with him some studies, on glass and paper, for the *Large Glass*, and several drawings, but (in accordance with his ascetic principles) little personal baggage. On 6 August 1915, he arrived in Bordeaux. From the great bridge which spans the Gironde he saw the *Rochambeau* waiting, her funnels belching black smoke. The sight filled him with escapee's relief.

Walter Pach met him off the boat in New York. They journeyed uptown through the blinding August heat to the Pachs' small apartment in Beekman Place, where Duchamp was to stay until he found somewhere to live. This soon materialized in the form of a duplex apartment at 33 West 67th Street belonging to Walter and Louise Arensberg, who were summering out of town.

Arensberg was one of Duchamp's greatest fans. He was the wealthy son of a Pittsburgh steel-magnate, but business interested him not at all. He and his even wealthier wife preferred to devote themselves to the life of the mind – literature, poetry, and, since the Armory Show, art. He had caught the show in New York only on its closing day, but such was the impression it made that he followed it to Boston, where he visited it several times more. He was particularly struck by Duchamp's work – and was, indeed, to become one of his most devoted collectors. However, by the time Arensberg got there, most of the works he coveted, including Duchamp's – *especially* Duchamp's – had been bought.

For Duchamp had arrived to find himself, to his astonishment, famous. 'Every time I met someone, they would say, "Oh! Are you the one who did that painting?" '[32] Had he been inclined to paint more pictures, he could have sold every one. But that was just what he did not want to do. He preferred to make what money he needed giving French lessons; that way, he would learn English. Later, he took a job working from two to six every afternoon in J. P. Morgan's private library for one hundred dollars a month. When the Arensbergs returned to New York he rented a studio for forty dollars a month in the Lincoln Arcade building on Broadway and 66th Street – a square room looking out onto a narrow court, with an alcove containing a double bed (usually unmade), two chairs (generally covered with clothes), and 'canvases in disorder everywhere'.[33] He spent his time playing chess, in which he was becoming increasingly interested, and working, desultorily, on the *Large Glass*. 'It interested me,' he explained, 'but not enough to be *eager* to finish it. I'm lazy, don't forget that. Besides, I didn't have any intention to show it or sell it at that time. I was just doing it, that was my life. And when I wanted to work on it I did, and other times I would go out and enjoy America.'[34]

New York enchanted him. 'It was different from Paris. A little bit provincial. There were many small French restaurants, small French hotels, which have disappeared. Everything changed in 1929 with the crash. Taxes were introduced . . . I saw a little of what America must have been like in the nineteenth century.'[35] He loved its democracy – the way wealthy and poor alike used the subway to travel around town. He loved the relaxed life of Greenwich Village, with its chess players and artists. 'I wasn't getting "so much per month" from anyone. It was really *la vie de bohème* in a sense, slightly gilded.'[36] In Paris he had been very much on the fringes of artistic life, working in the library, living in his small apartment in the Rue Ste Hippolyte, on visiting terms with a few artists – Picasso, Braque, Delaunay – but never part of their intimate circle. But in New York he found himself, because of the *Nude*, at the centre of attention. He abhorred Mabel Dodge's 'evenings', but was soon taken up by a group of poets, painters and musicians, American and European, which met three or four times a week after dinner at the Arensbergs', to gossip, play chess (another link between Arensberg and Duchamp), listen to music, discuss art and relax. There was always a loaded sideboard (especially appreciated by the penurious poets), and sometime after midnight, Louise would wheel in a trolley of cakes and puddings, to act as blotting paper for the whisky which was also liberally to hand. The gathering would end in the early hours, sometimes riotously.

The Arensberg group included representatives of all the arts: writers and poets such as William Carlos Williams, Mina Loy and Alfred Kreymborg (who also played chess to professional standard), painters from the Stieglitz circle, musicians like Louise Arensberg herself. There was also, as the months went by, a strong French contingent, which as well as Duchamp included the Picabias, the painter Alfred Gleizes, who had been a member of the Puteaux Cubists, and his wife Juliette Roche, and the composer Edgard Varèse, the originator of concrete music. And it is clear from all accounts that Duchamp, 'this extraordinary and popular young man', as William Carlos Williams called him, was absolutely the star of the show. He was now twenty-seven years old, with 'the charm of an angel who spoke slang . . . frail, with a delicately chiseled face and penetrating blue eyes that saw all. When he smiled the heavens opened. But when his face was still it was as blank as a death mask.' This enigmatic emptiness at his core puzzled everyone. Did it reflect some mysterious childhood hurt?[37]

He hypnotized them; and at the same time eluded them. Henri-Pierre Roché, whose *Victor* is an attempt to analyse this attraction, ascribes it partly to celebrity ('He was, after Napoleon and Sarah Bernhardt, the most famous Frenchman in America'), partly to positive virtues ('He had beauty and a central, incendiary, negative idea'), and partly to the impossibility of pinning him down. 'Everybody loves him,' says Patricia, the novel's heroine 'He's everyone's and no-one's. Wherever he goes he becomes the centre, the leader.' (Patricia was a portrait of Beatrice Wood, then in love with Roché and Duchamp's fond friend; later the lover of both. 'The three of us were something like an *amour à trois*,' she remembered in old age. 'It was a divine experience of friendship.'[38])

All this – his notoriety, his impenetrability, his easy charm and starry status – made him a potentially intimidating figure; and it seems clear that a large part of his magic lay in the fact that this awestruck expectation was not generally fulfilled. On the contrary, what struck most people about Duchamp was his absolute lack of side or pomposity. He could be very kind and tactful. When Beatrice Wood found herself penniless he pressed a sealed envelope into her hand at the end of an evening, adjuring her to open it only when she was alone in her room. ' "Do not open it in front of anyone." . . . Then he kissed me goodnight and walked quickly away . . . I hurried up the stairs and breathlessly opened the envelope. Inside was fifty dollars . . .'[39] But Wood, besides being a woman (always helpful where the flirtatious Duchamp was concerned), spoke fluent French. Communication between the French contingent and the Americans was not always so easy. This was partly because of the language barrier, but also because of a certain defensiveness among the young American avant-gardists, who were always conscious of being, as William Carlos Williams put it, 'for the most part beginners in matters of art, no matter how we might struggle to conceal the fact'. The result was a certain ambivalence regarding the 'sophisticates from Montmartre'. The Arensberg salon, said Williams, 'disturbed and fascinated me. I confess I was slow to come up with any answers.'[40]

Williams found it impossible to get on terms with Duchamp. One especially disastrous encounter remained imprinted on his memory, '[filling] me with humiliation so that I can never forget it'.

> Seeing on Arensberg's wall a recent picture by Duchamp showing five heads ... (I think it was a portrait of his own sisters), I wanted to say something to him about it. He had been drinking. I was sober. I finally came face to face with him as we walked about the room. I said, 'I like your picture,' pointing to the one I have mentioned.
>
> He looked at me and said, 'Do you?'
>
> That was all.
>
> He had me beat all right, if that was the objective.
>
> I could have sunk through the floor, ground my teeth, turned my back on him and spat ... I realized then and there that there wasn't a possibility of my ever saying anything to anyone in that gang from that moment to eternity ...[41]

And yet, in that instant repulsion lie the seeds of Duchamp's phenomenal success in America. One could hardly imagine anything further removed from the earnest, almost religious social idealism and artistic enthusiasm of Williams and his fellow-poets than Duchamp's unrelenting detachment and indifference. They were intent on delving into their own and each other's souls: Duchamp's whole artistic endeavour was dedicated to concealing his, if any. But that same American enthusiasm which, repulsed, took so violently against him, was equally ready, if allowed, to flame up in his favour. Those whom he did not repel were enchanted. It is not every day that one is accepted on equal terms by a phenomenon; and as a result, his impact on America (and eventually the world) was far greater than anything he might have achieved had he stayed home amidst the cynics of Europe.

No wonder he felt New York was home, a place where he might spend his life. It must have seemed like a dream. Viewed from the perspective of Paris, it *was* a dream; just as France, from New York, was a nightmare – with all a nightmare's unreality. Henri-Pierre Roché describes a visit to a cinema at which the newsreel showed French troops bursting from the trenches. The audience applauded. The same newsreel went on to show German troops of the imperial guard goose-stepping through the burning ruins of a French village; and the audience applauded once more. The war existed in another world. Political edge, even of the most general sort, is noticeable by its absence from the mockery of Duchamp and Picabia. Duchamp reserved his scorn for art; as for Picabia, there is fury there, all right, but it is a personal, inturned fury: 'What I like least in others', he wrote, 'is myself.'[42]

*

Picabia, unlike Duchamp, was passed fit for active service. It seemed at first as though he would have to spend the war in uniform, 'to which', as his wife observed, 'no-one could have been less suited'.[43] He tried to extricate himself from the artillery by offering his services as a military artist. Then his father-in-law (an ex-cavalry colonel) stepped in: a general of his acquaintance needed a chauffeur. Francis moved down to Bordeaux with the government in exile, while Gabrielle volunteered as a nurse's aid. After a while, however, the prospect of the front line loomed once more. And once more a friend came to the rescue. Picabia was sent to Cuba to negotiate supplies of sugar and molasses for the army. He left for

67

Havana on 15 April 1915, but never arrived there, for his ship's first port of call was New York. Nonchalantly disregarding his mission, he launched himself once more into the round of gaiety. The war, Havana, sugar and the French army might never have existed.

Things had changed since his last visit. The seemingly endless war had invested the New York party with a doomsday edge, even though (for the present at least) it remained half a world away. The Arensbergs' civilized evenings were not typical of the violent fare to be found elsewhere. Gabrielle Picabia, who followed her husband in October to remind him of his mission and the dangers of disregarding it, describes

> a motley international band which turned night into day, conscientious objectors of all nationalities and walks of life living in an inconceivable orgy of sexuality, jazz and alcohol ... It was a brutal life from which crime was not excluded. We knew, for example, the hero-victim of a fatal drunkenness induced by companions with a view to stealing his identification papers ... Seen from Broadway, the massacres in France seemed like a colossal advertising stunt for the benefit of some giant corporation.[44]

Spy-fever was rife. Gabrielle was introduced one evening to Count Bernstorff, the German ambassador.

> Next morning Picabia was called to the French Commission. It was already known that we had met Bernstorff at Mrs. X's. We learned that our hostess' husband was one of the principal manufacturers of arms and other war materials for France, while Mrs. X. herself was generally held to be the mistress of the German ambassador – in short, a dubious situation. The French Commission asked Picabia to profit by Mrs. X's friendliness towards him to learn more about her and clarify her role ...[45]

He refused to be drawn in; but the perceptive Gaby saw that they had not escaped the war by merely absenting themselves. New York Dada, which was in effect the creation of Duchamp and Picabia, was as much a product of war as anything written under fire. Would Duchamp have stood so firmly by his decision to cease all artistic creation, would Picabia have been drawn so far down the path of relentless nihilism, without the constant consciousness of slaughter? 'The unknown is an exception, the known a deception,' Picabia wrote in his review *391*, signing himself: *FP, who knows nothing, nothing, nothing.*

Calmly going his own way amid the maelstrom, Duchamp presented his usual enigmatic figure. His extraordinary quietism – his complete and unbudgeable indifference, to money, reputation, the supposed pleasures of creative work – contrasted with his genial manner. For Gabrielle Picabia, the secret of his attraction lay in this unexpected and beguiling disjunction. 'Despite the pitiless pessimism of his mind, he was personally delightful, with his gay ironies. The attitude of abdicating everything, even himself, which he charmingly displayed between two drinks, his elaborate puns, his contempt for all values, even the sentimental, were not the least reason for the curiosity he aroused, and the attraction he exerted on men and women alike.'[46]

The women, especially, found him irresistible. He had by now quite lost his pre-war reticence and was happy to oblige them sexually, though always declining, in accordance with his principles, to commit himself emotionally. His friend Henri-Pierre Roché remembered him at this time as constantly surrounded by girls, 'like a great flower of fragrant dresses that constantly renewed itself'.[47] He slid his hands dexterously under their bodices, he whispered in their ears. And what did he whisper? Only the wittiest obscenities. ' "*On peut dire*," he began, his beautiful streamlined face pressed to mine,

"*Madame, vous avez un joli caleçon de satin. On ne peut pas dire*," he concluded with a whimsical kiss, "*Madame, vous avez un sale con de catin*."[48] The rather prudish William Carlos Williams describes a typically louche party including ('of course') Duchamp, at which he saw

> a French girl, of say eighteen or less, attended by some older woman. She lay reclining upon a divan, her legs straight out before her, surrounded by young men who had each a portion of her body in his possession which he caressed attentively, apparently unconscious of any rival. Two or three addressed themselves to her shoulders on either side, to her elbows, her wrists, hands, to each finger perhaps . . . and some to her legs. She was in a black lace gown, fully at ease. It was something I had not seen before. Her feet were being kissed, her shins, her knees, and even above the knees, though as far as I could tell there was a gentleman's agreement that she should not be undressed there.[49]

This mode of multiple embrace was evidently fashionable among the Arensberg crowd: Mina Loy describes something very similar going on 'in Walter's parlor': 'every now and then a man would rise, giving his place to another'.[50] Nothing could have expressed more graphically the current mood of decadent sensuality, nor been more calculated to offend a youthful idealist. Duchamp also enjoyed taking American girlfriends to the Café du Brevoort on the corner of Fifth and Eighth Avenues, which had a French proprietor and staff, and teaching them French *gros mots*, to shock the barman. (In *Victor*, Roché's novel, Beatrice Wood's character Patricia, on first meeting Pierre (Roché), suggests they sit down on the bed, which is the room's only comfortable seat, with the words, '*Foutons-nous sur votre lit comme divan – c'est Victor qui a fignolé mon français.*' ('Let's relax on the bed, since you don't have a sofa. Victor's been fixing my French.') But *foutre* means fuck, a word unthinkable for any well-brought-up American miss, and one whose meaning clearly passes Patricia by.)

Inevitably, in this supercharged atmosphere, the urge brutally to destroy comfortable preconceptions, in ways that had more to do with ferocity than art, became irresistible.

The most notorious such gesture took place in and around the Exhibition of Independent Painters, organized in 1917 by Katherine Dreier, a large blonde German-American approaching middle-age who was passionately committed to the cause of modern art. Miss Dreier was dazzled by Duchamp, who always treated her kindly: it was for her that he executed his very last painting, *Tu m'*, the following year. This, the occasion of their meeting, was to be an exhibition without censorship: anyone might exhibit, on payment of six dollars. Duchamp, who was on the jury, anonymously submitted a urinal, which he stood upside down and entitled *Fountain*. He signed it *R. Mutt*, possibly alluding to the Jordan L. Mott Iron Works, the company which pioneered the manufacture of plumbing equipment in the States. Then, keeping his authorship secret, he sat back to await the verdict of his fellow-jurors.

He was not disappointed: their outrage fulfilled his wildest hopes. Most of them, unaware of Mr Mutt's true identity, voted to reject the work. Despite the fact that Mr Mutt had paid his six dollars, it was banished from the exhibition and placed behind a partition so that no one was aware of its existence. 'You would really have been disappointed had the Fountain been welcomed,' Pierre Cabanne said to Duchamp years later. He replied, 'Almost. As it was, I was enchanted.'[51]

Duchamp at once set about making the most of this wonderful scandal. In *The Blind Man*, a sheet published to defend and celebrate Mr Mutt's contribution, the 'Richard Mutt Case' was exhaustively discussed.

What were the grounds for refusing Mr. Mutt's fountain: -
1. Some contended it was immoral, vulgar.
2. Others, it was plagiarism, a plain piece of plumbing.

Now Mr. Mutt's fountain is not immoral, that is absurd, no more than a bath tub is immoral. It is a fixture that you see every day in plumbers' show windows.

Whether Mr. Mutt with his own hands made the fountain or not has no importance. HE CHOSE it. He took an ordinary article of life, placed it so that its useful significance disappeared under the new title and point of view – created a new thought for that object.

As for plumbing, that is absurd. The only works of art America has given are her plumbing and her bridges.

This was not Duchamp's first 'readymade'. There had been several in Paris, including the bicycle-wheel and the bottle-rack which his sister Suzanne had thrown out with the garbage when he left, and more in New York – for example a snow shovel entitled *In Advance of the Broken Arm* which he bought one wintry day and carried proudly back to his studio. New York gossip told how Duchamp 'walked daily into whatever store struck his fancy and purchased whatever pleased him – something new – something American. Mr Mutt described these objects as "ordinary articles chosen and placed so that their useful significance disappears under the new title and point of view".'[52] They were on no account to be regarded as objects of aesthetic pleasure. Duchamp, speaking as himself, complained how difficult this was. 'It's very difficult to choose an object, because, at the end of fifteen days, you begin to like it or to hate it. You have to approach something with an indifference, as if you had no aesthetic emotion.'[53]

Readymades were, rather, expansions of the idea of chance, which interested him at this time, as it interested many others. Why this rather than that, a bicycle-wheel, a bottle-rack, a snow shovel, and not an umbrella, a shoe, a flat-iron? Aesthetics emphatically had nothing to do with it. Randomness was in the air: chance, pure chance, had led him to these objects. It was an idea whose time had come. Duchamp's first experiment with chance had been in connection with the *Large Glass*: the section known as *Three Standard Stoppages* consisted of three threads, each a metre long, dropped from the height of one metre onto a horizontal plane, and preserved in the positions in which they fell. 'Each of the *Stoppages* [made] its own deformation,' he explained. 'This amused me. It's always the idea of "amusement" which causes me to do things ... My "Three Standard Stoppages" is produced by three separate experiments, and the form of each one is slightly different. I keep the line, and I have a deformed meter. It's a "canned meter", so to speak, canned chance; it's amusing to can chance.'[54] Later, the titles became as important as the objects: the miniature French window stood on a wooden base, its panes covered with black leather, entitled *Fresh Widow*; the ball of string squeezed between two brass plates joined by four screws called *Secret Noise*. They, too, in their new incarnations, were 'canned chance'.

The readymades are oddly disturbing. This is partly because the dissonance between what they were and what they are undermines our view of ordinary life as well as art. Samuel Taylor Coleridge adduced the same explanation for his friend Wordsworth's early non-acceptance: 'In opinions of long continuance, and in which we have never before been molested by a single doubt, to be suddenly convinced of an error is almost like being convicted of a fault ... the distinct sense ... of the connection between two conceptions without the sensation of such connection ... feels as if [one] were standing on his head though he cannot but see that he is truly standing on his feet.'[55]

R. Mutt's *Fountain*, however, disturbs for other reasons, too. It may be ready-made, but it is far from pristine. On the contrary, it is loaded with associations. In Art's very own sanctum Mr Mutt pissed on the notion of Art. What, then, could he think of art collectors? And how secret, after all, was his identity? Certainly the Arensbergs – those avid collectors – were in on the secret: Walter Arensberg defended the work in the jury, and bought it for his collection; Louise wrote a cod-critical article for *The Blind Man*. They and Miss Dreier were under Duchamp's spell; they clamoured for anything he might care to produce. What, though, beneath that inscrutable and charming surface, did he think of them and their all-American enthusiasm for Art? Duchamp veiled himself: he hid behind aliases. R. Mutt was only the first of many. The Arensbergs and Miss Dreier resolutely refused to hear the voice behind the veil. But William Carlos Williams heard, and hated it.

*

Picabia had spent the past year in Barcelona, recuperating from the excesses of New York. There he had launched a review, *391*, to follow on from Stieglitz' now-defunct *291*. 'It's not as well done, but it's better than nothing, because really, here, there is nothing, nothing, nothing,' Picabia wrote Stieglitz from Barcelona announcing his new venture.[56] In *391*, along with current gossip, poems and comment, he developed his new style of machine portraits. Marie Laurencin, for example, who was sitting out the war in Barcelona with her German husband Otto von Watgen, was portrayed as a ventilator fan, representing her freshness. (The portrait's subtitle, *Four in Hand*, refers to the men in her life, of whom Picabia was one.) *Américaine* was a light bulb, the element sandwiched between Flirtation and Divorce, waiting for a screw in order to light up. In the overheated wartime atmosphere, these pictures caused a certain amount of trouble. Picabia, with his dubious military status, was unable to enter France; contact between Barcelona and Paris was maintained chiefly by the female exiles. One of these, Nicole Groult, was stopped at the frontier: the first issue of *391* carried her story.

> Aiming to express the spiritual realities of this world, Francis Picabia remains resolute in borrowing only symbols from the repertoire of exclusively modern forms.
>
> A very intelligent censor recently made a mistake and thought he recognised, among paintings representing variously Love, Death and Thought, something like the working drawings of a compressed airbrake, or of a machine to crush peach stones.
>
> Everything stopped at the frontier while the luggage of a charming Parisienne – Madame Andrée Nicole Groult – was sent to M. Painlevé of the Institute, at the Ministry of Inventions concerned with National Defence, under a good escort.

But despite these small excitements, Barcelona, with its group of artistic exiles waiting for time to pass, was no substitute for real life. Deprived of Paris –

Years of genius and oriental sun
1914–1915[57]

– Picabia yearned for New York's coruscating energy. Restored (more or less) to health, he could no longer resist the allure of the glittering city. He landed on 4 April 1917. In two days the United States would enter the war. The New York party, however, would continue for a while yet. And Picabia was not about to let Duchamp take all the prizes for scandal. The vehicle for his big gesture was Arthur Cravan, an old Barcelona acquaintance also now in New York: another of those young men who, with a few extravagant acts and an early death to their name, would become Dada and Surrealist icons.

Cravan's real name was Fabian Lloyd, and he liked to hint

that he was an illegitimate son of Oscar Wilde. In fact he was his nephew by marriage: his father, Otho Lloyd, was the brother of Oscar Wilde's unfortunate wife Constance. His mother, Nelly, was Swiss. Brought up in Switzerland with his cousin Vyvyan, Wilde's son, he grew into a tall, strong, and brutally handsome young man. At the age of twenty he came into a little money and decided to launch himself in Paris. Making the most of his two main assets, he became Arthur Cravan, prizefighter and relative of Wilde, with whom he maintained a mysterious channel of posthumous communication. (The name Cravan is probably taken from Cravans, the home town of his then girlfriend. As for Arthur, it may be after Rimbaud, or perhaps Oscar Wilde's hero Lord Arthur Savile.)[58] He acquired a certain notoriety in literary circles, where he was described as an 'improvised man of letters and professional boxer – though who knows where, exactly? But to question one aspect of Arthur Cravan is to question the whole of him.'[59] One could meet him at Kees van Dongen's Thursdays, when all the critics came to drink liqueurs at his studio near the Boulevard Saint-Michel. One corner of the studio was devoted to boxing: Cravan was to be seen there 'sparring with Negroes'.[60]

In 1912, he launched a little review, *Maintenant*, written entirely by himself. In it, he published his poems and explored his obsessions – especially that with Wilde. One entire issue was occupied by an interview with the ghost of his celebrated uncle – or was the relationship perhaps closer than that? Wilde visits Cravan/Lloyd in his apartment under the adopted name of his final years, Sebastian Melmoth. He asks after Nelly, and Fabian replies, ' "She's my mother." The question made me feel strange, for had I not often heard half-hints about my mysterious birth?'[61] Cravan also published an invented interview with André Gide, a spiteful revenge for Gide's opinion of 1901 that 'one has to admit Wilde is not a great writer'. He recounted a dream he had had of Gide: 'He was dazzled by my height, my shoulders, my looks, my wit. He was crazy about me, he'd have done anything I wanted . . .'[62] Cocteau[63] thought Cravan might have been the inspiration for Lafcadio: *Les Caves du Vatican* was written in 1913, the year Cravan published his 'interview'. Certainly there is a random quality to Cravan's life and actions that recalls Gide's hero.

In April 1914, with issue no. 4, Cravan achieved the notoriety he craved. With all the subtlety of his *alter ego* the prizefighter, he set to and abused the painters exhibiting in the current Salon des Indépendants.

> *M. Delaunay*, who has the face of an inflamed pig, or perhaps a Duke's coachman, might be expected to paint like a brute. The exterior is promising, but the interior isn't up to much . . . Unfortunately for him, he married a Russian . . . I don't say I wouldn't fuck *Madame Delaunay* just once. Like most men, I'm a born collector, so it would give me a cruel satisfaction to debauch a kindergarten teacher . . . *Marie Laurencin* (haven't seen her picture) needs someone to pull up her skirts and give her a big . . . to teach her that art isn't just a little pose in front of the mirror. Oh! My dear! (keep your trap shut!) Painting is walking, running, drinking, eating, and fulfilling your natural functions. You can say I'm disgusting, but that's just what it is . . .

The war put paid to *Maintenant* along with so much else, and Cravan fled (on the proceeds of a fake Picasso) to Switzerland. But his mother refused to keep him there. He therefore decided to make for the New World, pausing awhile in Barcelona. Here he fought the most famous boxing match of his career against the black heavyweight champion Jack Johnson who, run out of America for sleeping with white women, was supporting himself by giving exhibition matches in Europe. Johnson defeated Cravan by a knock-out in the seventh round, after carrying him for the first six: a feat the more easily achieved as Cravan, anticipating humiliation, had arrived in the ring reeling drunk. All this, however, was of little consequence. The *fact* of the fight (and the purse) was what mattered. The Cravan legend grew apace. On the boat to New York, he told his fellow-passenger Leon Trotsky that he 'preferred crushing the jaws of a Yankee gentleman in a noble sport to letting his ribs be crushed by a German'.[64] When he finally appeared in New York, it was as the poet who had challenged the world champion to a bout: and, once there, he published his own account of the fight. 'I know he is generally reputed to have a knock-out punch,' Cravan told *The Soil*'s eager readers, 'but, having fought him, I realised that this was not true.'[65]

Picabia now set up a scandal of his own for which Cravan was to be the vehicle. It was announced that the *poète-boxeur* would speak on 'The Independent Artists in France and America' on the afternoon of 12 June 1917 – an event which, judging by the tone of his *Maintenant* outburst, promised to be interesting. The audience, of course, knew nothing of the speaker's habitual style of art criticism. It consisted principally of Fifth Avenue hostesses eager to learn the latest trends in 'futurist' art. Meanwhile Picabia and Duchamp took Cravan to lunch at the Brevoort, where they got him roaring drunk.

The appointed hour arrived, but the speaker did not appear. Increasingly restive, the audience waited. Arensberg, the chairman, pacified them by offering free drinks from the bar which ran along one side of the room. Every few minutes the phone would ring to announce, 'Don't worry! He's on his way!' Eventually his prayers were answered. The speaker staggered in, and the audience settled down to hear what he had to say.

Cravan sober was a charming fellow, reserved, courteous, a faithful lover and devoted friend. This was the *poète*. Alcohol, however, liberated the *boxeur*. He barely made it to the podium, where he sank down at the small table and began scornfully to address the audience. Then all of a sudden his voice fell. He muttered about suffering intolerable pain: he couldn't possibly go on unless he took his clothes off. No sooner said than done. He proceeded to remove his waistcoat, unfastened his braces, leaned over the table and began to hurl obscene epithets at the audience. At this crucial juncture, before the descent of the trousers, several policemen, alerted by a distressed member of the audience, entered the room, handcuffed him, and dragged him out. They would have taken him to jail, but Arensberg stepped in, stood bail and whisked the sodden lecturer away.

The scandal was complete: the audience dispersed in disarray. 'You can't curb a force of nature,' commented a lady. Gaby Picabia records a beaming Duchamp commenting, 'What a wonderful lecture.' But Roché remembers him staying on at the Arensbergs' that night after all the others had left and seeming to feel, for the first time, a certain self-disgust.

Picabia felt no such qualms. *391* (now being edited from New York) recorded that since Cravan's 'delightful chat about the Independent Artists was broken off by *force majeure*, the brilliant lecturer is proposing to finish his New York summer in Sing Sing'.[66]

In fact he finished it much further afield. It was by now clear that America would soon introduce conscription. Cravan fled to Canada; later, after a brief return to New York, he left once more for Mexico, this time accompanied by the British poet Mina Loy, whom he had met at the Arensbergs' and would eventually marry. They led a gipsyish existence there, subsisting on what Cravan could earn from boxing bouts and journalism. They decided to move on to Buenos Aires: Cravan acquired a small boat and began to refit it for the voyage.

What happened then? Nobody knows, everyone guesses. According to William Carlos Williams, 'One evening, having triumphantly finished the job, he got into it to try it out in the bay before supper. He never returned. Pregnant on the shore, [Mina] watched the small ship move steadily away into the distance. For years she thought to see him again . . .'[67]

So the myth was born. Some, given to assonance, resuscitate Cravan in the equally mysterious Mexican writer B. Traven. His mother continued to believe that he had, after all, arrived in Buenos Aires. Mina finally accepted that he must have drowned in the Pacific; but she insisted that it was suicide, not an accident, and that he had drowned himself to safeguard the inheritance of their daughter Fabienne. As the years passed, he became less and less probable.

> You know, he was so extraordinary. [Mina wrote.] His life was unreal, or surreal, in that he never *was* the things he became. For instance, he became *champion de Boxe amateur de la France* without boxing, because all the challengers sat in a row and he was presented and they all resigned . . . So he was champion . . . He used to walk about Berlin with four prostitutes on his shoulders. The police ordered him to leave, and he asked if they could give any reason for turning him out. They replied that there was no particular reason, merely, '*Sie sind zu auffalend*' – you are too 'noticeable'.[68]

Duchamp insisted that he was a work by Duchamp. Like Vaché, he lives on as Dada-Surrealist legend: but where Vaché was subtle, Cravan was merely crude; where Vaché was cruel, Cravan blundered. Cravan was Vaché blunted and enlarged: simplified and brutalized for the violent New York market.

*

By the autumn of 1917, it was clear that the great New York party was coming to an end. The war had reached out across the Atlantic to join them. Juliette Roche, Gleizes's wife, recorded the kind of thing one overheard at the Brevoort:

The Russians are doing a good job!
No, no! It's the Fifth Dimension!
You don't know the English!
My eye is nothing but a convention!
28,965,000 tins of jam . . .
92,567,300 tons of coal . . .
These are tragic times—
They've got the contracts, but not the ships . . .[69]

In October Picabia left never to return, destined for Paris, and thence (following another nervous collapse) a Swiss rest-cure. Duchamp, called before yet another French army board, was once more rejected for active service. He took a job as secretary to a captain at the French military mission in New York. But he did not enjoy this; and in the summer of 1918, having arranged six months' exemption from military duty, he left for Buenos Aires, arriving there on 21 September in the company of Yvonne Chastel, the ex-wife of his sister Suzanne's intended husband Jean Crotti. There, three weeks later, he received the terrible news that his brother Raymond had died, from blood-poisoning picked up at the front.

Faced with this awful blow, Duchamp retreated into chess. He began to play obsessively, to the point where Yvonne packed up and left for France. And in June 1919, disappointed with the bourgeois dullness and heavy *machismo* of Buenos Aires, he, too, embarked for Europe. He left more than one broken heart in New York – including that of Katherine Dreier, who even travelled to Buenos Aires to visit him.

But perhaps the person who most missed Duchamp in New York was a young artist who went by the name of Man Ray.

Duchamp had met Man Ray through the group of American poets – specifically, Kreymborg – that assembled at the Arensberg salon, and there developed between them an intimate confederacy that would last all their lives. A small man (he was hardly more than five feet tall) with pouchy cheeks and an inscrutable expression, Man Ray had begun life in Philadelphia as Emmanuel Radnitsky, the son of Russian-Jewish immigrants. Art had always been his main preoccupation, and he soon showed the technical facility which would in later life prove both a blessing and a curse. He found he could make a good living doing technical drawing. But this was never more than a means to an end. He attended art classes in his spare time, fell in love with a fellow-student's ex-wife, a Belgian poet named Adon Lacroix, and became another person. When, later, people asked him about his beginnings he would say: 'My first name is Emanuel, and my last name is no concern of anyone's.'

As Man Ray, he began to paint – notably, some attractive geometric landscapes obviously influenced by Cubism. He was on the edge of the Stieglitz group, and was hoping, as he would hope all his life, to make a name and career as a painter. At the time he met Duchamp he was living with Adon, generally known as Donna, in Grantwood, New Jersey. A group of modernist friends, including Kreymborg, practised the simple life there in a small artists' colony of clapboard shacks situated on a bluff. The shacks were primitive but cheap, and Man Ray, like most of this group, was broke. The winters were hard, but summer was delightful.

It was a Sunday afternoon late in the summer of 1915 when Man Ray noticed two visitors walking down the path towards the colony. They were Arensberg and Duchamp, come to see Kreymborg's country place. Man Ray spoke no French, and Duchamp's English was still non-existent. However, Donna's first language was French. She and Duchamp chatted away. Meanwhile Man Ray brought out two tennis rackets and a ball. He and Duchamp took up their positions; there was no net. 'I called the strokes to make conversation: fifteen, thirty, forty, love, to which he replied each time with the same word: yes.'[70] They felt an immediate sympathy for each other.

Man Ray was fiercely radical. He had received his art training at the Ferrer Center, named after the Catalan anarchist and radical educationalist Francisco Ferrer. Anarchism was active in America, and Man Ray moved in anarchist circles. Donna's first husband, Adolf Wolff ('Loupov' in Man Ray's memoir *Self-Portrait*), wrote for *The International*; Man Ray designed at least three covers for it, and two (August and September 1914) for Emma Goldman's magazine *Mother Earth*.

These activities, unsurprisingly, placed him, as far as patrons and public were concerned, firmly on the margins of American life. If he wanted to make a good living, he could do so through his professional drawing expertise; but this was not how he wished to spend his time. He therefore faced the age-old artist's dilemma: principle and poverty, or compromise and a sufficiency? And now here came Duchamp, an unrepentant iconoclast if ever there was one, a fellow-pacifist, a man who refused to repeat his previous work despite acclaim and the promise of wealth. And he had pulled off the trick: while Man Ray was living in a wooden shack in New Jersey, Duchamp had the run of some of Manhattan's wealthiest salons. Is it any surprise that Man Ray immediately fell under Duchamp's spell?

Not long after this meeting Man Ray came into some money, selling a number of paintings to the Chicagoan collector A. J. Eddy. On the strength of this coup he and Donna moved back to the city, and Man Ray and Duchamp began to see more of one another. Man Ray shared Duchamp's passion for chess; they were both interested in photography. Duchamp, already fulminating against the thrall of the 'retinal' in art, was suffering endless hours of tedium translating his *Large Glass* from project to actuality. Perhaps photographic techniques might achieve the same effect, but far more quickly? He told his new friend that he would stop painting altogether when it was finished. With any luck photography would soon bore people with painting – 'until something comes along which makes photography unbearable'.[71] Man Ray's approach was somewhat different: he was intent upon making the camera a pure medium for the expression of what was in his head. He said, 'I am trying to make my photography automatic – to use my camera as I would a typewriter – in time I shall attain this and still avoid the irrelevant for which scientific instruments have such a strong penchant.'[72]

Duchamp's living quarters, when Man Ray went to visit him, showed no trace of his fashionable success. He was then living in a ground-floor apartment that 'looked as if he had been moving out and leaving some unwanted debris lying around'.[73] On a pair of trestles near the window, Man Ray observed 'a large piece of heavy glass covered with intricate patterns laid out in fine lead wires'.[74] This was the Glass, then endlessly in progress; the walls were covered with notes and drawings for it. Man Ray offered to photograph it.

Duchamp did not take him up on this offer until sometime later. By then he had moved to another apartment, a large loft, with a naked bathtub standing in the middle of the floor and, hanging from the ceiling and against the wall, various paintings by and of members of his family. The Glass, covered with dust, stood on its trestles.

It was to be an important moment in Man Ray's professional life.

> There was only a single unshaded bulb hanging over his work, but from experience I knew this did not matter in copying still objects ... Looking down on the work as I focused the camera, it appeared like some strange landscape from a bird's-eye view. There was dust on the work and bits of tissue and cotton wadding that had been used to clean up the finished parts, adding to the mystery. This, I thought,

was indeed the domain of Duchamp ... Since it was a long
exposure I opened up the shutter and we went out to eat
something, returning about an hour later, when I closed the
shutter ... The negative was perfect – I was confident of the
success of my future assignments.[75]

Duchamp entitled this photograph *Elevage de poussière* –
'Raising dust' in the same sense, he explained, as one might say
'Raising pigs'. He had nurtured that dust – had protected it
from cleaners with a notice: ELEVAGE DE POUSSIÈRE – À
RESPECTER. Later he cleaned it off, all except one section in
which he mixed it with varnish to obtain 'an effect of blond,
transparent cones which I never would have obtained with
paint'.[76]

This wonderful photograph remains one of the best Man
Ray ever did, and is constantly reproduced. It embodies the
frustrating paradox of his career. As a photographer he was
unparalleled – brilliant, original and innovative, making unique
pictures, always experimenting with new techniques. At this
particular time he was in fact using a commercial photographic airbrush to produce paintings – a technique which the
critics, who had evidently still not separated the notions of
artist and *craftsman*, much disliked: they thought it smacked
of cheating.

But he wanted to be a painter, not a photographer: this
presented problems. The trouble with painting was that his
patrons wanted more of the same, while his restless spirit
constantly hankered after something new. After his hit with
Mr Eddy, he had had several more exhibitions of his paintings.
But his initial success was not repeated. Neither the airbrush
paintings nor his various other experiments sold as well as
the Cubistic landscapes he had abandoned. When he exhibited
his 'Rope Dancer Accompanied by Her Shadows' at the
Independent Artists show, a critic wrote: 'The person who

painted this picture is a drug addict, a pervert and a criminal!' Unwilling to move backwards artistically, he was forced to return to his draftsman's job to make a living.

Meanwhile Donna and he were drifting apart. He spent all his time working, either at the office or in his studio, while she was alone at home. Eventually, inevitably, she took another lover; and although they got back together for a while, it was clear that the marriage was doomed. Not without bitterness (on one occasion he even beat her up with a leather belt) Man Ray moved out. To complicate matters he was beginning to fall in love with Donna's daughter by her first marriage, Esther Wolff, whom he had first met as a child posing in the life class, but who was now a nubile and flirtatious teenager. 'She looked at me with questioning eyes and asked me if I was unhappy. I took her into the hallway, put my arms around her, said I did not know exactly what I felt ... I only hoped I would be a lasting friend, whatever came. There must have been a note of emotion in my voice – she put her arms around me and kissed me, ran up the steps calling back to me that she would speak to Mother. I called back for her not to do that.'[77]

Clearly his life needed a new direction. He was therefore delighted when, after a few months in Paris, Duchamp reappeared in New York early in 1920, bearing a chemist's sealed glass *Flask of Paris Air* as a present for Walter and Louise Arensberg. And indeed it was not long before Duchamp had drawn his friend into Katherine Dreier's latest enterprise: to set up a museum of modern art. For Duchamp, Man Ray's presence served to dilute Miss Dreier's Germanic intensity; for Man Ray, it was (among other things) an opportunity to earn some much-needed money taking photographs for the projected museum. He made other contributions, too: his first artefact, a work entitled *Lampshade*, made from an old lampshade which he had lifted from a dump and cut into a spiral; and (in a slightly different sphere), a name for the project, which he suggested (not knowing that the words meant, simply, 'incorporated') should be called Société Anonyme. Duchamp was enthusiastic, and Miss Dreier was swept along. Later, the word 'Inc.' was added, so that the project became, effectively, 'Inc. inc.'

'Paris seemed dull to me during the months I was in France,'[78] Duchamp wrote. But if Paris had palled by comparison with the remembered gaieties of New York, the New York he now encountered failed equally to live up to the memory of its former self. Prohibition was introduced a few days after his return, resulting in unsatisfactory extremes of public glumness and private excess. 'One doesn't drink any more here and it's quiet, too quiet,' he wrote to Yvonne.[79] He played chess as much as ever, and he and Man Ray tried out some projects. Duchamp was constructing a machine consisting of two rotating panels of glass painted with spirals and mounted on ball-bearings. Man Ray agreed to photograph it when it was completed. When the machine was set in motion, however, the panels of glass flew off and almost beheaded both artist and photographer. Undaunted, Duchamp ordered new materials and set about rebuilding his machine; in the meantime the two friends planned further collaborations. One was an experiment with two movie cameras, joined by gears, to see if a film shot simultaneously from two different angles would be stereoscopic when projected. Unfortunately, when the film came to be developed it swelled and stuck together. A little was salvaged, and there did seem to be an effect of relief. But, as Man Ray put it, 'capital was needed, as well as several other adjustments'.[80] The project was abandoned. Another was tried: a New York Dada magazine, inspired by some of the publications Duchamp had seen in Paris.

As Man Ray told it in his memoirs, this was an insignificant affair, 'as futile as trying to grow lilies in a desert'.

I picked material at random – a poem by the painter Marsden Hartley, a caricature by a newspaper cartoonist, Goldberg, some banal slogans. Stieglitz gave us a photograph of a woman's leg in a too-tight shoe; I added a few equivocal photographs from my own files. Most of the material was unsigned to express our contempt for credits and merits. The distribution was just as haphazard and the paper attracted very little attention. There was only the one issue.[81]

Doubtless all that was true. But *New York Dada* played a more significant role in Man Ray's life than he allows here. It was his first contact with the Dada scene, both via Duchamp but also in the person of a new correspondent: Tristan Tzara, writing from the Dada epicentre of Zurich. 'Dada belongs to everybody,' Tzara announced. '. . . I know excellent people who have the name Dada. Mr Jean Dada; Mr Gaston Dada; Francis Picabia's dog is called Zizi de Dada . . . Dada belongs to everybody, like the idea of God or the toothbrush.' Tzara looked forward to universal Dada: 'Dadaglobe.'

Man Ray found all this instantly sympathetic. Dada, in his view, was 'a state of mind . . . the tail of every other movement'.[82] It was, more importantly, his own state of mind. He added his name to the vast international list of Tzara's correspondents.

Duchamp was off once more to Paris. He suggested that Man Ray might like to join him there, and Man Ray realized that this was the chance he had been waiting for. What was to keep him in New York? Each preferred (or in Man Ray's case, was to prefer) the detachment of expatriate life. Like Duchamp, too, Man Ray preferred to travel light. It was yet another point of contact between them. He at once set about getting a passport 'to convince myself that I was going away', obtained a cheque for 500 dollars on account from a prospective buyer introduced by Stieglitz, and bought an old theatrical trunk and a large packing case to hold his works and equipment. As for his clothes, they were on his back. He spent his last American night dancing and drinking, and was poured into his bunk by friends an hour before the boat sailed.

In 1915, the sculptor Frank Macmonnies (just arrived from Paris) wrote in the *New York Times*: 'If only America would realize that European art is finished, dead, and that America is the country of tomorrow's art, instead of trying to refer everything back to European traditions! Look at the skyscrapers! Can Europe show anything more beautiful?'[83] And Jean Crotti, in grateful exile, reflected: 'It seems possible to me that New York is destined to become the artistic center of the world.'

Their refrain would re-echo through the coming decades.[84] But it would take another war before the world came round to this way of thinking. In the meantime the tide of ideas ebbed back to Europe, and the artists followed in its wake.

CHAPTER THREE

THE CELESTIAL ADVENTURE OF M. TRISTAN TZARA

SINCE EARLY 1916, the name *Tristan Tzara* had been spreading, virus-like, around the avant-garde in Paris and elsewhere. As a friend of his remarked, one of his main occupations was wrapping and posting.[1]

In February that year he wrote to Max Jacob from Zurich, enclosing a poem. He was editing a new review, *Cabaret Voltaire*, and requested books, poems, copies of *Soirées de Paris* – in short, anything Jacob might have to hand. But Max, living from hand to mouth, had nothing to offer.

Undeterred, Tzara tried elsewhere, enclosing another poem. This time he addressed himself to Paul Guillaume, an art dealer who had recently started a review of his own. Guillaume complimented him on the poem, passing on the interesting news that he had received it while in the company of, among others, Apollinaire, who was then back in Paris on account of his wound.

Encouraged (though evidently he needed little encouragement), M. Tzara at once wrote to Apollinaire, enclosing a copy of his review. Would the great man have a poem for *Cabaret Voltaire*?

Apollinaire blew first hot, then cold. He had not replied at once, he explained, 'because I was afraid that you considered yourselves *above the mêlée*, an impossible attitude when every sort of progress, material, moral and artistic, is under threat . . .' However, he was now reassured; Hugo Ball, Tzara's co-editor on *Cabaret Voltaire*, had also written to Paul Guillaume, assuring him that the review had nothing in it of the 'German mentality'. Apollinaire promised not only poems, but prose too, if he could lay his hands on some. And would Tzara mention his latest book, the *Poète assassiné*? He even offered his services as a paid collaborator in the journal (would it be monthly? Perhaps even fortnightly?) before signing off in suitably patriotic style: *'Vive la France! Vivent ses Alliés! Vive la Roumanie!'* (for Tristan Tzara, apparently, was Rumanian).

None of these plans came to anything, however. The review, which was now called *Dada*, was badly received in the French press. It was subversive, bolshevik – Germanic, even. Apollinaire, in his new incarnation as the embodiment of patriotism, decided he could have nothing to do with such a publication. 'Even though I am a wounded soldier,' he wrote nervously, 'I have to behave with the greatest circumspection. I'm afraid of compromising myself if I collaborate on a review with German contributors, however Ententophile.'[2]

*

It was undoubtedly true: *Dada* had German contributors. It even had a German co-editor, Hugo Ball. Born in the Rhineland in 1886 to a devout Catholic family, he studied philosophy at the University of Munich. There, in 1910, he met the Expressionist playwrights Herbert Eulenberg and Frank Wedekind, and his life changed. He abandoned his studies for the theatre, which seemed to him the perfect medium for his radical ideas, and departed for Berlin. Two years later he was back in Munich, having found a job as *Dramaturg* (artistic director) at an experimental theatre there, the Kammerspiele.

This was the year, 1912, when Marcel Duchamp also came to Munich. Unlike Duchamp, however, Ball was there because he wanted to participate in the city's brilliant artistic life. He already knew the leading playwrights; he now became absorbed in the philosophy of the Expressionist painter Wassily Kandinsky, who was working towards spiritual regeneration through all-embracing artistic experience. Kandinsky became Ball's revered hero. By 1914, they were planning a book about the new theatre. In a letter to his sister Ball wrote: 'If we succeed in bringing out the brochure before October 1

... we will found an "International Society of Modern Art", including not only theatre, but also modern painting, modern music, modern dance.'[3] Unfortunately other events intervened. Ball was destined to make his mark on modern art, but in a somewhat different – though equally comprehensive – way.

It was in Munich that he met two of those who would accompany him in his new adventure. One was the young Richard Huelsenbeck, a medical student. Huelsenbeck, though six years Ball's junior, soon became a close friend and ally, sharing his interests in literature and radical activism. The other was an actress and nightclub performer, Emmy Hennings, who would become his wife. Emmy was well-known in her world – well-known for unreliability, but also for the 'incendiary nature', the 'brain-tearing intensity' of her performances, whose effect she enhanced with morphine and absinthe.[4] She was only a year older than Ball but already had a chequered history, including a broken marriage, a term of imprisonment and a suspected homicide. Nevertheless, she would be his anchor during the difficult days ahead.

When war broke out, Ball was not a pacifist. On the contrary, he volunteered three times, only to be rejected each time on medical grounds, though without being granted a permanent discharge. Curious to see what was going on, he made a private visit to Belgium in November 1914. And all thoughts of patriotic gore were instantly banished by what he saw there.

Ball's and Emmy's lives now became bound up with anti-war protest. Emmy was imprisoned for forging false papers for men wishing to avoid military service; Ball got a job as a magazine editor in Berlin, and immersed himself in the writings of Bakunin and Kropotkin. He and his friend Huelsenbeck organized meetings and poetry readings to commemorate poets killed at the front. As the war went on, Ball felt increasingly unable to continue living in Germany. By May 1915, he and Emmy had fled to Switzerland, 'the great conservation park, where the nations keep their last reserves'.[5]

There, in and around Zurich, they lived for some months on the edge. Emmy earned a little money doing menial jobs, but they spent some weeks living in fear and destitution because Ball had heard the police were after them. He was terrified of being sent back to Germany as a deserter, and to avoid this had adopted a false name. This dual identity was, it turned out, the problem – a purely administrative one. The Swiss police were concerned only with their own laws – in this case, the one concerning the proper registration of aliens. *Why* the aliens were there, interested them not at all (an important factor for the motley inhabitants of the 'conservation park'). After twelve days in detention, they let Ball go. He retired to the country to lick his wounds, and eventually got a job playing the piano with a small theatrical troupe.

Returning to Zurich early in 1916, his thoughts now returned to his first love: radical theatre. With this in mind, he approached a Herr Ephraim who owned a milk bar (*Meierei*) in Niederdorf, 'a slightly disreputable quarter of the highly reputable town of Zurich'.[6] Disreputability, of course, meant cheap rents: this was the quarter favoured by many of the exiles then assembled in Switzerland. The revolutions hatched in the tiny Spiegelgasse would reverberate through Europe. Herr Ephraim's milk bar was at number one; at number six, 'opposite us, if I am not mistaken,' Ball remembered eighteen months later, in the June preceding the October Revolution, '[there lived] Mr Ulyanov-Lenin. He must have heard our music and tirades every evening; I do not know if he enjoyed them or profited by them ... Is dadaism as sign and gesture the opposite of Bolshevism? Does it contrast the completely quixotic, inexpedient, and incomprehensible side of the world with destruction and consummate calculation? It will be interesting to observe what happens here and there.'[7]

In fact Dada memories of Lenin are few. Tristan Tzara remembered playing chess with him, though he only realized years later whom his opponent must have been. Most of the exiles frequented the same cafés, notably the Café de la Terrasse, but Lenin preferred more proletarian establishments. Of his favourite haunt he said, 'You get to know what people are really talking about. Nadezhda Konstantinova is sure that only the Zurich underworld frequents this place.' Later in the same conversation, he mused philosophically: 'I don't know how radical you are or how radical I am. I am certainly not radical enough. One can never be radical enough; that is, one must always try to be as radical as reality itself . . .'[8]

Ball's enterprise was less deliberate and more immediate than Lenin's. As he tells it, nothing could have been more straightforward than Dada's beginnings. He was broke; all he had to sell were his and Emmy's talents. He could play the piano, she could sing; cabaret was the obvious possibility.

> I went to Herr Ephraim, the owner of the Meierei, and said, 'Herr Ephraim, please let me have your room. I want to start a night-club.' Herr Ephraim agreed and gave me the room. And I went to some people I knew and said, 'Please give me a picture, or a drawing, or an engraving. I should like to put it on exhibition in my night-club.' I went to the friendly Zurich press and said, 'Put in some announcements. There is going to be an international cabaret. We shall do great things.' And they gave me pictures and they put in my announcements.[9]

The announcement read: 'Cabaret Voltaire. Under this name a group of young artists and writers has been formed whose aim is to create a centre for artistic entertainment. The idea of the cabaret will be that guest artists will come and give musical performances and readings at the daily meetings. The young artists of Zurich, whatever their orientation, are invited to come along with suggestions and contributions of all kinds.'[10]

Ball had no idea who, if anyone, might turn up in answer to this, though he and Emmy already had one collaborator: Hans Arp, an Alsatian artist who had been working in Paris. Unfortunately, since 1871 Alsace had been part of Germany, which, when war broke out, made Arp an enemy alien. He therefore moved to Switzerland. Arp was developing a new style of sculpture involving superimposed layers of cardboard, and later wood, in organic shapes and bright colours; and he helped Ball with the décor for the new nightclub.

The cabaret was due to open on 5 February. At about six that evening, Ball, Emmy and Arp were busy hammering when 'an Oriental-looking deputation of four little men arrived'. ('Oriental' was the word Ball used when he meant Jewish. He had come into contact with anti-Semitic thinking as a student, and had in fact had an operation to straighten his nose because he thought it looked too Jewish.) 'They introduced themselves: Marcel Janco the painter, Tristan Tzara, Georges Janco, and a fourth gentleman whose name I did not quite catch ... Soon Janco's sumptuous Archangels were hanging with the other beautiful objects, and on that same evening Tzara read some traditional-style poems, which he fished out of his various coat pockets in a rather charming way.'[11]

There was, of course, a language problem – though not too great, for Tzara spoke French and German as well as Rumanian: he had been writing in French since leaving Rumania. Words flowed out of him in a ceaseless, bubbling stream. He was, as Ball had noted, 'oriental': born Samuel Rosenstock in Moinesti, Rumania, he was the original rootless cosmopolitan. He was at this time not quite twenty, ten years younger than Ball. But despite his youth he already had some literary experience. He and his friend Marcel Janco, a fellow-pupil at the Lycée Mihaiu Viteazul in Bucharest, had co-edited a review containing, among other things, Rosenstock's first poems, which he signed *S. Samyro*. In the autumn of 1915 the two of them, together with Janco's brother, left Bucharest for Zurich. Janco was to study architecture; Rosenstock enrolled in the university's Faculty of Philosophy and Letters and, for the first time, sported his new *nom de guerre*: Tristan Tzara – supposedly Rumanian for *sad in the country*. Certainly a more urban spirit can rarely have existed.

Hugo Ball and Tristan Tzara were unalike in every way. Ball was thoughtful, withdrawn, blond and very tall: Tzara, small, dark and loquacious. He wore a monocle; behind it his grey eyes sparkled with intelligence and animation – he 'might have resembled Leon Trotsky or James Joyce, if each had shaved off his beard'.[12] His lack of height (remembered Hans Richter, another member of the Zurich group) 'made him all the more uninhibited. He was a David who knew how to hit every Goliath in exactly the right spot with a bit of stone, earth or manure, with or without the accompaniment of witty *bons-mots*, back-answers and sharp splinters of linguistic granite ... the total antithesis between him and Ball brought out more clearly the qualities of each.'[13]

So the core personnel of the Cabaret Voltaire assembled itself: Ball, Hennings, Tzara, tall, gentle Janco, sweet-natured Arp with his shaven head, and finally the explosive Richard Huelsenbeck, Ball's old friend, who now also arrived in Zurich. 'The Cabaret Voltaire', Hans Richter wrote, 'was a six-piece band. Each played his instrument, i.e. himself, passionately and with all his soul.'[14]

The programme varied nightly, always playing to a packed house; for it was immediately clear that something extraordinary was happening in Herr Ephraim's Meierei. The chance combination of these six had coalesced into an expression of all the fury felt by their generation. In Tzara's words, 'Every night we thrust the triton of the grotesque of the god of the beautiful into each and every spectator, and the wind was not gentle ... bitterness laid its nest in the belly of the family man.'[15] Every night, that is, except Sunday. Sunday was Swiss night, left free for the natives. But not much happened then. How could it? The point of the Cabaret Voltaire was that it was *not* Swiss, but a product of war and exile. It drew its edge from the war: from its performers' consciousness that they were there, and alive, only by a combination of luck and chance.

And chance, having brought them together, began to work its magic. For here too chance was in the air. The Cabaret Voltaire had miraculously formed itself from the chance response to a newspaper advertisement. Arp, pleased by the pattern made by some scraps of torn-up paper, pasted them where they lay and entitled the result *Following the Laws of Chance*. Tzara had a recipe for making a poem:

> Take a newspaper.
> Take some scissors.
> Choose from this paper an article of the length you want to make your poem.
> Cut out the article.
> Next carefully cut out each of the words that makes up this article and put them all in a bag.
> Shake gently.
> Now take out each cutting one after the other.
> Copy conscientiously in the order in which they left the bag.
> The poem will resemble you.
> And there you are – an infinitely original author of charming sensibility, even though unappreciated by the vulgar herd.[16]

There were differences. Arp reserved the right not to preserve his fragments if the pattern they made did not appeal to him, while for Tzara choice played no part: the refusal of the conscious self was the essential thing. But these, though not insignificant, were details. Chance guided their pens, brushes, tongues, and through it they expressed their inner-most feelings. It was like nothing anyone had ever done before: it was a negation, the very antithesis of anything previously known as art. What had the straight line of thought, the limitations of logic, done for the world? They demanded a new world, and new worlds need new ways of thinking.

Tzara's description perhaps gives the best feel of what went on:

> Red lamps overture piano Ball reads Tipperary piano 'under the bridges of Paris' Tzara quickly translates a few poems aloud, Mme Hennings – silence, music – declaration – that's all ... February 26 – HUELSENBECK ARRIVES – bang! bang! bangbangbang ... Gala night – simultaneous poem 3 languages, protest noise Negro music / Ho osenlatz ho osenlatz ... Hü-ülsenbeck Hoosenlatz whirlwind Arp two-step demands liquor smoke towards the bells/ a whispering of: arrogance/silence Mme Hennings, Janco declaration, transatlantic art = the people rejoice star hurled upon the cubist tinkle dance.[17]

Huelsenbeck liked to read his poems to the accompaniment of the big drum, marking the beat with a riding-crop. He was obsessed with African rhythms, with which he and Ball had already experimented in Berlin. Tzara punctuated his performances with bells, drums, cowbells, blows on the table or on empty boxes; he screamed, sobbed and whistled, and jiggled his buttocks like a belly dancer. Simultaneous poems were read, perhaps for three voices, perhaps for seven. Janco made extraordinary masks, 'and they are more than just clever', Ball records.

> They are reminiscent of the Japanese or ancient Greek theatre, yet they are wholly modern ... We were all there

when Janco arrived with his masks, and everyone immediately put one on. Then something strange happened. Not only did the mask immediately call for a costume; it also demanded a quite definite, passionate gesture, bordering on madness. Although we could not have imagined it five minutes earlier, we were walking around with the most bizarre movements, festooned and draped with impossible objects, each one of us trying to outdo the other's inventiveness . . .[18]

Arp wrote poems in which he explored free association ('*The rubber hammer strikes the sea/Down the black general so brave . . .*') and made more and more of his lyrical abstract works, which poured out of him 'like my toenails. I have to cut it off and then it grows again.'[19] Emmy sang her shrill songs, and the enigmatic Ball, playing accompaniments, encased in bizarre cardboard costumes, liturgically chanting his sound-poems, bound all this anarchy together. He noted: 'With all the tension the daily performances are not just exhausting, they are crippling. In the middle of the crowds I start to tremble all over. Then I simply cannot take anything in, drop everything, and flee.'[20]

*

The world knows the Cabaret Voltaire and the movement to which it gave rise by the name of *Dada*. In fact the name did not appear until April 1916, three months into the cabaret's trajectory. In his diary entry for the 18th of that month, Ball wrote: 'Tzara keeps on worrying about the periodical. My proposal to call it "Dada" is accepted . . . *Dada* is "yes, yes" in Rumanian, "rocking horse" and "hobbyhorse" in French. For Germans it is a sign of foolish naiveté, joy in procreation, and preoccupation with the baby carriage.'[21]

Dada's date of birth is therefore identified, down to the nearest week. But who had hit upon it?

A still-unended war rages over this question. Ball's diary entry seems to indicate that it was him. Tzara claimed that, 'A word was born, no-one knows how.' Arp declared that, 'Tzara invented the word Dada on 6th February 1916, at 6 p.m. I was there with my 12 children when Tzara first uttered the word . . . it happened in the Café de la Terrasse in Zurich, and I was wearing a brioche in my left nostril.'²²

Huelsenbeck, however, would have none of this. He gave at least two versions of what happened. In one he said, 'The word Dada was accidentally discovered by Ball and myself in a German-French dictionary when we were looking for a stage-name for Madame le Roy, the singer in our cabaret. Dada is the French word for hobby-horse.' In the other, Madame le Roy doesn't come into it. In this version, Huelsenbeck and Ball were trying to think of a name for their publication; Ball was leafing through the dictionary, running his finger down the columns of words, when Huelsenbeck, struck by a word he had never heard before, cried, Stop! And he and Ball and Emmy agreed that Dada was the very word they needed for their new artistic direction.²³ A letter from Ball to Huelsenbeck dated 28 November 1916, seems to back up this account: '. . . and last of all I describe Dada, cabaret and gallery. So you have the last word on Dada as you had the first.'

A childish, trivial argument; but one important in its symbolism. As Huelsenbeck himself put it, 'I do not mean to over-estimate this service, for Dada has become the symbol of the totality of our artistic expressions. But . . . my idea of Dada was always different from that of Tristan Tzara.'²⁴

'There are five of us,' wrote Ball (apparently counting Emmy and himself as a single person), 'and the remarkable thing is that we are actually never in complete or simultaneous agreement, although we agree on the main issues. The constellations change. Now Arp and Huelsenbeck agree and seem inseparable, now Arp and Janco join forces against H., then H.

and Tzara against Arp, etc. There is a constantly changing attraction and repulsion . . .'[25]

It was hardly surprising. Dada was built on tension and paradox. They were artists; but they were anti-art. They rejected rationality. But their irrationality, their abandonment of themselves to chance, was neither directionless nor purposeless. Their intention was to undermine everything – including themselves. 'I'm writing this manifesto to show that you can perform contrary actions at the same time,' Tzara wrote.[26] That was something the Dadas did every second of the day.

Under these circumstances, the surprising thing is not that Dada began to fragment so soon after it was born, but that such a group ever achieved coherence. That it did was due to Ball's unifying influence. 'I have examined myself carefully,' he had written in 1915. 'I could never bid chaos welcome, throw bombs, blow up bridges and do away with ideas. I am not an anarchist.'[27] And yet (a typical Dada contradiction) he had, in his cabaret, let loose the most anarchic force art had ever known.

He held himself together, as his diary shows, only by unremitting effort. His large, uncompromising presence reconciled them to their differences. So Arp, who was no anarchist, could accept Tzara's 'final dissolution' as a means to an end: 'a new and brilliant weapon to destroy what was outworn and useless, to ward off the bourgeois and to strengthen the line that separated us from banality (even in ourselves)'.[28] And Huelsenbeck could enjoy Tzara's prodigious literary facility without being terminally affronted by its frivolousness, its political pointlessness.

But Ball was soon exhausted, both by the physical and mental effort of the daily show, and the emotional strain of binding these disparate comets into a steady constellation. On 14 July, just five months after the opening of the Cabaret Voltaire, he marked his break with the movement by reading his Dada manifesto at the group's first public meeting, held at Zurich's Waag Hall. 'Dada is a new tendency in art. One can tell this from the fact that until now nobody knew anything about it, and tomorrow everyone in Zurich will be talking about it,' he declaimed. '. . . How can one get rid of everything that smacks of journalism, worms, everything nice and right, blinkered, moralistic, europeanized, enervated? By saying dada. Dada is the world soul, Dada is the pawnshop. Dada is the world's best lily-milk soap.'[29] It was time to move on. 'When things are finished, I cannot spend any more time with them. That is how I am; if I tried to be different, it would be no use.'[30]

Exhausted, he and Emmy left for the Ticino countryside, with its blue mountains rising above lakes and rose gardens, landing in the village of Vira-Magadino from the Locarno ferry 'like Robinson on his island of parrots'.[31] And by the end of 1917 they were in Bern, a city seething with spies and intrigues, where Ball helped edit a democratic anti-Kaiser weekly. In his diary, he comments on the Bern conspirators. There were no socialists among them – 'or at least no well-known socialists . . . They are opposed to utopia, and it would be the utopia of all utopias to be living abroad when offices are allocated in Germany in the near future.'[32] But utopianism did not worry Ball – quite the reverse. He was in search of what he termed the 'supernatural', by which he meant something above and outside the ordinary; and found 'no other answer but in isolation, in desertion, in withdrawal from the age'.[33]

He was reading at this time not only Nietzsche and Bakunin, but also those embodiments of the Zeitgeist, Rimbaud and Sade. But Ball's Rimbaud and Sade – since our heroes reflect nothing if not ourselves and our desires – were not Breton's, nor yet Apollinaire's. For Breton and his friends, preoccupied with the overturning of the old cultural order, Rimbaud's importance lay in his use of language, his revolutionary concerns, and his decision to abandon all this without a second thought. For the visionary Ball, however, Rimbaud, too, was a visionary: 'he had a religious ideal, a cult ideal, and he himself knew only one thing about it: that it was greater and more important than a special poetic talent'.[34] (And for Huelsenbeck, whose vision of the Dadaist was as 'the robber-baron of the pen', Rimbaud was 'a hell of a guy' who 'jumped in the ocean and started to swim to St Helena' while literary gents 'sit in the cafés and rack their brains over the quickest way of getting to be a hell of a guy'.[35]) In the same way, Sade, for the young Parisians the philosopher of the *acte gratuit*, was for Ball a political and artistic exemplar, an early exponent of individualism and outrage: in short, a Dadaist.

*

The deepest split in the Cabaret Voltaire was that between Richard Huelsenbeck and Tristan Tzara. 'Tristan Tzara was devoured by ambition to move in international artistic circles as an equal and even a "leader",' Huelsenbeck was to write a few years later. He went on to comment that '. . . a Napoleon among men of letters is the most tragi-comic character conceivable'.[36]

As to Tzara's ambition, there can be no question. His every action, his entire trajectory over the next few years, proclaimed it. The chance that sent him to the Cabaret Voltaire had freed his anarchic talents, and with them the certainty that this was merely the first step towards a glittering career. Ambition fuelled his tongue, to impressive effect. Without his endless verbal and poetic felicity, without his terrific energy and enthusiasm, Dada would have followed a different path. This, of course, was exactly what angered Huelsenbeck. For Tzara's path was not his. 'While Tzara transformed Dadaism into an artistic movement', Huelsenbeck wrote, 'I felt it to be a volcanic eruption.'[37]

This is what things have come to in this world
The cows sit on the telegraph poles and play chess
The cockatoo under the skirts of the Spanish dancer
That is the lavender landscape Herr Mayer was talking about
when he lost his eye
Only the fire department can drive the nightmare from the
drawing-room but all the hoses are broken . . .[38]

For Tzara Dada was an opportunity; for Huelsenbeck, a matter of life and death. For while Bucharest sat on the outskirts of the war, all Germany was convulsed by it. In the event of defeat (and after America's entry in 1917 this became virtually certain) there would be revolution. The Kaiser would go: and then who would fill the vacuum? Right or Left, Fascists or Communists? The only certainty was that, whatever the solution, it would be extreme. Ironically, many of the two sides' aims – full employment, a renewal of national self-respect, the removal from power of the old order – were not so very different. Nor were the means by which, in Germany and Russia, they would try to attain them. Great public works are a universal economic tool, totalitarianism tempts zealots of every stripe. But in 1916 all that was still in the future. What was clear was that the battle-lines were drawn, not merely at the front, but inside Germany itself. On one side were those who gave and enforced the orders, on the other, those who obeyed them – or refused to. Revolution threatened. If it could happen in Russia, why not in Germany? The Spiegelgasse chickens were homing in to the roost.

In this harsh situation, the notion of 'art which found meaning in cubes and gothic'[39] was a nonsense, and the very idea of artistic politics, almost blasphemous. Art – or anti-art – was a weapon or it was nothing. 'To make literature with a gun in hand had, for a time, been my dream,' Huelsenbeck wrote.[40]

By 1916, the group which would crystallize this feeling,

and which would become known as Berlin Dada, was already forming. It consisted of two brothers, Wieland Herzfelde and John Heartfield (who had anglicized his name as an anti-war protest), and the artist George Grosz; and its productions were marked by a savagery quite unlike anything produced elsewhere.

The first meeting of Grosz and Herzfelde was almost an artwork in its own right. It took place in 1915, at the Berlin studio of the Expressionist painter Ludwig Meidner. Grosz was then twenty-two, Herzfelde, nineteen. Both had been discharged from the army – Grosz on grounds of ill-health, Herzfelde for insubordination – and both were passionately anti-war, as was this whole gathering. Grosz, however, did not appear as himself, but as a Dutch businessman who had devised a scheme to make millions by collecting shell-splinters from the battlefield, getting war cripples to paint them with patriotic emblems and slogans such as 'God gave us and saved us' and 'Every shot hit the spot', and selling them as paper-weights and ashtrays. The earnest pacifist intellectuals were appalled, both by the horrendous cynicism of the scheme and by its cold-hearted perpetrator. Grosz unblinkingly maintained his *alter ego* for the entire evening. Later, Herzfelde made it his business to visit the perpetrator of this 'sobering . . . shocking . . . and invigorating' joke.[41]

Herzfelde was just then trying to publish an anti-war magazine, and by the summer of 1916 he had succeeded, despite having no capital, no publishing experience and no means of obtaining a publishing permit from the authorities. The trick had been to buy up the name and permit of a magazine that was failing, called *Neue Jugend*. The first issue contained, among other things, drawings by Grosz and a poem by Richard Huelsenbeck.

Grosz's brutal drawings, Herzfelde's magazines and Heart-field's extraordinary photomontages (he was at this time a postman, part of his anti-war campaign being to deposit all the letters in storm-sewers, in the hope of stirring up anti-war anger among those families who failed to receive their mail) were all vital elements of Berlin Dada. But though all were against the war, this did not mean that their political positions were identical. Herzfelde and Heartfield were and remained unequivocal Communists. In their view, the blame for the present situation rested squarely upon the shoulders of the ruling class. But Grosz was not so sure. He felt that the masses had wanted war just as much as their rulers, and that even now it was not unpopular. The war absolved people from having to make a living; it allowed them to indulge their worst instincts. Sheer selfishness (the selfishness of Grosz's 'merchant from Holland') would prolong it, though it was surely lost.

This highly equivocal view of the masses is reflected in Grosz's terrifying drawings. The message is never in doubt: it castigates those in high places. Nor is the misanthropy, which is undifferentiated and universal. But the unspoken message is more complex. Where the bourgeois and officer classes are individually drawn in what, for want of a better word, one might call loving detail, the downtrodden masses are just that: masses. Grosz has no interest in them. They are a cipher, there for the propagation of a message, strident and sulphuric. For the undirected anarchy of Zurich could have no place here. When, at the beginning of 1917, Huelsenbeck returned from Zurich to Berlin, 'I felt as though I had left a smug fat idyll for a street full of electric signs, shouting hawkers and auto horns.'[42]

Hans Richter draws a distinction between Dada and Futurism, not so much in terms of techniques and enthusiasms – many of which (simultaneity, sound-poems, machines) they shared – but in point of programme. That is to say, Futurism had a programme which its works were designed to 'fulfil' whereas Dada 'not only had *no* programme, it was against all

programmes. Dada's only programme was to have no programme ... The frailty of human nature', Richter adds, 'guaranteed that such a paradisal situation could not last.'[43] To this
blank sheet Richter attributes Dada's 'explosive power to
unfold *in all directions*'.

But what he is describing is the politics of the vacuum.
Zurich in wartime, with its zoo of exiles and non-participators,
was the still eye of the storm. Richter's Dada, irreverently,
irresponsibly, absolutely creative, reflects this exceptional
situation. Anywhere else, a programme imposed itself.
For example, Huelsenbeck recalled that when he returned to
Berlin people were beginning to realize that the war was lost,
and that as a result (since 'it was only natural they should have
lost their enthusiasm for reality') they were turning to art.
'Germany always becomes the land of poets and thinkers when
it begins to be washed up as the land of judges and butchers.'[44]
It followed that Dada must be anti-art, and especially anti-
Expressionism, that 'opulent idyll'.[45] 'I thought the war would
never end, and I think it never really did end,' George Grosz
wrote in his autobiography.[46]

The Berlin Dadaists, unlike their counterparts in New York,
were not nihilists. They set out their stall in uncompromising
terms:

What is Dadaism and what does it want in Germany?
1. *Dadaism demands:*
1) The international revolutionary union of all creative and
   intellectual men and women on the basis of radical
   Communism
2) The introduction of progressive unemployment through
   comprehensive mechanisation ...
3) The immediate expropriation of property ...[47]

It seemed that Dada and Communism were now one.
Certainly this was Huelsenbeck's view: 'Dada is German

communism,' he said.[48] Elsewhere the movement was a war-time flower, nourished by anti-militaristic fury and withering (or metamorphosing) with the return of peace and normality. But in Germany this did not happen – for in Germany the end of the war did not bring peace. On the contrary, it signalled the start of a new war. On 9 November 1918, the Kaiser abdicated. A democratic republic was at once declared – in order to forestall the declaration of a Soviet republic by Karl Liebknecht. The soldiers of the old imperial troops were ordered to fire upon workers demonstrating in the streets. At first, wrote Grosz, 'to all of us, and to me, it seemed as if the gates opened and light streamed through'. But only too soon 'the gates were closed and shut with double locks. This alerted many of us to the necessity of defining our political position.'[49] At the Cabaret Voltaire the choice, in Huelsenbeck's words, had been between 'artists and bourgeois. You had to love one and hate the other.'[50] But now things had moved on, and politics rather than art took centre stage. For Grosz, 'There were the people and there were the fascists. I chose the people.'[51] On the night of 31 December 1918, Grosz, Herzfelde and Heartfield joined the Communist Party, receiving membership cards from Rosa Luxemburg herself. From this vantage point they watched as, during the next two weeks, the soldiers of the Democratic-Socialist Weimar Republic crushed the workers' revolution with machine guns, four-inch artillery, flame throwers and trench mortars. On 15 January 1919, Luxemburg and Liebknecht were brutally murdered by the same forces.

Now began the high point of Berlin Dada. During the hectic months of 1919, Herzfelde published a series of magazines, starting with *Jedermann sein eigner Fussball* (*Every Man His Own Football*, or *Every Man Can Kick His Own Head In*), which appeared on 15 February 1919. Herzfelde and his friend Walter Mehring hired a little band to play sentimental military tunes, dressed up in top hats and frock coats and rode in a horse-drawn carriage. Behind them walked *Jedermann*'s contributors carrying bundles of the journal, each shouting the title of his contribution. As they walked through Berlin's prosperous west end their reception was cool, but as soon as they arrived in the poorer districts they were greeted with great enthusiasm. By the time they were stopped at the Alexanderplatz, the entire edition of 7,500 copies was sold out. *Jedermann* was immediately and permanently banned; it reappeared under a new name, *Die Pleite* (*Bankruptcy*), which managed six issues, all containing the usual mix of drawings, poems, photomontages, manifestos and Communist propaganda before it, too, was suppressed, to be replaced by *Der blutige Ernst* (*In Bloody Earnest*).

The Dadas, of course, did more than publish magazines. They gave soirées and cabarets inspired by the Cabaret Voltaire, they produced artworks (notably the collages of Max Ernst and Kurt Schwitters), they mocked the swearing-in of the President of the Republic, showering flysheets from the gallery nominating one of their number, Johannes Baader (*Oberdada*) for President. Where they could not outgun, they outlaughed. The high point of Berlin Dada was the great 'First International Dada Fair' held in 1920 at the gallery owned by Dr Otto Burchardt (*Finanzdada*), whose centrepiece was a stuffed effigy of a German officer with a pig's head bearing the placard 'Hanged by the Revolution'.

After this, however, the great question could no longer be avoided. Was Dada an autonomous artistic movement or the offshoot of a political party? Dada's programme might, in the black and white days of the emergency, coincide with that of the Communist Party, but how long could this cohabitation last? For Dada's programme, as Richter had remarked, was fundamentally to have no programme. The Communist Party, on the other hand, had a very definite programme, and cadres were expected not only to work within it, but to subject their work to Party approval. Some gave up the struggle: Huelsenbeck left to become a ship's doctor. Others might offer, but would their offerings prove acceptable? Thus, in 1925, Grosz and Heartfield published an essay, 'Art is In Danger', which, dismissing the subjective option of bourgeois soul-searching, saw the artist as having to choose between class war propaganda and the development of engineering that was Constructivism. When this was translated into Russian, the translator interpreted Grosz as advocating Constructivism as the most desirable route for the revolutionary artist. But this conclusion was immediately dismissed by Lunacharsky, the Soviet Commissar for Education and Culture (and an enthusiast for Grosz's own work), because Constructivism had by then fallen out of favour in Moscow. Grosz's translator (Lunacharsky insisted) must have misread the text.

What, if they could not submit to such whims, were left-leaning artists to do? The choice was stark: one could either be an apparatchik or a class traitor. The conflict would dominate the next two decades. Among others, it helped drive the Russian Futurist poet Mayakovsky to suicide, baffled André Breton and split the Surrealists. Perhaps only Marcel Duchamp and Man Ray, suspended in mid-Atlantic above the fray, managed totally to ignore it.

The Berlin Dadas had no more easy answers than anyone else. As time went on, Grosz, repudiating his former self and donning another, became a bourgeois. So, too, did Huelsenbeck. It is interesting to note, in the light of these early hostilities, that during World War II Tzara, by then a devoted Communist, became a hero of the French Resistance, while Huelsenbeck emigrated to America and became a New York psychoanalyst with a large apartment on Central Park West.

*

Ball and Huelsenbeck might have disappeared (though Ball would return to Zurich and Dada for a few more months early in 1917), but for Tzara the Dada adventure had only just begun. And the first thing to do was pin it down. The Dada of the Cabaret Voltaire had been a fleeting thing. What survived after the show? A few masks, a few pictures, a few photographs. What was needed, as Tzara knew, was *publication*: something solid. That had always been his priority. Huelsenbeck hated the thought that Dada might be turned to individual advantage; Tzara, that this unique opportunity might be wasted.

The very first Dada publication, a magazine, *Cabaret Voltaire*, was more or less a communal affair, with Ball in charge. But after one issue it changed its name to *Dada*, and Tzara became its editor. To the suspicious eyes of Huelsenbeck this was but one more example of Tzara's overweening ambition: Dada, which belonged to everyone, was being used to further one man's career. 'What a source of satisfaction it is to be denounced as a wit in a few cafés in Paris, Berlin, Rome!'[52] Others, however, saw it differently. Hans Richter observed that 'Tzara . . . edited, directed, propelled, designed and administered the periodical *Dada*. Ball's plan of circulating the editorship was not carried out, simply because no-one but Tzara had so much energy, passion and talent for the job.'[53]

The first number of *Dada* appeared in July 1917, by which time Ball was back in Zurich, and Dada once again putting on its soirées, this time at the Galerie Corray, where a Dada exhibition, assembled by Tzara at three days' notice, could be viewed during the day. (With his usual organizational flair, Tzara had overcome wartime shortages of suitable materials by realizing that the governments of the belligerent nations were only too anxious to compete with one another in neutral Switzerland, even if it meant putting themselves in the hands of Dada. From France, Italy and Germany he sought and

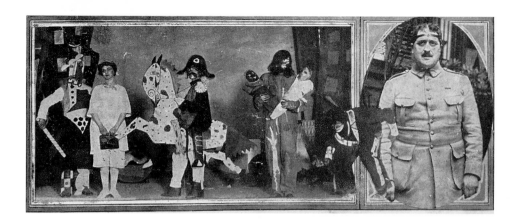

Above: Les Mamelles de Tirésias, showing Serge Férat's décor and costumes. The author is in full patriotic fig, and bandaged following his operation

Right: Unwilling soldiers: André Breton and Louis Aragon, WWI

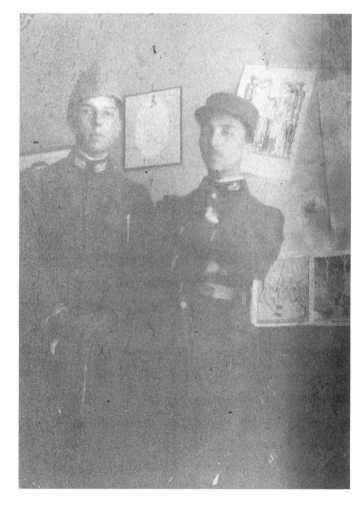

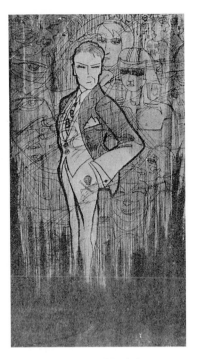

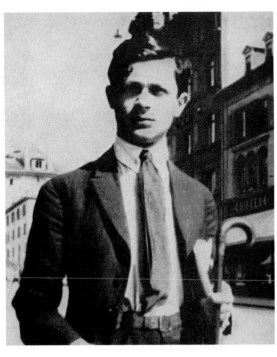

Jacques Vaché

Tzara with gloves and cane, the photo Breton found so reminiscent of Vaché

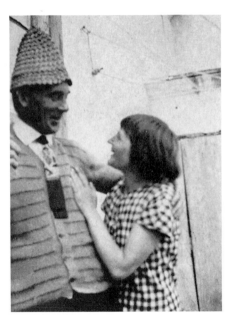

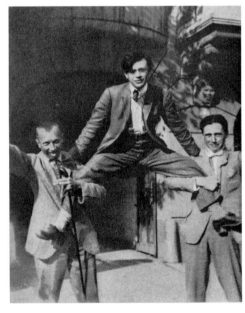

Hugo Ball and Emmy Hennings, Zurich, 1916

Hans Arp, Tristan Tzara, Hans Richter: borne aloft on Zurich's gales of laughter – 1916–17

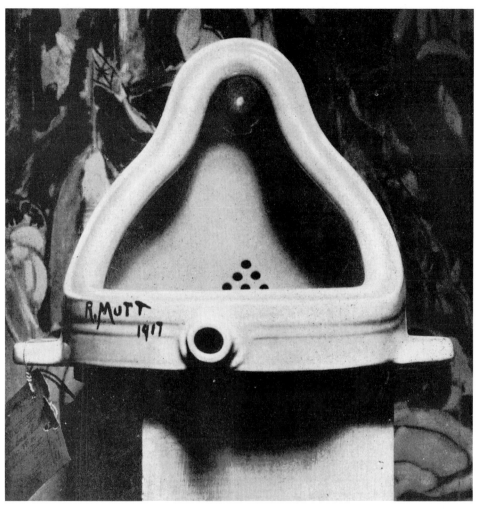

R. Mutt's *Fountain*: Duchamp pisses on Art, 1917

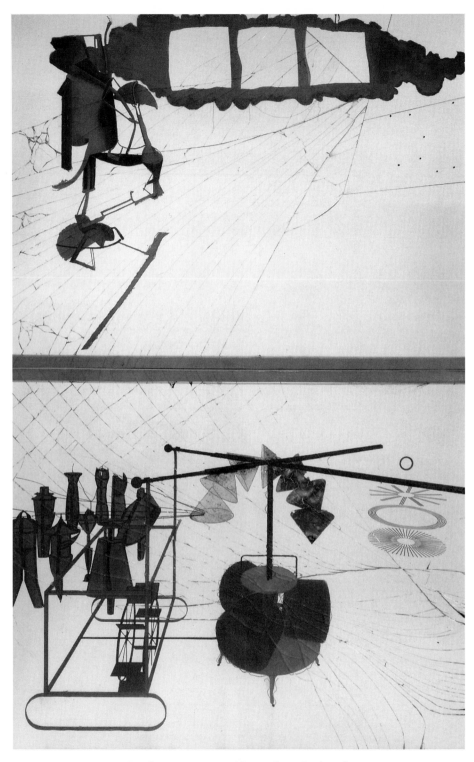

Duchamp's Large Glass, after the break

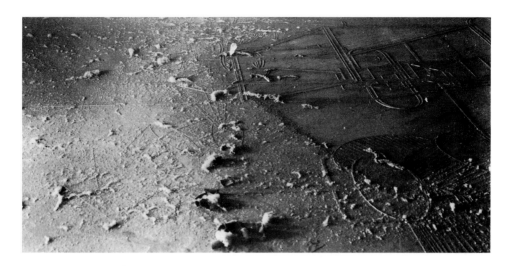

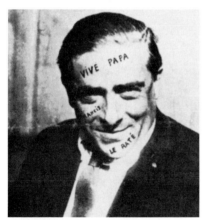

Above: Raising Dust on the Large Glass: Man Ray's famous picture

Left: Picabia – 'Long Live Papa Francis the Failure'

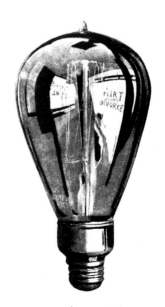

AMÉRICAINE

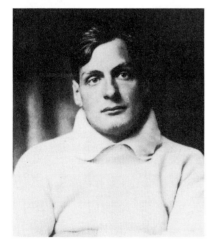

Arthur Cravan, *poète et boxeur*

Picabia: Portrait of an American girl – screw her and she lights up

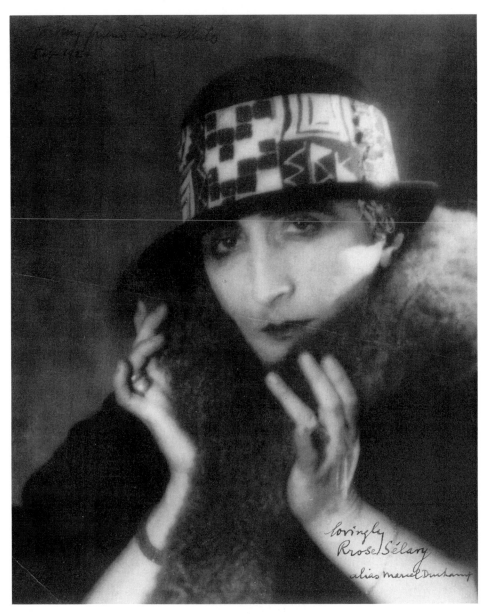

Rrose Sélavy, photographed by Man Ray, 1924

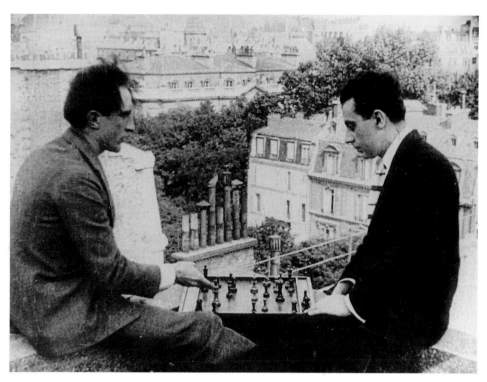

The chess players: Duchamp and Man Ray float above the fray

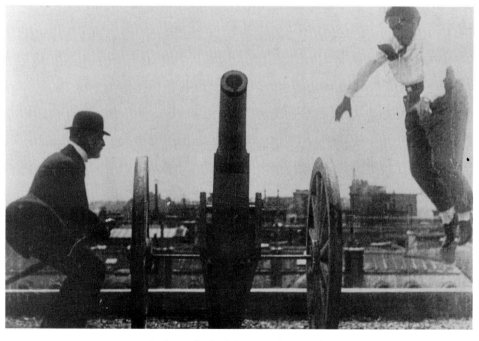

Satie and Picabia – Dada as joke

391

Au pluriel

"Une définition n'a jamais été qu'un mal pour un autre — et le commun des mortels s'appelle erreur".

De plus en plus, de moins en moins. Trois cent quatre vingt onze est un oiseau à poils, la Vierge satisfaite le tient dans ses bras, la pluie des grands jours, un biceps bien tendre, une ombre à plusieurs, les paupières comme des ongles ou les ongles comme des heures où.

Petit, petit trois cent quatre vingt onze de ma mère et des liqueurs de dessert, de plus en plus, de moins en moins, une lumière derrière un coup de poing, un coup de poing pour une lumière.

Je suis comme les autres, je vais au café. Aussitôt, j'entends : " Garçon un 391 des dimanches ". Je suis discret, je le répète jamais ce que j'écoute dans les water-closets.

Un aimable désordre sinsli or n'étant qu'un effet de l'art, j'ai pu enjamber deux ou trois fois dans ma vie une belle religieuse aux cornes d'ivoire, une belle, très belle.

Le livre sur lequel j'écris est ouvert à la page 202.

En le lisant, les Cubistes ont bien pleuré.

PAUL ÉLUARD.

Eh bien non, la lettre signée Paul Eluard n'était pas de Reverdy ! Je m'excuse infiniment auprès de celui-ci, d'une réponse qui ne peut s'adresser à lui mais bien au véritable auteur de la lettre. Ce dernier n'aura qu'à relire deux fois la note parue dans " Proverbe ", en remplaçant le nom du sympathique Reverdy par le sien, il sera frappé de voir combien cette note lui est facilement applicable !

FRANCIS PICABIA.

TABLEAU DADA par MARCEL DUCHAMP

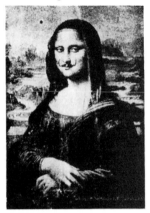

L H O O Q

Manifeste DADA

Les cubistes veulent couvrir Dada de neige ; ça vous étonne mais c'est ainsi, ils veulent vider la neige de leur pipe pour recouvrir Dada.

Tu en es sûr ?

Parfaitement, les faits sont révélés par des bouches grotesques.

Ils pensent que Dada peut les empêcher de pratiquer ce commerce odieux : Vendre de l'art très cher.

L'art vaut plus cher que le saucisson, plus cher que les femmes, plus cher que tout.

L'art est visible comme Dieu ! (voir Saint-Sulpice).

L'art est un produit pharmaceutique pour imbéciles.

Les tables tournent grâce à l'esprit ; les tableaux et autres œuvres d'art sont comme les tables coffres-forts, l'esprit est dedans et devient de plus en plus génial suivant les prix de salles de ventes.

Comédie, comédie, comédie, comédie, comédie, mes chers amis.

Les marchands n'aiment pas la peinture, ils connaissent le mystère de l'esprit...........

Achetez les reproductions des autographes.

Ne soyez donc pas snobs, vous ne serez pas moins intelligents parce que le voisin possèdera une chose semblable à la vôtre.

Plus de chiures de mouches sur les murs.

Il y en aura tout de même, c'est évident, mais un peu moins.

Dada bien certainement va être de plus en plus détesté, son coupe-file lui permettant de couper les processions en chantant " Viens Poupoule ", quel sacrilège !!!

Le cubisme représente la disette des idées.

Ils ont cubé les tableaux des primitifs, cubé les sculptures nègres, cubé les violons, cubé les guitares, cubé les journaux illustrés, cubé la merde et les profils de jeunes filles, maintenant il faut cuber de l'argent !!!

Dada, lui, ne veut rien, rien, rien, il fait quelque chose pour que le public dise : "nous ne comprenons rien, rien, rien".

" Les Dadaïstes ne sont rien, rien, rien, bien certainement ils n'arriveront à rien, rien, rien ".

Francis PICABIA

qui ne sait rien, rien, rien.

L.H.O.O.Q

received post-free propaganda material, which he then turned to his own use.)

But Tzara had already initiated a programme of Dada publication in 1916, beginning with a work of his own: *La Première Aventure céleste de M. Antipyrine*. (Antipyrine was a powerful painkiller: Tzara, who was prone to headaches, consumed it in large quantities.) Part of what M. Antipyrine had to say was delivered in the form of a manifesto – the first of many: the manifesto, in Tzara's hands, became an art form, defined as 'a communication made to the whole world, whose only pretension is to the discovery of an instant cure for political, astronomical, artistic, parliamentary, agronomical and literary syphilis. It may be pleasant and good-natured, it's always right, it's strong, vigorous and logical.'[54]

M. Antipyrine had his say at the same soirée in the Waag Hall at which Ball took his leave. But where Ball's manifesto was full of thought and fury, and deeply serious underneath the nonsense, Tzara's was gay and anarchic, overflowing with life and energy, just like its irrepressible author. 'Dada is life with neither bedroom slippers nor parallels,' M. Antipyrine declared. '. . . Dada remains within the framework of European weaknesses, it's still shit, but from now on we want to shit in different colours so as to adorn the zoo of art with all the flags of all the consulates . . .'

Having achieved print, Tzara set to work. 'He wrapped, pasted, addressed, he bombarded the French and Italians with letters; slowly he made himself the "focal point".'[55] In Paris Apollinaire received his copy of *Cabaret Voltaire*, and showed it (among others) to his friend Paul Guillaume (thus returning a compliment, since it was Guillaume who had first drawn Tzara to Apollinaire's attention). Guillaume wrote to Tzara demanding copies for himself and mentioning his friend Marius de Zayas in New York. Tzara sent de Zayas copies both of *Cabaret Voltaire* and *M. Antipyrine*; in return, de

Zayas sent *291* to Zurich. Duchamp, who saw a copy of *M. Antipyrine* in New York, recognized 'the spirit of Jarry, and long before him, Aristophanes – the antiserious attitude, which simply took the name of Dada in 1916'. But although he could see the resemblances between what was going on in Zurich and his own activities in New York, he insisted that there was a difference: the Dadas were committed to action, he thought; 'they were fighting the public. And when you're fighting you rarely manage to laugh at the same time.'[56] Duchamp, of course, absolutely declined to fight.

Among Tzara's targets, naturally enough, was Francis Picabia. Their correspondence opened in August 1918, with Tzara's form letter – the one with which he always opened a correspondence. He mentioned, if possible, an acquaintance – in this case the art dealer Felix Vallotton, who was, as it happened, a close friend of Arthur Cravan's mother. He then progressed to the meat of the letter, which was headed simply 'MOUVEMENT DADA, ZURICH'. He was the editor of 'a modern art publication, *Dada*' whose contributors he listed. He would very much appreciate Picabia's collaboration on the next issue, which would have a large format and print-run to match, with one part entirely devoted to drawings and woodcuts. 'As we don't have much money, we would be grateful if you could yourself see to the print-making.'[57]

Picabia replied cordially. It so happened he was in Switzerland himself, at Bex-les-Bains, with Gabrielle and their children. He was in a state of nervous collapse, and nothing soothed jangled nerves better than the anodyne Swiss air. The downside was that Switzerland was stiflingly boring. Tzara's letter offered the possibility of welcome diversion.

It is hardly surprising that Picabia was a wreck. His life was even more out of control than usual. Returning to Paris from the wild and alcoholic life of New York, he had met a young woman, Germaine Everling, who was in the midst of a depressing divorce. He had become obsessed with her and swept her off her feet. In his chaotic apartment, 'filled with a scattering of books, papers, golf clubs, skis, African masks and model boats, a large canvas reading Bonjour Picabia! in black letters on a cream ground, the carpet covered with papers and cigarette butts, leather divans and lots of mattresses to put up stranded friends',[58] Picabia spun Germaine the old, old story. His wife had gone off and left him all alone, with no one but the concierge to look after him ... When he set off for Switzerland and Gabrielle, Germaine followed him to the French-Swiss border.

He was still, despite all this, writing and painting, and in September (soon after the start of his correspondence with Tzara) Herr Wolfsberg, a Zurich gallery-owner, offered him an exhibition on very advantageous terms. Picabia sent a portfolio of his machine-paintings; and Wolfsberg, who had for some reason been expecting something less uncompromising, recoiled in horror and refused to show them. Before he could send them back, however, the Dadas contrived to see them. In his next letter Tzara recounted their enthusiasm, which was such that Arp wanted to buy one 'if it isn't too dear'. Wolfsberg, Tzara assured Picabia, was 'an abominable, pretentious insect ... If you opened a door into his belly you would find an entire shopful of alcoholic products ...'[59]

As a result of this mishap the correspondence between the two became decidedly warmer and less formal, and they were soon making tentative arrangements to meet. But this was not so easily arranged. Picabia's nervous exhaustion prevented him journeying to Zurich; crises at *Dada 3* (the printer was arrested just as the magazine was about to go to press) kept Tzara tied down. Picabia sent a book of his own poems, (*Athlète des panpos funèbres*) *The Funeral Athlete*, together with a promise to contribute to future numbers of *Dada* and introductions to some Paris friends who might also contribute. Finally *Dada 3* appeared. Despite Dada's loss of momentum, it was full of good things. Its cover was a Janco woodcut, and it contained Tzara's own *Dada Manifesto 1918*, a programme of forthcoming Dada events, book notes from Paris, Barcelona, Stockholm, Bucharest and New York, and poems by Picabia, Tzara, Huelsenbeck and Arp. (Despite their disagreements, Tzara continued to put his name to Berlin Dada publications, and Huelsenbeck to contribute to Tzara's magazines.) Picabia was delighted with it – 'at long last something Swiss which isn't crap'.[60] He requested more copies, and invited Tzara to visit him in Paris, 'where I have quite a roomy apartment'.

Tzara's excitement may be imagined. He had made it! He was recognized, Paris beckoned. The timing could not have been better. Zurich's great days had been a product of the war, and the war was now over: it was time to move on. More than a year would pass, however, before Tzara saw Paris. For a long time it seemed that he and Picabia would not even manage a meeting in Switzerland. Picabia was too tired, Tzara too busy and too poor . . . Finally, in January 1919, Picabia, en route for Paris, decided to break his journey for three weeks in Zurich. 'I can tell you frankly that the main idea is to pass some time with you,' he wrote.[61]

Many years later, Gabrielle remembered their short stay in Zurich as one of the high points of these nomadic years. The warmth of their welcome by the 'bande Dada' delighted them. Arp, Tzara, the Janco brothers and the rest were so young, so charming, so full of fun and plans and talent. This went not just for the men, but the girls as well. Except for Marcel Janco, who was married, the Dadas haunted the halls of Rudolf Laban's dance school. Laban's girls became the Dada paramours: Sophie Taeuber, who married Hans Arp, Maja Chruscek, who lived with Tzara, Maria Vanselow, who, after a spell with Georges Janco, became Hans Richter's girlfriend. Eventually the whole Laban school became involved with Dada, performing Laban's highly individual dances, with their revolutionary choreography, before abstract backdrops by Arp and Richter, while wearing Janco masks. 'We were known', remembered Hans Richter, 'to laymen and experts alike, more by our roars of laughter than by the things we were actually doing.'[62] Nothing could have been more different from the despairing laughter of New York than this Zurich hilarity. 'They were moralists, not immoralists,' Gabrielle concluded.[63]

The Dadas were equally delighted with their new friends. When Tzara and Arp met Picabia at his hotel, they found him 'very busy pulling a clock to pieces . . . He attacked his alarm clock ruthlessly till he got to the spring which he pulled out triumphantly. He stopped working to greet us, then taking the wheels, the spring, the hands, and other secret parts of the clock, he immediately impressed them on paper. He connected these imprints together by lines and added to the drawing sentences full of wit.'[64]

Between Picabia and Tzara, an immediate and enormous sympathy arose. No doubt this had partly to do with differences of age and stage. Picabia was almost forty, celebrated, well connected; Tzara, twenty-one, bursting with ambition and promise. Tzara needed a foothold on the next rung of the ladder; Picabia, in the throes of mid-life crisis, was anxious to identify with youth and remain in the swim.

But they were united by more than these comparatively crass and opportunist ambitions. Each contained within himself all the tensions and contradictions which marked Dada, professing (and believing) the deepest cynicism about 'art' and all its works while at the same time being, inescapably and fundamentally, artists. 'Art is a *PRETENSION* heated at the **TIMIDITY** of the urinary basin, **hysteria** born in the **studio**,' cried Tzara in his Unpretentious Proclamation;[65] but he could not prevent himself from writing a stream of poems 'as exquisite as freshly-picked flowers'.[66] Art might, as he constantly proclaimed, be shit, but he had a large stake in that shit. His *Dada Manifesto 1918*, written a year earlier, is (among other things) a rage at phony 'art' and a heartfelt defence of the real thing: 'There is one kind of literature which never reaches out to the voracious masses. The work of creative writers, written out of the author's real necessity, and for his own benefit. The awareness of a supreme egoism, wherein laws become insignificant.'[67]

Picabia, too, personified this paradox. Richter noted that the pictures he exhibited (or tried to exhibit) in the Galerie Wolfsberg 'did not, in our eyes and in spite of all his anti-art declarations, lie outside the sphere of art'. Picabia's violently and constantly touted contempt for art and its role as a medium for the 'communication of inner experiences', sprang from the very urgency described by Tzara: a deep and desperate need to express the nihilism which overwhelmed him at this time. 'Wherever in life the life-impulse might break through (as it does in art) it must be torn apart, disordered and disowned. The life-impulse as such was suspect.'[68]

The result of this sympathy was a new creative energy. Picabia sent Tzara drawings and prose for *Dada 4*; together in Zurich they produced a new issue of *391*, no. 8, whose cover celebrates and draws together all Picabia's friends and collaborators, old and new, from Apollinaire to Tzara, in one happy network. 'I really miss Zurich,' Picabia wrote Tzara from Gstaad. *'Those three weeks went in a flash ...* I hope the printer sends me proofs soon, I can't wait to paste them up.' He added: 'All the skiers here look like fried fish.'[69]

Their correspondence over the next year is warm but inconclusive. They exchanged poems, drawings, magazines. 'Have they sold lots of *391*s in Zurich? What do the papers say?' Picabia wanted to know.[70] Then came a nervous crisis, he was confined to bed, life seemed worthless: wouldn't Tzara come and see him? It was the only prospect he could contemplate with anything approaching enthusiasm. But before Tzara could reply, Picabia wrote again: he had been advised to leave Switzerland for Paris. Tzara must join him there. He regaled his new friend with Paris news: Cocteau had fallen out with everyone, Picasso was more and more impressive, Juliette Roche (Mme Gleizes) couldn't wait to get back to New York. But nothing interesting was happening. The only intelligent people, in Picabia's opinion, were Duchamp (just then paying his first visit home for four years), Georges Ribemont-Dessaignes and Tzara himself. All these letters echo with the same refrain. '*Come as soon as possible.*' 'Are you coming?' 'Come, do come, as soon as you can.' 'I'm really sorry that you're still not in Paris.'

But now that the moment had come, Tzara could not bring himself to move. Although obviously capable of a certain amount of activity, since the bumper issue of *Dada 4 & 5* appeared in May, it seems clear that, for much of 1919, he was incapacitated by some kind of nervous breakdown. He had conceived a horror of the room in which he lived, but appalling headaches and indefinable terrors and malaises prevented him from leaving it. In order not to see it, he got into the habit of dressing and undressing in the dark. Once, when he went out, he returned to find that a new occupant had moved in and piled all his papers and belongings in the corner of some dark closet: he moved in there with them.[71] For some months he didn't write, or, when he did, forgot to post his letters. In July Picabia finally received a letter, announcing a planned trip – back to the Balkans. Picabia heard no more until October: Tzara had not after all visited the Balkans, the stories coming out of there were too terrifying. He was still afflicted with anomie. Perhaps he might come to Paris in November ... It was not, however, until the end of December that he could bring himself to actually name a date, of sorts. He was busy with *Dada 6*; as soon as it was ready, he would come. Picabia remained unequivocally encouraging. 'You can be perfectly happy about coming to Paris, you will have *bed, bread and salt*. It's a very good time, things are picking up here ... Is ARP coming too?'[72]

*

By this time, Picabia was no longer living with Gabrielle in the chaotic apartment full of mattresses on the Left Bank, but had moved in with Germaine, in Rue (now Boulevard) Emile-Augier, in the extremely bourgeois 16th arrondissement. Not that this had clarified much: both Germaine and (to Germaine's fury) Gabrielle were pregnant. True to form, however, babies were the last thing on Picabia's mind. He was more concerned with cars, having just sold his old Singer and decided to buy a spanking new Mercer tourer from America. This was unloaded on 31 December 1919, a week before Germaine's baby was due. He spent hours standing in the street, stroking it, admiring its details, and intoning his new-car mantra (to be repeated sixty-three times over the course of the next twenty years): 'It's the most beautiful car I've ever seen!'[73]

The Mercer was not the only new and beguiling arrival in Picabia's life. Another was André Breton, who had first contacted him three weeks previously requesting contributions for his magazine, *Littérature*. Picabia sent two poems and an invitation to call one evening after dinner. The meeting was a huge success. Breton, who had long admired Picabia from afar, revelled in his brilliance and was flattered to arouse the enthusiasm of such a figure. As for Picabia, 'I like everything about you,' he told Breton, 'you're exactly the kind of person it's essential to meet from time to time in the course of a life if one's to have the courage to go on. I'm sure I'm not wrong in this.'[74] It was agreed that they would meet again after dinner on 4 January.

Breton was not the only visitor at the apartment that evening. Germaine's neighbours Georges and Dodo de Zayas (brother and sister-in-law of Marius de Zayas: it was they who had first introduced Germaine to Picabia) had also called round. They had all dined together the previous evening. Now Georges had stomach cramps, which he was inclined to attribute to their meal. So did Germaine; but it seemed likely that hers had a rather different cause. The midwife was called, and confirmed that the baby might arrive at any moment. This presented a problem. Not only was nothing ready for the new arrival, but the bedroom was occupied by Picabia and Breton, deep in conversation. They were talking about Nietzsche. De Zayas, despatched to dislodge them, was summarily dismissed. Germaine began to feel alarmed; de Zayas renewed his appeal. He plucked discreetly at Picabia's sleeve. 'Do fuck off!' said Picabia. 'Can't one have a quiet conversation anywhere round here?' 'Good God!' finally cried the unfortunate de Zayas, discretion cast to the winds. 'Germaine's having her baby! She needs the bedroom!' At this Breton jumped up 'as if a snake had bitten him'; he had only recently abandoned his medical studies, and (Germaine surmised) was afraid he might be called upon to act in a professional capacity. He seized his hat and coat and made for the door. Just in time: the baby made his entrance less than an hour later. The midwife, who had never met Germaine's boyfriend nor enquired as to who he might be, noticed the Mercer parked in the street, 'Goodness,' she said, 'that's M. Picabia's car. He was showing it to me only yesterday, he was there when I went to see his wife. I looked after her when she had her baby a few months ago. Really, what a household! . . . He wasn't even living with her, it turns out he has a mistress, and she's pregnant, too! Artists, I ask you! What on earth can he be doing in a respectable place like this?'[75]

A few days later, Germaine suggested that Picabia might

like to take the new car for a spin. There was nothing for him to do in the apartment; she and the baby were well. He had just driven off when the doorbell rang. She heard voices, but did not recognize them. Then a card was brought in. It was large and printed in a script so florid that the name could barely be deciphered. She read (with difficulty): *Tristan Tzara.*

Germaine, of course, knew who Tzara was: he had been a central topic of conversation for months. She was not, however, expecting him. Had Picabia not mentioned his standing invitation? It seems quite possible. Domestic consideration was not one of his virtues. Or perhaps, after all those false starts, he no longer really believed Tzara would actually take him at his word.

Germaine's first reaction, not unreasonable in the circumstances, was to send the visitor away. But he would not be sent: he insisted upon seeing her. 'In sidled a black and white young man, like a woodcut by his friend Arp. He was small, slightly round-shouldered, with short arms at the ends of which hung plump, sensitive hands. His skin was waxy, like a candle: his short-sighted eyes behind their pince-nez seemed to be seeking some resting-point . . .'[76]

Tzara apologized for any inconvenience, but his friend Picabia had told him he must come straight round. When was this, Germaine wanted to know. In Zurich, a year ago, Tzara told her. Germaine began to realize that he assumed he would be staying in the apartment. She explained the circumstances: since the baby's arrival there was no spare bed; Picabia himself was sleeping in the salon. She offered to find him a hotel room. He looked more and more miserable: she was afraid he would burst into tears. 'The trouble is', he said, 'I have no money.'

What could she do? Germaine offered Tzara the divan in the salon. Francis would have to find somewhere else to sleep for a few days. He immediately began to unpack, spreading his effects among Germaine's precious ornaments. He had very few clothes, but, making up for this, a mountain of papers: correspondence, manifestos, posters, magazines, manuscripts, were piled in every corner, a large typewriter was placed upon a delicate Louis Quinze console. Soon the salon was transformed into Dada Central. With every post, yet more papers arrived. They poured in, apparently from every corner of the globe. The cleaning woman was forbidden to touch any of them: they were far too important.

Happily installed, Tzara's life fell easily into its accustomed rhythm. He rose late, breakfasting around four in the afternoon, and when he was not out (for he was much in demand) worked at his correspondence all evening and far into the night. He enjoyed rocking little Lorenzo Picabia in his arms. 'Dada!' he would croon. 'Say Dada, little one.'

Bowing to *force majeure*, Picabia and Germaine left on 2 February for a few quiet weeks in the Midi. 14 Rue Emile-Augier was left to Tzara, Michel (Germaine's son by her divorced husband), the baby and his nanny. Picabia sent Tzara a card announcing their safe arrival at Martigues and giving their planned date of return. Tzara responded with relief. 'Thank goodness you're coming back, I can't bear the loneliness!' he complained, before plunging into an account of the latest artistic quarrels.[77] The Picabias returned on the 20th to find Tzara still installed. The few days stretched on. It would be many months before he moved out of 14 Rue Emile-Augier.

CHAPTER FOUR

DADA COMES
TO PARIS

THE NEWS OF Tristan Tzara's arrival soon spread round Paris. Breton, Soupault and Aragon were in a state of high excitement at the prospect of meeting this legendary personage.

It was a year since they had first become properly aware of Tzara. His *Dada Manifesto 1918*, published in *Dada 3*, had seemed to speak with their very own voice.

> I'm writing this manifesto to show that you can perform contrary actions at the same time, in one single, fresh breath; I am against action; as for continual contradiction, and affirmation, too, I am neither for nor against them, and I won't explain myself because I have common sense . . .
>
> No pity. After the carnage we are left with the hope of a purified humanity . . .
>
> Let each man proclaim: there is great destructive, negative work to be done . . .

Louis Aragon received his copy in January 1919, while still mobilized with the army medical corps in Sarrebrück. Next day a note arrived from Breton: 'I've been drunk on the wonderful manifesto in *Dada 3* . . .'

'To read this at Sarrebrück,' Aragon marvelled, '. . . while the 4th battalion captain warned, "It would be better, Doctor, if you didn't receive correspondence from Switzerland . . ."'[1]

Breton at this time was distraught on account of Jacques Vaché's death, which had occurred only two weeks previously. Tzara's manifesto uncannily echoed his dead friend's tone of insouciant iconoclasm ('*To launch a manifesto you must want A.B.C. and fulminate against 1,2 & 3 . . .*'). Perhaps the avenues Vaché had seemed to open were not, after all, entirely closed off. In Breton's first letter to Tzara, written on 22 January, there are hints of the role Tzara was to play for him over the coming year: 'I was just about to write to you when some bad news distracted me. I've just lost the thing I loved best in the world: my friend Jacques Vaché is dead. It's given me so much pleasure lately to think how much you would have liked each other: he would have recognised a kindred spirit . . .'[2]

The correspondence progressed. Tzara confided his plan to visit Paris; Breton begged to be among the first to welcome him when he arrived. Breton introduced himself and his friends. He was twenty-three, Aragon and Soupault twenty-two. They were starting a magazine whose first number was about to appear with the enthusiastic backing of no less a personage than André Gide! 'I feel as close to you as it's possible to be,' Breton concluded his third letter.[3] He, Soupault and Aragon sent poems for inclusion in *Dada*; Tzara sent two of his own for their new review, *Littérature*.

Breton's letters to Tzara were soul-baring and hero-worshipping, written with that terrifying freedom from guile and pretence which was one of his more unnerving qualities, a source, perhaps, of the magnetism he famously exerted on all around him. Tzara's replies were altogether more guarded and convoluted. Maybe he felt that the unadorned Tzara might not be the hero-material Breton hoped for – or perhaps the urge to embroider was just too deeply ingrained in him. At any rate, he allowed himself a few extra years, giving his age as twenty-seven instead of the actual twenty-two, and added a few heightening touches to his life. 12,000 people had visited an exhibition recently organized by him. If his nerves were in shreds, it was because the day before he had watched as a train cut to pieces a lady with whom he had been talking two minutes earlier . . . From time to time, however, there appeared some remarkable insight or flight of fancy. 'I think, my dear Breton, that what you're really looking for is *people*,' he wrote in one such passage.

Writing is nothing but an escape, from every point of view.
I don't think of myself as a professional writer. I would
have become a swashbuckling adventurer if I'd only had the
physical strength and nervous energy to achieve just the one
thing: to not get bored. One writes because there aren't
enough new faces and by force of habit, one publishes to
find people and to have something to do. And that's very
silly, too. The solution would be simply to resign oneself.
Just do nothing. But you need so much energy for that.
Complications are so essential to one's health . . .[4]

This passage tremendously impressed Breton, partly on
account of its echoes of Vaché (*I would be an adventurer . . .*),
partly because it reflected so exactly his own doubts. Why did
one write? Why did anybody write? He decided to make this
into a questionnaire, to be sent to 'the most appropriate
representatives of different tendencies in contemporary literature', which would feature in the forthcoming number of
Littérature. Somewhat to the surprise of the editors, replies
poured in. Breton liked only Valéry's: 'Out of weakness.' But
all were published, and as a publicity stunt it could not have
been bettered. Suddenly, all the critics (many of whom had of
course replied to the questionnaire) noticed *Littérature*. There
would be many more questionnaires. They suited Breton's
orderly mind, his curiosity, his passion for fixing and classify-
ing and ascertaining where people stood. Meanwhile he practised his technique on Tzara. He was working on a theoretical
study of seduction through the ages: What did Tzara think
about love? Marinetti was visiting Zurich: Who were the three
most interesting people of Tzara's acquaintance? 'It's always
nice to know.'[5]

Could Tzara – could *anyone* – possibly live up to Breton's
expectations in the flesh? Their burgeoning friendship, even
more than most pen-friendships, was founded upon an almost

inevitably false premise: Breton's idea of what Tzara must be like. He was Paul Valéry as a young man (a suggestion that had apparently come from Valéry himself, prompted by Tzara's poetry and Breton's effusions); he was a new Jacques Vaché. 'I suppose I'd better not read too much into this resemblance . . .'[6] Breton wrote, but did so notwithstanding. 'I think of you as I have never thought of anyone . . . but Jacques Vaché . . . (I mean, before I do anything, I try and imagine how you'd feel about it) . . .'[7] To Picabia he confessed, 'I'm waiting for him as I don't think I've ever waited for anyone before.'[8]

As the projected date of Tzara's arrival drew near the Musketeers began to feel distinctly nervous. 'Suppose he turns out to be some frightful provincial Swiss, what a let-down!' said the young musician Georges Auric to Louis Aragon, walking home from an evening at Breton's lodgings where the talk, inevitably, had been of Tzara.[9] The moment itself, however, was constantly postponed. Between 6 and 8 January, Breton went five times to meet trains at the Gare de Lyon, but Tzara, prostrated by nerves now that the fatal moment had come, was not on any of them.

His outriders, however, were. Marcel Janco stopped off in Paris to visit Picabia, en route for Nancy, where he was to pursue his architecture studies. At Rue Emile-Augier, Breton, Aragon and Soupault listened avidly to his stories of the Cabaret Voltaire's beginnings. If Janco was to be believed, the birth of Dada had been wholly fortuitous, with no particular idea in mind beyond that of earning some money amidst the spume of merchants, deserters, spies, propagandists and actors washed up in Zurich by the war. Janco spun tales of masked belly dancers and drugs, girls brought in to attract the clients . . . Could this random and apocalyptic vision really be the background against which the poetic ideas of a Tzara had developed? They were astonished and impressed by Tzara's multifarious activities as described by Janco, the exhibitions he organized, the shows in which he starred, the magazines he edited ... Picabia, detached and worldly-wise, watched with an ironic grin the open-mouthed astonishment of these serious young men.[10]

At long last it happened: the arrival was announced. Nervously they waited in the salon at the Rue Emile-Augier, where piles of Picabia's machine-pictures jostled the eighteenth-century furnishings. In a nearby room, a baby wailed. A door opened: and there was Tzara. Aragon, Breton, Soupault and their new friend Paul Eluard gaped, as at a rare zoological specimen.[11] He was very dark and very small. He took three hurried steps and stopped: they realized he must be short-sighted. 'I'd never imagined him like this, a young Japanese with glasses,' Aragon noted later. 'So this was the agitator we'd summoned to Paris, who looked so like Jacques Vaché in that photograph with the leather gloves, and whose poetry everyone compared to Rimbaud's ... He held his elbows close to his sides, his forearms horizontal, delicate hands held half-open ... like a frightened night-bird caught out by the daylight, with a lock of dark hair that kept tumbling into his eyes ...'[12] He was unnaturally pale: all his vitality, Aragon thought, was in his eyes, which were very beautiful. He spoke slowly; his French was fluent but strongly accented (the word 'Dada', for example, was pronounced in Slavic mode, with two staccato, very short 'a's). Self-conscious about his accent, for some time he could not be persuaded to speak in public. He laughed a lot: it was a defiant, challenging laugh.

Perhaps to counter a certain sense of anticlimax, Tzara continued the vein of rather childish self-aggrandizement which had been evident in his letters to Breton. He claimed acquaintance with Einstein and Jung, both of whom were indeed then in Zurich, but neither of whom he knew well, if at all. He liked to quote a saying of Einstein's: 'If you look into infinity, what do you see? Your backside.' It wasn't much, but such as it was it seemed to confirm Dada, which was something.[13] Soupault thought he soon realized how quickly he might come to dominate these correct young petit-bourgeois intellectuals.

Comparing notes after this first meeting, the four friends were disconcerted. What had they expected? Not, at any rate, what they had just met. For Breton, the hardest thing to swallow was the complete absence of any resemblance to Vaché. Nor did Tzara appear to be a new Rimbaud. He was – himself. Soupault, for one, did not take to him. It seemed that Aragon was the only one to retain any enthusiasm.[14]

*

Littérature had first appeared in March 1919. The three friends had been projecting a review of their own ever since they first met two years earlier. Walking endlessly up and down the boulevards they discussed their enthusiasms and mapped out a programme. The demise of Pierre Reverdy's established and respected review *Nord-Sud* finally decided them. A gap had been left, and they would fill it. By 1919 some backing had been found, and by the time this melted away Soupault had turned twenty-one and come into a little money. Now literary Paris spread itself invitingly before them. 'It was delightful to sniff the intellectual disarray and nervousness,' Louis Aragon wrote. 'I'd been told André Gide was dying to meet me (he was) and I was dying to meet Pablo Picasso ...'[15] Who would be the peacetime friends, who the intellectual foes? Which groups would be in, which fade away? Such frivolous preoccupations were far removed from the grim realities of Huelsenbeck's Berlin; but as Picabia's friend Georges Ribemont-Dessaignes observed, (and as Berlin itself so terribly proved), 'Liberation without laughter soon gets bloody.'[16] Where Hugo Ball's assemblage of chance arrivals had tapped directly but almost unwittingly into the spirit of the times with the wonderful accident that was the Cabaret Voltaire, nothing could have been more deliberate and thought-out than the launch of the magazine that was to become *Littérature*. Something new was in the air, and Breton, Soupault and Aragon wanted to seize it.

What should they call their new review? The first name hit upon was *Le Nègre*, because they wanted a sense of the pavement café's openness, 'admitting everyone, whatever their skin colour, however shifty-looking'.[17] *Le Nouveau Monde* was fleetingly considered. Reverdy suggested *Carte Blanche*, but this was rejected as being too precious and Cubist. It was Paul Valéry who suggested *Littérature*, which took its name sardonically from a line of Verlaine's: *'Et tout le reste est littérature . . .'*

Breton was enthusiastic – he still idolized Valéry. Soupault was uncertain – it could be so easily misunderstood. But Aragon liked the title's provocative, disagreeable, pretentious overtones. It was adopted; contributors were sought. Politicking began in earnest.

André Gide, as Breton had so excitedly boasted to Tzara, was their big catch. At this time he was going through a bad patch: a friend had made public his homosexual preferences, and his wife had retreated to Normandy and burned all his letters. Anxious to be in with the new young crowd, he invited the Musketeers to visit. They praised his novel *Les Caves du Vatican* and its hero Lafcadio, originator and practitioner of the *acte gratuit*. Gide laughed edgily at what they had left unsaid. 'You mean you don't like my other books?'[18] Nevertheless he promised a piece for the magazine. However, it failed to arrive. The ubiquitous Jean Cocteau, furious at their refusal to accept him on the editorial board, had been turning Gide against them. 'Beware of Cocteau,' Apollinaire had warned. 'He's a cheat.' He was certainly an arch-intriguer, and from then on a certified enemy, infuriatingly omnipresent in the small world of avant-garde Paris. 'He says you sent him a Christmas card,' wrote Breton to Tzara on 26 December 1919. 'I suppose it's possible; if so, you can't know him very well.'[19] Despite Cocteau, however, Gide returned to the fold. His prose fragments, *Les Nouvelles Nourritures*, opened the first issue of *Littérature*.

Tzara appeared in the books section of the first issue, where Aragon reviewed his *25 Poems* rather tepidly, but his *Dada Manifesto 1918* was received with great enthusiasm. He was there again with a poem in the second. His name was greeted with suspicion. Reverdy had published a few of his poems in *Nord-Sud*, but was put out at the importance accorded him by *Littérature*; Valéry, part of the xenophobic faction that still insisted upon Dreyfus's guilt and disliked Apollinaire, also disapproved of this new and suspect enthusiasm. When the establishment literary review *Nouvelle Revue Française* published an anti-German attack on Dada, Breton arranged for Tzara to reply in an open letter to the editor. It was ignored: Breton published it himself. So that even before his arrival, Tzara had become a player in the Paris game.

*

'The debut of Dada in Paris', Tzara declared, 'took place on the twenty-third of January, at the matinée organised by the Dadaist review *Littérature*.'[20]

This occasion had been mooted for some time. It was to be the first of a projected series of fortnightly poetry readings, at which some paintings would also be shown, and music by the group known as *les Six* (Auric, Poulenc, Milhaud, Arthur Honegger, Germaine Taillefer and Louis Durey) performed. But Tzara's arrival presented the possibility of springing a sensational surprise. The Musketeers had met Tzara on a

Tuesday; the matinée was scheduled for the Friday. It was decided to keep Tzara's arrival secret – a resolve made easier by his uncharacteristic bashfulness at the prospect of speaking French on a Paris platform. On Wednesday evening he accompanied the group to their usual café, where amid the crowd of habitués he went unintroduced and unnoticed. And on Thursday they met at Picabia's, to finalize the details of the next day's performance.

Tzara explained the techniques perfected by himself and his fellow-Dadas. A piercing noise or prolonged silence could drive people to the point where they would act regardless of the consequences – they had even, he said, used door keys to bombard the stage, without a thought for how they would get back into their houses afterwards. The Musketeers were not altogether convinced. The custom in Paris was for actors to speak the poems; they were dubious about Tzara's assumption that authors would (as in Zurich) read their own works – even long poetic manifestos. Manifestos? The Musketeers invoked the ever-hovering spirit of Vaché. One could hardly imagine *him* sitting quietly through some incomprehensible and interminable manifesto. Nor were they at this stage quite certain about missiles. It was decided to restrict Tzara and his anti-poems to one brief but violent manifestation, unannounced, which would create the maximum possible sensation when tossed into the gentle boredom of an evening's poetry reading.

The venue was the Palais des Fêtes in the Faubourg Saint-Martin, near les Halles, a building containing two cinemas, a café and a party-room complete with small stage, from which both cinema orchestras could be heard. An announcement had been printed in the previous evening's *Intransigeant*; the crowd began to arrive even before the chairs were properly set out. A number of serious shopkeepers came, hoping to hear the poet and journalist André Salmon speak on 'La Crise du change', an ambiguous title which they thought referred to exchange-rate fluctuations. There were also artier souls, hoping for poetic uplift.

The programme, which naturally started late, began in the lowest of keys, as befitted the polite poetry magazine *Littérature* still was. Salmon gave his talk, which was received respectfully but with some disappointment, since it turned on literary rather than monetary change (after the Symbolists, Apollinaire; after Apollinaire, *Littérature*). Some poems were read, some music played, in the palest of pale grey modes. A number of pictures were then presented, beginning with Cubist productions by Gris and Léger: the audience sat on its hands. The mood changed, however, when recent works by Picabia were unveiled, one consisting of inscriptions in large black letters on a light ground, including the letters 'L.H.O.O.Q.' which, when read aloud (*elle a chaud au cul*) form, as every French schoolboy knows, the phrase: she's got the hots. At the sight of this the audience began to get noisy, and the tumult was increased by the sight of another Picabia work, this time done in chalk on a blackboard. Part of this consisted of the words 'RIZ AU NEZ', which, read out loud, can mean either 'rice in the nose' or 'laugh in your face' (*ris au nez)*. The noise level rose further: at this point Breton, as had been arranged, wiped the blackboard clean of its transient Picabia with a damp sponge. More poems were read. And then it was announced that Tristan Tzara (one of whose poems had just been declaimed to the scandal of some ladies present) would present a recent work – in person.

A stupefied silence ensued: Tzara appeared, blinking in the lights. He proceeded to cut up an article by Léon Daudet, dropped the pieces into a hat, and read out the resulting 'poem'. In the wings on either side Breton and Aragon rang bells as he spoke, drowning out the words. 'For once,' says Aragon, 'expectation was fulfilled ... It was three minutes of indescribable hullabaloo, and the audience, which had never experienced anything so insolent [at that time it was disrespectful even to read poems sitting down], was furious. They yelled and threatened . . . After that, everything else was a bit of a let-down.'21

It was; and not only on-stage. Their first encounter with Dada in the flesh left the *Littérature* crowd feeling oddly out of sorts. What were they getting themselves into? Eminent backers of the older generation like André Salmon and Juan Gris felt betrayed, and were furious. Gris (one of whose pictures had been shown in the earlier part of the programme) threatened to punch Tzara's face in but ended up tamely shaking his hand. Fernand Léger, who had also shown a picture, pronounced it all too, too funny. Soupault found a number of pressing reasons to leave immediately for Geneva. Breton, Eluard and Aragon began to quarrel. Aragon was scolded for being too kind to Cocteau; Eluard made some malicious comments; Aragon retorted with some unforgivable remarks. 'Perhaps that was the real beginning of Dada, with its struggles and quarrels and the heavy atmosphere . . . which was the mark of that singular time and which doesn't really explain the sparks and the darkness.'22

*

Despite Tzara's turbulent irruption, the poetry reading matinée had still visibly been a poetry reading in the old style – albeit with frills. Only two weeks later, however, it became clear that the spirit of Zurich had taken over. The February issue of *Littérature* contained Dada poems by Picabia, Tzara and Ribemont-Dessaignes; a *Bulletin Dada*, emanating from Tzara and Picabia at Picabia's other address, Avenue Charles Floquet, announced a new matinée – this time of the Dada movement. It would take place at the Salon des Indépendants, the Grand Palais des Champs Elysées. The programme would consist entirely of manifestos, beginning with Picabia's (to be read by ten people) and ending with Tzara's (four readers and a journalist), and the next edition of *Littérature* would consist of the printed texts. In order to add appeal and draw the crowds, Tzara started a rumour that Charlie Chaplin in person would take part in the performance, and made sure it came to the ears of the press. 'Charlie Chaplin, the great Charlot, has just arrived in Paris,' announced the *Journal du Peuple.* 'He has just joined the Dada movement . . .'[23] 'Although we denied the rumour, there was one reporter who followed me everywhere,' Tzara reported, deadpan. 'He thought that the celebrated actor was up to some new stunt and was planning a surprise entrance.'[24] The reporter, however, had he but known it, was already dealing with the master of stunts and surprise entrances.

Chaplin's name, as Tzara had known it would, drew a huge crowd to the Grand Palais. Naturally he did not appear, nor was there any further mention of him. Perhaps for this reason, perhaps on account of the violence of the texts themselves (read, in fact, by their authors, and not as advertised), the room was quickly in uproar. 'Thousands of persons of all classes manifested very uproariously it is impossible to say exactly what – their joy or their disapproval, by unexpected cries and general laughter . . . The newspapers said that an old man in the audience gave himself up to behaviour of a character more or less intimate, that somebody set off flashlight powder and that a pregnant woman had to be taken out.'[25] Whatever else it did or did not achieve, Dada drew the audience into the show. They participated as they had never done at previous poetry readings – indeed, nothing had elicited such a reaction since the memorable première of Jarry's *Ubu-Roi.* 'That was the essential thing,' wrote Ribemont-Dessaignes. 'We had to provoke a hostile reaction, or else we were nothing but sinister imbeciles. After that, Tristan Tzara was called *Sinistre Farceur.*'[26] Tzara was jubilant. Picabia, however, lost his nerve. He disappeared as soon as the show began, and his manifesto had to be read by someone else. This was to become a regular feature of Dada performances. Picabia, for whatever reason, simply could not bring himself to participate. He pleaded his fragile nervous state, which would not allow too much excitement. 'He had the courage to sign the most audacious declarations, against his friends even, but he had no physical courage,' concluded the faithful Ribemont-Dessaignes.[27] Tzara remembered this failing with 'tenderness',[28] Breton dismissed it, asserting that physical courage was not particularly admirable, but others, notably Soupault, found it intensely annoying.[29]

Dada manifestations followed thick and fast. A few days after the Grand Palais excitements, they were invited to present their case at a workers' club, sharing the platform with (among others) Raymond Duncan, philosopher brother of Isadora, a well-known Paris figure who always appeared in ancient Greek garb. Breton solemnly read Tzara's lengthy and incomprehensible *Dada Manifesto 1918* ('*Ideal, ideal, ideal,/Knowledge, knowledge, knowledge,/Boom-boom, boom-boom, boom-boom*'). But this time it was Aragon who particularly infuriated the audience, looking, as he did, like 'a good little boy let out on parole'.[30] Long-haired Duncan, in his peplum, leapt to Dada's defence – not that he knew anything about it; but it had the right to be heard nevertheless. Then there was an appearance at the Université Populaire in the Faubourg Saint-Antoine; followed a few weeks later by a full-scale show at Lugné-Poë's Théâtre de l'Oeuvre. This consisted of a number of original works, including the first Parisian performance of *La Première Aventure céleste de M. Antipyrine*. There was a piano piece, the *Chicory Walk*, 'composed' by Ribemont-Dessaignes according to the laws of chance and performed with complete sang-froid by the pianist Marguerite Buffet, Gabrielle Picabia's cousin (the composer, a picture of drawing-room correctness, turned the pages for her); sketches by Ribemont-Dessaignes, Breton and Soupault, and a Picabia manifesto (read by Breton in the author's inevitable absence): 'You are all indicted; stand up! It is impossible to talk to you unless you are standing up ... Hiss, shout, kick my teeth in, so what? I still say that you are half-wits.'

To everyone's dismay, however, no teeth were kicked in, there were no hisses. The audience seemed unmoved, except perhaps by disappointment. They had come in hopes of outrage, they wanted to be shocked; instead, faced by a selection of avant-garde artistic events, they applauded politely. Even Picabia's other contribution, a stuffed monkey stuck to a canvas and framed by inscriptions reading *'Portrait of Cézanne – Portrait of Rembrandt – Portrait of Renoir – Still Life'* failed to rouse them. It was not until the final offering, a well-known singer named Hania Routchine who, in place of the advertised 'sung manifesto' offered a calming song entitled 'Clair de Lune' by a well-known composer, Duparc, that the desired ructions broke out. Included in such a programme, the item was an insult to Duparc and all who loved him. The room erupted in fury: the unfortunate singer burst into tears and rushed off.

'I thought it was a dreadful evening,' Cocteau told Picabia afterwards. 'Sad, timid, devoid of audacity, pleasure or invention.' It was clear where the fault lay: not with Picabia, who 'creates, or wants to, a "drama", a "misfortune", a "no", a "blasphemy", an atmosphere of new romanticism', nor with Tzara, who 'disorganises'. But 'a few college boys have made [the Dada spirit] as boring as Jarry, Duparc, Sacha Guitry, Bruant, Madame Lara or Ibsen'.[31] The reaction of the theatre's manager, Lugné-Poë, seemed to confirm this judgement. Dada had filled the house: clearly, far from outraging, it was a draw.

He offered to consider any manuscripts the Dadas might care to send him for presentation at l'Oeuvre.

Gide, like Cocteau, was unenthusiastic. His objections, however, were the opposite of Cocteau's. Where, for Cocteau, it was the 'college boys' who had undermined the true spirit of Dada, for Gide Dada was an alien influence which boded ill for *Littérature*'s future. In the April issue of the *Nouvelle Revue Française* he published a subtly malicious and unsubtly anti-Semitic article targeting Tzara:

> The unfortunate thing for the inventor of Dada is that the movement he began has run him down: he is crushed by his own machine.
> It's a pity.
> I'm told he's a very young man.
> Apparently he's charming. (Marinetti was irresistible, too.)
> I'm told he's a foreigner. – I find that easy to believe.
> Jewish. – Just what I was about to say.
> I'm told he doesn't use his real name; and I can well believe that Dada itself is nothing but a pseudonym.
> Dada – is the deluge, after which everything begins again.
> Naturally foreigners aren't much interested in our French culture. It's up to the legitimate heirs to protest: the former have everything to gain, the latter, everything to lose.[32]

Dada, however, rolled unstoppably on. What would they do next? By now this was the continual, unending question. Every outrage must be capped by something even more shocking: that, or anticlimax. Before every new manifestation they met at Germaine Everling's apartment, where Tzara had by now become a fixture. Picabia would preside; everyone in turn was expected to produce some properly scandalous ideas. 'The harvest was never very plentiful. The chief offering was inevitably the first, or second, or nth adventure of Tristan Tzara's *Monsieur Antipyrine*, performed … always in the inevitable cardboard cylinders (it was his favourite idea, Zurich had obviously been quite overcome by it),' Breton acidly remembered.[33] Tzara proved a hard taskmaster. He lived, Germaine reported, 'in a state of perpetual exaltation', a veritable Dada dictator. Dada was all, and any initiative which might distinguish any one participant to the detriment of the whole, sternly discouraged. As might be expected, morale began to sink. 'Two or three of us couldn't help wondering if this monthly battle of Hernani[34] … was really enough in itself.'[35] Expectations had been raised so high: by contrast, reality seemed distressingly meagre. And it all required immense effort, which (as he ruefully recalled) only the diligent Breton seemed willing to put in.[36]

The next Dada Festival was scheduled to take place on 26 May, in the Salle Gaveau, a highly respectable venue and one far larger than the Oeuvre (which had been forced to turn paying customers away). Press notices and sandwich-men announced that all the Dadaists were preparing to have their heads shaved in public. There would also be painless boxing, a Dada illusionist, a genuine con-man, a vast opera, sodomite music, a symphony for twenty voices, a stationary dance, two plays, manifestos and poems. At the end, Dada's sex would be revealed. M. Gaveau, the venue's proprietor, understandably nervous, wrote to Picabia demanding assurances that the evening would not undermine his hall's good reputation. Picabia, lying through his teeth, provided them.

Unknown to most of the participants, a terrifying cloud hung over the group as the festival approached. Among the advertised attractions (including the inevitable excursion of M. Antipyrine) was a sketch by Breton and Soupault, *S'il vous plaît*. This supposedly had four acts, of which the second had already been presented at the Théâtre de l'Oeuvre. The first and third acts also existed, but the fourth remained a mystery. The authors took Aragon into their confidence. Given Dada's current hysterical atmosphere of competitive shock, it was clear that this fourth act must, if it were to avoid anticlimax, be a real drama, the kind of thing that would one day be called a 'happening'. They had devised just such an event. When the moment came, the curtain would rise on the authors (who would also play the two male parts). While the audience watched they would write their names on slips of paper, fold them and drop them into a hat. They would then draw one of the papers out of the hat. Whoever was named would then shoot himself through the head with a revolver. Vaché himself could not have devised a more chilling dénouement, nor one more perfectly arbitrary. The presentation was planned for some time in April.

'For three weeks', Aragon wrote, 'death lurked among us. For three weeks, three weeks of unspeakable anguish, I had not a single doubt . . . I could not look at either of my friends without being filled with terror. I knew it was no use trying to dissuade them. Behind the carnival of those first Dada months in Paris lurked this dreadful, sinister secret.' The moment came – and passed. 'Simply, my two friends abandoned their plan.'[37] S'il vous plaît was published in Littérature the following September, still without a fourth act. The authors had directed that it should not be printed. None was published for another forty-eight years. What then appeared consisted of two lines: 'The authors are called for. Two actors enter instead, and take their bows.' As for Aragon, he kept his secret to himself until after Breton's death.

Had they really intended to do it? Perhaps not. Dada, born out of slaughter and disillusion, continually flirted with suicide, but only Vaché had so far delivered on the promise. On another occasion Breton appeared with two revolvers strapped to his head, but neither of them actually went off. In his recently-launched review *Le Coq*, Cocteau teased: 'Our principal reproach to Dada is that it's too timid. Now that the rules of the game are established, why so little action? Not a single Dada has killed himself or even a member of the audience. They give us *sketches*, we listen to *music*.'[38]

Even so, the house was full to bursting – Picabia had made sure of that by distributing a large number of tickets free of charge. The uproar began with the first number, the promised appearance of Dada's 'sex', a huge cardboard tube balanced on balloons (which slowly lost their air in the heat: 'The Sex is deflating!' yelled a panic-stricken Tzara in the wings) and continued uninterrupted until the end. The audience had come prepared with peanuts, assorted vegetables, fruits and rotten eggs, all of which ended up on-stage, together with a number of coins and paper darts. There were even beefsteaks, purchased during the interval. The Dadas preserved their stern mien throughout. Picabia (who had designed the set, but as usual declined to appear) watched from a box by the side of his new girlfriend, the singer Marthe Chenal. A member of the audience challenged him to a fight: Mme Chenal forbade it because there were ladies present. They agreed to meet outside after the show, but Picabia, true to form, vanished early.[39] At the end, by popular demand, Marthe Chenal sang the 'Marseillaise', for which she was famous. Tzara was triumphant, Picabia absent, Breton increasingly uncertain. Cocteau was not alone in his doubts. The college boys shared them too.

In the June issue of *Littérature* Soupault published a series of imaginary epitaphs for his friends, brilliantly and poignantly encapsulating their qualities. He caught Breton's passion for qualification:

Tu ne me diras plus
Tout de même, tout de même . . .

There'll be no more of your
Even so, even so . . .

and of Tzara he wrote, ominously:

On a beaucoup ri quand on a appris ta mort
On avait tellement peur que tu sois éternel

We laughed a lot when we heard of your death
We were so afraid you might be eternal

Tzara spent the summer in Zurich and the Balkans, with Arp and with his family. But these reminders of his old life were sadly diminished by his more recent memories of Paris. 'From this provincial hole Paris seems so wonderful,' he wrote Picabia from Zurich. 'I can't imagine how I stayed here for so long.' And from Bucharest: 'All I want is to get back to Paris. I find the Balkans and their mentality deeply disgusting.'[40]

But Paris – the Paris which had awaited him so impatiently six months earlier – no longer wholly reciprocated his enthusiasm. Paris could never be his as Zurich had been. Rumanian, Austrian, German – in wartime Zurich, the only irrelevance was to be Swiss. Intellectually, artistically, Zurich had been a city of exiles, for those few brief years the centre of the artistic world; and its pulse had been Tzara's pulse. That was what bewitched Picabia and (at a distance) Breton. Tzara's great Paris period had been 1919, before he ever set foot there. As soon as he actually appeared in person, the inevitable decline began. As Breton put it years later, 'The great disappointment of that time arose from the fact that Tzara wasn't what I'd supposed . . . The *Dada Manifesto 1918* had seemed to throw the doors wide open, but in the end we found they just led to a corridor which went round in circles.'[41]

Could it have been otherwise? The difficulty lay less with Tzara than with changing times and places. Tzara's manifesto had been written, his techniques evolved, in feverish wartime Zurich, where immediacy was all: antecedents, intellectual or national, counted for nothing. There was neither time nor need to analyse aims or motives. The same was true in the tenser milieux of Berlin and New York. Dada was a wartime flower. Its edge and fury derived from real, not literary, fighting.

But now the war had ended, and different qualities were needed. The Paris Dadas dismissed Tzara's enthusiasms and suggestions as provincial – fine for Zurich, but not up to sophisticated Paris standards. Perhaps they were not altogether wrong. It was not, however, the city to which he was unsuited, but the moment. The Zeitgeist had changed, he had not. Peace meant time to consider, and considering – 'tout de même, tout de même' – was Breton's forte. His reflex was always to 'draw conclusions'.[42] And Tzara's Dada was not about conclusions. It did not lead in any particular direction: simply, it was. Mindless iconoclasm – the anti-art that would shock people out of their parti pris – was its whole point. And then? At this point Tristan Tzara dropped out; and André Breton stepped in.

*

'All the members of the Dada Movement are presidents,' declared one of the many Dada manifestos. A partial list of these presidents, from W. D. Arensberg to Mary Wigman, was published in the Bulletin Dada, where it occupied the entire front page. Practice, however, was less simple. If all are leaders all are also followers, and neither Picabia nor Breton was any more a natural follower than Tzara. By the end of the first Dada season in Paris it was clear that the movement was divided into two camps, each with its own style and centre. On one side stood Picabia, Tzara and Picabia's faithful supporter Georges Ribemont-Dessaignes, unreconstructed devotees of the loud and aggressive Zurich style; on the other, the

Littérature group, led by Breton, unreadable, ambiguous, full of amendments and qualifications.

Breton and Picabia were matched in emotional ruthlessness. For Picabia, Dada was simply one more episode in a life of episodes, sentimental, intellectual and artistic. He had used it, as was his habit, 'for his own ends, adding a certain brilliance which perhaps it lacked. He kept it up as long as it suited him, and turned against it when it became boring – that is, when he ceased to play the leading role.'[43] This had personal as well as intellectual repercussions: the allies acquired with yesterday's enthusiasm were always liable to become today's enemies. Breton, too, was an unreliable friend, but for quite other reasons. For him, Dada – or the intellectual journey on which it was a stage – was a business so serious that it governed all aspects of life, including friendship. His whole austere philosophy was founded upon the unquestioned necessity of drawing conclusions – and acting upon them, regardless of repercussions. Friends, now and throughout his life, took second place to this inexorable logic.

Picabia preferred to receive at home, wherever that might happen to be: Gabrielle's, Germaine's, sometimes now Marthe Chenal's. He continued to publish his own magazine, *391*, which meant that he stood at one remove from *Littérature*. Cocteau, as well as Breton, was a frequent visitor to his apartment. 'What you do expresses yourself and amuses me,' Cocteau told Picabia. 'Tzara often moves me deeply, I could even say that he is the only poet to have this effect on me, though what he does is the diametric opposite of my work. Ribemont is pure, too, I'm certain. But Dada . . .'[44] By which, of course, he meant the Musketeers.

Breton, Aragon and Soupault did not inhabit the kind of apartments where it was possible to receive company. Breton had a room at the Hotel des Grands Hommes, Aragon lived with his family, Soupault was a young man about town. They preferred to conduct their social lives in cafés – a preference soon to become an immovable part of Breton's daily life. At this point, their chosen clubroom was a café in the Passage de l'Opéra called Certâ (soon to be immortalized, with its yellow curtains and assortment of unmatched cane chairs, in Louis Aragon's book *Le Paysan de Paris*). Breton and Aragon had discovered it one afternoon towards the end of 1919. It appealed 'because we hated Montparnasse and Montmartre, because too we enjoyed those equivocal passages'[45] with their underwater light which abound in the centre of Paris (though this one was soon to disappear under the extension of the Boulevard Haussmann). Certâ was the first of the Dada and Surrealist cafés, those legendary venues, those homes-from-home where, every evening, the chosen ones would assemble for the price of an aperitif. Louis Aragon confessed that, so alluring was the voice of the lady cashier, he would ring Certâ simply for the pleasure of hearing her say, 'No, Monsieur, no-one's been asking for you,' or simply, 'None of the Dadas are here, Monsieur.'[46]

This visible separation of styles had not yet developed into anything so irrevocable as a split. Picabia was a regular at Certâ, while Breton was often to be found at Rue Emile-Augier. Indeed, Breton had promised to write a preface for Picabia's latest book, *Jésus-Christ Rastaquouère* (*Jesus Christ the Wide Boy*). After the Dada Festival, however, he began to back off. Dada appeared to be descending into farce, and no one was ever less suited to farce than Breton. Besides, where, if anywhere, was all this leading? The only obvious way to cap a rain of tomatoes and beefsteaks was by ever larger and more violent demonstrations, inviting yet more flying victuals. It soon became clear he was avoiding Picabia. 'My "closest" friends, who aren't necessarily my best friends, know I prefer to be alone when I'm depressed,' he explained. '. . . I've had one or two very obvious reasons for depression this week, perhaps (and I find this astonishing) you hadn't realised. I know it's ridiculous, but it's all saddened me a lot . . . I still like you a lot even though I've been avoiding you. I sometimes need a long line of credit, why won't you extend it to me?'[47] But understanding was never Picabia's forte. Two weeks later he was complaining to Tzara that '*Littérature* doesn't give a fuck for us . . . Breton is a complete actor, he and his two little buddies think you can just change friends like you change a pair of boots.'[48] By the end of August Breton had concluded that he would not – could not – write the preface to *Jésus-Christ Rastaquouère*. 'That simply isn't where I am any more . . . I promised him I would, so Picabia and I will fall out. (I really liked Picabia.)'[49]

Nevertheless, the Musketeers were invited to the opening party for Picabia's new exhibition at Povolozky's gallery opposite the Beaux-Arts that December (1920). Not that this was a mark of especial favour: everyone he knew was invited; diplomats rubbed shoulders with Dadas, family friends fought for air with newspaper reporters, mistresses with wives. No one looked at the pictures – such was the crush, it was impossible to see them.

And what was the first sight to greet the three friends when they made their entrance? A snub in person: Cocteau, a top hat cocked over one eye, conducting a jazz ensemble of Auric on piano and Francis Poulenc wielding (among other instruments) a Klaxon horn. Cocteau made a short speech, plagiarizing (as Aragon noted) Tzara's poem-recipe: 'Mesdames, Messieurs, to make MODERN music, what do you need? Take some musicians, make them play a FOX-TROT with a few wrong notes added in, take a poet and make him "CONDUCTOR" – and everyone comes to see.'[50] The Musketeers assumed, rightly or wrongly, that Picabia was hoping for some violent reaction from them. They agreed the best thing would be to leave, quietly. 'Lamentable!' cried Breton.

'Lamentable,' Aragon agreed, and Soupault added, 'Imbecile!'[51] The party roared on without them.

Nevertheless, they decided to embark upon a new Dada season. It would consist, at Breton's suggestion, of a programme of 'visites-excursions'. This new season, Breton declared, 'will not resemble the last. Last year, the Dada programme was purely artistic (or anti-artistic, if you want – for me there isn't any difference.) This year, Dada proposes to raise the debate and to take the discussion into the moral plane ... We want to take our public to a place where, unlike a theatre, attendance in itself will be a real manifestation of good faith.'[52] The first venue selected was the churchyard of Saint-Julien-le-Pauvre, a piece of waste ground favoured by tramps and derelicts. Advertisements were placed in the weekly press. On the appointed day in April about fifty spectators and a couple of journalists turned up. It began to rain heavily. Ribemont-Dessaignes read the dictionary out loud. As the rain showed no sign of stopping, the crowd dispersed. A photograph shows the dripping Dadas, lined up like a football team.

The point of Dada was pointlessness. But this was pointlessness of a different order to anything that had gone before. Tzara was furious: in Soupault's opinion because they had departed from the Cabaret Voltaire routines. Dada, until now his life and (in large part) his creation, had been taken over. And the next 'manifestation' made this even clearer. This was a 'trial' of Maurice Barrès, billed to take place on 13 May 1921. Breton would preside, Ribemont-Dessaignes was the prosecutor, Aragon and Soupault spoke for the defence and Tzara would head the cast of witnesses.

Maurice Barrès? Who was Maurice Barrès, and what did he have to do with Dada?

In fact the 'Barrès trial' had nothing to do with Dada and everything to do with the exorcism of Breton's own obsessions. When Breton, Soupault and Aragon were schoolboys,

Barrès had been the standard-bearer of the young rebels, anarchistic, anti-authoritarian. Breton had described, in a letter to his classmate Theodore Fraenkel, the 'profundity and admirable philosophy' of Barrès's book *Du Sang, de la volupté et de la mort*.[53] But by 1914 (the year after this letter was written) Barrès had abandoned his liberal stance and, in a daily newspaper column, sounded instead the voice of belligerent nationalism, hymning war's 'redemptive fire', urging on the slaughter.

For Breton's generation, then, Barrès represented abject betrayal, and the Barrès Trial was an acting-out of this fury. But since it was paraded under the Dada banner, Tzara – to whom all this meant nothing – was necessarily included. And it is clear from the transcript that the acting-out extended not just to past betrayals but to present animosities. Called as a witness, Tzara reacted in bravura Dada style, making it quite clear what he thought, if not of Barrès, of the proceedings in general:

> Q: [from Breton, presiding]: What do you
>   know about Maurice Barrès?
> A: Nothing.
> Q: So you've nothing to say?
> A: Yes . . . Maurice Barrès is the most
>   repulsive man I've encountered in my
>   literary career; he's the biggest piss-artist
>   I've come across in my poetic career; the
>   biggest pig I've met in my political career;
>   the most worthless man Europe has
>   produced since Napoleon. I have no faith
>   in justice, even Dada justice. You will
>   agree, Mr President, that we're all of us
>   nothing but a collection of scoundrels.
>   Whether we're bigger scoundrels or
>   smaller scoundrels hardly seems
>   important . . .

Q: Do you know why you've been called as a witness?
A: Because I'm Tristan Tzara, of course.
Though I'm not completely sure of that.
Q: What is Tristan Tzara?
A: The diametric opposite of Maurice Barrès . . .

At the end of his evidence, Tzara sang a song:

Drink birds' milk
Wash your chocolates
Dada
Dada
Eat veal

after which he left the room, slamming the door behind him.

'I realised then', Philippe Soupault recalled, 'that two friends of whom I was extremely fond were beginning to oppose each other, and, sadly, to detest each other.'[54]

Tzara's attitude infuriated Breton. This was a serious matter for him, and he felt he had been made a fool of. The fact that Dada was – or had been – *about* laughing at serious matters did not mollify him. One of Breton's difficulties with Dada in general and Tzara in particular had always been that laughter of any sort did not come easily to him. On this occasion, he said, Tzara sounded 'the only discordant note . . . He kept on with his buffoonery and at the end he sang a stupid song. You only have to look at the transcript in *Littérature* to see how inappropriate that was in the circumstances – he was the only one to react like that.'[55]

On the day the Barrès Trial took place, Picabia wrote: 'I do not like illustriousness, and the directors of *Littérature* are nothing but illustrious men. I prefer to walk at random, the name of the street matters little, each day resembles the other if we do not create subjectively the illusion of something new, and Dada is no longer new.'[56]

*

Breton was clearly moving away from Dada, as Tzara understood it. He was encouraged in this by Simone Kahn, whom he had recently met and who would become his first wife. Writing to her cousin Denise she described Breton's 'extraordinary poet's personality ... [his] precise and penetrating intelligence even when he's dealing with the unconscious ... [his] enormous simplicity and sincerity, even in the midst of contradictions'.[57] She had found the Salle Gaveau Festival deeply depressing: 'the crudity and the lack of invention were equally inexcusable'.[58] What was such a man doing in such a setting? 'I am not a Dadaist,' she declared; to which Breton replied, half-joking but half-seriously, 'Nor am I.'[59]

Nevertheless, Dada's iconoclasm, its use of random chance, its expansion of art's boundaries and demolition of the traditional walls between painting and poetry, between artist and public, all remained profoundly sympathetic aims. It was the mindlessness he couldn't bear. But surely this was a contradiction in terms? Surely chance precluded thought? You either thought of your word *or* picked it out of a bag; drew your line *or* glued your string where it fell.

As it happened, there was another way; and before Tzara's arrival, Breton and Soupault had already begun to explore it.

It was not always easy for survivors to cope with the days and weeks following the war's end. 'We looked forward to ... endless parties, absurd illuminations, perpetual fourteenth of Julys,' wrote Louis Aragon of those days.[60] But not everyone shared this euphoria. For Breton, as for so many, the pleasures of cessation and survival were overshadowed by deaths: first Apollinaire's, then Jacques Vaché's, so brutal and unexpected. All his hopes and plans had been founded upon the joint enterprise which was to have been his and Vaché's future. Now only a blank remained. He spent much of his time wandering up and down the room he was renting at the Hotel des Grands Hommes, near the Panthéon, wondering what, if anything, he would ever bring himself to do. Doctoring was out of the question. He had made up his mind to abandon his medical studies, though he had not yet told his parents of this decision. He would not do so until more than a year later, in March 1920. They were, as he had foreseen, wholly unsympathetic. They declined to continue his allowance, and came to Paris to present their ultimatum, assuming that André would return with them to Lorient, in Brittany, where they were now living. He was actually in the act of packing his case when Philippe Soupault happened to arrive. This was the only time Soupault ever saw Breton's parents. He was struck by André's strong resemblance to his authoritarian and domineering mother, whom he hated, and the comparative insignificance of his father. Soupault dissuaded his friend from leaving.

Soupault, too, spent much of his time aimlessly wandering. The two 'met nearly every day, and talked about poetry and the impossibility of living'.[61] Sometimes Breton would try to recall certain phrases which came to him, complete with syntax and images, between sleeping and waking. They were elusive, often incomplete, but they seemed to him poetically interesting.

This was not Breton's first brush with depression: he had encountered it routinely (though in others rather than himself) at the shell-shock centre in Saint-Dizier to which he had been posted in the second half of 1916. He had been fascinated by the possibilities glimpsed there, particularly in the new realm of Freudian psychoanalysis (which he himself had tried out on a few patients). In Paris he had expanded this interest, taking up a post under Babinski, the famous neurologist. On their interminable walks around the boulevards, Soupault and

156

Breton (Aragon was then still in Germany) discussed these studies and their implications. For with that unerring instinct for the significant which he shared with Apollinaire, Breton had realized that here, in Freud's writings, lay the route-map for the great artistic journey of the coming century: the journey to the interior. Here lay the way out of the impasse created by photography for figurative art, and by Balzac, Dickens and the Romantics for the written word. Might the techniques he had learned at Saint-Dizier help pin down those fleeting, tantalizing images on the edge of mind? And might they, at the same time, help him through his distress as they had helped his patients?

There is some argument as to the source of Breton's early ideas on the unconscious. Breton always attributed them to Freud, but according to Soupault[62] they were derived at least as much from Pierre Janet, the leading French authority on these matters – who had, as it happened, been Raymond Roussel's doctor. In later years, says Soupault, Breton would never mention Janet because he derided Surrealism and reserved particularly harsh words for Breton's quasi-novel *Nadja* and its indictment of the treatment of mental patients.

It is true that Freud had not yet been translated into French. His work, however, was referred to in some French texts – *Précis de psychiatrie* by Dr Régis, and *La Psychanalyse* by Régis and Hesnard. Breton had read both these works at Saint-Dizier and even copied out some pages for his friend Theodore Fraenkel. And a notebook entry made at the time of Breton's and Soupault's experiments discusses Freud in the context of the work he and Soupault had just produced.

In fact, however, the technique Breton and Soupault picked for their experiment – automatic writing – would seem to indicate the influence of Janet as well as Freud, for he was a leading light of the spiritualist movement, and this was a technique frequently used by spirit mediums in their attempts to contact the dead. Spiritualism, for obvious reasons, had seen a huge renaissance during and after the war, and Janet was only one of many distinguished scientists – another was his friend the Nobel prize-winning biologist Charles Richet – who dabbled in it. Their aim was to bring scientific method to bear on the vexed question of possible contacts with the spirit world (though in the event it must be said that the spirits, or their earthly incarnations, generally outflanked the scientists).

The automatic writing of spirit mediums produced little of interest (many critics remarked on the notable inanity of even the most celebrated spirits when speaking through a medium in this way). Breton and Soupault, however, proposed to apply this technique with Freudian rather than occult intent. In later years Breton would become increasingly interested in aspects of the occult – astrology, for example, or the clairvoyant talents of mediums, weapons in his continuing war upon logic and lucidity, the twin enemies of the marvellous. But for the moment, the only spirits he and Soupault were interested in contacting were their own.

It was Soupault who began the experiment, 'my eyes half-shut'. Neither he nor Breton knew what, if anything, would happen. All they knew was that they did not want to write poems of the kind they had already produced. The first sentence to emerge was: 'Drops of water hold us prisoner, we are no more than perpetual animals.' When it was Breton's turn, he began: 'The story returns to the pricked silver manual and the most brilliant actors prepare for their entry . . .'

The book, Breton noted, 'was written in six days'.[63] 'For the first time, I think, writers actively refused to judge their work by simply not giving themselves time to look at what they had created.'[64] All that was needed was to abstract themselves from the world and let the words flow – which they did with such rapidity that '*we had to use abbreviations to get it all down* . . . The chapters simply went on until the end of the day brought them to a stop, and, from one chapter to the next, only changes of speed led to slightly different effects.'[65] The results contained 'events we had never even dreamed of, the most mysterious combinations; it was like walking through a fairy-story'.[66] The resulting prose and verse has an extraordinary and haunting quality, reminiscent of Rimbaud and, in particular, Lautréamont, whose bizarre and arbitrary images (such as the notorious 'encounter of an umbrella and a sewing machine on an operating-table') were to assume such importance for Breton and his friends. Indeed, it was later conjectured that Lautréamont might have used this same technique for his *Chants de Maldoror*. Breton and Soupault agreed to continue the experiment for a fortnight, separately, together, then separately again. They wrote all day, for eight or ten hours at a time. The resulting work was entitled *Les Champs magnétiques* (*Magnetic Fields*).

For both, this was a period of great happiness. The clouds of misery and uncertainty were suddenly dispelled. Aragon remembered that 'Philippe often told me how A.B., who just before the experiment of the *Champs* saw before him nothing but emptiness and despair, had changed while they were writing, bursting out laughing at certain images or phrases.'[67] Breton remembered 'the euphoria, intoxication almost, of our discovery. It was as if we'd stumbled across some rich seam.'[68] As for Soupault, he felt 'wonderfully *unburdened*. I'd found an exit, a possibility of progress.'[69] The therapy had proved successful. Vaché's death had been faced down, along with his parting message of nihilism and despair. *Les Champs magnétiques* is dedicated to him – but the dedication does not appear until the end.

Aragon, returning to Paris, found Breton drunk on poetry. He had recently copied out the hitherto unpublished *Poésies* of Isidore Ducasse, aka the Comte de Lautréamont, at the Bibliothèque Nationale, and the effect of this work on all of them was profound. Breton had undertaken the task 'out of simple literary curiosity, but . . . the shining light of that mind appeared to us as a fundamental text . . . seductive as the fire which fell one Thursday on the heads of the apostles . . .'[70] But it was clear that this was not all. Something else had happened – 'something faceless and nameless'. His friends were evasive: whatever this something was, it was not easily discussed – certainly not when they were all together. Finally Breton, alone with Aragon in a café on the Boulevard Saint-Germain, told him and showed him.

'It was written in school exercise books,' Aragon remembered many years later. 'André had placed himself so that, from where I was, I couldn't see the writing, to know who had written the different parts . . .'[71] He was eager to know if Aragon could spot which were his passages, which Soupault's. To his disappointment, this was almost always possible. 'But did it really matter?' Aragon wondered. 'It's certain that André, alone, could never have written Les Champs magnétiques. He would never have had the courage to venture into the unknown by himself . . . As time has passed, [it] has become the work of one two-headed author, and this double vision is what enabled Philippe Soupault and André Breton to advance along that unknown path, into the shadows where they spoke out loud.'[72]

Characteristically, the introspective Breton had been more unnerved by their experiment than Soupault. What, he wondered as always, would be the consequences? Where was all this leading? And did it really have any value? He was soon persuaded that it did, and was eventually to conclude that 'nothing we say or do has any value except when we obey this magic dictation'.[73]

The first three chapters of Les Champs magnétiques were published in the October, November and December 1919 issues of Littérature, to be followed by Breton's tribute to his dead friend – the publication of Vaché's *Lettres de guerre*. But by that time Breton was already corresponding with Tzara and Picabia and bewitched by the vitriolically energetic *391*. The spell they cast, the exciting prospect of meeting these new heroes, the novelty of their message, occupied his mind to the exclusion of all else. The thread of automatism was broken, the path momentarily lost.[74]

Now once again his mind returned to Freud. It was the summer of 1921. The world was on holiday. Tzara, Arp and their friend Max Ernst, a German Dada from Cologne, were at Tarrenz-bei-Imst in the Tyrol with their wives and girlfriends, enjoying a jolly time that recalled the heady days of Zurich. Ernst's work – witty, delicate collages, unbridled animal and vegetable fantasies, the exploration of new techniques such as *frottage* that brought chance by yet another route into the world of the visual arts – had little in common with the screaming brutalities of Berlin Dada, and he himself, tall, thin, bird-like, resembling nothing so much as his own creation Lop-lop, King of the Birds, seemed oddly un-German. France, however, offered him a welcome. Breton, his fiancée Simone, Soupault and Aragon had recently arranged an exhibition of Ernst's paintings in Paris – 'a revelation,' said Soupault.[75] This, however, had been organized at a distance, packets and parcels of work arriving by every post; the exhibition's organizers had never actually met Ernst in person. Since then Breton and Simone had married. They decided, on the strength of an alluring postcard, that Tarrenz would be a fine place for a honeymoon, and Paul Eluard and his wife agreed to join them there.

Both Breton and Tzara had suffered recently at the hands of Picabia, and this, for the moment, had drawn them together again. Even so, Tzara was uncertain about Breton as holiday company. The latter's increasing intensity was reaching epic proportions. 'We're awaiting the moment when he will reach the point of compression at which, like dynamite, he explodes,' read 'Dr Serner's Notebook' in *391* no. 11. Ribemont-Dessaignes wrote reassuringly to Tzara: 'Saw everyone at Certâ . . . All in a very good mood. No brewings-up or conspiracies . . . The wedding has lightened things up for the moment and Breton was all smiles. Eluard and his wife were there too. Charming.'[76] However, by the time the Bretons arrived in September the others were about to leave. It was probably just as well: when Breton tried to read aloud from Lautréamont, Tzara and Ernst were openly bored: his arrival, Ernst commented, was 'like a hair in the soup'.[77] The Eluards arrived to find all except Breton and Simone already gone. Eluard, who had especially looked forward to meeting Ernst, soon followed him to Cologne; Breton decided to make for Vienna, where he would beard Dr Freud in his lair as one researcher to another. He had sent Freud a copy of *Les Champs magnétiques*, which he considered a significant step in the exploration of the literary unconscious, avoiding the self-censorship of such authors as Shakespeare and Goethe, however celebrated they might be.

Breton's expectations of this interview were enormous. For some days he 'prowl[ed] around Freud's house without finding the courage to knock', carrying the great man's photograph.[78] Finally he was granted an appointment for three one afternoon, 'though I have very little free time these days'.[79] Leaving Simone waiting in a café Breton set off in a state of high excitement.

He was soon – too soon – miserably back; he would not speak to Simone about what had happened. His bitter disappointment is reflected, however, in the brief account published some months later in *Littérature*:

> At last the famous door half-opens for me. I find myself in the presence of a little old man with no style, in the shabby

162

office of a poor local doctor. He has no great love of France, the only country still indifferent to his work ... I try to get the conversation going by mentioning the names of Charcot, Babinski, but perhaps because these are already distant memories, or perhaps because he's unwilling to commit himself with someone he doesn't know, he lets drop nothing but generalities: 'I've never received anything more touching than your good letter,' or, 'Luckily, we can count upon the young people of today.'[80]

*

In January 1920, Breton had nervously awaited the coming of the Dada Messiah from Zurich. Tzara had seemed to promise nothing less than – the future. Now, two years later, Dada had become a dead weight, an intellectual void within which no progress was possible. What had changed? Nothing – and that was the trouble. In Tzara's words, 'Dadaism has never based itself upon any theory and is nothing but a protest.'[81] But this static position was intolerable to Breton, with his incessant urge to keep moving forward. 'Excuse me for thinking that, unlike the ivy, I die if I attach myself.'[82]

Breton therefore decided to try for a grand gesture which might pole-vault him out of the Dada cul-de-sac. He would organize a conference, the Congrès de Paris, which would cover all aspects of 'l'esprit moderne', within which he lumped Dada, together with Cubism and Futurism, as three aspects of 'a more general movement whose direction and breadth are not yet certain'.[83] From these deliberations would emerge the next step: they would be a crucible (in Picabia's image) for 'a wonderful nugget which he'll pull along behind him on a little trolley and sign André Breton'.[84] As for the congress's themes, they too would emerge. In a circular to newspaper editors and critics, Breton sketched two possibilities: 'Has the spirit which we call modern always existed?' And

'Among modern objects, is a top hat more or less modern than a locomotive?'

After the experience of the Barrès Trial, the Dadas, though in principle supporting Breton, were doubtful of this new venture, threatening, as it did, another collapse into bathetic wordiness. Picabia doubted whether it could succeed; Tzara, in the politest and most conciliatory of terms, begged to dissociate himself from it.

At this brush-off from one who (as he saw it) had been included only as a matter of courtesy, Breton saw red. He presented the congress's next committee meeting with a text destined for the press, and soon to become notorious. 'The committee of the Congress of Paris ... is making active progress ... From now on the undersigned, members of the organising committee, want to warn against the manoeuvrings of a person known as the "promoter" of a movement from Zurich, whom it is not useful to name in any other way and *who has nothing to do with any current reality.*' The document concluded with a postscript intended, among other things, to separate Tzara from one of his natural allies: 'We learn that Francis Picabia has just announced his support for the Congress of Paris.'[85]

To attack Tzara in such terms was anyway unforgivable; in France's xenophobic, post-war, post-Dreyfus atmosphere, doubly so. A number of Breton's erstwhile colleagues on the congress's organizing committee called a meeting in the Closerie des Lilas, at which Breton would effectively be tried for his offence.

More than a hundred people packed into the café's upstairs banqueting-room. It was the show of the season. Everybody was there – not just the Dadas and their associates, but such figures as Matisse, Picasso, Constantin Brancusi, and (of course) Cocteau. 'Never in my experience were words of such passion and flame hurled at each other by men without coming to blows,' said an American witness, Matthew Josephson. 'If they had been Americans, they would have butchered one another.'[86] But this was Paris: the damage was verbal and emotional rather than physical. Tzara screamed abuse; Soupault tried in vain to reconcile the warring parties.

Picabia was not present: he had left the scene, preferring as usual to watch the altercations from a safe distance, namely, Saint-Raphaël on the Côte d'Azur. For some time his relations with Breton had been cool; now, however, since Tzara had come out formally against Breton, Picabia was veering in the other direction. Breton wrote long letters outlining Tzara's dastardly manoeuvres, the interviews he was giving the press, the meetings he had called to discuss Breton and the congress. He invited Picabia to join himself and six or seven of the faithful in a new review – they might even stage some manifestations in the old style? 'The formula is still to be decided, naturally.'[87] Whatever they fixed upon, however, the decision should be taken before the congress.

'I'm happy we're still friends,' Picabia replied. He did not, however, take up Breton's suggestion of a new review, being about to publish one of his own, *La Pomme de pins* (*The Pine cone*). 'There's lots in it about the Congress.'

In fact the *Pomme de pins*, a four-page folded sheet, was not *about* anything, consisting, rather, of a scatter-shot of abuse and aphorisms – 'Cubism is a cathedral of Shit,' 'Tristan in his cotton cap thinks he's still at Zurich,' 'Heads are round so that thoughts can change direction,' 'Saint-Raphaël bazaar – Grand Sale of ideas – end-of-season thoughts – Genuine bargains – Unheard-of prices,' 'Picabia has invented a gyroscope for brains suffering the vertigo of celebrity . . .' – and so on. When it arrived in Paris, Tzara and his friends published their own broadside, *Le Coeur à barbe, journal transparent* – an inappropriate title, since it was an exercise in rebuttal comprehensible only to initiates.

The Congrès de Paris had lost momentum. Each passing day made that clearer. Even Breton's oldest allies – Soupault, Eluard, Theodore Fraenkel – allowed their names to appear as collaborators in the *Coeur à barbe*. Breton, weary, resigned himself to failure. In the April number of *Littérature* he published his farewell to Dada:

> Drop everything.
> Drop Dada.
> Drop your wife, drop your mistress.
> Drop your hopes and your fears.
> Toss your children into the woods.
> Drop the prey in the shade.
> Drop, if you must, your easy life and plans for the future.
> Set out on the road.[88]

His eyes were fixed on the future. Whatever it might contain, it would invariably take precedence over present loyalties. 'It's been said that I discard old friends like old boots,' he wrote, referring to Picabia's *mot* recently made public by Tzara. 'It's a luxury, I admit it, one can't wear the same pair for ever: when it doesn't fit me any more I leave it to my staff.'[89]

*

In the summer of 1923, more than a year after the fiasco of the Congrès de Paris, Tzara decided to put on one last grand manifestation. In order to do so, however, he had to ally himself with a front organization, since, after the chastening experiences of previous Dada events, no theatre manager in Paris would take him on. He found a Russian group called 'Tcherez' (meaning 'across' or 'above') whose leader, Zdanevitch, succeeded in leasing the Théâtre Michel in the Rue des Mathurins for Friday 6 and Saturday 7 July. The evening would be called *Le Coeur à barbe* – The Bearded

Heart – after the sheet produced in answer to Picabia's *Pomme de pins*.

A mixed programme was projected, containing some odd bedfellows. There would be a sketch, *Le Coeur à gaz*, written and performed during Dada's heyday three years previously; some films, including an abstract one by Hans Richter and a very short one, *Retour à la raison*, by Man Ray, now living in Paris, who at Tzara's request had cobbled together some footage in the course of an evening (Tzara came one day and said, 'Tomorrow is a Dada manifestation and we need a film.' Man Ray, always willing to oblige a friend, went out, bought a few hundred feet of film, and made Rayographs on it with thumbtacks and nails and salt and pepper, adding in a few shots of his mistress Kiki for good measure); music including Satie's *Trois Morceaux en forme de poire* and Milhaud's '*Shimmy' caramel mou*, executed by Marcelle Meyer; and some poems, including works by Soupault and Eluard, whose permission had not been sought and whose names were followed in the programme by that of the enemy-in-chief, Jean Cocteau. These would be read by the actor Marcel Herrand. The performers were drawn from the new generation of young men who had joined Dada over the past couple of years: René Crevel, Jacques Baron and, surprisingly, Pierre de Massot, who had been Breton's faithful lieutenant during the Congrès de Paris preparation and who had recently written a slighting article about Tzara in the Belgian review *Ça ira* referring to him as 'that little Rumanian Jew'.

Evidently Tzara expected trouble.[90] Before the show he let it be known, in most un-Dada fashion, that anyone interrupting would be thrown out. Serge Romoff, one of the Tcherez group, told Breton as he came in, 'All right, Breton, we're letting you in, but you've got to be quiet.' To add insult to injury, Breton had actually paid for his seat (twenty-five francs): the *Littérature* group had all had to pay (despite protestations of friendship and gratitude from Tzara) when free tickets were being handed out to 'all the Americans he knew'. Clearly relations had not improved during the past year. Eluard announced his determination to prevent his name being dragged in the mud; Aragon, anticipating the worst, warned that his support could not be counted on in the event of a fracas, as he would be with a friend – presumably a lady.

The evening began with some music, politely applauded. Then Tzara introduced Pierre de Massot, who proceeded to read a proclamation:

> André Gide, died in battle
> Sarah Bernhardt, died in battle
> Claude Terrasse, died in battle
> Francis Picabia, died in battle
> Pablo Picasso, died in battle . . .

Picasso, in the stalls, folded his arms and caught Eluard's eye. Breton rose and shouted, 'That's enough!' Cane in hand he climbed on-stage and ordered de Massot off. De Massot stammered something, and Breton hit him so hard that he broke de Massot's left arm. By this time the theatre was in uproar, the performers rushing to de Massot's aid, the audience on its feet. 'I can't tell you how much I admire what he did,' enthused Aragon. 'André Breton doesn't bother with small gestures which might attract unwelcome sympathy.'[91]

Everyone sat down again, but Tzara could be seen signalling, and several policemen, who had clearly been stationed at the ready, advanced into the room. 'A truly stupefying spectacle: Tristan Tzara, yesterday's anarchist, the impenitent Dadaist, calling the police against people who wanted to *prevent* something – and what people! People who had defended him against not just Paris, but the world!'[92] Tzara indicated Breton and his friends Benjamin Péret and Robert

Desnos. He also indicated Eluard, who had not (yet) so much as opened his mouth, but Eluard was not thrown out.

The performance continued, though the pianist was visibly nervous. Finally it was time for the *Coeur à gaz*. This had been costumed by Sonia Delaunay, using cardboard, which left the actors effectively immobile. Eluard called on Tzara to come forward and explain his actions. When he appeared Eluard jumped on-stage and slapped both him and René Crevel, trapped inside his cardboard costume. A general riot ensued. The performance was abandoned, the next day's show cancelled. The theatre was torn apart: Tzara sued Eluard for 8,000 francs damages. Before the case could come to judgement, however, Eluard (for, as we shall see, a variety of reasons) had left for the Far East.

As for Breton, the evening gave him the excuse he had been looking for. Between himself and Dada, all was over. He had literally beaten it into the ground. In 1928, when he published his autobiographical fragment *Nadja*, he was still flourishing his grudge: 'M. Tristan Tzara would no doubt prefer it if no-one knew that on the evening of the *Coeur à barbe* in Paris he handed Paul Eluard and myself over to the police, even though such a gesture is deeply significant and, in this light, which will inevitably be that of history, *25 Poems* [the title of one of his books] becomes *25 Élucubrations of a Police Agent*.'[93] It was not until two years later that the quarrel came to an end. At that point Breton inscribed Tzara's copy of *Nadja* with the words: 'To Tristan Tzara, by a singular turn of events which makes me see him again as I did when I first knew him. What a wonderful laugh he has!'[94]

CHAPTER FIVE

A SEA OF
DREAMS

MARCEL DUCHAMP, ZIGZAGGING between continents, arrived in Paris from Buenos Aires in August 1919. He at once gravitated to Picabia's apartment (which he located with difficulty, having previously known only the matrimonial home on Avenue Charles-Floquet). But if he had been restive in New York, Paris, too, offered few attractions. It was too painful: back in France his brother Raymond's death, which he had not fully grasped in far-off Argentina, suddenly acquired a terrible reality. He fled back to New York on 27 December, leaving behind him an aura of mystery and legend.

During this short stay Duchamp made three new works. All have since passed into myth (the invariable fate of Duchamp's works, there being so very few of them). One was the *Tzanck cheque*, made out to his dentist, Dr Tzanck, every line of which was laboriously and minutely drawn by Duchamp, and which was soon worth far more than its face value. Another was the *Flask of Paris Air*, which he took back to New York as a present for the Arensbergs. The third, and by far the most famous, made in October 1919, was the postcard of the Mona Lisa which Duchamp decorated with a beard and moustache, inscribing at the bottom five letters: L.H.O.O.Q.

This, of course, was the source of Picabia's joke at the *Littérature* matinée in February 1920. Picabia habitually filled his work with arcane (to outsiders) allusions to his friends, making his inscriptions and magazines more or less impenetrable to all those lacking the key of intimacy. A few weeks later *391*[1] published the complete work under the heading 'TABLEAU DADA par MARCEL DUCHAMP' (just above Picabia's own 'Dada Manifesto', which he signed, characteristically: '*Francis PICABIA who knows nothing, nothing, nothing.*'). Picabia did not have the original to hand, so he made his own version: it had a slightly bolder moustache but lacked the beard. (Much later, Duchamp went one better, publishing a Mona Lisa without either beard or moustache, over the one word '*Rasée*' (shaved).)

This schoolboy joke has engendered a vast literature. The Milanese scholar and collector Arturo Schwartz, for example, concentrates upon Duchamp's (undoubted) alchemical interests. Duchamp's own translation of the phrase was 'There is fire down below'; this (says Schwartz) refers to the base of the pelvis – 'sacrum' – the vestigial (and, by extension, *sacred*) *queue* or tail, which is also the last letter – Q – of the rebus. Alchemically, 'bottom' is linked to the earth, passivity, the moon, water, femininity – it is the eternal feminine. L.H.O.O.Q. thus juxtaposes the polarities: fire/sun/masculinity, water/moon/femininity. It describes, firstly, the *coniunctio oppositionis* in which sun and moon unite; leading, secondly, to a higher awareness because of the increase of fire (down below), and thirdly, to the third stage of the magistery, when bride and bachelor are happily brought together in the androgynous adept, 'a fact which in turn explains the addition of the moustache and goatee which complete the no longer enigmatic smile of the Mona Lisa'.[2]

Schwartz also draws parallels between Duchamp and Leonardo da Vinci, the Mona Lisa's creator. Both (he observes) were notary's sons; both left few surviving works; the major works of both were all abandoned or unfinished; Leonardo, like Duchamp, was interested in puns and anagrams; Leonardo used mirror-writing while Duchamp was interested in mirrors; both had an androgynous psychology (as L.H.O.O.Q. proves). Schwartz additionally notes that in Argos, brides would put on a false beard on their wedding night . . .

The Leonardo connection was also made by the gallery-owner Julien Levy. He draws a parallel between Duchamp's notes on the *Élevage de poussière*:

> To raise dust
> for 4 months. 6 months which you
> close up afterwards
> hermetically – Transparency
> – Difference. To be worked out

and a passage in Da Vinci's *Notebooks*:

> Concerning the local movements of flexible dry things
> such as dust and the like
> I say that when a table is struck
> in different places the dust
> that is upon it is reduced to various shapes
> of mounds and tiny hillocks.

When this comparison was submitted to Duchamp, he gave 'what I can only describe', says Levy, 'as his Gioconda smile.'[3]

For some, an alchemical riddle; for others a smutty joke. For Breton, a new hero was heralded. 'What I'd seen of his intelligence made me think he must be some sort of amazing prodigy.'[4]

What, in fact, had Breton seen? Not yet the man himself: he had left for New York some days before Breton's first meeting with Picabia. As to the works, little of Duchamp's limited production was available in France, and when Tzara invited him to send a work from New York for a 'Salon Dada', he sent a characteristically gnomic refusal: a telegram reading *'Pode Bal'*, or *'peau de balle'* – balls to you: another instant Dada/Duchamp legend. (He told his brother-in-law Jean Crotti that he had nothing to exhibit, and anyway, the verb *exposer* (to exhibit) sounded too much like *épouser* (to marry).) Blank cards bearing the catalogue numbers of the missing exhibits were put up in their place. For the rest, there were fleeting esoteric references in *391* ('Marcel Duchamp, Professor of French at Washington Square University, has resigned from the committee of the Independents . . .'); a few risqué puns: '*Du dos de la cuillère au cul de la douairière*' ('From the ladle's bump to milady's rump'); '*Conseil d'hygiène intime: Il faut mettre la moelle de l'epée dans le poil de l'aimée*' ('Tips on intimate hygiene: Put the pork of the sword in the fork of the broad'); and the *Tzanck Cheque* and L.H.O.O.Q., both of which Picabia had already reproduced.

These childish jokes and smutty wordplays (a knack first developed as a seduction technique in the orgiastic atmosphere of wartime New York) could not have been further removed from anything produced by the perfectly humourless and innately prudish Breton. Indeed, a large part of Paris Dada's failed chemistry was due to Breton's unremitting solemnity, which pervaded even his jokes. No wonder Tzara's antics, the product of Zurich's gales of laughter, had fallen so flat. But what we seek in our heroes is not merely ourselves – it is ourselves as we should like to be: and Breton, though humour-less, coveted humour. Or rather 'Umor'; not humour *per se* but a particular humour – Vaché's: the variety he christened *humour noir*. And Duchamp's humour, though light and charming, was nothing if not *noir*. Those seemingly artless little games were far from innocent. The laughter has a cutting edge; it emerges, despite Duchamp's disclaimers, from some deeper well than the top of the head, its apparent source. Tolstoy observed that 'When we read or look at the artistic production of a new author the fundamental question that arises in our soul is always of this kind: "Well, what sort of a man are you? . . . What can you tell me that is new, about how we must look at this life of ours?" '[5] And although Duchamp would undoubtedly have laughed at the very notion of a soul, Tolstoy's observation held as true of anti-art as of art. Duchamp's games reflected his absolute refusal to engage with life. They were directed not only at the myths upon which art is founded, but at the criticism which seeks to explain them: a double distancing.

Both Duchamp and Picabia were older than André Breton's generation, Duchamp by nine years, Picabia by seventeen. 'We were the old men. Still, in the eyes of the young people, we represented a revolutionary element . . . They found that we represented the spirit that they, too, wanted to represent, and they were drawn to us.'⁶ But Duchamp and Picabia were two very different propositions, and it showed nowhere more than in their relations with Breton.

The difficulty with Picabia and Breton was that they were, in important respects, too alike. Breton was determined to assume direction of the new thought: he dictated events, or did not participate. That had been part of his problem with Tzara, who, when he proved not to be a hero, became, immediately and inevitably, a rival. But the notion of being led was equally inconceivable to the volatile and headlong Picabia. He had wealth, fame, enormous creative talents; Breton had none of these things. Why, then, should he declare allegiance to Breton?

Duchamp, however, would never compete, any more than he would disappoint. In fact, he would never 'do' anything. In his perfect unconcern he was ready to submit not just his work but his very life to the laws of chance. In front of the marvelling Breton, he tossed a coin in the air with the words, 'Tails I go to America tonight, heads I stay in Paris.' 'Not the slightest question of indifference,' Breton commented. 'He would infinitely have preferred to go, or to stay.'⁷ It was terribly attractive, even though, for Breton as for all the disappointed New York ladies, there was something fatal about the attraction. In a letter to the couturier and maecenas Jacques Doucet (then employing him as an advisor to help with the creation of a collection of avant-garde artworks) Breton described Duchamp as 'the man from whom I would be the most inclined to expect something, if he wasn't so distant and deep down so desperate'.[8]

Distant? Absent might have been a better word. Duchamp was not to be found; he was always hiding. Breton describes his 'face whose wonderful good looks are not marked by any particularly outstanding detail; nothing you say to him makes any impression on that polished surface'.[9] It was, in fact, nothing but a mask: which of Duchamp's many identities was he wearing today? You turned around, and when you turned back he had become someone else. 'I was really trying to invent, instead of merely expressing myself,' he said. '. . . My intention was always to get away from myself, though I knew perfectly well that I was using myself. Call it a little game between "I" and "me".'[10] There was the Marcel Douxami whose letter in *The Blind Man* described how the works of 'a certain Picabia have particularly irritated me' – to the point of apoplexy. There was his near relative Marchand du Sel, creator of puns. There was the chess player, retreating into a cerebral haven safe from reality. And, if these were not enough, there was the most celebrated of them all, Rrose Sélavy (who always saw *la vie en rose*).

'I wanted to change my identity,' Duchamp told Pierre Cabanne, describing Rrose's birth, 'and the first idea that came to me was to take a Jewish name: I was Catholic, and it was a change to go from one religion to another. I didn't find a Jewish name that I especially liked, or that tempted me, and suddenly I had an idea: why not change sex? It was so much simpler. So the name Rrose Sélavy came from that.'[11] In fact she was not born with a double r, but acquired it in 1921 in Cocteau's nightclub Le Boeuf sur le Toit for which Picabia had done a painting, *l'Oeil cacodylate*, signed by all his friends. Duchamp signed it with one of his customary wordplays: '*Pi Qu'habilla Rrose Sélavy*', part of which contains a subsidiary

178

wordplay on *arroser* (making water) *c'est la vie*. There is also an erotic play: the double r, pronounced in the French way (erre) turns Rose into Erose. Duchamp celebrated Rrose's birth with a new work, a miniature French window with eight glass panes covered in black leather. He entitled this *FRESH WIDOW COPYRIGHT RROSE SÉLAVY 1920*, and it embodies Rrose's attributes[12]: she is French, fresh (i.e. pert), widowed (so available), easily opened, in mourning maybe, but in leather rather than crepe. Rrose figures seductively in a number of photographs, making her first appearance on the cover of Duchamp and Man Ray's sheet *New York Dada* under yet another punning pseudonym, Belle Haleine (Beautiful Breath – or Belle Hélène), whose photo adorns the label on a bottle of *Eau de voilette* (*tiolet water perfumed with voilets*).

How was it possible to fall out with such a person? You couldn't: your adversary melted away before your very eyes. Even when you thought you knew him, you were liable to find out that your acquaintance was merely with a facet. In 1941, the Russian Constructivist sculptor Pevsner met Mary Reynolds, Duchamp's mistress for the past twenty years. Pevsner couldn't believe it. He had had no idea of her existence, yet he had seen Duchamp almost every week of his life throughout those years.[13] *As I was going to the fair/I met a man who wasn't there./He wasn't there again today ...* Clearly the man in the song is Marcel Duchamp. 'You're looking for a man,' Tzara had told Breton. It was true: and the danger always was that (as in Tzara's own case) he would find him. With Duchamp, however, as with Vaché, there was never any risk of that. Like the unicorn, he was a mythic creature.

Duchamp at this time had only a tourist visa for the States, which had to be renewed after six months' residence. Rather than bother with that he preferred to leave for a while. He returned to Paris in June 1921, for eight months, and in 1923 came back for three years. Until the outbreak of World War II, Paris would be his main base. He would hover around the edges of Breton's group, influencing it in many ways without ever actually belonging to it. 'I [was] borrowed from the ordinary world by the Surrealists,' he explained. 'They liked me a lot; Breton liked me a lot; we were very good together. They had a lot of confidence in the ideas I could bring to them, ideas which weren't antisurrealist, but which weren't always Surrealist either.'[14]

Was it merely a coincidence that the only two Surrealists never to fall out with André Breton were Duchamp the honorary American and his friend Man Ray, soon to become an honorary Frenchman? Hovering in mid-Atlantic they never became 'enemies', never suffered excommunication at Breton's quasi-papal hands. For Americans, it was hard to take quite seriously the splits and crises which punctuated the lives of their friends. The group of Dadas, soon to become Surrealists, was in their view simply a delightful club full of like-minded fellow-artists. For the paramountcy of theory – as Karl Marx had already found out – is something no anglophone can easily comprehend. Matthew Josephson, the little magazine *Broom*'s new Paris correspondent, had been introduced to Man Ray by a mutual New York friend and had soon got to know Aragon and Soupault. He became an enthusiastic group member. But when he contributed some doggerel to Tzara's polemical *Coeur à barbe*, Aragon 'assured me that I had not the least understanding of what I was doing. I replied that while I could not possibly follow all the raveled plots and counterplots of the warring factions, I did not believe they were serious.'[15] Not serious! For Breton, Tzara and their friends, this was the stuff of life itself. Before Josephson's eyes, yesterday's bosom friends became today's bitter enemies. And still he could not quite believe it. Breton, for instance, declared writing for the commercial press unacceptable, citing Rimbaud's dictum that the hack is no better than the ploughman. On pain of expulsion, or at the very least a severe reprimand, activities must be confined to acceptable outlets. Josephson, however, assumed that 'in secret, they were writing their own personal literature'.[16] That, at any rate, was what *he* would have done.

> We Americans knew the cold statistics of the war in Europe, indicating that some twenty or more millions were casualties; but we could not calculate its unexpected human consequences, [Josephson observed.] The greater part of Aragon's generation had been killed or maimed; those who survived, at the coming of peace, had been left not merely with the sense of being 'lost,' but with the consciousness that they must drive for an all-out revolt against the civilisation that had brought forth this long orgy of destruction.[17]

For Aragon, Breton, Tzara and the rest, the essence of Dada and what would become Surrealism lay here. These were no optional games, but a strategy for survival. Art was no longer merely an expression of civilization's heights and progress. Between Apollinaire's generation and their own, that was what had changed. In that sense, the Americans remained pre-war.

Partly, of course, it was a question of personality. Neither Duchamp nor Man Ray was capable of the intense friendship between men which marked Breton's circle, and upon which much of his power rested, making excommunication, when it occurred, such a traumatic experience. Duchamp, though a man of many friends, was passionate only about the avoidance of intensity. As for Man Ray, the lens of his camera stood between him and the world he recorded. Intensity was reserved for his work and for women, whom Breton's circle excluded from serious intellectual consideration. And because they were uniquely immune to this aspect of Breton's power, Man Ray and (especially) Duchamp acquired a power of their own.

181

'Dada cannot live in New York,' complained Man Ray, writing to Tzara in June 1921, just before he left America for what turned out to be twenty years. 'All New York is dada, and will not tolerate a rival.' On 22 July, he disembarked at Le Havre. Later he always gave the date of his arrival in France as 14 July, Bastille Day – much as grateful Americans like Louis B. Mayer adopted 4 July as their birthday. In each case, the chosen date symbolized, in its significance, the relationship between the man and the place.

*

'I will try to be at the train in Paris when you arrive,' Duchamp had written. 'If you do not see me at the station, take a taxi to 22 rue de la Condamine and ask for me downstairs. [This was Yvonne Chastel's apartment, where Duchamp was staying.] I will be in or leave the key (6th floor, *top floor*, right hand door when you get off the elevator) . . . I have arranged a room for you in a little hotel where Tzara lives. He may be gone when you arrive.'[18]

This was the Hôtel de Boulainvilliers, near Rue Emile-Augier, where Tzara had moved when, finally, he vacated Germaine Everling's salon. As Duchamp had supposed, Tzara had indeed left for the summer; for the moment, Man Ray took over his room. Later that evening, Duchamp took him to Certâ. 'Half a dozen young men and a young woman sat around a table in an isolated nook. After introductions some attempt was made at conversation. Jacques Rigaut, who spoke a few words of English, interpreted questions and answers. It was rather summary, yet I felt at ease with these strangers who seemed to accept me as one of themselves, due, no doubt, to my reputed sympathies and the knowledge they already had of my activities in New York.'[19] He was right: everyone knew of Man Ray. In that culture of little magazines, *New York Dada* had passed from hand to hand; and Man Ray had also sent works for the Salon Dada so categorically ignored by Duchamp.

Breton was there, of course, 'carrying his imposing head like a chip on the shoulder', Aragon, Eluard with his wife Gala, Soupault – the usual crowd. To Man Ray's surprise, there were no painters – Picabia and Breton were currently at odds, and the other Dadas were almost all writers. Even the painters – Ernst, Arp, Picabia – also wrote poetry.

From the café the group adjourned to a restaurant, and from there to a funfair.

> My friends rushed from one attraction to another like children, enjoying themselves to the utmost, ending up by angling with fishing-poles with rings on the ends for bottles or wine or cheap champagne. I looked on, bewildered by the playfulness and the abandon of all dignity by these people who otherwise took themselves so seriously . . . Once I ventured on the dizzy swings with the Eluards; we were violently thrown upon each other and I wondered fleetingly whether they sought a physical extension into the realm of strong sensations.[20]

He was almost certainly right: the Eluards, as we shall see, were always on the alert for new sexual possibilities.

This search for 'strong sensations', whether sexual (as Man Ray characteristically implies) or otherwise, was a vital aspect of Dada. As Soupault put it, 'Writing seemed too limited, I wanted to convert poetry into action.'[21] He was in the habit of stopping passers-by to ask if they knew where Philippe Soupault lived. Some shrugged and walked on; others tried to help him find out. Sometimes he would ring the doorbell of some unlikely building and ask whoever answered the same question – 'Does Philippe Soupault live here?' 'I don't think he'd have been surprised to receive the answer Yes,' Breton commented. 'He'd have gone to knock on the door.'[22] On one spectacular evening, Soupault and Jacques Rigaut, forgetting the number of the apartment where they were invited to dine, found the door opened by complete strangers. Evidently large numbers of guests were expected, for

> to our joy and amazement we were warmly welcomed and immediately offered an aperitif. Jacques Rigaut was delighted by this mix-up and signalled me to say nothing to undeceive our involuntary hosts. He talked brilliantly during dinner, told stories, invented influential connections. The mistress of the house . . . was charmed. It was an evening she would not soon forget. I did my best to play the same game. Then, without warning, he had had enough, and, very politely, left. They were obviously sorry to see us go. Jacques Rigaut was delighted. When we got into the street he burst out laughing. 'We must do it again,' he said.

And they did, but with a more polished technique. When they spied a flow of arrivals signalling a party, they would buy flowers and chocolates and join the happy guests. On one occasion, however, the host threatened to call the police. 'We're going,' said the unperturbed Rigaut, 'but we want our flowers and chocolates back.'[23] Man Ray watched these *actes gratuits* wide-eyed. 'I feel like a new-born baby,' he wrote in a letter to his family. His first French artwork was a collage, *Transatlantique*, showing burned shreds of American newspaper and spent matches scattered in a Paris street.

He was at once accepted into the group: Duchamp's recommendation guaranteed his welcome. Breton was less enthusiastic than the others, distrusting both Man Ray's anarchism, which made him resistant to group discipline of the kind Breton was trying to impose, and also the friendship which had sprung up between him and the current arch-enemy, Tzara. Tzara was promoting his new friend internationally, arranging exhibits in Brussels (through Clement

Pansaers) and Cologne, where Max Ernst was all enthusiasm. But Man Ray declined these: 'I want to make my first show in Paris so that I do not appear provincial,' he told Ferdinand Howald, a wealthy American patron from whom he was receiving financial support. And before long he could report that his 'new French friends', having viewed his work in the hotel room, were arranging an exhibition for the fall.[24] Soupault was about to open a small bookshop and art-gallery, the Librairie Six, and suggested that its first exhibition might be devoted to Man Ray. A catalogue was assembled, with quotable quotes from Max Ernst, Ribemont-Dessaignes, Soupault, Tzara – 'Monsieur Ray was born one day he no longer knows where. After having been successively a coal merchant, several times a millionaire and chairman of the chewing gum trust, he decided to respond to the invitation of the dadaists and show his latest canvases in Paris' – and Thoughts on Art from Man Ray himself: 'After dressing a medium-sized carp from the Seine, you cut it in slices (taking care to remove the gallbladder from the base of the head). Among artists, 281 have been put out to a wet-nurse, of which only one lives in Paris; on the other hand, it should be noted that, of this number, only 4 were breast-fed.' The works included, besides objects such as the spiral *Lampshade*, several examples of his latest technique, airbrush painting. 'It was wonderful to paint a picture without touching the canvas,' he commented. 'This was a pure cerebral activity. It was also like painting in 3D; to obtain the desired effects you had to move the airbrush nearer or further from the canvas.'[25]

Man Ray was happily surprised by the numbers attending, though they were not large by the standards of earlier Dada events. Picabia arrived draped in sweaters and scarves, defying the icy December wind in an open Delage. The ceiling 'was festooned with brightly coloured toy balloons, [Soupault was very fond of balloons] which were hung together so closely that one had to brush them aside to see the pictures ... At a given signal, several of the young men in the crowd applied their lighted cigarettes to the ends of strings attached to the balloons overhead and all of them went popping off, while the crowd of about fifty persons became as merry as if it were Bastille Day.'[26] In the middle of it all, Man Ray recounted, 'a strange, voluble little man in his fifties came over to me and led me to one of my paintings ... with a little white beard, an old-fashioned pince-nez, black bowler hat, black overcoat and umbrella, he looked like an undertaker or an employee of some conservative bank.'[27] This was Erik Satie. Man Ray was cold and tired, having spent most of the night hanging the show; Satie led him out of the gallery and sat him down in a nearby café, where he ordered hot grogs, and then more hot grogs. 'Leaving the café we passed a shop where various household utensils were spread out in front. I picked up a flat-iron, the kind used on coal stoves, asked Satie to come inside with me, where, with his help, I acquired a box of tacks and a tube of glue. Back at the gallery I glued a row of tacks to the smooth surface of the iron, titled it, The gift, and added it to the exhibition.'[28] Thus was born one of the most famous of all Dada objects, *The Gift*. Man Ray had intended his friends to draw for it, but it disappeared that same afternoon – he strongly suspected Soupault. This was to be its fate on many occasions. Undaunted, he always made a new one. Like many of Man Ray's artefacts – the eye/metronome *Object of Destruction*, made after Lee Miller left him, is another – it hauntingly encapsulated the Surrealist aim of reaching the unconscious through a disturbing and unexpected conjunction. This was no coincidence. Man Ray knew the work of Lautréamont, the poetic originator of this technique: he had been one of Donna's favourite poets when they were first together in Grantwood. In Man Ray's objects, the metaphor was made flesh. He liked to say of his *Gift* that 'anyone could *make* an iron adorned with a row of tacks, but only one person could have come up with the original *idea*'.[29] With his friend Duchamp he inhabited the brave new world of concepts, in which the retinal was merely incidental. Despite his high hopes, however, none of Man Ray's artworks sold. In Paris as in New York, it seemed he would have to make his living by his camera.

'I am still in the experimental state in photography, and the results are largely accidental,' he had told Miss Dreier earlier that year.[30] And in an important sense, this would never cease to be true. Part of Man Ray's genius was his ability to pin down the possibilities of darkroom accidents and turn them into techniques. This talent manifested itself from the start of his Paris career. Gabrielle Picabia provided an introduction to the famous couturier Paul Poiret, who gave him carte blanche to take whatever photographs he wanted, and even (since Man Ray was still living in a hotel) allowed him to use an attic darkroom. Developing his first batch of photographs for Poiret, he stumbled upon one of his most famous accidental innovations.

One sheet of photo paper got into the developing tray – a sheet unexposed that had been mixed with those already exposed under the negatives . . . and as I waited in vain a couple of minutes for an image to appear, regretting the waste of paper, I mechanically placed a small glass funnel, the graduate and the thermometer in the tray on the wetted paper. I turned on the light, before my eyes an image began to form, not quite a simple silhouette of the objects as in a straight photograph, but distorted and refracted by the glass more or less in contact with the paper and standing out against a black background, the part directly exposed to the light.[31]

Thus – accidentally, as with so many of Man Ray's techniques, including the famous 'solarisation'[32] – Rayographs were born. 'Is Photography an Art?' Stieglitz had famously asked. 'It doesn't need to be an art,' Man Ray would reply. 'Art has been surpassed. We need to use light now. It is light that I create. I sit before my sheet of photographic paper and I think.'[33] Man Ray, with his magic lens, was to become the wizard of Surrealism.

Tzara helped make more Rayographs, and Poiret bought some. It was not long before Man Ray found himself much in demand. Fashion houses were impressed by his work for Poiret, and artists wanted to collaborate on books and magazines. 'They crave America. So we are making a fair exchange, for I love the mellowness and finish of things here,' he told Howald.[34]

In more than one way, Man Ray's experience in Paris paralleled that of Duchamp in New York. Duchamp's stunning success with the *Nude Descending a Staircase* in New York bore no relation to the modest reputation he had up till then sustained in Paris: and this success opened liberating doors which transformed his life, so that New York became his true home. In the same way, many of Man Ray's works, which were now delighting Paris, had been made in New York but now acquired new meanings as complements to his friends' texts. Marius de Zayas grumbled that he was enjoying a 'false success among the intellectuals',[35] but that only went to confirm Man Ray's growing feeling that Paris was where he belonged. For a while he contemplated a dual life, like Duchamp's. 'New York is sweet but cold. Paris is bitter but warm,' he wrote enigmatically to Howald.[36] But Paris's rich and varied *vie de bohème*, its ramshackle tolerance unlike anything to be found in New York, soon enfolded him.

Brancusi the Rumanian sculptor gave memorable dinner parties in his white studio, with its white-painted brick stove, its table that was a white plaster cylinder six feet across, the hollowed-out logs that served as seats. Brancusi's cooking was famous: he would set a leg of lamb upon the embers in the stove and prepare Rumanian cornmeal to accompany it, with slivovitz and large amounts of wine. 'The meal finished, Brancusi piled up the dishes and carried them to a corner sink, came back with a stiff steel brush and scraped the table clean and white again. Our clothes were more or less white with the plaster, but he said not to worry – it was perfectly clean stuff.'[37] On one of these occasions a fellow-guest, a rich baroness famous for supporting the avant-garde, began to complain of feeling ill. Brancusi told her to go and lie down; after a while he sent Man Ray to see how she felt. 'I sat down beside her and began stroking her temples; when I stopped she seized my hands and told me to continue – I had a magic touch, she said. I became more emboldened . . . the inevitable happened. When I came down again I said simply that the baroness was much better and would come down presently. The group was silent; no remarks about my prolonged absence. I was very grateful for the tact displayed.'[38]

Sitters began to flood in. The Marchesa Casati was so delighted with a blurred picture he took of her, in which she appeared with three sets of eyes, that she distributed copies all round Paris saying Man Ray had portrayed her soul. He left the hotel for a studio – a room with a sleeping-gallery in the Rue Campagne-Première, in which 'a difficult stairway [led] to the path of dreams'.[39] And he acquired a mistress – the mistress of every American boy's bohemian dreams. This was Alice Prin, better known as Kiki de Montparnasse, a country girl from Burgundy who had come to Paris and achieved notoriety as an artist's model. They met one night at the Rotonde, not long after Man Ray's arrival – he had not yet learned to speak French: Duchamp (speaking from experience) had recommended getting a French girl as the best way to learn. Man

Ray took Kiki to the cinema. On the way back 'I explained
that I was a painter but could not work directly from a model
– it was distracting, she especially would be too disturbing,
she was so beautiful, I was already very much upset and
troubled.'[40] Kiki, however, refused at first to be photographed.
Photographers, like photography, worked too fast; besides
which she had a distressing physical defect about which the
camera would not lie as paint might. After a great deal of
persuading, however, she agreed. Man Ray was consumed with
curiosity about Kiki's defect. What could it be? Her face and
body were visibly exquisite. It turned out that she had no
pubic hair. Nothing – no pomades, no massage – had ever
succeeded in producing any, try as she might. A previous
lover, the Japanese painter Foujita, had made her neurotically
conscious of this deficiency. 'He often used to come over and
put his nose above the spot to see – if the hair hadn't started
to sprout while I'd been posing. Then, he'd pipe up with that
thin little voice of his: "That's funny – no hairs! Why your
feet so dirty?"'[41] Man Ray comforted her. 'I told her that was
fine, it would pass the censors.' Soon Kiki moved in with him:
they would be together for six years, which was as long as his
marriage to Donna.

It became clear that he could not work with Kiki constantly around the studio. They rented an apartment; she
would stay there during the day while he went to work in the
studio. Unusually for Paris at that time it had heat and a
bathroom, and every night before they went out the same
ritual would be followed. Kiki would take a long bath, after
which Man Ray would design her a face for the evening. Her
eyebrows were completely shaved: he drew her new ones, and
made up her eyelids in blue, copper, silver or jade. As much as
any painting or photograph she became his creation, a vision
of his imagination. Their closest friends, and frequent com-

panions on these excursions, were Tzara and Robert Desnos, a young poet who was becoming one of André Breton's closest associates.

Unused to having time on her hands, Kiki took up painting, for which she showed considerable aptitude. An exhibition was arranged for her; it was a success both artistically and financially – most of the pictures were sold. But she did not continue – 'had none of the instincts of a career girl, could never turn her talents to profit'.[42] Would he have preferred it if she had done so? Unlike some of the other Dadas and Surrealists Man Ray had no problem thinking of women as colleagues – though he never expected them to be *sexless* colleagues, as his correspondence with a later mistress, Lee Miller, makes clear. 'I have tried to justify [my] love by giving you every chance in my power to bring out everything interesting in you,' he wrote to her. 'The more you seemed capable the more my love was justified . . . In fact it was a much more satisfactory form of realisation, for me.'[43] He was, after all, American, and used to those bold and direct American career girls who had so amazed and enchanted Duchamp and Roché.

But the relationship between Man Ray and Kiki could never be an equal one. She might be bold, she was certainly shameless: she once did an impromptu impersonation of Napoleon by pulling up her skirt (she never wore knickers) so that her bare white thighs could represent his white breeches – with no anomalous pubic hair to spoil the image. But she was comfortable only within the narrow limits of her own world. The ménage clearly puzzled those whom Man Ray refers to as 'my more intellectual friends'. They bored her, and she made no effort to hide the fact. 'Unlike the wives or mistresses of the others, who tried to keep up with the current or kept silent, she became restless. I took her back to her beloved Montparnasse. Someone once asked me whether she was intelligent. I replied shortly that I had enough intelligence for the two of us. Kiki told me some of my most intellectual friends had propositioned her.'[44]

In fact, as her memoirs show, although uneducated she was no fool. Even so, their relationship was never an equal one. For Kiki, despite all diversions, sex was life, while for Man Ray sex was only one part – though an important part – of the deal. Describing the self-same circumstances, he wrote: 'The balcony was the bedroom where Kiki had to remain quietly while I was receiving.'[45] And she wrote: 'He photographs folks in the hotel room where we live, and at night, I lie stretched out on the bed while he works in the dark. I can see his face over the little red light, and he looks like the devil himself; I am so excited that I can't wait for him to get through.'[46] Alas for Kiki, work endures, but sex is fleeting.

*

When Man Ray wrote from New York asking Tzara's permission to name his magazine *New York Dada*, Tzara replied: 'You ask for authorization to name your periodical Dada. But Dada belongs to everyone.' Tzara, however, had been displaced; and Breton, who was no anarchist, approached life in a very different way. Josephson, while remarking on the group's warmth and comradeship, spoke wonderingly of their quasi-religious discipline – like 'the Franciscans, or more nearly the Jesuit societies'.[47] Where in America such a group would have been constantly in turmoil, each one intent upon his own programme, here full agreement apparently reigned as to what was or was not acceptable, who was in or out, what should be done to sow the requisite confusion and disorder. Everyone would gather daily at Certâ or its annexe Le Petit Grillon, where, around the usual table, Breton would survey his troops. At twenty-five he had become a formidable figure, with 'a huge head, like one of the old Jacobin leaders, a mass of wavy brown hair, pale blue eyes and . . . jaws of granite. Like the men of 1793 he had in him a combination of fanatical idealism and ruthlessness.'[48] Josephson noted Breton's 'passion for morally dangerous experiment',[49] and the way in which it held his young disciples enthralled.

The new generation now gravitating to the movement was clearly overwhelmed by this grave presence and the coldly penetrating intelligence behind it. Josephson recalls an evening when he and his wife invited the Bretons to dinner at their apartment.

> No sooner had we finished eating than Breton's younger disciples dropped in (as if they had been told to report there), and literally sat at the feet of the master, for there were few real chairs, while he reclined comfortably in the only armchair. The nonchalant young giant, Vitrac, sprawled full length; with him was Benjamin Péret, a troubled, sullen-looking youth; and together with two or three others there was Jacques Baron, a slight, blue-eyed boy of seventeen . . . Breton used to catechize these young people with the air of a schoolmaster who was being kindly for the moment, but could be severe if he chose to. 'And what have you been doing with your time?' he asked of each in turn. It was plain that he cast a spell over them . . .

Not long after this dinner-party, Jacques Baron ran away from home with a boxer and his sister: Baron was supposedly in love with the sister. His frantic parents called the police, who hunted the boy everywhere.

> Shortly, I heard through secret channels that Jacques had made his way back to Paris and remained hidden in André Breton's apartment. He had not a sou; Breton and his wife fed and sheltered him in their home, which the boy dared not leave for a time.[50]

When the police hunt drew too near, Jacques slipped away with Aragon under cover of darkness. Aragon took him to a cheap hotel; he dared not leave his room. Cold food and chocolate were smuggled in by the conspirators. He only emerged when Aragon negotiated a truce with M. Baron senior. But, as Baron told Josephson later, Breton was the person he really regarded as his 'father'. And this was not entirely surprising. Breton was propounding a whole new set of values – anti-family values – and in this shifting world, he was the young man's sole guide and anchor.

Breton raises – to the power n – the whole vexed question of charisma. He was dictatorial, he was humourless, he was in many ways inhuman and impossibly pompous; not, on the face of it, attractive qualities. And he was implacable. Once expelled from the magic circle, quondam Surrealists remained untouchable. Matthew Josephson, returning to Paris a few years after his first meeting with Breton, was not only ignored by him – 'he saw me come in, scowled, and turned his back'[51] – but was cut off, on Breton's orders, from all his other friends of earlier days – those, at least, who still remained inside Breton's sphere of influence. Aragon, once so close, crossed the street in order to avoid meeting him. After a chance encounter they arranged to talk in the secrecy of Josephson's hotel room: a secrecy essential if Aragon's own relations with Breton were not to be ended. Simone Breton, after her marriage ended, received the same treatment. Yet despite all this, no one, having once basked in the warmth of Breton's approval, could bear to be cut off from it. One of the many paradoxes surrounding this difficult man – difficult to be with, to satisfy, above all to understand – was this: however badly he behaved – and he behaved monstrously – the threat of excommunication was a terrible one. Partly this had to do with the intensity of group life. For Dadas and Surrealists, the group *was* life: expulsion was therefore a sort of death sentence. But Breton himself was the centre, the sun around which they all revolved. 'All of us who knew him experienced that vertiginous double movement: fascination and centrifugal separation.'[52]

Duchamp explained the phenomenon with another paradox: 'I have never known a man with a greater capacity for love, or a greater power of loving life's greatness,' he said after Breton's death. 'It's impossible to understand his hatreds if you don't see that, for him, it was a question of protecting the quality of that love ... Breton loved as a heart beats. He was in love with love in a world which believes in prostitution. That was what he was about.'[53] His inner flame burned with an intensity that, said Robert Desnos, 'I can only call genius.' Such was its strength that it warmed all who met him: 'He will breathe into a chance acquaintance enough warmth and ostensible talent to make an instant poet out of a dummy – though he'll be the first to throw away the carcase when some more worthy visitor arrives.'[54]

So it was only to be expected that the young men should be extremely jealous in their relations with him. Like siblings, each wanted Breton to himself. And there were many young men – a constant influx: as yesterday's heroes were discarded, today's crowded in. Faced with a need to find new directions, Breton looked, as always, to new faces. 'We still have Picabia, Duchamp and Picasso,' he wrote in September 1922. 'Do you remember Guillaume Apollinaire or Pierre Reverdy? Isn't some of our vitality due to them? But already Jacques Baron, Robert Desnos, Max Morise, Pierre de Massot are waiting for us.'[55] And the answer – whatever it was – would lie with them.

The most immediately significant figure of the new intake was Robert Desnos. Desnos was the son of a wholesale butcher. He wanted to be a poet, and had followed Dada from afar since 1919; his parents, unsurprisingly, were not enthusiastic. During 1920 and 1921 military service kept Desnos far from Paris (in fact, in Morocco). He kept in touch with Dada doings through Benjamin Péret, whom he had known for some years, and whose letters, which arrived in 'immense envelopes covered with obscene and anti-militarist slogans',[56] did nothing to make Desnos's army life any easier.

Péret was 'a tall boy, quite fat, with a stupid-looking face'. He came from Nantes, where an acquaintance, knowing of his literary ambitions, had given him Breton's name. He was painfully shy: on his first journey to Paris his mother came too, determined to make sure her son took up this useful introduction. Their train arrived in the early hours; at six in the morning they knocked on Breton's door at the Hotel des Grands Hommes. 'Monsieur,' said Madame Péret, 'I know your name and I've been told you can do something for my son who wants to be a writer.' She then disappeared, leaving the tongue-tied Benjamin with an embarrassed Breton. The acquaintance did not take: quite apart from his shyness, Péret's looks were against him. It was not until some years later that he really found his feet with the group, where he was to remain one of Breton's closest and most uncritical supporters.

Desnos and Péret had met not long after this embarrassing introduction. Péret told Desnos he knew Breton slightly (without, however, describing the circumstances of their meeting), and had an introduction to Picabia. It was natural, then, that Desnos, passing through Paris in 1921, should ask Péret for an introduction. But it was at once obvious that Péret did not wish to oblige. In fact his standing with the group was still very uncertain; his shyness made him seem stupid, he was constantly teased and ignored.

> Nevertheless, he arranged to meet me at five o'clock on the corner of rue Richelieu and the Boulevards, to go on to Certâ. He did not show up. About half past five, tired of waiting, I made my own way to the Passage de l'Opéra. At the back of the bar, at a round table, sat a group of young men. Péret was among them. I was very depressed by this

196

betrayal. I sat down at a far-off table and waited for Péret to notice my presence. But he didn't want to . . .

Finally, fed up with waiting, I went up and tapped Péret's shoulder. He introduced me, not too unwillingly, but with little enough enthusiasm to ensure that the ice remained unbroken and I was horribly embarrassed . . .

There were Breton, Aragon, T. Tzara, Rigaut, Ribemont-Dessaignes and two visitors . . . At about seven everyone left . . . and there remained: Breton, Tzara, Péret and I.

We had dinner at a cheap restaurant in the passage de l'Opéra. [Desnos describes how Tzara spent the meal making rude remarks about passing women, while Breton talked single-mindedly of Dada and writing.]

It was terrible. The only word I could say was 'Absolutely' . . .

Finally it came to an end. Breton and Tzara went one way, Péret and I buried ourselves in a cinema . . .[57]

It was not until 1922 that Desnos was able to get on terms with the *Littérature* crowd, when he was reintroduced by Matthew Josephson: in his baggy blue conscript's uniform and his scarlet fez, he 'came to my table at a café where I regularly met my French friends, saying that he had seen me with Aragon and Breton, and earnestly begged me to present him to them'.[58]

This time the moment was propitious. Following the collapse of the Congrès de Paris, almost everyone in Breton's immediate circle was, in one way or another, contaminated by its shadow. This one had committed the crime of writing articles in the press; that one's attitude was in some detail suspect. Thanks to Péret's churlishness, however, Desnos retained the untarnished bloom of novelty. Finally he had his place in the sun. And he did not waste it.

In March 1922, *Littérature*, which had ceased publication the previous August with an issue dedicated to the Barrès

Trial, began a new series. Previously it had sported a modest yellow cover; now it blossomed out in bright pink, with a top hat design by Man Ray. On the first page appeared the inevitable *enquête*: 'What do you do when you are alone?' All, it seemed, was as before. But no: on page five an important new direction was signalled. It carried detailed accounts of three dreams dictated by the dreamer (Breton).

'Insight such as this', wrote Freud in his preface to the first English edition of *The Interpretation of Dreams*, 'falls to one's lot but once in a lifetime.' No one would have agreed more heartily than Breton. As we have seen, Freud's perception of the journey inwards as the great journey of the coming century had instantly spoken to him. For a while he had been diverted by Dada, which shared his rejection of the 'artistic' life and his desire to explore the possibilities of chance. But Tzara's route had proved a dead end. Now he returned to the path he had begun to explore with Soupault. Were there perhaps other ways of developing what they had begun in *Les Champs magnétiques*? Having published his anti-Dada polemic 'Drop Everything' in April 1922, he turned towards these new possibilities. And in his wake rushed Robert Desnos. Some months later he, too, published three 'Dreams', one of which is the purest wish-fulfilment: 'I am in bed and I see myself just as I really am. André Breton comes into the room, the official journal in his hand. "*Cher ami,*" he says, [Breton's habitual form of address] "I'm pleased to announce your promotion to the rank of sergeant-major," then he makes a half-turn and leaves.'[59]

Dreams are a mappable route to the subconscious: that was Freud's great aperçu. But how to grasp them? And how to use them in an artistic rather than a therapeutic sense? Breton and Soupault had experimented with one possibility, but although the group continued to practise automatic writing the words never flowed for them again in quite the same dazzling way. And Breton's published dreams were just that – dreams: a starting point, a declaration of interest. What, then, was the next step? Once more, as he had with Saupault, Breton turned to the techniques developed by spiritualism. Although he was adamant in his refusal to admit that 'there can be any communication whatever between the living and the dead',[60] these techniques now became very interesting as a means of plumbing the subconscious.

What became known as 'the period of sleeping-fits' began with one of Breton's new young acolytes. René Crevel (whom Eluard had beaten up on the occasion of the *Coeur à barbe*) was a beautiful boy with golden curls and angelic features. He had had an adventure which was to point the new way forward:

> At the edge, the start, of this sea, there had been a beach, of sand by day and of skin by night. On the land side of the beach, in an orchard with too many flowers, a girl had thrown herself down . . . In the evening, she had invited me to her mother's, her mother being chock-full of theosophy and occult sciences. In the dining-room of the little house, there was also an old woman . . . Madame Dante.

Madame Dante announced a séance, with materializations. In the traditional manner, the four joined hands round a heavy table. Crevel remembered nothing more: his head dropped forward onto the table, he was asleep. Next day he had to leave for Paris to resume his military service, 'and there I spoke to Breton of the adventure'.[61]

Breton encouraged him to try and repeat the experience. 'On Monday 24 September, at nine in the evening, in the presence of Desnos, Morise and myself, Crevel falls into a hypnotic sleep.' He began to speak, declaiming, sighing, sometimes almost chanting; he seemed to be talking about a woman accused, perhaps wrongly, of murdering her husband. On waking, Crevel could remember nothing of what had been said. Another experiment was tried, this time excluding him: to no effect. And then Desnos offered himself as a subject, 'though he considered himself a most unpromising candidate, an opinion strengthened by the fact that only a few evenings before he had, in my company, resisted the efforts of two public hypnotists . . .'[62] Desnos's head fell onto his arms and he began convulsively scratching at the table. A few seconds later he awoke, convinced that he had never been asleep. His career as a sleeper had begun.

A number of techniques were evolved for finding out what went on in the sleepers' heads. (Péret and others soon began to join in the séances, though Desnos and Crevel remained the principal 'mediums'.) Crevel said that the action of scratching the table might mean that the subject wanted to write: accordingly, on the next occasion (Breton, Eluard, Péret and Ernst were present) a sheet of paper was placed before Desnos, and a pencil placed in his hand. At first this was unproductive: he wrote only '14 juillet – 14 juill', and covered the words with crosses or pluses. They then interrogated him in turn, the questions spoken, the answers written.

> Q: Desnos, this is Breton. What can you see?
> A: The equator . . .
> Q: Is he going on a journey?
> A: (indicating No with his hand) Nazimova
> . . . [a film star then much in vogue]

Other exchanges were less impenetrable. Paul Eluard replaces Breton:

> Q: How do you see Eluard?
> A: He's blue.

Q: Why is he blue?
A: Because the sky's in (an unfinished word, illegible, the whole phrase is crossed out furiously.)

Péret's hand replaces Eluard's:

Q: What do you know about Péret?
A: He will die in a carriage full of people.
Q: Will he be assassinated?
A: Yes.
Q: Who by?
A: (he draws a train, a man falling out of the door) By an animal.
Q: Which animal?
A: A blue ribbon my lovely vagabond.
(Long silence, then) Don't talk about her any more, she's going to be born in a few minutes.

Everyone wanted to try this new craze, though not all were suitable subjects. On one occasion Crevel returned to his story of the terrible murders; on another, Péret, apparently asleep, suddenly burst out laughing. Eluard, Ernst, Morise and Breton were unable to fall asleep. The séances began to take over their lives. Aragon wrote:

They live only for these moments of oblivion when, all lights extinguished, they speak without knowing what they say, like drowning men. Every day these moments become more numerous. Every day they want to spend more time sleeping. Their words, recorded, intoxicate them. Everywhere, anywhere, they fall asleep ... In the café, amid the chatter, in bright daylight, jostled on all sides, Robert Desnos has only to close his eyes, and he speaks, and amid the beer-glasses, the saucers, The Ocean itself crashes down with its prophetic rumblings and its foamy banners.[63]

All eyes were upon Crevel and Desnos, the chief sleepers: a tremendous rivalry grew up between them. Crevel had, after all, started the whole business; now he saw it being snatched away from him – and with it, Breton's attention. If both were present at a séance, Crevel was desperate to fall asleep before Desnos – 'because I thus score over Desnos, my mediumistic competitor. Otherwise I should not care.'

> At night-time my sleep is hollow. My wakings are not up to much, either. I have no sexual life all the while I am present at and joining in these seances. I don't want one. I don't even think of having one.
> ... Desnos and myself very quickly came to suspect each other, our suspicion developing into an enmity which I thought might lead Desnos to scratch out my eyes ... for that matter, I myself once gave him a push which made him knock his head against a mantelpiece – [yet] when I met Desnos on occasions other than those of the seances, they of course were the only things we could talk about.[64]

'I have never stopped sighing for that time,' he concluded. And indeed he spoke of it in the poetic terms of one recalling a heavenly experience, writing 'in letters of phosphorus', recalling Desnos's rather prominent eyes as 'his two oysters in their shell-like lids as they used to reflect in all their glaucous and raucous passivity the motion of the sea'.[65]

In this duel of psychics, it was Desnos who won. When it came to sounding the subconscious he seemed gifted with extraordinary powers. In another era, Aragon thought, he might have founded a religion, or a city.[66] Breton went even further. Once more – as with Vaché, with Tzara, with Duchamp – he projected upon the beloved of the moment the qualities he desperately sought for himself. 'Only exaltation counts ... and you never get that without fanaticism on the part of the author,' he wrote. '... In our time, in the intellectual domain, there exist, to my knowledge, three fanatics of the first water: Picasso, Freud and Desnos.'[67] Desnos's astonishing powers of self-hypnosis had got him where he dreamed of being. He was the hero of the moment: the field was his.

Except for a single rival: a man who wasn't even there – who wasn't, in this instance, even a man. The enigmatic Rrose Sélavy with her puns and wordplays, witty, unexpected, naughtily erotic, was busy exercising her wiles. 'RROSE SÉLAVY TROUVE QU'UN INCESTICIDE DOIT COUCHER AVEC SA MERE AVANT DE LA TUER; LES PUNAISES SONT DE RIGUEUR,' declared the opening page of the October 1922 *Littérature*. ('Rrose Sélavy thinks an incesticide should sleep with his mother before killing her: bedbugs obligatory.') Rrose's use of words, declared Breton, introduced a whole new chemistry, full of hitherto unsuspected autonomies and colours. Words had lost their innocence: they 'are no longer merely playing. Words are making love.'[68] Examples of her work were scattered throughout the issue, which also contained Breton's adulatory essay on the ever-evasive Duchamp – much of it couched in metaphoric reference to those questions of spiritualism and materialization which were so much on his mind: 'The day her riddle is solved, the sphinx will throw herself into the sea ... We may be as ridiculous, as touching as spirits, but let us not, my friends, put our faith in materialisations, whatever they may be. Cubism is a materialisation in corrugated cardboard, Futurism in rubber, Dadaism in blotting-paper. But, I ask you, what could be less welcome than *materialisation*?'[69] What, indeed? Duchamp, ducking and weaving between his many personae, offered no such crude prospect. Rrose's work, mathematically rigorous ('exchange of letters within a word, exchange of syllables between two words') and without (in his view) any lowering taint of 'the comic element which seemed inherent in this form' was, Breton declared, 'the most remarkable thing to

have appeared in poetry for a very long time'.[70] Isidore
Ducasse had dazzled with his subtly altered proverbs (changing, for example, La Rochefoucauld's 'Love of justice, for most
men, is simply the fear of suffering injustice' to 'Love of justice,
for most men, is simply the courage to suffer injustice'). Now
Rrose was playing similar games with syllables, extending the
poetic possibilities of these new games of chance.

How could Desnos possibly compete? The answer was –
by swallowing Rrose whole. On the immaterial plane where
he reigned uncontested Desnos met Rrose: Desnos *became*
Rrose. She spoke through his mouth, she wrote with his hand.
Together they produced eight pages of her characteristic work,
one hundred and fifty new puns. '*Dans un temple en stuc de
pomme le pasteur distillait le suc des psaumes.*' ('In a palmy
pleasaunce the priest distilled the psalmy essence.') '*La solution
d'un sage est-elle la pollution d'un page?*' ('Is the wise man's
solution the page's pollution?') – and so on – and on, and on.
'Who dictates these phrases to Desnos?' Breton wondered. 'Is
[Desnos's] brain really joined to Duchamp's as he says it is, so
that Rrose Sélavy only speaks to him when Duchamp is
awake?'[71] Some years later, in his novel *Nadja*, he recalled the
excitement of those days:

> I can still see Robert Desnos as he was in the days which
> those among us who have known them call the *period of
> sleeping-fits*. He 'sleeps', but he writes, he speaks. It is
> evening in my studio above the Heaven nightclub. 'Come in,
> come in to the Chat Noir,' they're shouting outside. And
> Desnos goes on seeing things I can't see, things I only see as
> bit by bit he shows them to me. He takes on the personality
> of the most rare, the most unfixable, the most disappointing
> of living men, the author of the *Cemetery of Uniforms and
> Liveries* – Marcel Duchamp. He has never seen him in the
> flesh. That aspect of Duchamp which seemed the least
> imitable through a few mysterious 'plays on words' (Rrose

Sélavy) appears in Desnos in all its purity and suddenly acquires extraordinary breadth. Whoever has not seen his pencil mark on the paper, without the slightest hesitation and so incredibly fast, those extraordinary poetic equations, without being sure, as I am sure, that they could not have been prepared beforehand, even if he can appreciate their technical perfection and wonderful talent, can have no idea of what that meant to us then, of the absolute oracle it seemed.[72]

Did Breton really believe Desnos was 'possessed' by Duchamp? Did Desnos believe it himself? The answer seems to be yes; and possessed not just by Duchamp – by others, too. At this period he was producing poems 'by' Apollinaire, Germain Nouveau, Villon, Lautréamont – almost the entire Surrealist pantheon. Though Breton was careful not to commit himself ('As things stand, I can't explain it'), he observed that, once he was awake, Desnos 'seems as incapable as the rest of us . . . however hard he tries'.[73]

Duchamp himself was unenthusiastic. 'Had a note this morning from Crotti [Jean Crotti, his brother-in-law] enclosing 50 lucubrations by Desnos,' he wrote Breton. 'I usually sleep till noon – can't get back to sleep after that – what a telepath! Or rather, "psychic" – In any case, it'll be very useful for Littérature – I'll take him on at once as my Paris correspondent – Why doesn't he ask Rrose to marry him? She'd be delighted.' Rrose, he added, had just opened a dress shop. 'Practical fashion – Creations Rrose Sélavy – the Oblong Dress, designed exclusively for ladies afflicted by the hiccups—'[74] Decidedly, psychic transports were not for the ironic Marcel.

From the standpoint of Freudian New York there was little new in all this. 'Everybody in Greenwich Village . . . was doing just that – they were having themselves "psyched" – six or seven years ago!' exclaimed Matthew Josephson when

Aragon invited him to a séance.[75] And despite Aragon's assurances that 'It's different with us' he could never really take the séances seriously. For the last hundred years, he told Tzara, who was feeling depressed and excluded by this bizarre turn of events, France had followed the latest American fashion – but ten or twenty years later. After Poe, the French Parnassians. After Whitman, 'energism'. And after Mary Baker Eddy, occultism. 'Really, that old maids' game? I suppose they're doing it as a joke. You mustn't get so awfully down about it. They'll grow up one of these days.'[76]

Josephson was wrong there: joking they certainly were not. Things got to the point where Desnos would turn up at Breton's apartment almost every evening and fall into one of his sleeps. 'He'd just go off, even in the middle of a meal. What was more, it got harder and harder to wake him by the usual methods. One evening I absolutely couldn't, and he was getting more and more carried away – it must have been three in the morning – I had to go out and get a doctor.'[77] The doctor was greeted with insults; the sleeper awoke without his intervention. But what would happen next time?

There were even more alarming manifestations. On one astonishing occasion, recalling nothing so much as Mesmer's fashionable soirées of mass hypnosis 150 years previously, a large party of guests was invited to a grand house belonging to Marie de la Hire, a friend of Picabia's. The rooms were cavernous and dimly lit, and before long ten or more of the guests were entranced, sleepwalking, gesticulating, uttering strange prophecies. At about two in the morning, Breton suddenly realized that a number of them had disappeared. 'I finally discovered them in some dark anteroom, where they were trying to hang themselves from the coathooks. They had plenty of rope . . . Crevel was one of them, it was apparently he who had put the idea into their heads.'[78] On another occasion, Desnos chased Eluard with a knife while in the trance state and had to be forcibly disarmed. The sleepers lost weight. The sleeping-fits got longer and longer. 'They don't want to wake up any more. They fall asleep at the mere sight of another sleeper, and speak from a far, blind world . . .'[79]

People now began to ask out loud questions that had been lurking for some time. Was it possible that the sleep was not always genuine? That the trance state was sometimes faked? Not that that necessarily devalued it. 'If you simulate something, don't you still think it? And what is thought, exists . . . And what can explain the aura of genius in those spoken dreams which unfolded before me?'[80]

But however induced – and even if faked – such a state was, once attained, by definition out of control. They had 'thrown themselves into it as into a sea, and . . . [it] threaten[ed] to carry them away to a place on the borders of madness'.[81] Desnos was a regular drug-user. All he needed (in Josephson's opinion) was a shot of opium and an audience, and he was away. Crevel's was a precariously-balanced and unpredictable personality. Who could guarantee that one day things might not take some irretrievable turn? The experiments, Breton decided, must be curtailed, if not brought to an end.

Desnos was mortified. The sleeping-fits were his speciality, they assured him of Breton's attention. Without them, how long could he expect to maintain his place in the sun? And without that, how would he survive? 'My affection for you is as great as ever,' he wrote to Breton (in a letter which in fact was never posted). 'But I am perfectly aware that I no longer arouse that burning curiosity in you which was, though I never admitted it, one of my reasons for existing.'[82]

The situation was not immediately as clear-cut as he had feared. He had opened the gates to a new array of possibilities, and Breton, intent on following this new path, remained grateful. He would soon extol Desnos as 'the one among us who has perhaps come closest to surrealist truth'.[83] But his

interest, as Desnos recognized, was directed at the phenomenon, not the man. A few years later, after a bitter quarrel, he
was to distinguish brutally between the two: 'Desnos, unable
to control the powers which once uplifted him, and whose
dark possibilities he seems not to understand, unfortunately
decided to confine his operations to the real world, where he
was nothing but an ordinary man, lonelier and poorer than
most . . .'[84]

This disillusionment was still five years into the future. But
although not yet disenchanted with Desnos in person, Breton,
too, was depressed. How, now, would he access the dream-
world which had seemed to promise so much? The spectre of
Vaché's suicide surfaced to haunt him once more. 'Only
unfinished things appeal to me,' he wrote in January 1923,
when the sleeping-fits had turned sour. In the essay 'La
Confession dédaigneuse', which was his great tribute to Vaché
and their relationship, he wrote of 'the lovely shade . . . at the
edge of that window through which, every day, I begin once
more to throw myself'.[85]

As his continued existence indicated, he could not quite
bring himself to commit the act itself. But there remained the
example of his other hero, Rimbaud, who at Breton's age had
long since renounced poetry. Why should Breton, too, not
commit artistic suicide? There was no need to go so far as to
extinguish life itself. All that was necessary was to put down
his pen. In April 1923, he declared that he, Eluard and Desnos
had taken a decision to stop writing – 'perhaps in a couple of
months' time . . . We shall publish a manifesto over our three
names. We're deciding upon a text.' As to his reasons for this
drastic move, 'I see the situation of everything I defend as
desperate. In fact the game seems altogether lost . . . as far as I
can see the possibilities of literature and of politics are about
as boring as each other. Only spontaneous powers interest me
. . . From now on all I want is to ignore it all – reviews, books,

newspapers, the lot. I shall avoid all literary activity.' How, then, would he live? 'I don't want to work. Work's out of the question,' he declared loftily. 'The mind gets its best results when it functions in a vacuum. Obviously it needs a basic minimum of nourishment, which it will find in love – of the most unbridled variety.'[86]

The indications are that this remained a theoretical rather than a practical resort. *Dérèglement* was not part of Breton's repertoire. Josephson recounts an evening around this time when Soupault, in response to Breton's constant cry – 'This is so dull, I'm bored with everything. Hasn't anyone any ideas?' – suggested that they repair, wives and all, to a nearby rather classy brothel.

> 'Show us your tricks,' one of our party said. The girls in a group knelt down on the floor and began to make lascivious movements and gestures towards us, clumsily and mechanically. Soupault kept encouraging the girls in comic spirit; but Breton became, or pretended to become, angry. He had with him, as always, his heavy knobbed cane which he tapped on the floor impatiently. Everyone in our party felt uncomfortable, and no-one knew what the next step was to be ... 'This is disgusting,' Breton cried out at length, 'a shameful spectacle – how could you take us to such a place?'

Breton's vexation, comments Josephson, 'was not at all feigned'.[87] And when Picabia took Breton to the Marseille red-light district (on the way to Barcelona, where Breton was to give a lecture at the opening of a Picabia exhibition) he was terminally embarrassed. Simone had to ask Picabia not to take André to such places, as they 'depressed him terribly'.[88]

Perhaps it was not entirely coincidental that Duchamp, too – a living hero, and still uncompromised – had just forsworn all future artistic production. After eight years of work, he had declared his *Large Glass* definitively unfinished. The

Arensbergs had bought it while still in his studio, but now they sold it to Miss Dreier, since they were about to move to California and were afraid it might break in transit. Duchamp supervised its move to her apartment on Central Park West: the two panels were installed one above the other in a free-standing wooden frame he had designed for them. On the back of the lower panel he inscribed the words: '*LA MARIEE MISE A NU PAR/SES CELIBATAIRES MEME/Marcel Duchamp/1915–1923/inachevé.*' (On a subsequent journey it did indeed break. Duchamp remained stoical. He had liked to proclaim at the Arensbergs' that 'a stained-glass window that had fallen out and lay more or less together on the ground was of far greater interest than the thing conventionally composed *in situ*'.[89] What was true for a stained-glass window remained true for his own Glass. Painstakingly he pieced it back together and declared it greatly improved – indeed, finally completed – by the web of break-lines.) He now moved back to Paris and methodically set about becoming a chess player of international standard. 'Dada was a very useful force for vacuity,' he commented years later. 'Dada says, "Don't forget you're not as empty as you think!" ... [It] was a very useful purgative. And I think I was deeply conscious of that at the time, and I felt the need to purge myself.'[90]

Duchamp would maintain his vow of artistic silence for another thirty years (until the unprecedented experience of falling in love broke through his shell of detachment). Breton's, however, was broken almost as soon as it was made. Some months after the interview in which he had made it, he published an eclectic collection of poems, dreams and automatic texts called *Clair de Terre*, significantly rounded off with a gnomic utterance dedicated to Rrose Sélavy:

> *André Breton n'écrira plus.*
> (Journal du Peuple – Avril 1923)

J'ai quitté mes effets,
Mes beaux effets de neige!

I've abandoned my clothes,
My beautiful snow clothes!

The next step beckoned, and was not to be resisted. There were always consequences, and they must be followed through.

*

Despite Breton's return to writing, a sense of crisis continued to pervade the group of which he was ever more clearly the leader and inspiration. For instance, it was all very well for him to decree that 'work is out of the question', and to anathematize the life of the literary hack, but how were these literary young men supposed to live if not by writing books and articles? Breton himself had (for the moment) solved the problem by marrying a rich woman (another aspect, perhaps, of that nourishment which he hoped to find in love). Several other Surrealists also tried this route. Aragon had an affair with the shipping heiress Nancy Cunard; Soupault married, *en secondes noces*, the wealthy and intelligent Marie-Louise le Borgne; Tzara married Greta Knutson, a beautiful Swede related to the Nobel family; and the despairing dandy Jacques Rigaut, banished by his family to America, married a rich widow and acquired a Rolls-Royce 'in the true Dada spirit'.[91] But this solution was at best temporary. Nancy Cunard soon lost interest in Aragon, with catastrophic consequences. Soupault's marriage did not last. Tzara and Greta soon divorced; and Jacques Rigaut committed suicide.

Another possibility was picture-dealing. Breton and Eluard, in particular, had built up spectacular collections. Eluard, whose family was well-off, put his capital into pictures

211

partly to form a collection, partly in order to make some money dealing. Breton, whenever he had the funds, made the most of his unfailing eye for the potentially significant, acquiring some pictures cheaply before the artists were known, being given others by friends, and making it a rule, when asked to write a catalogue introduction, always to request a picture in payment and always to choose the largest and most valuable. When Picasso's dealer Kahnweiler was forced to sell up during the xenophobic days which followed the end of the war, Breton (though he was then short of money) made a point of attending the sale and advised all his friends to do likewise. In an emergency these pictures could always be sold. Duchamp also dabbled, having acquired (with Henri-Pierre Roché) a job lot of twenty-nine Brancusis on the death of the American collector John Quinn; he would sell one from time to time, when money was short.[92] But generally speaking it was almost impossible to adhere to Breton's rule and live. Breton himself was prepared to endure dire poverty in the name of principle: writing to Salvador Dalí some years later he declared himself unable to afford the price of a stamp, and it was not unknown to find him sitting amid his magnificent collection in the Rue Fontaine with the electricity and even the water disconnected. As he would put it, Surrealism had nothing to offer those 'concerned with their place *in the world*'.[93] And if the Pope backslides, where does that leave his moral authority? Others, less hardy, had to run the risk of his almost certain displeasure.

A different crisis occurred in March 1924 when, without warning, Paul Eluard vanished. His collection of poems *Mourir de ne pas mourir* (*Dying of not dying*) was just about to appear; it carried the sinister epigraph 'I am dying...' and the even more sinister dedication: 'To simplify things I dedicate my last book to André Breton.' Had he merely departed ('*To disappear is to succeed*', he had written in his review *Proverbe*), or had he, too, killed himself – as his last utterances seemed to imply? A Vaché, or a Rimbaud? In the collection of automatic writings, *Poisson soluble* (*Soluble Fish*), which he was putting together at this time, Breton's distress at his friend's disappearance is apparent:

> What is he? Where's he going? What's become of him? . . . I am no stronger than he, my jacket has no buttons, I don't know the order, I won't be the first into the town . . .[94]

In fact the explanation was more earthbound than Breton imagined. For some time now Eluard, his Russian wife Gala and Max Ernst had been living in a *ménage à trois*. Gala and Ernst had begun their affair during a second group holiday at Tarrenz-bei-Imst in 1922 ('Why must that Gala Eluard make it such a *Dostoievski drama!*' Tzara had expostulated. 'It's boring, it's insufferable, unheard-of!' And Eluard himself sighed, '*Ah, vous ne savez pas ce que c'est d'être marié avec une femme russe!*')[95] Bewitched by Gala, Max had left his wife and son in Cologne and moved in with the Eluards just outside Paris.

For a while Paul had done his best not to mind. He enjoyed group sex, and was something of a voyeur. And he liked to say, 'I love Max Ernst much more than I do Gala.'[96] But, as his friends knew, it was not quite as simple as that: he was, in fact, besotted with Gala. 'I don't move/I don't look/I don't speak,' he wrote despairingly.[97] Finally unable to take any more, he withdrew, without authorization, a large sum of money from his father's business, and disappeared. 'He's been wanting to leave more and more, spending the nights drinking champagne with Noll and Aragon . . . afraid to go home to sleep alone. Now he's gone. André says we shan't see him again. Gala's left with 400 francs, the baby [their daughter Cécile] and in an impossible situation because of Max Ernst.

Her in-laws will only help her if he leaves . . .' wrote Simone Breton to her cousin Denise Lévy.[98]

Breton need not have worried. Eluard had fled to Monte Carlo, doubled his stake, and embarked in Gauguin's footsteps for Tahiti. But he soon became bored there, and cabled Gala to join him, with Max, enclosing their fares. He was starting west by boat and would meet them in Saigon. Back in Paris he arranged to meet Breton at the Cyrano, the café in Place Blanche where the group now regularly met. (The passage de l'Opéra, and with it Certâ, had been demolished.) After all the emotion the meeting was an anticlimax. 'He's just the same. It was nothing but a holiday,' Breton commented acidly.[99]

Faced with all these tensions Breton turned once more to the consolation of automatic writing. 'I absolutely must get back to the accidental,' he told Simone. Plunging alone into the subconscious, he now felt a need to define and discuss this strand of experimentation more systematically. The possible was his true realm: he must learn at all costs how to 'outplay the probable'.[100] And the name of that realm was *Surrealism*.

For some time now, Apollinaire's word 'Surrealist' had been appearing in the writings of Breton and (especially) Aragon. 'It was thrown at us from outside,' said Aragon, 'and finally I persuaded Breton to accept it. So then he said, Fine, but in that case we've got to . . . say what we mean by all this.'[101] In fact the word had always been naggingly present; throughout the Dada days 'there reigned a vague and sentimental notion of the surreal in the back of our minds, a kind of foretaste of the abyss, anonymous, faceless. One fine day the spectre tore itself apart with its bony hands, from top to bottom. A long period of stupor followed this parting of the clouds.'[102]

The first mention had been as early as 1920, at the end of the first Grande Saison Dada, when Jacques Rivière had published an article, 'Reconnaissance à Dada', in the *Nouvelle*

Revue Française. 'Even though they don't dare admit it, the Dadas continue to develop that Surrealism which was Apollinaire's great ambition,' Rivière had written; which, since he was an establishment figure writing in the establishment's review, and trying, moreover, to claim Dada for the mainstream of French literary tradition, had aroused more indignation than gratitude among the Dadas in question.

In reply, Breton wrote an article, 'Pour Dada'. In it he mentions all those, from Valéry to Tzara, who have helped him along the road, and quotes them all at some length. It includes the following passage:

> There has been talk of a systematic exploration of the unconscious. It is no novelty for poets to abandon themselves to the inclination of their spirit. The word inspiration, fallen I don't know why into disuse, was quite acceptable a short time ago. Almost all images, for instance, strike me as spontaneous creations. Guillaume Apollinaire rightly believed that clichés such as 'coral lips' . . . were the product of that activity he liked to call *Surrealist*. Words themselves doubtless have no other origin. He went so far as to assert that one should never abandon a former invention, the prerequisite for scientific development, for 'progress', so to speak.[103]

Breton had used the word again in his essay on Desnos and the sleeping-fits: 'Entrée des Médiums' ('Enter the Mediums'). 'Up to a point, we know what we mean by *Surrealism*, my friends and I,' he wrote then (in 1922). '. . . We use it to indicate a certain psychic automatism which corresponds to the dream-state, a state to which it is, these days, very hard to assign limits.'[104]

Now, once more, Surrealism was in the air. People were thinking about Apollinaire; the magazine *Esprit Nouveau* was preparing a special Apollinaire issue, for which writers and artists were being asked to contribute either statements or artworks for a sale whose proceeds would go towards a tomb. It was clear that Breton saw himself in Apollinaire's role, as centre and spokesman for artistic innovation, whether verbal or visual; his appropriation of the dead poet's word was all part of this assumption. Two other poets, Paul Dermée and Ivan Goll, were also trying to stake a claim to it, but they were beaten off in short order.

Picabia, characteristically nettled, could not resist the opportunity to poke some fun:

> Q: Is there a new movement coming on?
> A: Certainly! There is always a movement, but it is impossible for me to specify it for you. What I can tell you is that it will be beyond those who seek to fabricate it. Artificial eggs don't make chickens . . .
> Q: Don't you like Lautréamont?
> A: I read Lautréamont when I was 19 and it bores me to talk again of a man whom my friends have discovered twenty-six years later.[105]

At the same time, he announced a new run of *391* – an announcement whose groupings, tone and timing were all clearly designed to cause Breton maximum annoyance:

> The famous review *391*, which astonished the world at the time of the dada movement, will reappear monthly under the unique direction of its former director, Francis Picabia, with the collaboration of MM. Erik Satie, Man Ray, Marcel Duchamp, Rrose Sélavy, Pierre de Massot, Robert Desnos, Stieglitz, Cassanyes, Huelsenbeck, Serner, Jacques Rigaut, Lila Robertson, Igor Stravinsky, Marthe Chenal, F.T.Marinetti, etc. etc,
>
> MM. André Breton, Louis Aragon, Roger Vitrac, Max

Morise, Marcel Noll, etc. are cordially invited by the master of the house.

It will be consecrated to Surrealism . . .[106]

Breton, annoyed, sent Picabia a letter in his usual pedantic style ('I don't intend to amuse you, nor instruct you; you know what I think of your recent activities . . . There's no point in telling you I decline your cordial invitation with all the force at my command, and will urge all my friends to do likewise . . .'). Picabia printed it in full in the revived *391*, under the heading 'A Letter from Grandpa' and followed by the brief and brutal comment: 'When I've smoked a cigarette, I'm not in the habit of keeping the butt.'[107] So ended the on-off-on friendship between Breton and Picabia. Most of the quondam Dadas would become, in one form or another, at one time or another, Surrealists: Picabia was not among them.

*

It was time to explore further both the new word and its implications. At first it seemed as though Breton, Soupault and Aragon might write 'something in collaboration, a sort of manifesto of our common ideas'.[108] In fact Soupault did not contribute: the two works that would emerge were Aragon's *Une Vague de rêves* (*A Sea of Dreams*) and Breton's *Manifeste du surréalisme*. The latter was at first designed as a preface to the automatically-written *Poisson soluble*. However, fuelled by the various rows over the rights to and meaning of 'Surrealism', it acquired increasing length and polemical steam, finally overtaking *Poisson soluble* altogether. Although they are always printed together, it is the manifesto that has become the principal work.

In it, Breton revisits his idea of 'pure psychic automatism'. Both he and Aragon situate Surrealism firmly in the realm of the non-rational, to be achieved by any number of routes –

217

physical fatigue, drugs, extreme hunger, dreams, mental illness
– all inducing similar hallucinatory phenomena, and leading to
'a hypothesis which, alone, explained and brought together all
these manifestations: the existence of some mental matter . . .
different from thought, of which thought was, perhaps, just
one special example'.[109] Or, in the famous phrase with which
Aragon ends his *Vague de rêves*: '*Faites entrer l'infini.*' ('Enter
infinity.')[110] Here, in the subconscious, was the seat of Surrealism. Breton cited the example of the poet St-Pol Roux who,
when he went to sleep, put a sign outside his door: THE
POET IS WORKING.[111] He and Aragon agreed that Surrealism was wholly word-led rather than thought-led, and that
this new world of language was sought not merely for itself,
but as a route to another way of being.

Both Breton and Aragon list the names of revered ancestors
and associates – Vaché, Roussel, Freud, Chirico – but it is
noticeable that where Aragon leaves them firmly in the realm
of inspiration – 'your portraits hang on the walls of the
chamber of dreams'[112] – Breton enlists them firmly as members
of the gang – *his* gang: 'Swift is surrealist in malice./ Sade is
surrealist in sadism. /Hugo is surrealist when he isn't stupid/
Rimbaud is surrealist in the conduct of life and in other
respects . . .'[113] Anxious as ever to confirm both group-identity
and the identities of group members, he includes in his affirmation the names of all the current members of his circle:
'MM. Aragon, Baron, Boiffard, Breton, Carrive, Crevel, Delteil, Desnos, Eluard, Gérard, Limbour, Malkine, Morise,
Naville, Noll, Péret, Picon, Soupault, Vitrac, have made an act
of ABSOLUTE SURREALISM.'[114] He mentions the old
illuminati Flamel and Lulle: Desnos, he declares, is of their
company[115]: 'Today, Desnos *speaks surrealist* at will.'[116]

Surrealism was, above all, to do with the marvellous, the
magical. 'The marvellous is always beautiful, anything marvellous is beautiful, in fact only the marvellous is beautiful.'[117]

Instants of magic, coincidence, prophecy, were the supreme Surrealist moments. There was Breton's first meeting with Eluard, and the realization that this young man had already accosted him once under a misapprehension. There was the evening when, seated at a café with the young woman, Nadja, she pointed randomly at a window: ' "Do you see that window over there? It's dark now, like all the rest. Look at it. In one minute it's going to light up. It'll be red." The minute passes. The window lights up. And there are, indeed, red curtains.'[118] There was the chilling moment, in an 'Open Letter to Clairvoyants' written in 1925, when he wrote: 'Some people like to think the war has taught them something; but they aren't as advanced as I am – for I know what the year 1939 has in store for me.'[119] There was the moment when he and Aragon discovered that each, earlier that day, had vainly followed the same unknown girl . . .

Earthbound realists might advance explanations for these phenomena, but explanation was just what Breton eschewed. Enchanted by the magical phenomenon of a jumping bean, he steadfastly refused to admit that the movement might be due to an insect hidden within.[120] 'Lucidity', he was to write, 'is the chief enemy of revelation.'[121] But to experience revelation, he had first of all to fight his own lucidity. Surrealists submitted themselves to chance – that key word. Thus from its inception Surrealism was a paradox: a methodical attempt to pin down the most fleeting of human experiences, the moments when two worlds, inner and outer, sleeping and waking, meet and coincide.

From now on, Breton's life would be an act of abandonment. It is impossible to imagine a greater test of will for this most self-conscious, most logical – most *lucid* – of men. If he was stern with others, he was sternest of all with himself. He *would* be abandoned. And in this way, his life would be a continuing memorial to his dead friend: '*Vaché est surréaliste en moi.*'

CHAPTER SIX

DREAMS AND COMMISSARS

LOUIS ARAGON WAS as enthusiastic as Breton in his exaltation of the dream-world. No work so eloquently expresses their state of mind during this period of sleeping-fits as *Une Vague de rêves*. But he had not personally taken part in the adventure. He had been trapped in the army during the first excursion into automatism, while Breton and Soupault wrote *Les Champs magnétiques*; now the pattern was repeated. Returning to Paris from a stay in Normandy he had found a *fait accompli*, with which he hastened to identify himself.

And what exactly had he been doing in Normandy? Writing a novel.

A perfectly normal occupation for a literary young man. But not something to boast of in Surrealist circles. 'No more novels,' Breton had proclaimed in 1918, at the start of their friendship. 'Purity, purity.'[1] Lautréamont's great aperçu had been life's lack of inherent shape: rather he saw it as a series of paradoxes and contradictions. Surrealism sought to exploit these: the novelist sought to impose a pattern. What is a novel without a story, a meaning – a shape? So Breton proscribed novels, in all their plodding realism. 'Everyone has their own little "observation" to make ... We're not spared a single detail: is the character blond, what is his name, is it summer? ... And the descriptions! I've never seen anything so meaningless: a recital of catalogue images, more and more of them, with the occasional postcard thrown in ...'[2]

Aragon, of course, knew all this. Yet here he was doing the very thing Breton condemned. How could he live two such different lives, wear such different faces?

The question goes to Aragon's very heart. Who was he, what was he? His life was ruled by secrets. Nothing was what it seemed. In 1922 his close friend Matthew Josephson

223

observed that Aragon was on holiday 'with his mother and his sister' – information he could only have had from Aragon himself. In fact, these two holiday companions were his mother and grandmother. Why the pretence? What was so shameful about the truth? Where did he come from, what (behind the brilliance and the charm) were his real opinions, his true predilections? How he would have liked to know!

Aragon's mother, Marguerite Toucas-Massillon, was the eldest of three sisters. The family was well-connected but poor, Marguerite's father having walked out when she was sixteen. Her mother was too much of a lady to find work, even *in extremis*. So it was Marguerite who earned the family living, such as it was, by painting flowers on china. And then came another disaster. At the age of twenty-four, she found herself pregnant. Her lover was fifty-seven, married, with a family of his own. What was to be done? Abortion, in this correct and Catholic family, was out of the question. There was only one thing for it: to conceal both the pregnancy and the birth. The first was achieved by moving between a number of different addresses; the second, by sending the child to be reared in Brittany for the first thirteen months of his life. When he returned to Paris, he was passed off as his mother's youngest brother. His father, Louis Andrieu, contributed a little money and his Christian name. As for his mother – she was, then and always, Marguerite; never, ever, Maman. In 1942, after she died, Aragon published a poem called 'Le Mot' ('The Word'):

> The word never crossed my lips
> The word never touched my heart . . .
> I never said it except in my dreams
> This heavy secret dangling between us . . .
> To call you my sister leaves me unarmed
> If I pretended, it was only for you
> Playing the innocent to the very end . . .

I shall go on sinning
My first sin was to live.

Despite this web of pretence, in which all was known but nothing spoken, Aragon remained very much tied to this family of women. Until 1923 – he was by then twenty-six – he lived at Neuilly with his sister/mother, sisters/aunts and mother/grandmother. They – narrowly respectable in their straitened circumstances – did not like the turn his life was taking. They had supposed him safely settled in a medical career: he had confounded them by following his friend Breton's example and abandoning his medical studies. Ever since they had been nagging him about his future. What was he going to do? How did he propose to live? Once again, as so often, the enlightened couturier Jacques Doucet came to the rescue. He already employed Breton as his advisor. Now he arranged to pay Aragon a small stipend in return for his *Projet d'histoire littéraire contemporaine*. It wasn't much, but it kept the women quiet: 'What a bore always to have to make such a fuss for a bit of peace,' Aragon grumbled. 'I don't ask much from THEM. Oh, well.'[3]

That was written in the summer of 1922. Soon afterwards, Aragon accepted a job as editor of a flagging literary magazine, *Paris-Journal*, which would, it was hoped, sail back into the mainstream under his editorship. The salary, added to what Doucet paid him, enabled him to live relatively comfortably; he was free to do what he liked with the paper and give work to his friends. It was, in fact, an ideal job. But on 15 April 1923, he suddenly resigned.

Once again (and not unreasonably) his family blamed Breton's malign influence. Aragon had resigned his job because it transgressed the Surrealist interdict against journalism in general and literary journalism in particular. 'They kept getting at me,' he told Doucet. 'I realised they'd never really trust me so long as I stayed at *Paris-Journal*.'⁴ Indeed, had the sinner been anyone other than Aragon the limits of acceptability would long since have been overstepped. But Breton could not – yet – turn his back on Aragon. Their friendship was stronger than principle – or at any rate, than this principle. His rigidity had already alienated Soupault, the third Musketeer, who had lost patience with Breton's interdicts and was drawing away from the group. How would he survive without Aragon? In the uncertain new life upon which they had embarked, they were each other's constants.

But, not for the first or last time, Aragon, wanting to satisfy everyone, satisfied no one. His resignation might appease his friends, but it infuriated his family. Once again, though on another front, his life was not worth living. Abruptly, he left Neuilly. But where (and how) would he live now? Doucet agreed, against the promise of the resulting manuscript, to provide enough money for a short stay in the country, to be devoted to writing. Aragon left Paris for Giverny on the Seine, to join a group of American friends – and commit treason. He had already published one novel, *Anicet ou le Panorama, roman*; now he began another. 'I was almost sure I had reinvented the novel. I began to write, determined to push it to its craziest limits.' Between lazing and a love affair (with Clotilde Vail, a wealthy American) he began to amass a heap of pages which, over the next four years, would acquire massive proportions. Its title was *La Défense de l'infini* (*The Defence of the Infinite*) – a name picked, he said, 'out of the air'.⁵

Aragon said nothing of this enterprise to his Surrealist friends. It proceeded by fits and starts, masked and interrupted by other works – for example, *Une Vague de rêves*: another secret to add to those many secrets with which he had always lived.

And here was yet another: despite *Une Vague de rêves*, Aragon was not, as Breton was, overcome with enthusiasm for

automatic writing. For Breton, spontaneity and the abandonment of control implied hope and possibility. Chance, which
for Apollinaire had represented modernity, and for the Dadas
anarchy and anti-art, was for him endowed not only with
unique poetic possibilities but with connotations of personal
salvation. Twice now – with the *Champs magnétiques* after
Vaché's death, and with the sleeping-fits when Dada was
fading and his Congrès de Paris running into the sand –
automatism had opened a new way forward, a therapeutic
unlocking of creativity, a direct route to the emotions, a means
of bypassing stifling lucidity.

But this was not true for Aragon. Automatism unsettled
him. It meant chaos and the abandonment of self – exactly
those things he could least cope with. As he would put it in
the *Défense de l'infini* itself, 'I can't think without expressing
the thought, so that writing is my way of thinking.'[6] And forty
years on his view had not changed: 'Ever since I can remember
I have belonged to the zoological species of those for whom
thought takes shape as I write.'[7] Only by the opposite of
automatism – by writing as lucidly as possible, by sustained
intellectual application – could he make sense of life. On all
the levels which mattered to him – of exactness, of self-
expression – automatism failed. Years later, reading through
the many notebooks full of his own efforts at automatism, he
was struck by their lack of subtlety and personality. 'When
you're in full sleeping spate, when you're no longer speaking
to anyone – not even to yourself – you suddenly assume a
rhetorical tone which you would never use consciously . . .
You pick up a whole lot of oratorical linguistic tricks and
aggressive conventions.'[8]

But he could not say this openly: not yet. For Aragon,
with his '*petites mensonges*', truth was always less important
than love. 'I betray myself from moment to moment, I argue
with myself, I contradict myself. I wouldn't trust someone like

me,' he announced in *Littérature.*[9] For Breton, words 'are making love';[10] for Aragon, they 'make love to the world'.[11] He was desperate for love, he would do anything to be loved. Especially, he could not risk the loss of Breton's love. Breton had shaped his life; for Breton he had thrown up his medical studies and his ideal job, for Breton he lived now from hand to mouth. How could he say what he thought? He would lose Breton's friendship, and who would he be, what would he do then?

In his novel *Anicet* Aragon paints the Breton of those early years as Baptiste Ajamais – a name taken from 'Façon', the first poem in Breton's collection *Mont de Piété*, where the girls *'font de batiste/A jamais!'* Jacques Vaché also appears, under the name Harry James – one of the signatures he sometimes used. And Anicet/Aragon always feels himself at a disadvantage vis-à-vis Baptiste by comparison with the dashing Harry James.

> 'I can see just what you're like,' [Baptiste assures Anicet.] 'It's amazing how I can absolutely see. One of these days I'm going to lose my temper. You're always talking, you never do anything ... Tell me, what actually do you ever do? You just let yourself live. You're terrifyingly docile. Look at Harry James: he and I can't be three days together without quarrelling ... The thing about Harry James is, you never know if he'll go and kill himself tomorrow, or commit some wonderful crime ... But with you, one never need worry: you'll never kill yourself.'...
>
> 'How do you know?' said Anicet. 'I might have something in mind. Would I tell you in advance?'
>
> Anicet knew he was lying ... but he keenly felt the humiliation of being compared with Harry James. He knew that once again he would follow as he was directed, that he was under Baptiste's influence ... But what was the power over him of that authoritarian personage? In the shadows, you could guess at the fascination of his look, his slight frown. There was nothing for it: Baptiste subjugated Anicet ...[12]

Three years later, all that was still true.

*

The final issue of *Littérature* appeared in June 1924. Dada was long dead; Breton's group, in the meantime, had been known as the '*Littérature* group' or (after Aragon's text) the '*Vague* movement'. But now they definitively assumed the new name that had for so long been hovering in the wings. On 1 December 1924, the first issue of a new review appeared. It was called *La Révolution surréaliste*.

For most of the world, the word 'revolution' at this time could have only one meaning. It was just seven years since the Dadas' erstwhile neighbour on Spiegelgasse had overthrown the Tsar of all the Russias. Where would the contagion spread next? Germany was in turmoil; only eighteen months later, a general strike would paralyse Britain.

The Surrealists, however, barely registered all this. Dada (at least that part of it which had taken root in France) ridiculed all politics, and Dada's descendants saw no reason to do otherwise. 'Censorship was very strict during the war,' Breton pointed out later. 'Politically significant events like the Zimmerwald and Kienthal congresses made very little impression upon people like us, and even the Bolshevik revolution was very far from being recognised for what it really was. If anyone had told us that our attitudes to the implications of these events would spark off conflicts between us, we should have been totally incredulous. We simply didn't possess what's usually known as a "social conscience".'[13] When a Surrealist spoke of revolution, insofar as he thought of politics at all, it was the politics of 1789 – 'Robespierre's curls, Marat's bath.'[14] When the first *Révolution surréaliste* announced that 'We are on the eve of a REVOLUTION' and urged readers to take part, the upheaval they had in mind was wholly cultural. As to its contents, they remained unsure. 'This first number ...

offers no definitive revelation ... We must wait to see what the future holds.' Meanwhile emphasis was laid on dreams and automatism. 'Only dreams offer man real liberty ... Every morning, in every family, men, women and children, IF THEY HAVE NOTHING BETTER TO DO, tell each other their dreams.' There would be experiments and inquiries, beginning with the question which had been hanging over Breton's head ever since that fateful January day in 1919: 'Is suicide a solution?' Replies should be sent to 15 Rue de Grenelle, a mansion that had once belonged to the La Roche-foucauld family, now the property of the Navilles, whose son Pierre was one of Surrealism's latest intake of young recruits. The ground floor of the house was established as the Bureau Central de Recherches Surréalistes, open every day between four thirty and six thirty (after which the staff repaired to the Cyrano for aperitifs).

This all sounded relatively tame. But the group had recently demonstrated a savagery of which the fieriest Dada might have been proud. This was the pamphlet *Un Cadavre* (*A Corpse*), a series of diatribes against the eighty-year-old novelist Anatole France, prepared in October while he was dying, and published on the day of his death.

France, who had won the 1921 Nobel Prize for literature, was the country's most celebrated novelist. He embodied the French spirit, scepticism, irony; he was admired from the Kremlin to the Elysée. Even before his death, the papers were full of him: it was clear that the actual event would trigger a flood of patriotic outpourings. He represented, said Breton, 'the prototype of everything we loathed. For us, if ever a reputation was undeserved, it was his. We were completely impervious to the celebrated limpidities of his style ... He had done everything possible to curry favour with both right and left. He was rotten with honours and wealth. We felt absolutely no compunction.'[15]

The idea for *Un Cadavre* originated with Aragon and his friend Drieu La Rochelle. Drieu was not a member of the group, though he knew them all. He had a certain amount of money – not, however, as his name suggested, because of aristocratic forebears: in fact his uncle owned a pharmacy in the suburbs, a detail he tried to keep to himself. His cover was blown by Cocteau, who took a party of young friends to see the name *Drieu La Rochelle* written over the pharmacy door. ('He went crazy,' Aragon remembered.)[16]

Drieu offered to pay for the printing; Eluard, Soupault, Breton and Aragon provided the text. It was an exercise in supreme tastelessness. 'Your kind, corpse, we don't like,' proclaimed Eluard. 'Let someone on the quays empty out a box of those old books "he loved so much" and put him in it and throw the whole thing into the Seine,' advised Breton. As for Aragon, his piece was headed 'HAVE YOU EVER SLAPPED A DEAD MAN?' and concluded, 'There are days I dream of an eraser to rub out human filth.' 'Next time, there will be another *Cadavre*,' they announced.

The *Cadavre* was a peculiarly French production. It is hard to imagine literary questions arousing such passions among the anglophones, while in Germany, Spain or Russia the threat of dire consequences, in terms of career if not personal safety, tended to invite relative prudence. (By 1924, even George Grosz was becoming less savage.) But in France the revolution had shown, firstly, that intellectuals mattered, and secondly, that they might go to considerable extremes and nevertheless continue unhampered in their careers. *Un Cadavre*, though it caused a tremendous scandal, did not bring upon its authors the retribution that might have been expected had it (or its equivalent) appeared elsewhere.

It was, however, important and interesting in political terms. Important, because it clearly aligned the Surrealists with the Left: the only group to support *Un Cadavre* was a circle of young pacifists and Communists who published a magazine called *Clarté*, devoted to the undermining of bourgeois culture. And interesting for what it reveals of the attitudes, at this moment, of Louis Aragon, later to become the French Communist Party's leading intellectual. For in it he excoriates both Right and Left, referring even-handedly to 'the imbecile Maurras' (Charles Maurras was a pillar of the extreme Right) and 'doddering Moscow' ('*Moscou la gâteuse*').

The editors of *Clarté*, as might be imagined, found this phrase highly offensive. While praising Eluard ('a true poet') and Breton ('the most fanatically honest mind of his generation') they remonstrated with Aragon. Perhaps Moscow was over-impressed by the prestige of Anatole France, but (wrote Jean Bernier, one of *Clarté*'s editors) 'that was simply a question of politics, and that, my dear Aragon, does not concern you'.[17] To which Aragon replied indignantly: 'My dear Bernier, You prefer to dismiss as an exaggeration a phrase demonstrating my lack of sympathy for the Bolshevik government, and communism in general. But you know I'm not *stupid* ... I can only shrug my shoulders at the Russian revolution. On the scale of ideas, it's about on the level of a ministerial crisis ... The problems of human existence', he declared in a 'bravura performance' that even his friends found slightly shocking,[18] 'have nothing to do with the miserable little revolutionary activity which has been going on in the East these past few years.'[19] For him the object of revolution could only be individual freedom, as absolute as possible. 'The Marquis de Sade, a target of abuse for the past hundred and forty years, never left the Bastille: and in the same way nearly all those *who refused all limits* and who should be, as he is, called *divine*, are held prisoner by ignoramuses.'[20]

For some months, the Surrealists and *Clarté* circled each other watchfully. The Surrealists were still far more anarchist than Communist. The first issue of *La Révolution surréaliste* featured a photograph of the anarchist Germaine Berton, recently convicted of assassinating Marius Plateau, editor of the right-wing *Action Française*, surrounded by pictures of the Surrealists and those they admired (such as Picasso). The second carried the banner: 'OPEN THE PRISONS. DIS-BAND THE ARMY. THERE ARE NO COMMON-LAW CRIMES'. And the fourth declared 'WAR ON WORK', which provided copious ammunition for those Communists who wanted *Clarté* to dissociate itself from the Surrealists.

In January 1925, the Surrealists clarified their position vis-à-vis the revolution:

1 We have nothing to do with literature; but we are quite capable, if need be, of using it for our own ends.
2 *Surrealism* is not a new or better means of expression, nor even a metaphysic of poetry; it is a means of total liberation of the mind *and anything resembling it.*
3 We are absolutely set upon Revolution.
4 We have joined the words *Surrealism* and *Revolution* purely in order to demonstrate the disinterested, detached, and altogether despairing nature of this revolution . . .[21]

By the summer of 1925, however, events had begun to move the group away from this naked anarchism. That July, the tribesmen of the Moroccan Rif rose against the government and, as Morocco was a French protectorate, the French army was sent to help quell the uprising. Naturally both Surrealists and Clartéists supported the Rif; and that same July they published a joint declaration, 'REVOLUTION FIRST AND ALWAYS!' in which unconditional support was set out for 'the magnificent example of immediate, integral and unanimous *disarmament* given the world in 1917 by LENIN at *Brest-Litovsk*, a disarmament of infinite revolutionary value which *your* France will never be capable of following'.

Your France belonged to the 'Priests, doctors, professors, litterateurs, poets, philosophers, journalists, judges, lawyers, policemen, academicians of every stripe, all you signatories of that idiotic paper "Intellectuals in support of the Father-land" . . .' In particular it belonged to Paul Claudel, poet, politician, and French Ambassador to the United States of America, who had not only recently been at pains to claim Rimbaud for Catholicism, but had dismissed the Surrealists as 'pederasts', which was ironic considering Breton's bitter homophobia. They responded with an open letter declaring that 'We very much hope that revolutions, wars and colonial insurrections will wipe out this Western civilisation' and seiz-ing 'this occasion to dissociate ourselves publicly from every-thing French, be it words or acts'. This letter was signed by Aragon, Antonin Artaud (at this period an active Surrealist), André Breton, René Crevel, Paul Eluard, Philippe Soupault, and twenty-two others.

All this anti-patriotism drew a protest from Drieu La Rochelle. He had been flirting with both the Surrealists and Cocteau; now he positioned himself definitively on the Right – a journey which would lead him, during the next war, to Fascism and suicide. Drieu's piece, published in the *Nouvelle Revue Française*, was addressed specifically to Aragon, in the name of God and their ten years' friendship:

> Politics or literature, it's all the same, fag ends from here and there, Freud, Einstein, Caligari, literary painters, *poètes mau-dits*, every sort of rationalist mysticism – and now neo-orientalism . . . Just as some people feel the occasional urge to murmur, Long live the King! . . . you bray out: Long live Lenin!
>
> Long live Lenin! I know you, Aragon, you'll tell me that the Communists are fools, that you're an old republican, an old anarchist, an old this, an old that (an old Frenchman, even!)[22]

Aragon replied the following month, characteristically combining indignation with a perfect ambivalence regarding his political position: 'I don't want to say that I've never shouted: Vive Lenin! I'll *bray* it tomorrow, since you won't let me shout it – after all, it recognises genius, and the sacrifice of a life.'[23]

Breton, meanwhile, was moving nearer to the Party. He had never been entirely happy with Aragon's silly belittling of the Russian revolution. Now, during a summer holiday in Provence, he read Trotsky's little book on Lenin, written between the latter's death in January 1924, and April of that same year. Despite (or because of) his ignorance of what was actually going on in Russia, he immediately recognized both a new hero and a new way forward. Dreams, sleeping-fits and automatism had led the way out of Dada's dead end, but now something else was needed if they were not to become just another literary device, a dead end in their turn. Trotsky's book was a 'revelation', Simone told Eluard; Breton himself spoke of 'this wonderful book'. He at once wrote a long article about it for the *Révolution surréaliste* in which he 'tried to move forward and commit myself as far as I possibly can'.[24] He was wildly enthusiastic, lauding the book to the skies ('the brilliant, *true*, definitive, magnificent pages of refutation devoted to the Lenins of Gorky and Wells . . .') and with it, in a jumble of superlatives, its principal protagonists. He took the opportunity to distance himself from the unreconstructed Aragon. 'For my part, I absolutely refuse to maintain solidarity with any friend who attacks Communism, in the name of whatever principle – even one so seemingly legitimate as the non-acceptance of work . . . Louis Aragon is perfectly free to tell Drieu La Rochelle that he's never shouted: Vive Lenin! but that he'll "*bray* it tomorrow since they won't let him shout"; in the same way I too am free to find that this isn't a good enough reason for such behaviour, that it makes things far too easy for our worst enemies, who are also Lenin's, to let them think we only act in this way out of defiance. On the contrary, Vive Lenin! just *because of Lenin!*'[25]

*

In fact there was more than politics behind Drieu's attack on Aragon.

For some years Aragon had been in love with an American woman, Elisabeth (Eyre) de Lanux. The affair was complicated for many reasons. One was that Eyre was married. More to the point, she was lesbian, though not exclusively so. But the real difficulty, which Aragon realized only after he had become irretrievably entangled, was that Eyre was already the mistress of his close friend Drieu La Rochelle.

For a long time he did his best to deny this love. 'I forbade myself to love her, I turned away from her with a terror which admitted everything . . .' And then, one night, 'She did this extraordinary thing, she called me to her: and I went.'[26]

It is notable, in this context, that all Aragon's serious liaisons were with foreign women: Clotilde Vail and Eyre de Lanux, both Americans; Nancy Cunard, half-American, half-English; and finally Elsa Triolet, who was Russian-Jewish. Only with them could he feel secure from embarrassing probes into family affairs, such as any French girl would inevitably make. All his vulnerability lay there, all his insecurities stemmed from his ambivalent and irregular family situation. As he put it (during one of the Surrealist investigations into sex): 'For a very long time, shame for me was a social feeling directed against my family (the notion that it was inferior).'[27]

Eyre's sudden move in his direction seems to have been primarily a form of vengeance. Drieu had been treating her shabbily, talking about her to his friends 'coarsely and discourteously . . . Aragon didn't like this barrack-room side of him . . . [He] told [Jacques Baron] Drieu behaved like a cad towards her.'[28] Perhaps she always intended to tell Drieu what had happened; perhaps Aragon could not resist boasting of his coup. At any rate, Drieu heard of it and their friendship ended – as the extraordinary personal bitterness of Aragon's reply to Drieu's article showed only too clearly:

> You're just an ordinary man, you're pathetic, you couldn't lead the way anywhere, you're lost and I'm losing you. You're fading, you're invisible in the mists. There's nobody else out there, but it's what you wanted, shade, so off you go, bye bye . . .[29]

Aragon now found himself in a hopeless position. Drieu and Breton, his two oldest, closest friends, were each demanding the impossible. For Drieu he must give up Eyre, for Breton, the novel. What was he to do? Writing to his friend Denise Lévy, a one-time love and the witness of his travails with Eyre 'at this moment in my life when EVERYTHING must be decided', he continued: 'Denise it seems that I'm considering *myself* at this moment for the last time. That's it . . . Tomorrow will be terrible, and Tuesday, and Wednesday. And after that, implacable existence. I've lost my youth, that's really what I've lost.'[30]

We do not know what Eyre de Lanux really meant to Drieu. His bitter comments twenty years after these events (Aragon was by then a happily married man and a war hero, Drieu a condemned collaborator in hiding to escape arrest) imply that the real hurt lay in the loss of Aragon. 'I once loved her for a few months. I didn't have the strength to snatch her away from her impotent husband, her dykey friends, all that . . .' He added: 'I'm dying friendless . . . It's twenty years since I cut myself off from Aragon who hates me more and more . . . Sexually, I found him out: I can understand that he's never forgiven me that.'[31]

But sex, for Aragon as for all the Surrealists, was always

something more than a mere social or physiological transaction. It was part of a sign-system, a search for significance beneath or behind the apparent, which was part of their approach to transforming the world. Eroticism, like the occult, was a path towards both the scandalous and the transcendent. For Aragon, as we have seen, the occult had little attraction. Sex, though, was another matter. This was what he wanted to explore and express in *La Défense de l'infini*. But while Breton's experiments with the occult were (in Surrealist circles) uncontroversial, Aragon's literary sallies into sex had a rougher ride.

The trouble was that, because *La Défense de l'infini* was a novel, Aragon felt continually on the defensive, constantly aware of the insecurity of his position in the group. He might be Breton's oldest ally, but this guaranteed nothing. If in *Une Vague de rêves* and *Un Cadavre* he went further than anyone else, this was the reason. 'André's power over me was even greater since the formation of a real Surrealist group, with newcomers, younger than us, always trying to prove their orthodoxy against Philippe, Paul or me.'[32]

It seemed for a while that he had managed to reconcile his and Breton's viewpoints on this subject. Breton, discussing automatic writing, 'began to say that the *dictation* for him began with a *heard* phrase. At which I cried that it was just the same for me at the beginning of a novel . . . that there was exactly the same necessity, the same arbitrary link between the opening phrase and the Surrealist text as between the novel and the usually absurd phrase which starts it off.'[33] But this was at best a sophism, and the truce to which it led could only be uneasy.

At this time Aragon was engaged upon two books: the *Défense de l'infini* and the book that would become *Le Paysan de Paris* (*Paris Peasant*). '[The *Défense de l'infini*] stopped, started, acquired worrying proportions. I tried to fit everything

I wrote into this ghost of a book ... It was a secret at first, masked by poems, and that sudden exercise I began one day, as though searching for a new language, and which became *Le Paysan de Paris.*'[34]

Le Paysan de Paris is an exploration of the wonderful, that cornerstone of Surrealist experience, as it is found in Paris. Aragon showed Breton the first part and was encouraged to read it aloud to the group, which consisted largely of the young newcomers who made him feel so uneasy. His unease was at once justified. They clearly hated it. There was an embarrassed silence; they coughed, shuffled their chairs, exchanged glances. 'Finally, very kindly, someone – it was a woman – said, "Really, darling, why are you wasting your time writing stuff like this?"'[35] Such an unlooked-for response unnerved poor Aragon, as it would any author. Nevertheless, he continued to write.

Le Paysan de Paris is pervaded by glimpses of a hidden world. The book consists of two parts, one entitled 'The Passage de l'Opéra', one the 'Sentiment of Nature in the Buttes-Chaumont'. In the first part especially, the marginal, seedy, allusive Paris so beloved of the Surrealists is evoked with tremendous vivacity and dexterity. Everything is magical and sexual, and the sex is for sale. The Passage de l'Opéra contains both a down-at-heel burlesque theatre and a brothel:

> The door opens, and, wearing only her stockings, the girl I've chosen advances mincingly. I'm naked, and she laughs because she can see I like her. Come here darling I'll wash you. I've only got cold water, d'you mind? That's what it's like, here ...[36]

The second part is less straightforward. Three young men – Aragon, Breton and Marcel Noll – visit the Buttes-Chaumont park, which is pervaded by the unattainable spirit of love personified in the Dame des Buttes-Chaumont – Eyre de

Lanux. And at the end of the book, a lament is addressed (anonymously – neither Eyre nor Denise is ever named) to Denise Lévy, Aragon's confidante.

Whatever this might be – prose poem, essay on chance encounters, autobiographical fragments – it was not a novel. Even so – despite its Surrealist themes, despite the appearance in it of Breton himself – it had attracted the group's displeasure. How, then, could he risk anything more? For the moment he said nothing about the *Défense de l'infini*.

Meanwhile he had found a new love. This was Nancy Cunard, the rebellious daughter of Sir Bache Cunard the shipping magnate and his socialite wife Emerald. Nancy had been living in Paris since the early 20s, and was a familiar figure in artistic circles, both among the Americans and the French. She had suggested the title for Tzara's play *Le Mouchoir de nuages*, was a friend of Ezra Pound and William Carlos Williams, an habituée of Cocteau's nightclub Le Boeuf sur le Toit, and a poet in her own right: her first collection, *Outlaws*, was published in 1921, followed by *Sublunary* in 1923 and *Parallax* in 1925. She was rich, beautiful and stylish, with a predilection for armfuls of heavy bracelets and a frequently-changing cast of handsome men. In London she had been the lover of Michael Arlen, celebrated author of *The Green Hat*. The affair had led to an abortion, followed in short order by a hysterectomy, appendicitis, peritonitis and gangrene, from which, against long odds, she had recovered. Now she was thirty, and voraciously in her prime.

In some ways the two were well suited. He was, she said, 'beautiful as a young god, but terribly shy'.[37] However, that was not an insuperable hurdle. Nancy was bold enough for two – which, for Aragon, was all part of her attraction. Shrinking violets held no allure for him. 'I have a horror of virgins,' he said. 'I have only had relations with real women who know what love is and make no bones about it.'[38]

Apparently so effortlessly confident and successful (*'Tes petites amies/Font une ronde...'*), he was in reality as uncertain in this area as in all others. The front he showed the world was a dazzling one. He was, said his friend Luis Buñuel, 'so handsome, you can't believe'.[39] He was dandyish, with a famed collection of several hundred ties and cravats – two thousand, Breton claimed – vivacious, hyper-intelligent, 'icily polite in the best eighteenth-century manner'.[40] Numerous enraptured ladies asked no more than to search for the 'real self' hidden behind this façade; but it remained elusive. For, unlike them, Aragon knew that it consisted largely of weaknesses – and nowhere more than in the sexual field. That was his secret, and he was not anxious to share it. 'For a long time I assumed all women must hate me,'[41] he wrote in *Paysan de Paris*. The least distraction, he confessed, was enough to destroy his powers: 'An already precarious success is at the mercy of the first thought to enter my head.'[42] 'If a woman touched my sex only when it was erect it wouldn't get that way very often.'[43] What he enjoyed most was 'coming when I am performing cunnilingus'.[44] However, the hyper-sophisticated and experienced Nancy was not (at least in this instance) looking for a five-times-a-night man. In fact she later confessed to finding Aragon 'too demanding sexually'.[45]

The affair with Nancy also solved Aragon's housing problem. Ever since leaving Neuilly he had been not just jobless but homeless. At first he led a peripatetic existence, moving from hotel to hotel, preferably ones whose name ended in 'or' – such as the Grosvenor – since they belonged to the family of his friend Marcel Duhamel and he could often stay for free. Later a girlfriend, tiring of this makeshift existence, arranged for him to have the use of a ramshackle studio. But picturesque poverty was not for Nancy, and nor were peasants, from Paris or anywhere else. Together she and Aragon ricocheted between her numerous residences in London and Paris, New

York, Normandy and the Perigord. Of course she paid for everything. Aragon's stipend from Jacques Doucet had been cut off after the scandal of *Un Cadavre*, and although Doucet agreed to renew it against the promise of the new novel, 800 francs a month went nowhere in Nancy's world.

In many ways, however, the affair with Nancy deepened (or echoed) rather than alleviated Aragon's mood of despair. She was a gambler (Doucet specified he would have nothing to do with any gambling debts), an exhibitionist and a drunk. Late into the night she would trail from *boîte* to *boîte*, dragging Aragon in her increasingly foul-mouthed wake until, almost senseless, she was ready to be carried home. He was enthralled by her, but how could he avoid being demoralized by the humiliations she inflicted upon him? He tried consoling himself with other women, but his depression only deepened:

> As he went from cunt to cunt
> He became terribly sad
> As he went from cunt to cunt
> *Terribly sad*[46]

His one constant refuge in all this was *La Défense de l'infini*, the great work-in-progress. The sheaf of pages continued to mount. Wherever he found himself, 'in a café, early for a meeting, he'd pass the time writing a page or two of his great novel which nobody ever saw ... "Listen to this!" he'd say when you arrived, and on the spot he'd read out what he'd just written.'[47]

Such a project could not stay secret for long. Apart from anything else, Aragon (like any young writer excited about his work) actively desired an audience. Extracts were published here and there: one, 'Entry of the Succubi', in *Révolution surréaliste*; another, the 'Black Notebook', in Soupault's *Revue Européenne*, where it was billed as an extract from a forthcoming novel. Finally, the pre-publicity for *Paysan de Paris*, in

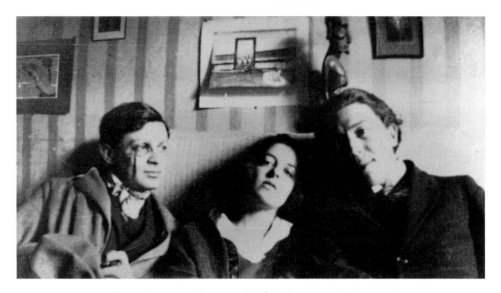

Tzara, Simone Breton, André Breton: Paris, 1920

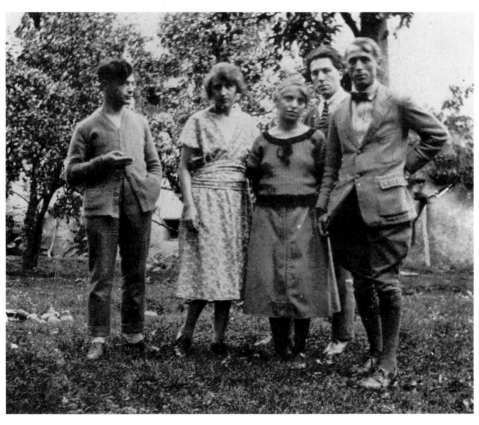

Dada en plein air: Tzara, uknown girl (possibly Maja Chruscek), Lou Ernst, Breton, Max Ernst, at Tarrenz-bei-Imst, 1921

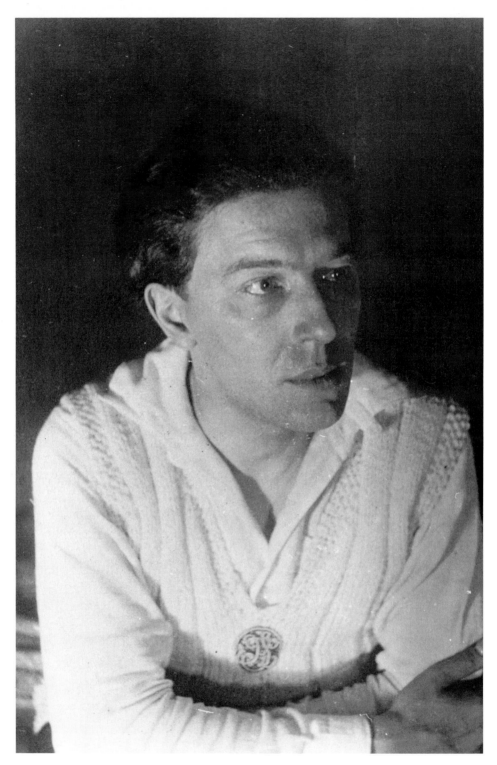

André Breton

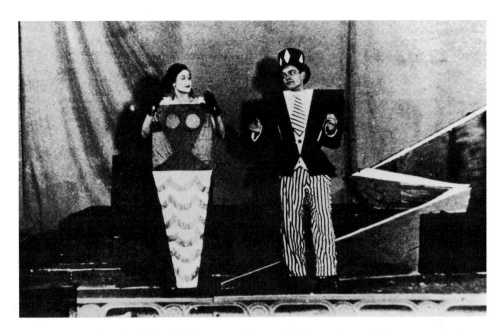

René Crevel and Lizica Codreanu perform *Le Coeur à gaz*. They are wearing Sonia Delaunay's cardboard costumes

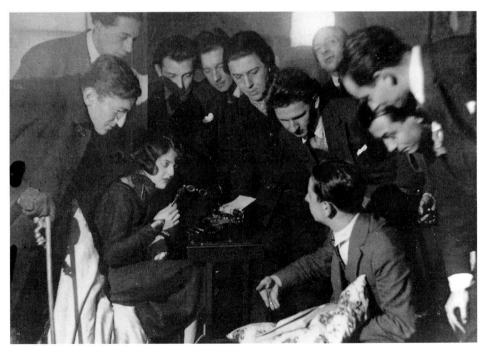

Simone takes dream-dictation. (Max Morise, Roger Vitrac, Jacques Boiffard, Paul Eluard, André Breton, Pierre Naville, Giorgio de Chirico, Philippe Soupault, Robert Desnos, Jacques Baron. Centre, Simone Breton.)

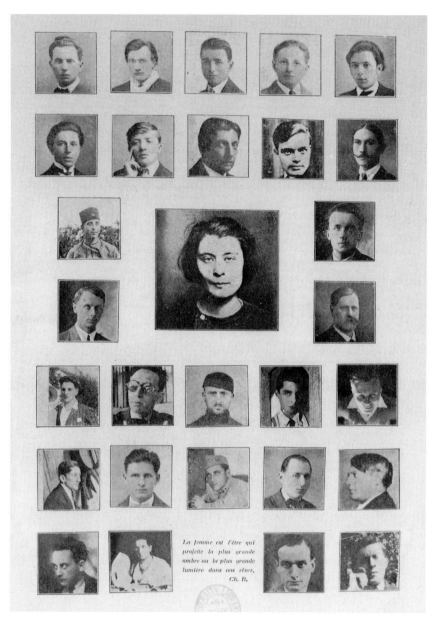

Surrealists and those they admired, 1925. Centre, Germaine Berton, 'that altogether admirable woman' jailed in 1923 for shooting the right-wing editor Marius Plateau. The pictures are arranged in alphabetical order from Aragon (top l.) to Vitrac (bottom r.): Louis Aragon, Antonin Artaud, Charles Baron, Jacques Baron, J. A. Boiffard, André Breton, Jean Carrive, Giorgio de Chirico, René Crevel, Joseph Delteil, Robert Desnos, Paul Eluard, Max Ernst, Freud, Francis Gérard, Georges Limbour, Matthias Lübeck, Georges Malkine, André Masson, Max Morise, Pierre Naville, Marcel Noll, Benjamin Péret, Picasso, Man Ray, Alberto Savinio, Philippe Soupault, Roger Vitrac. *Révolution surréaliste* no. 1

THE
SURREALIST
WOMAN:

(The head
is separate)

A) Man Ray:
*Hommage à
D.a.F. de Sade*
(SASDLR no. 2)

B) Brassaï:
Nu
(*Minotaure*
no. 1)

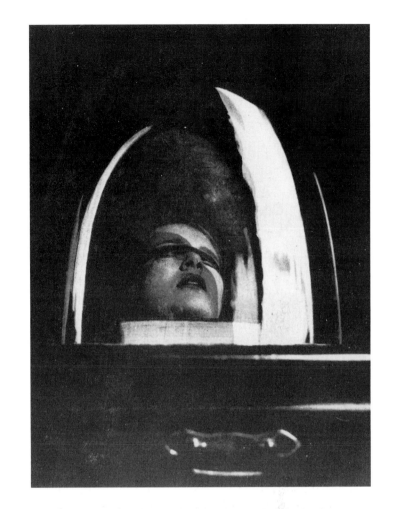

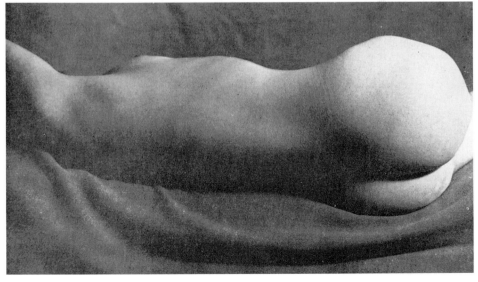

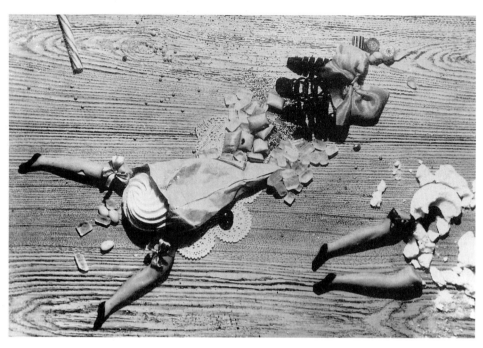

C) Hans Bellmer: Composition (*Minotaure* no. 7)

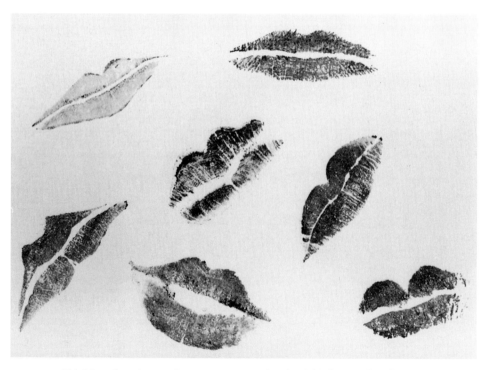

D) Mouth-prints – Suzanne Muzard, Elsa Triolet, Gala Eluard, Jeannette Tanguy, Marie-Berthe Ernst

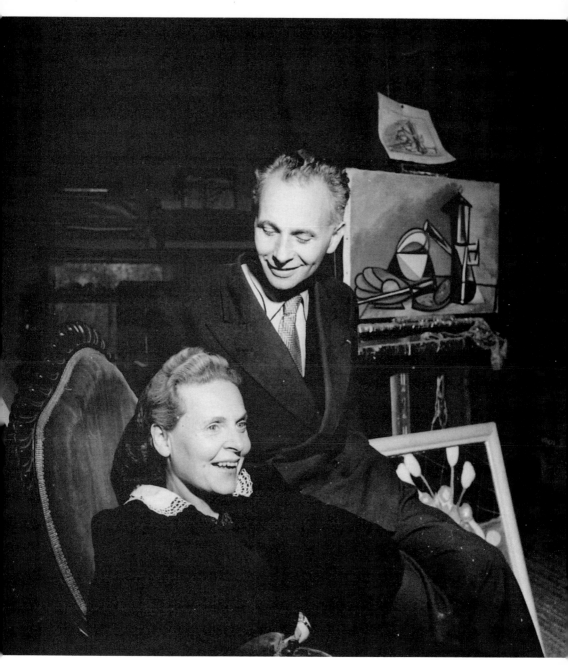

Louis Aragon and Elsa Triolet after the liberation of Paris, 1944

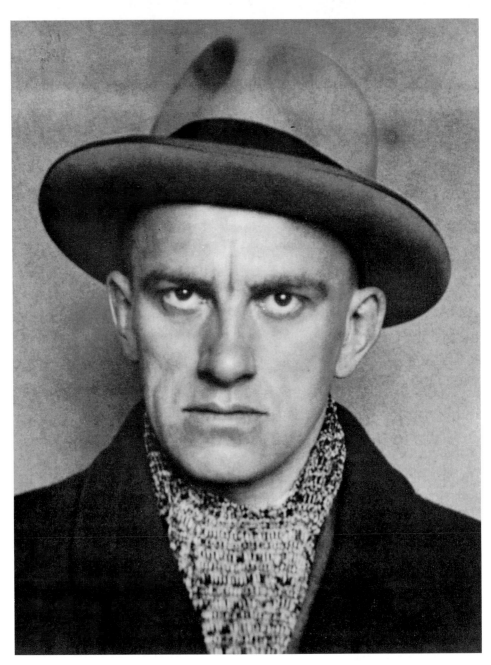

Mayakovsky

October 1926, referred to a novel 'in preparation'. It could no longer be ignored.

The great question among the Surrealists at this point was whether or not they should join the Communist Party. The argument centred upon the rocky question of autonomy. Did the Surrealists' support for the Party mean that their own intellectual activity must be abandoned in pursuit of the greater good of the masses? How far should the Party dictate what they might or might not do? And did their protestations of support mean anything if they stopped short of actually joining the Party, and putting themselves at its disposal? Pierre Naville, co-editor of the first two issues of *Révolution surréaliste* and owner of the premises which had housed the Bureau de Recherches Surréalistes, had left the Surrealists and become a militant Communist. He had recently published a pamphlet attacking Breton on these contentious issues. In his reply, Breton talked of the Surrealists' revolutionary literature, which 'belongs to that enormous enterprise of recreating the universe to which Lautréamont and Lenin dedicated themselves entirely', following in the glorious tradition of the poet-revolutionaries Rimbaud, Baudelaire and Petrus Borel. They had a special task to perform: 'something great and obscure tends imperiously toward expression through us'.[48] Aragon, however, was not writing this kind of literature, but indulging himself with fiction, and Breton now summoned him to explain himself in relation to both Surrealism and Communism.

A definite air of the witch-hunt hung over this meeting, at which the inquisitors were Breton (eager to prove himself politically), Naville, and Jean Bernier, editor of *Clarté*.[49] The implication was that unsatisfactory explanations would lead to expulsion. This institutionalized intolerance was a relatively recent introduction. There had been disagreements previously, but however violent, they had not been set in stone. Tzara and

Picabia, for example, though frequently in bitter conflict with Breton, had continued to contribute to *Littérature* until the very end. But times were changing. Life was less fluid, positions were hardening. You had to decide where you stood.

Aragon was not the first to be called to account: Antonin Artaud, who had found in Surrealism a congenial home for his black and iconoclastic introspection, preceded him. Artaud's sins were those of unacceptable work and company. He had recently, with Roger Vitrac (a Surrealist expellee) and Robert Aron, opened the Théâtre Alfred Jarry. He had also done some film acting – notably taking the role of Marat in Abel Gance's *Napoléon*. Asked whether he 'gave a damn' about the revolution, he snapped, 'I don't give a damn about the kind of revolution you mean,' and stalked out.[50] Then it was Aragon's turn. Breton reminded him that he had already pledged his loyalty to the Party's principles, even if he had not yet joined. 'I've been told', he continued pompously (of course this was something he knew perfectly well) 'that Aragon is continuing with literary activity: for instance, the publication of a six-volume work entitled *La Défense de l'infini*. Personally I can't quite see why. The passages I've read don't make me particularly desperate to see the rest.'

'The only published extracts have been in the *Révolution surréaliste*,' Aragon replied (which was not true). 'If there's any problem about publishing the book, then it won't be published. So there's no need to worry.'

What connection was there, Bernier asked, between Aragon's literary work and his revolutionary activity?

Aragon replied, 'I should say, it's a pastime relevant only to Surrealism.'

Breton concluded: 'What alarms me is the size of the project – six volumes, after all . . . It's got to interfere with the time you're free to devote to revolutionary activity.' The nature of this activity was not specified. These arguments continued throughout the following months, at the end of which Breton, Aragon, Eluard and a relative newcomer, Pierre Unik, officially joined the Party. (Péret was already a member.)

Party membership further encouraged Breton's impulse to control. A strict discipline was established among the Surrealists, and those who refused to submit were formally expelled – starting, in November 1926, with Soupault and Artaud, neither of whom was interested in political commitment. ('Today we have vomited up this vile dog,' wrote Breton of the unfortunate Artaud, in language violent even for him. 'We don't see why this stinking corpse . . . waits any longer to declare himself a Christian.')[51] The daily meetings at the Cyrano became more than ever ritualized:

> Those who failed to show up regularly for the meetings – and these took place every day – ended by being suspected of being lukewarm . . . A *good* Surrealist could not refuse the daily 'communion' . . . The excluded Surrealist could not fail to fall into an abyss of desolation because at the same time, he lost his friends, . . . Breton, and the gathering-places they frequented, and was forced into solitude, or into the mediocre games of the 'literary life'.[52]

In fact Aragon was often absent from the Cyrano, being almost permanently on tour with Nancy. During the first half of 1927, however, he remained in Paris, perhaps feeling the need to consolidate his position. And once again he found himself on the defensive. Drieu La Rochelle, writing about *Paysan de Paris*, regretted the politicization (and subsequent silence) of one who could produce such a resounding work of art. Whether this was the genuine regret of an old friend or mere mischief-making (probably a bit of both), the piece was deeply embarrassing for Aragon. Once more he was stigmatized as a *littérateur*, once more obliged to absolve himself from any such sin. He spent the summer writing *Traité du style*, a furious and dazzling analysis of his political and literary position (beginning with a disquisition on the verb *chier*: 'I shit on the French army in its entirety').

Traité du style was written at Varengeville in Normandy, where Aragon and Nancy spent that summer. Breton was staying nearby, in the Manoir d'Ango. He, too, was working on a book – the magical-autobiographical musings on love and chance which would become *Nadja*. Every evening, he and Aragon would meet at Pourville in the inevitable café to read their day's work to Nancy and each other.

This was not easy for Breton. His words came slowly – painfully so by comparison with Aragon's playful facility. Aragon 'set himself to write ten pages a day, and that was only about half an hour's work, if you could use the word work for those gymnastics, they were a game really'.[53] Faced with such fluency, Breton felt daunted. 'What Aragon is writing, what he reads to me nearly every day, stops me from writing very much of my own,' he confessed to Simone. 'It's so, so brilliant; you have no idea.'[54] His own production felt very flat by comparison, 'especially as storytelling isn't my strong suit'. The one consolation was that Aragon had confessed 'that by comparison with me, he feels he writes very hollowly'.[55]

Simone had not accompanied Breton to Normandy. They were drifting towards divorce. Breton had for some time been hopelessly and unsuccessfully in love with another woman, and, although Simone had no objection in principle, her husband's recent depression and bad temper had been more than she was prepared to put up with. He was the only guest at the Manoir. If he failed to write his new book, it would not be for lack of peace and quiet.

Aragon and Nancy were also having problems. Their relationship continued to deteriorate. But Aragon could not turn to his closest friend for comfort. For part of the trouble was that Breton was sleeping with Nancy.

André Breton, and *Nancy Cunard*! One would be hard-put to imagine a more ill-assorted pair than the earnest poet and the brittle heiress. The mere fact of such a coupling, and in such a situation, speaks of the mood of that Normandy summer. But there seems little doubt that it happened. Aragon, at least, was sure of it. Towards the end of his life he published an account of those days in which he hinted at this ultimate betrayal:

> And I can still hear, in that house with its cardboard walls where Nane [Nancy] and I were already beginning to ... quarrel, where I suddenly discovered jealousy ... I can still hear André laughing at the pages of the *Traité*, without knowing that that forced gaiety of mine already hid that of *Othello* which I was secretly reading and re-reading in the original English ...[56]

Another text refers to memories of a steamy summer night at Dieppe (near both Ango and Varengeville) with 'a window open onto the sea so as not to hear through the thin partitions the sighs, the heavy breath of love'.[57] And in yet another – this time a poem – Aragon finds himself all alone at Dieppe, on the day Sacco and Vanzetti were executed – a day when all good Communists were supposed to be out protesting. Unaccountably, no one else is there: his friend is absent. From which we may deduce, although Aragon never said it directly, that Breton and Nancy found more alluring ways to spend their time that day – thus replicating the scenario between Aragon, Drieu and Eyre de Lanux which had marked the beginning of the *Défense de l'infini*.

To whom should he turn in his despair? In the absence of his closest friend and his mistress, who were the problem, the obvious person was Aragon's long-standing confidante Denise Lévy. Denise was the cousin of Breton's wife Simone. They had met some years earlier, and Aragon had fallen fancifully in love. Denise, however, was married, and lived in Mulhouse, a long way from Paris. Safely unattainable, she became an idealized figure whom Aragon could love and trust. His letters to her are confessional and intimate. But now that avenue, too, suddenly closed.

The problem this time was Pierre Naville. Naville was a particular friend of Aragon's – one of the few ever to penetrate the Toucas family home at Neuilly. It had been arranged that he would visit Normandy from Paris to discuss the latest edition of *Révolution surréaliste* with Breton. But when he arrived, he was not alone. With him was Denise.

In principle, Aragon had been aware of this attachment. He had seen Denise's photograph at Naville's house as long ago as 1924. But that had been bearable: she was still married, still as available (or unavailable) as ever. Now, though, all that was changed. She and Naville were travelling together, a recognized couple; she had officially left her husband. There was no more hope for Aragon (for whom, during all these long years, she had *not* left her husband).

One by one, his sources of comfort were being cut off. And Denise's defection meant that even his final refuge – his real work, *La Défense de l'infini*, the work of his heart – was no longer available to him. Much of the book had been written with Denise in mind, was addressed to her, was set in the small town in eastern France (Commercy) where they had often met. How could he go on with it now? In a manuscript note, written in the margin of his account of the house with the 'cardboard walls', Aragon speaks of 'the other drama, the jolt to that monstrous manuscript at the end of 1927'.[58] The drama in question was Denise's defection to Naville, and the jolt proved terminal.

Despairing now, he took his novel apart. Its centre, *Le Con d'Irène* (*Irène's Cunt*), is a virtuoso piece, perhaps one of the most allusive, poetic – and unbridled – evocations of sex in the

French language. This Aragon now decided to publish on its own, botched into a more or less free-standing piece of transcendent pornography. As such it appeared, privately and under the counter, the following year. What remained was a shell. But he still carried it with him in a suitcase, a sort of talisman as he and Nancy set out on a wild chase across Spain.

Of what happened next Aragon never spoke in so many words, not at all until after Nancy's death, and not in any direct way until after Elsa Triolet's. His biographer Pierre Daix reconstructs the events from a long-lost poem and some late reminiscences.

The poem is 'Chant de la Puerta del Sol', written in (or about) Madrid, of which the Puerta del Sol is the central square. It recounts the burning of a manuscript in a hotel room:

> So I tore up four years of my life
> With my trembling hands With my knotted hard fingers
> On my knees dragging my legs bare feet
>
> Shut the window there's a bitter wind The leaves
> Will fly away . . .
> Four years four years' leaves piled up
> For the planned fire the flames soon
>
> She motionless staring Her beautiful hands
> Fingers raking her uncombed hair . . .
>
> Caesar the one you're going to kill salutes you
> Cries muted in the flying ash . . .

In fact evidence suggests that Nancy, far from standing by tearing her hair as implied here, succeeded in saving a considerable number of pages from the flames. In one of these pages, rescued after the war from the wreckage of her house in Normandy, Aragon describes the conscious departure he was making in *La Défense de l'infini*. 'I'm not following the rules of the novel or the rhythm of the poem. I'm writing and speaking as though Gustave Flaubert had never lived ... Marcel Proust bores me to death and M. Giraudoux is a rabbit's fart. As for the poets, if you'll forgive the expression, they spend their time buggering flies ... When I think of Honoré [de Balzac] I can understand why people like Paul Valéry and André Breton pour scorn on novels. But after all, I'm spitting in Balzac's face.'[59]

He had said he intended to re-invent the novel; and if anyone could have done so that person was Aragon, for whom words turned somersaults on command. 'Aragon's writing is as good as ever, but it's always rather inhuman,' wrote Breton to Simone from the Manoir d'Ango, referring to the gymnastics of *Traité du style*. In the same letter he remarked, 'It isn't just the human that you have to aim for, and that so few achieve, it's the essence of life.'[60] But in *La Défense de l'infini* – and above all in *Le Con d'Irène* – Aragon, uniquely, achieved precisely that. The writing has a fluidity, a spontaneity, an abandon, which he would never achieve again.

*

Some think *Le Con d'Irène* one of the great masterpieces of the French language.[61] What is indisputable is that the Aragon of that extraordinary fragment and the Breton of *Nadja* are opposite poles.

The central pages of *La Défense de l'infini* are devoted to a close-up description of Irène's orgasm:

> So tiny and so large! Here you are at home, man finally worthy of that name, here's the true measure of your desires. This is the place, bring your face close, already your gossiping tongue is loosened, this is the place of shady delights, this ardent patio, within its pearly borders, the lovely image of pessimism. O crack, sweet humid crack, dear vertiginous abyss ...[62]

If any passage in literature can be described as truly abandoned, it is surely this. The thought of Breton writing anything comparable is simply laughable. The policeman always sat so heavily upon his shoulder; try as he might for *dérèglement*, his intellect ruled his emotions with the iron fist he turned upon his Surrealist colleagues.

Ironically, never was this clearer than on the one occasion he broke free. The poem 'Union Libre' (Free Union'), written in May 1931, is an erotic celebration of his then mistress, Suzanne Muzard, and possibly the best poem he ever wrote.

> My wife whose buttocks are sandstone and asbestos
> Whose buttocks are the back of a swan and the spring
> My wife with the sex of an iris
> A mine and a platypus
> With the sex of an alga and old-fashioned candies
> My wife with the sex of a mirror
> My wife with eyes full of tears . . .

But having written it, he found himself in a terrible quandary regarding publication. For by now the policeman had returned, and he felt unusually and uncomfortably exposed. So he published it as a pamphlet, in a limited edition of seventy-five copies identifying neither author nor publisher, and showed a copy to Aragon and Eluard, claiming to have received it anonymously in the post. Eluard, entranced, wanted to run a classified ad to trace the author, but Aragon pulled Breton aside and asked if he took them for fools. 'You recognised me?' Breton said. 'No, but I recognised the woman,' Aragon replied.[63]

In *Nadja*, the work on which he was engaged at the Manoir d'Ango, the policeman was still fully in command. Even so, it has a freshness which saves it from being stifled beneath the weight of style and ideas, as is so often the case with Breton's work.

Nadja is not a novel, that forbidden breed. It is not a work of fiction: the events which it recounts all took place. However, it does have a plot. This follows Breton's encounter with a young woman, the eponymous Nadja. She catches his eye in the street one day; his glance is returned. He notes her almost incorporeal frailty, her curiously unfinished make-up; she is blonde, but her eyes are heavily ringed with kohl, like a film vamp's. He speaks to her 'without hesitation'; she responds, they sit together in a pavement café. In other words it is a quintessentially Surrealist chance encounter. They continue to meet. Nadja, it transpires, is quite without means or support; she lives from encounter to encounter. Breton shows her his work; it becomes clear that she is overwhelmed by this new acquaintance, so very different from her usual seedy pick-ups. She pretends to be, or is, clairvoyant: she 'sees' Breton's wife, small and dark. '*Tiens!* There's a dog with her. Perhaps a cat too, but somewhere else (true).' Against the background of Paris, their story continues. He runs into her when they had not arranged to meet, perhaps by coincidence. Another time she stands him up. They dine together: she predicts, correctly, that a particular window will light up, that it will be red. Max Ernst declines to paint her: the *voyante* he and Breton patronize, Mme Sacco, has seen him meeting a Nadja or Natacha whom he will not like and who will physically harm the woman he loves. Finally she and Breton spend the night together. He at once realizes things have gone too far, he must back off, she is becoming too dependent, she expects more from him than he can give her. She writes to him, she sends him her strange, sad drawings. All are reproduced in the book, along with photographs of Breton's Paris and paintings by his friends. She fades from his life. And some months later, he hears that she is confined in a mental hospital, where he does not visit her. The book ends with a phrase to become among the most famous in Surrealism: '*La beauté sera CONVUL-*

252

SIVE ou ne sera pas' ('Beauty will be CONVULSIVE or will not be'), with resonances of abandon, instantaneousness, of Mesmer's *convulsionnaires*, and, mockingly, of political pronouncements.

It is a strange and evocative tale. Chance and coincidence abound and dictate. It is, like all Breton's work, highly personalized, addressed to particular people, filled with his friends, his habits, the circumstantial framework of his life. It is about woman as muse – that constant theme of Surrealism: *l'amour fou*, all for love, man's destiny in woman. But it is not erotic. Nor, despite Breton's stated aims, is it particularly human. Humanity implies emotion, and there is little of that in *Nadja*. It observes rather than participates, thinks rather than feels. Breton, in short, is describing his own life – one in which abandonment was achieved only by suppressing, at enormous effort, the overweening superego. *Nadja* is juiceless where *Le Con d'Irène* brims over.

For Aragon, disoriented, in thrall to language, the signs led to eroticism, sexuality, and release in the unchained libido. For Breton, inhibited, intellectualizing, they pointed in the direction of the occult – coincidence, prophecy, clairvoyance and astrology. Each sought the direct route to the inner self, and each, in his own way, found it. An ideal, after all, is no less shared because it is tailored to fit personal compulsions. But this was something neither André Breton nor the commissars could ever accept; and the result was destruction.

Aragon's hotel room auto-da-fé resolved, if nothing else, the problem of his inclination to novel-writing. Like Breton four years earlier, like Duchamp and Rimbaud, desperation had led him to a sort of intellectual and artistic suicide. 'Those flames destroyed all possibility of writing novels IN ME for six years.'[64]

The romance with Nancy, however, was not quite finished. They returned to Normandy, where she was buying a house;

then, in 1928, voyaged through Italy. But the relationship had changed. Aragon's side of the bargain, his weighting in the scales, had been his intellectual prestige. Now that was finished – he was no longer writing poems, he had destroyed his novel. But he would at least pay his way. He sold a Braque, bought cheaply years before on the advice of Breton, and waited for the money to arrive.

In Venice, however, more misfortune awaited. Nancy fell for a black American jazz pianist, Henry Crowder, there on tour. Naturally she had to have him; at once. Why should that make any difference to Aragon? Simply, from now on there would be Henry too. *'Im Banden'*, laconically reads the post-card Aragon sent Denise (Madame Pierre Naville) from Man-tua on 9 August 1928: *with the group.* But he could not take things so lightly. He had none of Nancy's neurotic horror of fidelity. On the contrary, he could not survive without it.

And still he was dependent upon her: still his money had not arrived.

Some time later – perhaps in mid-September – he took an overdose of sleeping pills and lay down to die in his hotel room.

Perhaps he miscalculated the dose. Or perhaps, as he himself insisted, he was simply found too soon. At any rate, he was found, taken to hospital, and revived to face the unforgiving world. But in a sense he had succeeded. His youth, whose loss he had prematurely mourned in 1925, had now definitively evaporated. The carefree charmer, the glittering wizard of words, had vanished never to return. Between them, Breton and Nancy had finished him off.

*

In October, Aragon surfaced in Paris, and at once made for a house in the Rue du Château, near Montparnasse, belonging to his friend Duhamel (the one whose family owned the hotels ending in 'or'). This was a sort of Surrealist outstation, with a shifting population of young men and their girls of the moment. Jacques Prévert, Yves Tanguy, Raymond Queneau and Benjamin Péret all lived there at one time or another, mostly rent-free. At this moment the main residents were Georges Sadoul and André Thirion. The decor was triumphantly scandalous, the prize exhibit being a lavatory-chain whose handle was a crucifix stolen from a church. The residents particularly enjoyed the effect of this detail upon visiting family members. Breton rarely came there; despite his louche aspirations he found it hard to shed his formal manners, and felt uncomfortable in the presence of genuine sexual anarchy such as prevailed in the Rue du Château. His mistress, Suzanne Muzard, also preferred to keep away. Perhaps the memories it reawakened were too painful. When she and her friend, another Suzanne known (to distinguish her) as Suzanne-Hélène, had first arrived in Paris from the country, they had been forced to hold body and soul together by prostitution. They had gravitated to a brothel regularly visited by Drieu and Aragon, and had moved on from there to become habituées of the Rue du Château, house-girls in every sense of the word.[65] (Hence, presumably, Aragon's instant recognition of Suzanne in Breton's poem.) As a dazzling blonde, she was now living with Emmanuel Berl, from whom Breton was currently trying to woo her, with intermittent success. The intensity of his passion frightened her: she knew she could never reciprocate it, however much they might be physically attracted. Sadoul, when Aragon arrived, was hopelessly in love with Suzanne-Hélène (who rewarded his devotion with a dose of clap) but she did not return his affection and preferred to sleep with almost anyone else.

This clamorous atmosphere suited Aragon, who wanted anything but solitude. His money had finally come through, and he set himself to spend it as fast as possible. He, Thirion and Sadoul, all at that moment crossed in love, spent almost every night in the Montparnasse bars, the Dôme, the Coupole, the Rotonde. These were the haunts of the international crowd: Man Ray, now rather prosperous – 'he dazzled us all with his cars and his beautiful girls';[66] Kiki, still his *maîtresse en titre*, 'very blooming, very made-up, very low-cut, very sweet, very noisy';[67] the Japanese painter Foujita and his wife Youki, with whom Robert Desnos was about to fall in love; Clotilde and Laurence Vail, Aragon's friends from Giverny; the sculptor Brancusi; a colony of Russians centred around Ilya Ehrenburg, who would be one of the great survivors of the Stalin years . . . It was a milieu Breton hated, too smart, too self-consciously arty, too full of people he didn't want to meet, not conducive to mystery or chance. But it suited Aragon's brittle mood. He picked up another girl, foreign as always – a Viennese dancer called Lena Amsel. But she was a flirt with many admirers: clearly this, too, would end in tears.

And then Elsa appeared. She was with the Ehrenburg group, 'a small, red-haired woman, with a full bust and a milklike complexion . . . neither beautiful nor ugly; her face was serious and far from relaxed . . . A woman who could look men straight in the eye but didn't seem to pay them any particular attention.'[68]

Elsa was Russian, born Elsa Kagan, the daughter of a wealthy Jewish merchant in Moscow. Her family hated the racist Tsarist regime, and hoped for a democratic replacement – her elder sister Lily had married a Menshevik, Osip Brik, who later occupied various posts in the Bolshevik government. Lily also became the mistress of the famous and flamboyant Russian Futurist poet Vladimir Mayakovsky, a big, gentle, vigorous man, star of the post-revolutionary Agitprop days, whose journal, *LEF*, Brik edited. But those heady times were now drawing to an end. The brilliant Russian avant-garde was increasingly assailed by socialist-realist critics as Stalin, having seized power after Lenin's death, began to tighten the reins.

Elsa hated the Bolsheviks and had no taste for revolutionary disorder. She had met her husband, André Triolet, in Moscow during the early days of the revolution. He was wealthy and well-connected, and (like Jacques Vaché) had been assigned to the English army as an interpreter during the war. Disgusted by the incompetence of the Allied generals he joined the Allied mission to the new Russian government, but despite a certain sympathy for the Bolsheviks, he felt no temptation to remain in Moscow. He fell in love with Elsa and literally carried her away, across Siberia to Japan and thence to San Francisco, where they married. After demobilization they returned to France via Tahiti. But Triolet, whose motto was 'You can't spend more than three years with the same woman', was by then tired of Elsa, who, for her part, was happy to have reached France. They remained on excellent terms, though now separated: Triolet gave Elsa 3,000 francs a month. Meanwhile Lily and Mayakovsky found her a job as Paris correspondent for a Moscow newspaper. In the summer of 1925, she went back to Russia, where she remained until the following spring. She was not inclined to stay, but if she were to live in Paris, she would need a new man. It was clear, as soon as she set eyes upon him, that she had determined this must be Louis Aragon.

Aragon did not return her infatuation. She flirted; he resolutely failed to notice her. So she arranged an introduction. But this, too, misfired: with his Surrealist taste for mystery and distaste for the police, he assumed she must be a police spy – how else could she manage to maintain a foot so conveniently in both east and west? In any case he was preoccupied with Lena. However, Elsa refused to be discouraged. Aragon avoided her, but whenever Thirion or Sadoul appeared at the

Coupole she would call them over and sympathize with their misfortunes in her soft, steely voice, inviting them in their turn to sympathize with hers. This tactic soon began to pay off.

> At first, [Thirion remembered] I found her extremely pushy and indiscreet; she was almost impossible to shake off and I didn't like the perfume she wore. Little by little, though, I began to find her charming and appealing. I was often alone in the Coupole for hours on end ... waiting for Sadoul or Aragon to come so that I would have the heart to go home to bed – and she and I had long conversations. By repeating our talks to Aragon, I became part of her plans. The possible spy gradually gave way to a woman who was madly in love and had vowed to get her man.[69]

She soon had her opportunity. That November Mayakovsky visited Paris. He was following a new girlfriend, who hated life in Soviet Russia even more than she loved Mayakovsky. She fled to France; he did not succeed in persuading her back. Asked what he would write when he returned to Russia, he replied with sad irony, 'I'll go where the Party sends me. I'll receive my assignments from the Guild of Proletarian Writers.'[70] Two years later, in 1930, unable to work as he wished, unhappy in love, threatened by the authorities who were beginning to expel and deport his friends, forbidden to leave Russia, he would commit suicide.

But that was still in the future. In 1928, Mayakovsky was the hero of the hour. Aragon, who like all the Surrealists wanted to meet him, decided to throw a party at the Rue du Château. So Elsa must be invited; and with her usual vigour and determination she made the most of her opportunity. Following Aragon into a quiet corner, she threw him onto a conveniently situated sofa and made love to him. 'Neither party was disappointed,' Thirion observed.[71]

Nevertheless, things were not yet quite settled. For another month Aragon refused to choose between Lena and Elsa. The day of reckoning, however, could not be indefinitely postponed. One evening Aragon and Lena entered a nightclub called Le Jungle to find an anguished Elsa awaiting them. Aragon, appalled, abandoned both women and ran back to the Rue du Château, where he took refuge in drink. Some time later they arrived together, apparently on the most cordial terms. 'It was a misunderstanding,' Elsa announced. 'Lena now realises I love you and that my feelings for you have nothing to do with what she's looking for and what she feels. She also knows you love me; she didn't know it before.'[72] Lena left; Elsa stayed.

That was it. Elsa Triolet had entered Aragon's life, never to leave it. For a while they continued at the Rue du Château, but that soon palled: there was no hot water and no privacy. Aragon had meanwhile rented a large studio on Rue Campagne-Première, in the same block as Man Ray. Elsa insisted they move there together. Once installed, she systematically disconnected him from his many girlfriends. In particular, all mention of Nancy Cunard was forbidden. But while she soon succeeded in organizing Aragon's life vis-à-vis other women, making sure they felt thoroughly unwelcome in Rue Campagne-Première, she was unable, at least for the present, to detach him from his male Surrealist friends. If she was his emotional life, they were everything else: he could not do without either.

Aragon did not rebel. In Elsa he had found what he needed. Aragon, for all his gifts, was weak; Elsa was strong. She had her talents, but they were chiefly organizational. She had long since realized that the most important step in obtaining your heart's desire is to know what it is. After that, all you need is determination. She would be not just his wife, but his enabler. In return he would provide her with the life she desired. She would even, on his back, ride to literary fame in her own right.

At long last Aragon had a family, a strong woman who would accept him for what he was, on whom he could rely utterly, with whom there need be no more pretence. She was his, for ever. And from now on, he would be hers.

*

Although Breton, Péret, Aragon, Eluard and Unik were now members of the Communist Party, they were very far from being wholeheartedly accepted. Breton in particular was regarded with the deepest suspicion. From time to time he would be summoned before a committee of inquiry. These took place very early in the morning, in a school hall or trade union office.

> These committees consisted of three members, always unknown to me, introduced by their first names only. They were usually foreign, with a very poor command of French. It was more like a police interrogation than anything else. Sometimes they went on into the afternoon, with a very short time allowed for lunch. It didn't take long to explain things satisfactorily, but there always came a moment when one of the interrogators brought out a number of the *Révolution Surréaliste* and we started all over again. Looking back, the funniest thing – if you can call it that – was that some of the illustrations made them speechless with rage, especially the Picasso reproductions. They couldn't find anything sarcastic enough to say about them: how was one supposed to look at them, could I tell them exactly what it was 'meant to be' ... In the end they always endorsed my membership, but then for some reason a new committee would set itself up to examine me and the magazine ... would be carpeted again ...[73]

Meanwhile he was attached to a cell of gas industry workers, who asked him to make a report on the situation in Italy, concentrating on statistics '*and above all no ideology.* I just could not do it.'[74] It was possible that, as one observer put it, 'the good gas workers, having for once an "intellectual" in their midst, certainly must have believed they were doing the right thing by charging him with an intellectual task'.[75] Breton, however, saw only another example of malign manoeuvring, another put-down for the useless intellectual.

He became extremely depressed, the more so because his domestic life was a mess. Between Simone and Suzanne he never knew who or what he might expect to find at Rue Fontaine. At Suzanne's insistence he had asked Simone for the divorce which had been so long pending. Simone had left – she was now living with Max Morise – but continued to use the Rue Fontaine apartment from time to time, occasionally removing objects and papers she regarded as hers. Suzanne, moving in, marked *her* territorial rights by rearranging furniture and pictures and removing some of Breton's manuscripts altogether. Once, when Suzanne and Breton had been away for a week's holiday, they returned to find that Simone had changed all the locks. Breton, fuming, had to take a room at the nearby Terrass Hotel until the situation was sorted out. But Suzanne would not agree to commit herself to Breton, and on 1 December 1928, announced that she had married her old boyfriend, Emmanuel Berl.[76] His divorce had come through first, and she was concerned with security, not sentiment. Amid the confusion, Breton wrote Eluard gloomy letters on the futility of life. 'Less and less exchange of ideas or conversations worth having. Endless games. The phonograph. What's the use of it all.' 'Don't even ask what I'm doing, whatever you guess is more than the reality.'[77] 'What sort of hope do you place in love?' enquired the 1929 number of *Révolution surréaliste*. 'How do you picture the passage from the *idea of love* to the *reality of loving*? Would you, willingly or unwillingly, sacrifice your freedom for love? Have you ever done so? ... Do you believe in the victory of love's glory over the sordidness of life, or in the victory of the sordidness over love's glory?' If only he knew the answers! The title page of the magazine sported the lipstick mouth-prints of Suzanne, Elsa, Gala Eluard, Jeannette Tanguy and Marie-Berthe Ernst.

Chaos reigned, and Breton's reaction was a savage tidying-up and reassertion of control in those areas where this was possible. The daily meetings at the café of the moment – still generally the Cyrano – were increasingly formalized and severe. Extremely good excuses had to be found for non-attendance, and more than one acolyte approached the cocktail hour with trepidation. Potential recruits were subjected to a polite but merciless grilling before being accepted – or dismissed. There was even a hierarchy of acceptable drinks: at the top, anise-based absinthe-substitutes such as Pernod and Ricard; then sinister black mandarin-curaçao and Picon-*citron*; at the bottom, beer and Aragon's favourite Noilly-Prat vermouth. Burgundy might also sometimes be drunk, should Breton happen to feel like it.[78] When he arrived, the waiters hurried to fetch the green colouring with which he liked to tint his drinks (not, presumably, the Burgundy).

But these were details. Matters of substance were more problematic. Abandoning his emotional life as a lost cause, Breton decided that the question of Party membership and co-operation between accredited members and fellow-travellers must now be sorted out once for all, along with the question of Surrealist loyalties.

On 12 February 1929, Breton and Aragon sent out a joint letter to seventy-six persons. These included Surrealists old and new, even such expellees as Artaud and Vitrac (though not Soupault); old Dada friends such as Tzara, Picabia and Ribemont-Dessaignes; the *Clarté* group; another group named L'Esprit; Georges Bataille whose magazine *Documents* had recently been publishing the work of several ex- and semi-detached Surrealists; and a group of young poets who had been hanging around the Surrealist fringes calling themselves *Le Grand Jeu* (and publishing a magazine of that name). Did they think, the letter asked, that activity ought to be limited to an individual level? If so, would they like to explain, briefly, why? If not, what communal activity should be undertaken, of what sort, and with whom?

From the replies, Breton set about weeding out undesirables. Out went Artaud (again), Michel Leiris, Bataille ('too many idealist assholes,' he had replied), Desnos ('all literary or artistic activity is a waste of time'), Vitrac and Jacques Baron. The rest – fifty-seven of them – were invited to the Bar du Château, across the street from Duhamel's house, on 11 March, ostensibly to discuss Leon Trotsky's recent forced exile from Russia. But Thirion, for one, recognized that this was merely a pretext. He thought the meeting was designed to force a break with the *Grand Jeu* group, by whom Breton felt threatened – they were too uncontrollable and presented too much potential competition. And indeed the meeting centred upon two recent escapades by members of the group. One concerned a violently anti-militaristic petition recently signed by students of the elite Ecole Normale Supérieure, obtained by a member of the group named Gilbert-Lecomte and promised to Aragon for possible publication. But at the last minute Gilbert-Lecomte had got cold feet and destroyed the document. The other concerned an article published by Roger Vailland, another *Grand Jeu* member, at that time working as a stringer for a number of Paris newspapers. This was suspect in itself, but Vailland had stepped beyond the pale by describing the extremely repressive and right-wing Paris police chief, Jean Chiappe, as 'the purifier of our capital'. Chiappe was bent on suppressing anything he disliked, from excessive noise to immigrants and suspicious foreign films, though he was notoriously corrupt and open to a well-placed bribe. Everyone knew that he was just waiting for a pretext to descend upon the Surrealists. Vailland's piece could not have been more ill-judged.

On the appointed day, after a reading of the responses to the 12 February letter, with comments, Breton announced that, since the views expressed were so divergent, it would be useless to raise the Trotsky question at that particular moment. With that he moved the meeting on to consider the questions of Vailland and Gilbert-Lecomte. He played with Gilbert-Lecomte, first getting him to agree that he had behaved badly, then turning the meeting against the entire *Grand Jeu* group, then trying to create a split between Gilbert-Lecomte, Vailland and their erstwhile friends. At this point Ribemont-Dessaignes leapt to his feet, accused Breton and Aragon of acting like 'court justices' and stormed out. Amid continuing uproar the *Grand Jeu* group found themselves outmanoeuvred on all fronts, made fools of and reduced to impotence by Breton's remorseless logic. Next day, Ribemont-Dessaignes sent Breton a furious letter. 'So this is where all your collective inclinations lead: judgement, judgement, judgement – and what judgement! Your revolutionary action: a clean-out of people. And have you really ever done anything else? When has any collective venture led to anything but personal problems and schoolboy bullying? When are you going to stop loyalty-testing everyone who's close to you? ... Arrogance, that's your problem, Breton.'[79]

If Breton had wanted a clean-out, the Bar du Château meeting certainly achieved it. Even some of those who had not initially been against what he was proposing now drew away from him, sickened by his bullying tactics. These included Desnos, Michel Leiris and Raymond Queneau (whose OUL-IPO group, though retaining Surrealist enthusiasms such as Raymond Roussel, would be notably unjudgemental, and devoted to extreme formalism: all those things Breton was *not*). Such was Breton's fatal attraction, however, that even under these circumstances Leiris experienced withdrawal symptoms after their break, suffering a period of alcoholism before undergoing psychoanalysis and then escaping on an expedition to the Sahara, during which he had a wet dream in which he and Breton were reconciled.[80]

Breton now set about formalizing the current state of affairs in his *Second Manifeste du surréalisme*, published in the only *Révolution surréaliste* to appear that year. It reflected Surrealism's maturity, but also his current dark and savage mood. Where four years earlier the first manifesto had been filled with a brilliant enthusiasm, this one began as it was to continue: in fury. In a despairing and nihilistic sentence which has remained notorious ever since, Breton defined the 'simplest Surrealist act'. '[It] consists of going into the street, revolver in hand, and shooting at random into the crowd for as long as you can.'[81] He went on to distance Surrealism from its ancestors, Rimbaud, Sade, Baudelaire, Poe – 'what, after all, is more sterile than this perpetual interrogation of the dead?'[82] In his current mood even his greatest heroes lost their lustre. Rimbaud was chided for his deathbed conversion to Catholicism, Sade accused of counter-revolutionary acts, Baudelaire had been caught praying, Poe was no more than a detective-story writer. Only Lautréamont remained untainted – saved, like Vaché, by an early death. Among living ex-heroes, Desnos had capped his list of transgressions (journalism, cheap gossip, stagnation) by opening a nightclub impertinently named Maldoror (after Lautréamont's *Chants* of that name); Duchamp had abdicated into chess. 'Artaud, Delteil, Francis Gérard, Limbour, Masson, Soupault, Vitrac. This time it's official, each one drowned, with some scurrilous justification hung round his neck like a stone. The politicals, liquidated ... Desnos, liquidated, all those who flirted with Surrealism without actually belonging – Picabia, Duchamp, Georges Bataille, [Ribemont-Dessaignes] liquidated. Only Tristan Tzara escaped the mass drowning.'[83] (This was not quite true. Still pursuing the divide and rule tactics of the Bar du Château, Breton also made a point of praising René Daumal, one of the *Grand Jeu* group, whom he admired and wanted to attract into Surrealism.)

The way forward led along the twin tracks of Communism and the occult. Breton demanded a *'PROFOUND AND TRUE OCCULTATION OF SURREALISM'*,[84] mentioning in this connection the 'Metapsychics' of Charles Richet (recently the perpetrator of a series of bizarre spiritualist experiments in Algiers)[85] and such *illuminati* as Nicolas Flamel and Alphonse Rabbe. As for Communism, he reiterated Surrealism's special role: 'I really can't see, with all respect to some narrow-minded revolutionaries, why we should refrain from raising [under a common revolutionary banner] ... the problems of love, dreams, madness, art and religion.'

It was hardly to be expected that such wholesale anathemas would go unanswered, and they did not. Ribemont-Dessaignes, Jacques Prévert, Raymond Queneau, Roger Vitrac, Max Morise, Jacques Baron, Michel Leiris, J. A. Boiffard, Robert Desnos, Alejo Carpentier and Georges Bataille produced an insulting tract entitled (with echoes of 1924) *Un Cadavre*. But this time the corpse was not the dead Anatole France but the living André Breton. On the first page he appeared crowned with thorns, and a series of accusations and insulting verses followed. Morise declared that if Breton should suddenly acquire a taste for *'pieds de mouton sauce poulette*, you would suddenly see them consecrated revolutionaries ... How could the revolutionary opinions of a Breton be anything other than a joke?' Prévert: 'He could not play without cheating, and cheated quite badly, what's more, and kept billiard balls hidden in his sleeves; when they fell to the ground with a disagreeable sound before his embarrassed disciples, he said that was humour ...' and so on.

These sallies, though hardly unjustified, left Breton more depressed than ever. To add to his woes Suzanne, currently at the Breton end of her Breton/Berl/Breton pendulum swing, was nervy and unwell. (The situation eventually became impossible for her as well as the two men. She solved the problem by running away to Tahiti with a taxi-driver.)[86] Eluard succeeded in dragging him out to the Luna-Park fun-fair, where they spent two happy hours on the bumper-cars, but this provided only a temporary respite.[87] He published a new edition of the second manifesto listing in two columns – *before* and *after* – previous extravagant expressions of admiration from the *Cadavre*'s authors set opposite their current insults. But this was not really much of a reply, and the unpleasant taste remained. Years later he reflected apropos his savage attacks on Desnos and Artaud that 'those who were worst treated were those from whom Surrealism had expected most'. As ever, the seemingly impossible standard by which he measured others was no more than he expected of himself. 'At all costs our *marching wing* had to avoid getting bogged down in the problems of individual life.'[88]

*

Elsa, as her lipstick kiss implied, was still at this point trying to draw nearer to the Surrealists. The choice was simple: either Aragon's friends must become hers or she must pull him away to more congenial circles. At the moment both possibilities remained open. In 1929, she and Aragon travelled to Berlin to meet her sister Lily and Osip Brik, whom he did not yet know, and also Mayakovsky, who was staying there with them for a while. Elsa still felt more Russian than French, and it would help her standing in Russia if Aragon could be made the official French interpreter of Soviet literary initiatives. Lily and Brik were still in Berlin when, on 14 April 1930, they heard the terrible news of Mayakovsky's suicide. As he himself had said, 'In this life it is not difficult to die,/It is more difficult to live.'

In retrospect, it seems clear that what finally made the difficult impossible was a combination of unrequited love and Stalin's ever-tightening censorship and control. But the Surrealists knew nothing of this: instead they blamed individual feuds and cabals of the sort rife among themselves. Their faith in Stalin's Communism still retained its new-minted lustre. They had just begun a new magazine, *Surréalisme au service de la révolution* (*SASDLR*), whose first issue opened with a significant exchange of telegrams between the International Revolutionary Bureau and the Surrealists concerning the anti-Soviet war which everyone believed imminent:

> International Revolutionary Bureau requests reply following question what would be your position if imperialism declares war on Soviets

To which Breton and Aragon replied:

> Comrades if imperialism declares war on Soviets our position will conform directives Third International to French Communist Party
>
> If you feel can use us better in such a situation we are at your disposal for mission needing us in intellectual role Stop To submit suggestions would be to presume upon our role and circumstances
>
> In situation of armed conflict useless to wait before putting our particular talents at service of Revolution

This declaration, evidently intended to prove the Surrealists' revolutionary credentials beyond a peradventure, went much further in its unconditional commitment than any comparable group in France. But in the increasingly paranoid context of Soviet political manoeuvring mere good faith (as so many were fatally to discover) was not enough.

Mayakovsky, for one, had already made this discovery. In the same issue of *SASDLR* Breton made a passionate defence of the dead poet under the title 'The ship of love has foundered against the current of life' (a line from one of Mayakovsky's poems referring to his rejection by Veronica Polonskaya, who had refused to divorce her husband in order to marry him). Breton vehemently identified with Mayakovsky: clearly they had encountered the same dilemmas. 'Mayakovsky's suicide ... points up the problem, inescapable for even the best of men, of the relationship between his commitment ... to a just *cause* – specifically, here, the revolutionary cause – and the fate life has in store for him as an individual ... To love or not to love, that is the question.' He took issue with those who 'had tried to exploit the suicide of Mayakovsky at our expense and generally at the expense of all those who, with Mayakovsky, proclaim the absolute inanity of literature that pretends to be proletarian. Again we say, show us a real work of "proletarian art". More than ever, with Mayakovsky dead, we refuse to weaken. We shall not abandon the spiritual and moral position that he took ... On this, we shall make no concessions.'[89] A sentiment which was unlikely to endear him to the commissars, who had by now (10 January 1928) expelled Breton's hero Trotsky from the Party, along with thirty of his followers, and who were in no mood to encourage either independence of mind or Trotskyism.

Elsa, familiar as the French comrades were not with current Soviet machinations, could see the danger of such naïve pronouncements both for Surrealist hopes of admittance into Communist good graces and (more immediately) for her sister, who was after all associated with the group through Elsa and Aragon. Lily had now returned to Moscow, and Elsa desperately wanted to visit her there in her terrible grief (made worse by the fact that it was not for Lily that Mayakovsky had killed himself). But how was this to be arranged? Triolet's subventions had now ceased, and she and Aragon were broke – so much so that she was reduced to making necklaces for the Paris couture houses. She showed a considerable flair; Worth, Molyneux, Chanel, Schiaparelli, all used Elsa's creations in their collections. After the shows Aragon fitted up a commercial traveller's case and hawked the necklaces around the jewellery shops of the Rue de Rivoli with considerable aplomb and success – which his friends found slightly shocking.[90]

At this point a congress of revolutionary writers was announced, to take place that autumn in Kharkov. It was organized by the same International Bureau which had telegraphed Breton in the spring. Elsa saw an opportunity not to be missed. Could not Aragon attend it as a Surrealist delegate? André Thirion decided to organize this, together with a second ticket for his friend Georges Sadoul, threatened with three months' imprisonment for a stupid letter of incitement to mutiny he had written to a cadet at Saint-Cyr, the French military academy. This visit was to have dire consequences, unforeseen by all except (in Breton's opinion) Elsa. 'She demanded and got everything she wanted,' he said.[91]

The changes that took place during the course of the visit, particularly within Aragon, were apparent almost from the start. One of his recent literary commissions had been to write an (anonymous) introduction to Apollinaire's sprightly pornographic fantasy *Les Onze mille verges*. He had been in the habit of giving nightly readings from this at the Rue du Château, striding up and down as he declaimed (just the kind of thing Elsa wished to discontinue). Now he asked Thirion to send ('by registered post, remember') a couple of comparable volumes from his bookcase, *Maisons de société* and *Le Marseille curieux*. In the next breath he wrote: 'Don't put jokes in your letters, I wouldn't get them, my wits are slowing down. I'm having a lot of trouble expressing myself.'[92]

Aragon, slow-witted? It was hardly credible. But these were nothing less than birth-pangs and death-throes, simultaneously experienced. Aragon – the old Aragon, witty and irreverent – could have no place in Stalin's party. He must be disposed of. Meanwhile the altogether different person who would take his place – the loyal Party mouthpiece – was being born. It was enough to render even Aragon temporarily speechless.

It seems clear that he stepped into a trap almost as soon as he arrived in Russia. One of the puzzling aspects of the visit was the signature, by both Aragon and Sadoul, of an abject paper of 'self-criticism' in which they enumerated previous literary and political mistakes and promised not to repeat them. In the opinion of Pierre Daix, Aragon's biographer, it was 'almost certainly written by a French hand, using French information, that is, the result of an exchange of views on the issue between the French Party and the Soviets'.[93] It certainly showed a circumstantial knowledge of the Paris left-wing literary scene. 'As Party members,' it began, 'we recognise that we should have asked the Party to regulate our literary activity ... This error is the ultimate cause of the mistakes we have made and those with which we have associated ourselves.' The former consisted mainly of failing adequately to support the Party and its members. As to the latter, the texts in question were Surrealist in general and the second manifesto in particular, its idealism, its Freudianism, its Trotskyism ... From all this Aragon and Sadoul promised to dissociate themselves. 'Our one desire', it concluded, 'is to work as effectively as possible following Party instructions. We promise to submit our literary activity to Party discipline and control.'[94]

This document, the source of enormous subsequent controversy and embarrassment, was dated 1 December 1930, just before their departure from Russia. But recent research[95] indicates that in fact it was signed by Aragon and Sadoul at the very start of their visit, and as a condition of their being allowed to attend the congress. They could not refuse, because this would have compromised not only their own positions but those of Elsa and Lily. It was a classic trap; they could not have escaped it even had they wanted to.

But did they want to? To Aragon, at least, this loyalty test was perhaps not entirely unwelcome. Finally – with Elsa, in the bosom of the Party – he might find the identity for which he had searched all his life. In that sense offending the Surrealists was unpleasant, but not fatal. It *had already been* fatal: that Aragon had already died, in a hotel room near the Puerta del Sol. Now new prospects opened. And if he could not prove his loyalty to the Party, where would he be? Back in limbo. No doubt he felt he could talk himself out of his difficulty vis-à-vis Breton when the time came.

Meanwhile he and Sadoul set off for Kharkov, where it was soon apparent that they were more than mere observers. They spoke as representatives of France, for the Surrealists – and against their old adversary from *Clarté*, Henri Barbusse, who was also at Kharkov representing his new periodical *Monde* and determined to take control (and be seen to take control) of the French left-wing literary scene: a scenario which Aragon was determined to prevent. Much time and energy was spent in these manoeuvres – which failed: in the end Barbusse, not Breton, was given control of the French revolutionary writers' association. At the time, however, it looked as though Aragon had won. The conference gave him an unaccustomed sense of empowerment. He even felt free to make position statements in the name of Surrealism, going so far as to declare that revolutionary literature 'cannot have any other purpose than systematic preparation for the speedy establishment of the proletarian dictatorship'.[96] 'What ideological rubbish did he think he was pulling off at Kharkov?' furiously demanded the horrified Surrealists when, later, the extent of Aragon's indiscretions became clear.[97]

But Kharkov could be nothing more than an interval. The conference ended, and the two had to return to Paris to face the consequences of their actions. 'I can still see Sadoul's terrified expression when he got back, and the embarrassment he felt at my questions,' Breton said.[98] Breton told Aragon he proposed to publish the shameful document of renunciation, at which Aragon threatened to kill himself, evidently hoping (as Eluard coldly saw it) that this 'sentimental blackmail' might substitute for good faith. 'That's when I felt it was all over with Aragon,' said Eluard.[99] The Surrealists were now split into two factions, poets and politicals, and Eluard, leader of the poets, felt very bitter about Aragon.

Even now, however, the bridges were not quite burned. Breton had too much invested in Aragon – and vice-versa. If they could avoid a break, they would. 'I need you so much to help me get my ideas in order, such as they are,' Aragon wrote in the third issue of *SASDLR*. His article was entitled 'Surrealism and the Revolutionary Future', but much of it read more like a personal plea to Breton. '. . . Isn't it natural that I should turn to you, that I should ask your help, you who have set out the problems that concern me most, for a scientific adaptation of this method [dialectical materialism]. That's what we call Surrealism, a way of knowing the *real* mechanism of thought, the *real* links between expression and thought, and the actual relations between thought as it is expressed and the world it really affects.'

Desperate to reconcile the two warring factions, to reunite their political and intellectual identities, Aragon and Sadoul issued a manifesto, *To the Revolutionary Intellectuals*, justifying themselves and apologizing to the Surrealists. 'Surrealism implies the adherence, totally and without reservations, to the principle of dialectical materialism,' it announced hopefully. 'In the hands of the Surrealists, the psychoanalytic method is a weapon against the bourgeoisie . . . Also, none of them has the slightest connection with Trotskyism and it is insulting . . . to interpret certain phrases of André Breton to mean that he has ever taken the part of Trotsky against the International.'[100] But despite all these efforts, the writing was on the wall. Aragon could not help being aware of 'the extraordinary reduction of common ground' between himself and his Surrealist colleagues.[101] To add to his other uncertainties, his father/grandfather was dying. His mother/sister, called in to help look after him ('It saved the cost of a nurse'),[102] asked Aragon to visit. He did so, and found the old man protesting his lifelong atheism and vainly rejecting the Christian obsequies which inevitably awaited him (he was buried with a crucifix on his breast).

It would be another forty years before Aragon could speak of any of this; before, many would say, he found his voice again. Meanwhile he began a novel, part polemic, part fantasy, in the glittering inhuman manner of *Traité du style*, and gave a reading at Breton's apartment. But Breton was unenthusiastic. He could not see that it added anything at all to Aragon's existing work; he saw no point in publishing. Aragon abandoned it, and it was never heard of again.

Nor was all smooth on the Communist front where, in spite of everything, the Surrealists remained suspect. In December 1930, the PCF (French Communist Party) announced the creation of an Association of Revolutionary Writers and Artists. Breton had long been trying to organize such an association: now it existed, similar in every detail to what he had planned, except that only Party members would be able to belong – which at this particular moment ruled him out. Breton was outraged. 'It's only too obvious what this is about. We must know at once what Alexandre, Aragon, Sadoul and Unik think. Will they agree to leave us waiting at the door? Will they accept the depressing little jobs they'll be given under these conditions? I think we should demand to enter ... the Association of Revolutionary Writers.'[103] 'So that's where we are after all the ridiculous manoeuvrings of the past months,' he commented bitterly to Eluard. '...For this we've thrown Freud, Trotsky and the rest onto the rubbish-heap.'[104]

It was at this point that, at the request of Breton and Eluard, Aragon wrote his article in *SASDLR*, 'Surrealism and the Revolutionary Future'. They wanted him to define his position. But he could only reaffirm its ambiguity. 'And the future of the Surrealists ... is it possible to think it different from my own? My friends, it makes me sad – sadder than I like to admit – when I think of ... all those who want to separate me from you. It's true that I have been asked again and again to distance myself from you. It is equally certain that, indirectly ... the same people have also asked you to believe that it's already happened, that they've succeeded in separating us. Apparently this is all because I took a trip.' This was of course disingenuous in the highest degree: the 'trip' – to Kharkov – had hardly been a mere sightseeing tour. But Aragon would always remain wonderfully unclear on the subject of Kharkov. It was as though the ambivalence of his position simply prevented him from formulating any thoughts on this subject. In the same article he wrote, 'Towards the end of 1930, as everyone knows, Georges Sadoul and I were in Russia. We wanted to be there more than anywhere else, much more. That's all I have to say about the reasons for our journey.'

It was at the end of this year, 1931, that Aragon wrote his enormous poem 'Front Rouge', 'that poem which I hate'.[105]

The old Aragon, the pre-Kharkov Aragon, would hardly have recognized 'Front Rouge' as a poem at all:

Bring down the cops
Comrades
Bring down the cops
Further further to the west the homes
Of rich children and expensive whores . . .
Fire on Leon Blum
Fire on Boncourt Frossard Déat
Fire on the trained bears of social-democracy . . .

Unemployment is no longer known here
The sound of the hammer the sound of the sickle
rise from the land is it
the sickle is it
the hammer the air is full of crickets
corn-crakes and caresses
USSR
Shots Whiplashes Shouts
Heroic youth
Steelworks cereals SSSR SSSR . . .

'Front Rouge' was published at the end of 1931 in *Literature of the World Revolution*, a review published in Moscow under the direction of Barbusse, where hardly anyone noticed it. It was then reprinted in Aragon's next collection, published by Surrealist Editions, *Persécuté persécuteur*. After this had been on sale several months the French police seized the remaining copies, and in January 1932, indicted Aragon on two charges: incitement to murder and provoking insubordination in the army. If he were convicted, he might have to serve five years in jail.

The Surrealists at once leapt to his defence, even though relations between Breton and Aragon, and between the Surrealists and the Party, were at this point muddier than ever. The French Communist newspaper *L'Humanité* had just published an article condemning Surrealism as the ultimate in 'art for art's sake' absurdity. Breton wrote Aragon a stern letter:

I've had enough of these ridiculous games. I'm sure you recognise that these last few months I've refrained from doing anything in public that might embarrass you personally ... But I can't lend myself, even by staying silent, to the destruction of everything I hold honest, revolutionary and *true*. I hope we shall still be able to agree and fight this evil together. If you don't think this is possible, please let me know at once and give me back my liberty. Affectionately yours.[106]

Nevertheless, he persisted with Aragon's defence. He published a tract, *l'Affaire Aragon*, but this made little impact. So he turned to and wrote a pamphlet, *Misère de la poésie*, published in March 1932.

It was not an easy task. Once more stern principle compelled him to override his personal feelings – not, this time, to turn his back on a friend, but on the contrary to defend, only because a friend had written it, a piece of work he despised. Breton did not personally like 'Front Rouge'. Poetically it was a step back from automatism to 'controlled thought'. It was a *poème de circonstance*, occasional verse, referring to particular incidents and moments. 'So I'm compelled to consider it ... not as an acceptable solution to the problem of poetry but as an exercise on its own, captivating maybe but leading nowhere.'[107] He therefore organized the defence along two more general lines: philosophical, in which the Surrealist position regarding poetry is defined, and polemical, attacking various targets such as Gide and Barbusse's associate Romain Rolland, not forgetting to take several sideswipes along the way at *L'Humanité* and various other objects of displeasure such as the newly established Association of Revolutionary Writers and Artists. This was published alongside more than three hundred signatures garnered from among Surrealism's supporters worldwide (including the French section of the International Red Cross). There were also a number of attached texts: the poem itself; a letter of non-support from Rolland; a letter of application from Breton to the organizer of the AEAR; an especially ghastly example of proletarian literature; and a dialogue between René Crevel and André Gide in which '*André Gide nous parle de "l'Affaire Aragon"*' – explaining at great length why he can't add his signature:

GIDE:	I've been talking to some people about Aragon. Nothing's going to happen.
CREVEL:	He's been summoned before the examining magistrate.
GIDE:	Yes, but I've been to the Ministry of Justice and they don't want to pursue it. Interior's decided to retract its complaint. It's true that with the cabinet changes . . . But the new cabinet will be more left-leaning. Anyway, why should literature go scot-free? When I published *Corydon* I was prepared to go to prison. Thoughts are just as dangerous as actions. We are the dangerous ones. It's an honour to be condemned by a regime like this . . .[108]

Misère de la poésie was still in proof when the fourth number of *SASDLR* appeared. This contained, amongst other things, a text by Salvador Dalí entitled *Rêverie*, featuring an eleven-year-old girl called Dulita. As often with Dalí it was pornographic in the highest degree, a meticulously realized masturbatory fantasy in which he detailed the steps which would culminate in his sodomizing Dulita on the shitty straw of a stable floor (shit and masturbation being his two constant obsessions). It might have been especially designed to horrify the puritanical Party.

Aragon, anxious not to complicate the political situation any further at such a delicate moment, urged Breton not to publish *Rêverie*. But Breton refused to listen. Instead he mounted his high horse. How dared Aragon take such a line? Had he not (as Eluard pointed out) privately published three pornographic books of his own? So saying, Breton printed Dalí's text. And the Party reacted just as Aragon had feared. The four Surrealists who were also Party members – Aragon, Pierre Unik, Sadoul and Maxime Alexandre – were summoned to explain themselves.

It was an unpleasant experience. Before the interrogation began, they were left to sweat for a very long time while nobody took any notice of them – a hackneyed but nonetheless effective tactic. And the questioning which followed was so hostile that they could barely get a word in. Afterwards Aragon went to Breton and recounted all that had been said. Breton was particularly enraged by the phrase, 'all you're trying to do . . . is complicate simple, healthy relations between men and women'. 'As though', he commented later, 'in a bourgeois society those relations were ever healthy or simple!'[109]

It is indeed a deeply discomfiting phrase, and not just because it is moronic. More worrying is the whiff of compulsory lunacy, a sort of trial by ordeal. To accept such a phrase implies the acceptance of a mad and unreal world. Why, then, did these brilliant men subject themselves to such humiliation? For they all did it. Breton as well as Aragon endured and accepted his fill of such rebukes – for example, during his regular carpetings over the subversive content of the *Révolution surréaliste*. On other occasions, of course, he played the interrogator, administering rather than suffering the third degree. And although his demands and decrees might be less stupid, the difference was cosmetic rather than intrinsic. Breton might be a poet, but he had the spirit of a commissar. It was a fundamental contradiction, central to both his achievement and his tragedy.

A commissar, or perhaps an inquisitor: Breton is often

referred to as the Pope of Surrealism. The sobriquet refers to his assumption of infallibility, but it is telling in more ways than one. Whichever side of the carpet you stood, whatever the contentious creed – Communism, Surrealism, Fascism – more than politics were at stake on these occasions. It was no mere chance that they required you to accept the impossible, the illogical, the ridiculous, to reconcile the irreconcilable; for they concerned not logic but faith. They recalled the Inquisition, the search for heretics, the initiation into the Mysteries: the sectarian necessity of proving *at all costs* that you belong, body and soul. For soul, that indefinable essence, does not disappear simply because religion is abolished, any more than does the urge to belong. Who would have Aragon's soul, and Breton's? The Party claimed them. Breton obstinately refused to relinquish his. But that required a strength Aragon did not possess. Between Breton and the Party he was torn in two.

Despite their grilling the four 'tumultuously'[110] refused to renounce Surrealism. But Aragon found himself seriously discomfited. In a way his position vis-à-vis *Rêverie* neatly mirrored Breton's with regard to 'Front Rouge'. Each found himself obliged, for external reasons, to lay himself on the line for a piece of work he disliked. But while Aragon and Breton were old allies, so that Breton's inclination was to support Aragon if he could, the same was by no means true of Aragon and Dalí. On the contrary, they had already had one highly embarrassing encounter, over Dalí's plan for a 'Surrealist object' consisting of an armchair covered with shot-glasses full of milk. Aragon, to the astonishment of all present, had assumed his newly humourless Communist persona and priggishly condemned the waste of milk. There were children in the world who needed it, he said. 'We could hardly believe our ears,' said Breton.[111] And now here he was defending a man he disliked, called to account over a piece of writing he deplored and whose publication he had tried to prevent.

In his embarrassment he reacted with an outbreak of fury, not against Breton, nor even Dalí, but against the Party blockheads who had landed him in this impossible position. He would bring their stupidity to the attention of the highest quarters; he would telegraph Stalin himself to complain. (In the event he contented himself with sending a cable to the Revolutionary Writers' International.) Then he went to tell Breton what he had done. As it happened, Breton was just then correcting the proofs of *Misère de la poésie*. He immediately decided to include an account of the whole *Rêverie* affair, to show the bad faith and poverty of thought with which the Surrealists had to contend.

Aragon was appalled. His one wish was to put *Rêverie* and all its consequences behind him, not to court yet more trouble. 'He absolutely refused,' Breton recalled. 'He said it was an internal Party matter, which couldn't be made public. When I persisted – because of course all that meant nothing to me – he said that if I put that sentence in, then it was all over between us.'[112]

The balancing act was over. Finally Aragon was on the spot. For years – ever since he had first begun to write *La Défense de l'infini* – he had ducked and weaved, bent over backwards, used all the sophistry at his command in order to avoid this moment. He might be writing a novel – but he was not *really* a novelist. He might have signed a paper condemning Surrealism in the name of the Party – but that was not *really* what had happened. All he wanted was to be universally loved; all he wanted was to please everyone. But that was the one impossible thing.

According to Aragon, Breton actually marked the offending phrase for deletion in the proofs. When the pamphlet was published, however, there it still was. Aragon responded with an anonymously inserted notice in *L'Humanité*: 'Our comrade Aragon informs us that he has absolutely nothing to do with the publication of a pamphlet entitled *Misère de la poésie* . . . He wishes to make it clear that he entirely disavows both the contents of this pamphlet and the attention it has drawn to his name, every Communist being duty-bound to condemn the attacks contained in this pamphlet as incompatible with the class struggle.'[113] 'So paradoxically,' Breton mused, 'the break happened at the very moment the pamphlet was published – in his defence.'[114] Aragon and Breton never spoke to each other again. 'That shit', wrote Eluard, 'with his whimperings and his suicide threats . . . He deserves no pity.'[115]

'When I returned from Russia,' Aragon wrote, 'I was no longer the same man, no longer the author of *Paysan de Paris*, but of *Front Rouge*. Yet there still remained a thousand ties to be broken, and that was very hard. If I had the strength for it, it was, I know, thanks to the practical work, the political work in which the proletariat of my country involved me.'[116] Eluard agreed. 'He has become *someone else*, and his memory is of no more interest to me.'[117]

Who had he been before? That was something he had never been able to find out. He had been condemned to the wilderness of uncertainty. But now he had an identity. He was Elsa's, and through her Stalin's; he spent the rest of their life together loudly proclaiming his twin loves. Without her, he was lost. In 1932, when she walked out after a quarrel, he sent a despairing *pneu* to the Spanish film-maker Luis Buñuel, who, like Aragon, belonged at that time to both the Surrealists and the Communist Party. The *pneu* arrived at seven thirty one morning: ' "Come at once, I need to speak to you urgently." Buñuel arrived to find him furiously pacing the room. "She's left me all alone! And the Party's throwing me out because I'm a Surrealist! And our wonderful Surrealist comrades are putting out this garbage" – and he handed me a pamphlet, *l'Affaire Aragon* – "where they excommunicate me for being a Communist." '[118]

'Without Elsa,' he said later, 'I would have been silent' (*'je me serais tu'*). A phrase which, as his biographer Pierre Daix points out, differs only by one letter from *je me serais tué*: I would have killed myself. It seems not improbable. He had tried it once, after all. Another recruit to the ranks of celebrated Surrealist suicides, another literary reputation salvaged by a timely death. Jacques Vaché had thought suicide a solution; so, possibly, had Arthur Cravan, and, most recently, Jacques Rigaut, who in 1919 gave himself ten years to live and in 1929, for no reason other than the attraction of the act itself, gracefully fulfilled his own prophecy. 'Real freedom . . . is the revolver with which we can kill ourselves tonight should we happen to feel like it,' he wrote; and did so.[119] Elsa saved Aragon from both suicide and Surrealism. Only his reputation died.

For forty years he hid behind Elsa and the Party. 'Political engagement is a refuge and a mask,' says Julia Kristeva, 'and Aragon's life is the proof.'[120] Elsa's Aragon became a national monument. Not until she died could the mask be dropped. Then for the first time Aragon stood alone, as himself. He was, it transpired, homosexual. It was something he had never dared admit, not to Elsa, not to the Party, certainly not to the puritanical homophobe Breton – though there had been hints. After a visit to Madrid in 1925, when he gave a talk on Surrealism at the Residencia de Estudiantes, a story circulated that he had shocked the Residencia's principal by enquiring if there were any interesting urinals in town.[121] And even though the bearer of this tale was Buñuel – at that time pruriently fascinated by such matters – it seems, given his later history, not improbable. If so, it was part of a familiar pattern. In Madrid he knew no one; in Madrid he was safe. But once back home he preferred to excise part of himself rather than risk giving offence. Only when there was no one left to offend could he admit the truth.

When Matthew Josephson met Breton in America during World War II, he asked after his old friend. Aragon was by then a Resistance hero, a national poet. Had Breton heard from him? Breton replied, 'If I had power I would have Aragon shot tomorrow at dawn!'[122] According to Breton's biographer Mark Polizzotti 'he was still telling friends in the 1960s that he would not speak to Aragon if they were alone on a desert island'.[123]

Josephson concluded that Breton was 'a good hater'. But this is surely too literal a conclusion. Such continuing fury rather reflects the depth of the hurt. Eluard said, 'I trusted [Aragon] absolutely ... I loved him, I respected him, I defended him.'[124] The love – that was what made his actions so unforgivable. As for Breton, 'It's true that I've had to cut myself off from some people who were dear to me, and others have left me. The memories remain with me, they torment me from time to time, and I won't hide from you that the wound is reopened every time.'[125]

And Aragon? While Breton was alive he could feel no warmth for the unbending friend of his youth, describing him as 'a great poet, no-one can deny that, a very intelligent man, but an unpleasant character'.[126] But writing after Breton's death, he remembered a day when he and Breton, after walking Soupault home, had wandered past the Tuileries in the setting sun talking about the future.

> How old were we? Twenty, twenty-one? Not children any more ... B. outlined the enterprise of destruction we were going to undertake, anyone could join, but between us two a secret understanding ... All life before us, short most probably, but if a companion weakened ... then ... we would cast him out, ruin him, discredit him – use any weapon available ... We were talking about a programme of the utmost rigour, not something that could be achieved over just a couple of years. We'll finish them. Until the day

when we have to go even further, when one or the other will abandon the other or one . . . No weakness. No sentimentality. You know that the other will strike you down. You know it . . . 'Who'll be the one?' said A.B.[127]

CHAPTER SEVEN

ANDALUSIAN DOGS

It was appropriate that Dalí's *Rêverie* about Dulita should occasion the final break between Breton and Aragon. For Surrealism's early impetus was long exhausted, its early heroes (of whom Aragon had been one) all, in Breton's eyes, squeezed lemons. Something new was needed – new life, new faces, new ideas. And in 1929, the very nick of time, they appeared.

The cover of the twelfth and last edition of *La Révolution surréaliste* showed a Magritte nude captioned '*Je ne la vois pas cachée dans la forêt.*' ('I see no woman hidden in the forest.') Bordering it were photomaton photographs of the sixteen Surrealists in good standing, eyes closed. Included were the two new faces in question. Towards the top left-hand side a smooth-faced young man with prominent ears and a cad's pencil moustache: Salvador Dalí, author of the controversial Dulita text. And second from the right in the top row, a handsome, heavy-faced young man whose rather protuberant eyes were surrounded by impressive bags: his friend and collaborator Luis Buñuel.

Buñuel and Dalí were only a little younger than Breton and Aragon (Buñuel born in 1900, Dalí in 1904). But the Spain which produced them was not part of the modern world. Not only was it isolated from international politics, so that uniquely in Europe their generation was untouched by the Great War; it was, to a large extent, still mediaeval in the arrangement of everyday life. The Church, autocratic and backward-looking, dominated all aspects of life. This was especially true in the countryside, where it ran most of the thinly-scattered schools. When Primo de Rivera's dictatorship was toppled in 1931 and the Republic was established, 32.4 per cent of the 25 million Spaniards were illiterate. There was, however, an increasing awareness that elsewhere, things were different.

Luis Buñuel, Salvador Dalí and their great friend Federico García Lorca, the three outstanding Spanish artists of their generation, were – not by coincidence – all members of the same educational institution and the same class: the moneyed bourgeoisie. Buñuel and Lorca were *señoritos* – sons of rich country gentlemen: Buñuel from Aragon in northern Spain, Lorca from Andalusia in the south. Dalí's father (like Duchamp's: notaries' sons made a disproportionate contribution to the Surrealist movement) was a notary from Figueras, near Barcelona in Cataluña. All were educated largely or wholly in Catholic schools, little else being available, although Lorca's father was a keen secularist. All, when the time came for university, gravitated from the provinces to Madrid. And, once there, all were natural candidates for the Residencia de Estudiantes, established in 1910 by Don Alberto Jiménez Fraud. This was, as the name indicates, a student hall of residence. But it was also a focus for advanced thought, and for everyone who was anyone in Spanish intellectual life.

The Resi, as everyone called it, was a spacious, simple group of modern brick buildings situated at the northern end of Madrid's Paseo de la Castellana. Jiménez Fraud, the warden, had spent some time in England before returning to Madrid to open it, and his intention was to model it upon the Oxbridge collegiate system, providing the students with pleasant, clean lodgings, a stimulating atmosphere and easily available tutorial advice from the best minds. Austerity and concentration were the order of the day. Tea was the preferred beverage; no wine was served with meals. Dogs were not allowed in case their barking should disturb the students. In fact the Resi, with its sparse, simple furnishings, its high-mindedness, its secular yet missionary spirit, was strongly reminiscent of the women's colleges – Girton, Vassar, Somerville – also founded around this time. In Madrid, however, the residents were all men, though women often visited. Lorca, theoretically, was studying philosophy; Buñuel, agronomy. Alone of the three, Dalí's family recognized and supported his talent from the first, and he was enrolled to study painting at the Royal Academy of San Fernando.

Jiménez Fraud liked to expose his students to the very latest ideas. H. G. Wells spoke to them on the emancipation of women, Maynard Keynes on economics, and Einstein on relativity. Other visitors included Marie Curie, Paul Valéry, Marinetti, Max Jacob, Blaise Cendrars, Paul Claudel, G. B. Shaw, Le Corbusier, Walter Gropius, and (as we have seen) Louis Aragon.

Aragon must have found a receptive audience: Resi students were enthusiasts for the Surrealist heroes. In 1922 the works of Freud had begun to appear in Spanish translation. They were devoured by Buñuel and Dalí, both instantly entranced by this new world of insights and imaginative possibilities. 'My discovery of Freud, and particularly his theory of the unconscious, was crucial to me,' Buñuel wrote,[1] while for Dalí, *The Interpretation of Dreams* 'presented itself to me as one of the capital discoveries in my life'.[2] There was also a strong French influence: Apollinaire and Cocteau were much read and discussed. So was Lautréamont, to whose work (like Freud's translated into Spanish in the early 1920s) Dalí had been introduced by Breton's Barcelona lecture in 1922. Lorca, too, had discovered him, through a commentary by the great Nicaraguan poet Rubén Darío.

So the young Spaniards were up with the very latest in modern thought and writing. But the consciousness they brought to bear on all this was, at least in part, not modern at all. It embraced ideas and emotions long since vanished from educated circles elsewhere in Europe. For example, they possessed a fierce sense of regional identity, viscerally informing

291

everything they thought, wrote or painted. Lorca's Granada permeates his poetry. Dalí's umbilical attachment to Cadaqués, his beloved home, affected his entire emotional, artistic and intellectual life. Buñuel's Calanda and Zaragoza are imprinted upon his films, however divergent their scenarios. By comparison, Breton's Paris is simply a background. In this as in almost all other respects his work is a product of the intellect, theirs of something far less controllable. The Spaniards had no need to resort to automatism in order to access the inner man. They brought new qualities to Surrealism, among them an emotional force not seen since the early Dada days in Zurich.

The other big difference had to do with religion. For the Frenchmen the revelations of Freud and Lautréamont were chiefly intellectual and artistic. But for the Spaniards they were tinged with the guilty and deep-rooted delights of subversion and sin. Religion, for them, was a live issue, anticlericalism one of Surrealism's chief pleasures. Their distaste for the Church was of a quite different order from that of their French colleagues. Anticlericalism was, after all, nothing new in post-revolutionary France. Individuals might be pious, but the French Surrealists were products of the most consciously secular educational system in Europe. But for Dalí and (especially) Buñuel, products of harsh Spanish Catholicism, of the Marists and the Christian Brothers, rejection of religion held the deepest and most seditious of resonances. This was especially true for Buñuel who, before he lost his faith at the age of sixteen, had been deeply religious, serving at Mass and taking Communion every day. Then, suddenly, he became disgusted with the Church, its illogicality, its power, its wealth. Religion, sin, sex and death formed a murky and potent brew which would pervade the whole of his work. Both in Spain and (later) in Paris, he enjoyed nothing so much as roaming the streets disguised as a nun or priest. Part of the fun lay in the cross-dressing and religious aspects of this particular dis-guise. But a large part of the pleasure was erotic. 'Religion is full of eroticism,' Buñuel said to his friend Max Aub.

> 'What do you mean by that?'
> 'The sense of sin.'
> 'And what do you mean by sin?'
> 'The sense of sin in the sexual act, for example. In anything relating to sex.'
> 'But what's that got to do with religion?'
> 'Everything, everything. That's the world's sin: sin exists because religion exists – doesn't it?'[3]

Elsewhere he describes his sense of sin as 'voluptuous'. 'And although I'm not sure why, I also have always felt a secret but constant link between the sexual act and death.'[4] As Dalí put it on seeing Buñuel's *La Voie lactée* (*The Milky Way*): 'In spite of all his antireligious and more or less blasphemous pretensions, I have always said that Luis Buñuel will end up in holy orders.'[5]

*

Lorca and Buñuel arrived at the Resi some time before Dalí. Buñuel got there first. He was a sportsman, obsessed with physical culture, exercising every morning, a keen runner and boxer. But he also belonged to a *peña*, an intellectual circle of writers and poets which would meet at various cafés, including one whose marble-topped tables had eventually to be replaced, so covered were they with writers' graffiti. Madrid's intellectual life, which was entirely male, was constructed around the *peña*. In a particular café, on a particular day, you would find a particular group of people. Madrid might be the capital of Spain, but it was still a small town. You walked everywhere, and knew everyone. In his memoirs Buñuel relates how, one day, the dictator Primo de Rivera was expected for dinner in a café he often visited. To preserve the great man's privacy, the room was divided by screens. 'The first thing he did was to order the screens removed. When he saw us, he shouted, *"Hola, jóvenes! Una copita!"* The dictator was buying the leftists drinks!'[6]

Lorca arrived in Madrid two years later. Unlike the somewhat loutish and overbearing Buñuel, with his undirected energy, heavy features and round, exophthalmic eyes, Lorca, although physically clumsy, was grace, charm and talent personified:

> [He] was like a swan: heavy and graceless out of the water, but as soon as he was on the lake, extremely beautiful, lighting up everything around him ... When he found himself outside the kind of circles he preferred ... his rather hard and preoccupied expression was still intelligent and full of life, but neither his rather heavy, square face nor his clumsy movements were very attractive. But as soon as he entered a sympathetic atmosphere ... his whole being was pervaded by a perfect elegance. Mouth and eyes harmonised admirably and it was impossible to resist his charm. The words flowed, apt and incisive, the intonation of his rather hoarse voice was uniquely beautiful ...[7]

Buñuel was instantly entranced.

> Of all the human beings I've known, Federico was the finest. I don't mean his plays or his poetry; I mean him personally. He was his own masterpiece. Whether sitting at the piano imitating Chopin, improvising a pantomime, or acting out a scene from a play, he was irresistible. He read beautifully, and he had passion, youth and joy. When I first met him, at the Residencia, I was an unpolished rustic, interested primarily in sports. He transformed me, introduced me to a wholly different world. He was like a flame.[8]

By the time Dalí arrived towards the end of 1921, Buñuel and Lorca were ensconced at the centre of the Resi's (and Madrid's) intellectual life, part of the modernist *Ultra* group.

Dalí's upbringing differed from that of Lorca and Buñuel in several particulars. For one thing, there was never any doubt as to what he would do in life. His talent for painting was recognized and encouraged from childhood on. By a happy accident, he happened to have been born in the best possible place for the furtherance of his artistic ambitions. Zaragoza, Granada, even Madrid, were isolated provincial towns; Barcelona, on the other hand, was a centre of modern culture. The 1888 International Exhibition had left it with a lasting legacy in Gaudí's extraordinary architectural variations on art nouveau. Picabia, Gleizes, Cravan, Marie Laurencin had spent the war years there; in 1922, when Dalí first went to Madrid to live, the Dalmau Gallery was preparing a Picabia exhibition, for the opening of which Breton wrote his seminal text 'Modern Evolution and Those Who Participate in It'. Furthermore, Figueras, where Dalí's father worked, and Cadaqués, where the family spent its summers by the sea, was also home to the bohemian and welcoming Pichot clan of painters and musicians. Ramon Pichot, an Impressionist who had helped the young Picasso during his early days in Barcelona, introduced Salvador to paint's infinite possibilities. An adoptive Pichot daughter, Julia, (later to appear as the controversial Dulita of Dalí's fantasies) gave him early glimpses into the terrifying and enticing vistas of sex. And the very existence of such family friends as the Pichots meant that a painting career could be possible and acceptable. By the time he set out for Madrid at the age of seventeen, Dalí was already recognized as a potentially important artist.

With the unique mixture of panic and exhibitionism which was to mark his entire life, Dalí made sure that his first entry onto the Madrid scene was an unforgettable one. The style affected in the Residencia was in keeping with its Oxbridge origins – quiet tailoring, neat haircuts. Dalí, when he arrived in Madrid in September 1921, to take his art school exam and check out the Resi, cut a flamboyantly bizarre figure. He was a thin, feline youth with a narrow face, fine features and an unexpectedly deep voice. His lank black hair hung down to his shoulders, his cravat was tied in an enormous *lavallière* bow, he wore a black beret of long-haired wool, a cape, a hunting jacket and baggy breeches buttoned at the knees. His lower legs were clad in puttees as worn by Catalan muleteers, exposing strips of hairy skin.

Who could this extraordinary person possibly be? For some months after this spectacular arrival, nobody was able to find out. Little or nothing was seen of the newcomer, who for some reason was known as 'the Czechoslovakian painter'.[9] In fact Dalí was paralysed by shyness: when not at his studies he kept to his room, where he spent his time painting and whose floor was so covered with sketches that it was impossible to know where to put one's feet. He was 'discovered' by accident one day when the chambermaid left his door open and a passer-by – in Buñuel's account, Buñuel, in Dalí's, a genial medical student called Pepín Bello – happened to glance in.

> He could not wait to divulge this discovery to the members of the group ... At the time I became acquainted with [them] ... they were all possessed by a complex of dandyism combined with cynicism, which they displayed with accomplished worldliness. This inspired me at first with such great awe that each time they came to fetch me in my room I thought I would faint. They came all in a group to look at my paintings, and with the snobbishness, which they already wore clutched to their hearts, greatly amplifying their admiration, their surprise knew no limits. That I should be a cubist painter was the last thing they would have thought of! They frankly admitted their former opinion of me, and unconditionally offered me their friendship.[10]

Dalí, like Buñuel, at once fell under the spell of the bewitching Lorca. 'The poetic phenomenon in its entirety and "in the raw" presented itself before me suddenly in flesh and bone, confused, blood-red, viscous and sublime, quivering with a thousand fires of darkness and of subterranean biology . . .'[11] And his fascination was returned. Lorca fell passionately in love with Dalí, and at once set about trying to seduce him.

*

As is now well known, Lorca was homosexual. However, even as late as 1989, when Ian Gibson published his enormous biography of the poet, this was not something that could be admitted in respectable Spanish circles. The book resounds with Gibson's frustration at the impossibility of extracting such an admission from the poet's friends and acquaintances. Another book on the subject of the Lorca–Dalí friendship, published in 1981,[12] took it for granted that the person Lorca was in love with was Dalí's sister Ana Maria (a view obstinately shared by Ana Maria herself).

If this was still the case in the 1980s, years after Franco's death had released Spain into the modern world, one may imagine how much more impossible was such an admission during the early 1920s. For the aggressively heterosexual Buñuel, it was unthinkable. In his memoirs, he recounts what happened when he put the question directly to his friend:

> I remember someone once telling me that a man named Martín Dominguez . . . was spreading the rumor that Lorca was a homosexual, a charge I found impossible to believe. One day, we were sitting side by side at the president's table in the Residencia dining room, along with Unamuno, Eugenio d'Ors, and Don Alberto, our director.
>
> 'Let's get out of here,' I suddenly said to Federico, after the first course. 'I've got something I *must* ask you.'
>
> We went to a nearby tavern, and there I told him that I'd decided to challenge Dominguez to a fight.

'Whatever for?' Lorca asked.

I hesitated a moment, unsure how to put it.

'Is it true you're a *maricón*?' I blurted out.

'You and I are finished!' he declared, shocked and hurt, as he stood up and walked away.[13]

By that evening, Buñuel assures us, the two were once again the best of friends. But even in 1982, he felt compelled to add that 'There was absolutely nothing effeminate or affected about Federico.' He insisted, too, that even though Lorca was homosexual by inclination, he was not active because he was impotent. In his friend Aub's view, Buñuel's later hatred of Dalí stemmed from Dalí's insistence, in his memoirs, upon Lorca's homosexuality.

On Dalí's side, the situation was even more complicated. 'Dalí is completely asexual, androgynous as an angel,'[14] Buñuel said. This is arguable: what is certain is that Dalí was obsessed with sex, and that his own sexuality was (as all his paintings show) a matter of intense puzzlement and distress to him. There is some suggestion that he may have had incestuous feelings, or even relations, with his mother and sister.[15] He certainly felt deeply ambivalent about his father. Even after the problem was, up to a point, solved by the advent of Gala Eluard in 1929, masturbation was, and remained, his chief source of sexual pleasure. This, and his attempt to come to terms with it, was part of the great attraction of Freud, and hence of Surrealism: 'I was seized with a real vice of self-interpretation, not only of my dreams but of everything that happened to me, however accidental it seemed at first glance.'[16]

One of the sexual possibilities most terrifying to Dalí was the thought of homosexuality. Whatever he might be, he was not a *maricón*. But at the beginning of his friendship with Lorca, this was not a problem. Lorca was disturbing as well as attractive, but this was more on account of his immense personal magnetism than his sexuality. The difficulty for the narcissistic Dalí was in dealing with such competition for the centre of attention.

> I avoided Lorca and the group, which grew to be his group more and more. This was the culminating moment of his irresistible personal influence – and the only moment in my life when I thought I glimpsed the torture that envy can be. Sometimes we would be walking, the whole group of us, along El Paseo de la Castellana on our way to the café where we held our usual literary meetings, and where I knew Lorca would shine like a mad and fiery diamond. Suddenly I would set off at a run, and no-one would see me for three days.[17]

Gradually, however, their friendship burgeoned, and in 1925 Dalí invited Lorca to spend Easter with his family in Figueras and Cadaqués. It was the beginning of an idyll in which the entire Dalí family would become enchanted by Lorca, while he fell more and more in love with Cadaqués and Dalí. He read the family extracts from his work in progress, *Mariana Pineda*, and was delighted by their evident emotion. They strolled through Figueras to the plangent notes of the *sardana*, they feasted on sea urchins and grilled chops on the beach terrace at Cadaqués. On his return to Granada, the poet bombarded the Dalís with delighted letters. Ana Maria thought, rightly, that they were love letters and, wrongly, that she was their subject. That April, Lorca began his 'Ode to Salvador Dalí':

> Oh Salvador Dalí, of the olive voice!
> I speak what your person and your pictures tell me.
> I don't hymn your imperfect adolescent paintbrush,
> But I sing the firm direction of your arrows.
>
> I sing your lovely strength of Catalan light,
> Your love for all that has a possible explanation.

I sing your astronomical and tender heart,
A French playing-card, unwounded.

I sing your yearning for the statue ceaselessly pursued,
Your fright at the excitements awaiting in the street.
I sing the sea's siren, serenading you
From her bicycle of corals and shells . . .

Confronted by this burgeoning idyll, Buñuel was consumed with jealousy. Three is always a difficult number in questions of friendship, let alone love. And not only was he excluded from his friends' growing intimacy, but also from a certain professional momentum that was beginning to gather pace for both Dalí and, to a lesser extent, Lorca. In May 1926, Dalí participated triumphantly in the inaugural exhibition of the Sociedad Ibérica de Artistas, designed to create a forum for modern painting in Madrid. And that autumn the Dalmau Gallery in Barcelona gave him his first one-man show – also a triumph. He sent Lorca a copy of the only adverse review: 'the others are so unconditionally enthusiastic that they're of no interest'.[18] Lorca, too, though he would not become established until the publication of the *Romancero Gitano* in 1928, was beginning to make a name. The 'Ode to Salvador Dalí' had attracted a good deal of attention. They were striding firmly into the future: their paths seemed (comparatively) clear.

Buñuel, on the other hand, could see no very apparent way forward. The cinema had not yet presented itself as a possibility. 'I would really have liked to be a writer,' he reflected in old age. '. . . You need so many people to make a film. I envy the painter or writer who can work alone at home.' Painters and writers have other advantages too. No capital is needed to produce a book, while the spectre of raising money haunts every would-be film-maker. Buñuel would not be free of it until the very end of his life. But writing, as he had already

300

found out, was not for him. 'I repeat myself. What would take a writer two minutes takes me hours.'[19]

Nevertheless, he must do something – or return to Calanda and the life of a *señorito*. But modern life was what he wanted, not a return to the Middle Ages; and there was only one place for that – Paris, home of Lautréamont, Apollinaire, Cocteau and the Surrealists. On the recommendation of Don Alberto he offered his unpaid services to Eugenio d'Ors, the Spanish representative at the Society for Intellectual Co-operation recently set up by the League of Nations. He was told to go to Paris, improve his French and English by reading the papers, and await instructions. His father had died in 1923; his mother, scenting a diplomatic career, promised a monthly cheque. In January 1925, Buñuel arrived in Paris. The franc had recently been devalued: living was cheap, a bottle of champagne cost eleven francs – one peseta.

Buñuel at this time was a correct proto-diplomat, spatted, suited, bowler hatted. However, he had few official duties. How, then, was he to pass the time? He soon found the answer: by going to the cinema, sometimes as often as three times a day. 'Thanks to a press pass I'd inveigled out of a friend, I saw private screenings of American films in the morning at the Salle Wagram. During the afternoon I went to a neighborhood theatre, and in the evenings to the Vieux Colombier or the Studio des Ursulines.'[20] *The Battleship Potemkin* aroused such emotion in the audience that 'when we left the theatre, on a street near Alésia, we started erecting barricades ourselves'.[21] But the real revelation was Fritz Lang. 'When I saw *Destiny*, I suddenly knew that I too wanted to make movies . . . something about this film spoke to something deep in me; it clarified my life and my vision of the world.'[22] At the age of seventy-two Buñuel, by then as celebrated as his hero, finally met Lang, then over eighty, and couldn't resist asking him for his autograph.

At last he knew what he wanted to do. 'My life has taken an unexpected turn,' he announced in February 1926. 'I'm going to dedicate myself to film-making. I'm going to start helping Jean Epstein around the set to learn the job. Perhaps in a couple of years ... I shall be able to work independently.'[23]

Epstein was then a well-known director. He ran a small acting school on the side, in which Buñuel enthusiastically enrolled; but his enthusiasm waned when he discovered that all his fellow-students were White Russians and the whole thing was little more than a scam. Somewhat to his surprise, Epstein agreed to let him assist on his current production, *Mauprat*. 'I did a little bit of everything; I operated a waterfall, and even played a gendarme during the reign of Louis XV (or was it XVI?)'[24] Buñuel was fascinated to see that the cameraman, Albert Duverger, had no assistant, but changed his own film and developed his own prints. Duverger would be Buñuel's cameraman on both *Un Chien andalou* and *L'Âge d'or*.

The collaboration with Epstein would continue into the next film, *The Fall of the House of Usher*. But there it faltered. One day, just as everyone was packing up, Epstein said, 'Stay a minute with the cameraman, Luis. Abel Gance is going to audition two girls, and you might be able to give him a hand.' But Buñuel refused.

> With my usual abruptness, I replied that I was *his* assistant and not Gance's, that I didn't much like Gance's movies (except for *Napoléon*), and that I found Gance himself very pretentious.
>
> 'How can an insignificant asshole like you dare talk that way about a great director!' Epstein exploded ... adding that, as far as he was concerned, our collaboration had just come to an end ... 'You be careful,' he said. 'I see Surrealistic tendencies in you.'[25]

Despite his enthusiasm for the movement, tendencies were, for the moment, all Buñuel's Surrealism amounted to. He would have liked to join the group – his letters home implied that he knew the Surrealists well – but in real life he could never muster up the courage to approach them. The nearest he came to flesh-and-blood Surrealists was in passing by the Closerie des Lilas soon after Péret and a friend had insulted Madame Rachilde at a banquet given there in her honour, leading to a riot and much broken glass. Péret was always the Spaniards' favourite Surrealist (as a poet, not as a person, Buñuel insisted),[26] perhaps because his anti-clerical fervour was almost as great as their own. Buñuel had been particularly struck by a photo in *La Révolution surréaliste* of 'Benjamin Péret insulting a priest'. (This Iberian affinity seems to have been mutual. Péret spent many years in Latin America and married a Mexican: his son Geyser Péret became a general in the Brazilian army.)

The issue of *La Révolution surréaliste* containing this photograph also carried one of the perennial inquiries into sexuality ('What's your favourite place to make love? With whom? How often do you masturbate?'), and not only the questions, but the frankness with which they were answered, seemed incredible to Buñuel. One of the great cultural shocks of his move to Paris had been the sight of couples kissing in the street, and the realization that seemingly respectable men and women frequently lived together without being either married or ostracized. His Marist education had left him terminally afflicted with the madonna/whore syndrome. Either a woman was totally chaste, or she was fallen and deserved no respect.

On the occasion he first met his future wife, this almost led to a fatal misunderstanding. It was 1926. He was visiting a painter friend, Hernando Viñes, who shared a studio with another artist, Joaquín Peinado. Peinado arrived back from an anatomy class with two fellow-students, Hélène Tasnon and Jeanne Rucar. Jeanne taught gymnastics, and had won a bronze medal in the 1924 Olympics. Luis was immediately attracted. He took Peinado aside and whispered: 'I've got some of those pills that get women excited if they're dissolved in wine. Let's give them to these girls.' 'He thought we were tarts,' Jeanne remembered. In Madrid, it was impossible for a respectable woman even to sit down with the men in a café *peña*: any girl who would visit an artist's studio unchaperoned must be a whore. This, however, was not Madrid but Paris. 'These are respectable girls from good families!' Peinado replied indignantly. 'Jeanne's father is a friend of mine!'[27] At once the other set of attitudes clicked in. Formally, Luis called upon Jeanne's parents and asked permission to take her out. They began regular Sunday afternoon walks, chaperoned by Jeanne's sister Georgette. Georgette sympathized, and left them to it: but nothing more than kisses ensued, and then rarely out in the open. Jeanne grumbled that Luis was always dragging her to the cinema, but this was only partly to do with his passion for film. 'That was where you went to neck with your girlfriend,' he explained. 'It was the only place where that was possible. There was absolutely nowhere else you could be alone. You couldn't even hold hands. It would have been a scandal. But the cinema was something else.'[28] Another possibility was dancing. Jeanne said, 'I taught Luis the tango in the kitchen of my place in Paris. Although [he] played the violin he couldn't keep a beat, so we compromised with the fox-trot. To tell the truth Luis didn't like to dance. He liked to get me in his arms. That was what I liked, too.'[29] The public dance halls served the same purpose, but of course no respectable girl could be seen there.

Once Jeanne had agreed to marry him, Luis became (in Parisian terms) extraordinarily, outlandishly proprietorial. After watching one of her gymnastics classes he decided that such displays in such garments were indecent and must cease: 'Everyone can see your legs. I don't like my fiancée making an exhibition of herself.'[30] She agreed to resign. But how, in that case, was she to earn a living? He suggested she take a job as an assistant at Juan Vicens' Spanish Bookshop. It paid 300 francs a month – less than she had earned teaching; but she agreed. After she had been working there for a while she noticed that her salary did not appear in the cash-book. Vicens, confronted, confessed that Luis was paying it out of his own pocket. And this was by no means all. There was the question of her piano lessons. Jeanne was learning the piano; Luis knew her teacher, a rather attractive man. He would escort her to the door, and collect her again afterwards. Who was present during the lesson? Was her teacher married? 'The way you play,' he concluded, 'I don't see why you bother.' Jeanne never played the piano again.

It seems astonishing now, and it was fairly extraordinary even then – though Jeanne's own parents were scarcely less strait-laced than Luis himself in these matters. But she was prepared to put up with it because she was madly in love with him, and he with her. He was quite simply the most beautiful young man she had ever seen. Meeting him after an absence, the sight of him struck her dumb – she had forgotten how attractive he was. 'A tall, handsome fellow, slightly con-strained, like a boxer in a suit that's slightly too tight ... His face was olive-skinned, open, generous, lit by two soft green eyes. His wide square jaw was the only indication of possible hidden violence ...'[31] They remained together for sixty years. But when, after his death, Jeanne published her memoirs, she called them *Memoirs of a Pianoless Woman*.

Clearly, though Buñuel might be living in Paris, emotion-ally he was still in Spain. And in Spain Lorca and Dalí were getting up to – who knew what? Perhaps in order to reassert his claims, he urged Dalí to come to Paris for a visit.

Dalí needed little persuading. He had been thinking about Paris for years; it had been the home of his old mentor Ramon Pichot; he had recently read *Le Bal du Comte d'Orgel*, a *roman-à-clef* by Cocteau's young protégé Raymond Radiguet about Parisian high society. He and his sister Ana Maria arrived, escorted by their stepmother/aunt, in April 1926. Buñuel met them at the station, overjoyed to see his friend's familiar and beloved face.

Dalí in Paris was his usual mixture of abject impracticality and professional ruthlessness. He could hardly bring himself to cross the road: in order to achieve this operation the aunt had to take Salvador and Ana Maria by the hand as if they were four years old. 'Alright, children, let's go!' she would say, and hurry them across to safety.[32] But once arrived on the other side, he knew exactly what to do and whom to see. Through the Barcelona gallery-owner Josep Dalmau, who had put on the Picabia show, he had the Surrealist introductions Buñuel lacked. Dalí's goal, however, was not Breton but Picasso. A meeting had been arranged by Lorca's friend, the painter Manuel Angeles Ortiz.

'I have come to see you,' I said, 'before visiting the Louvre.'

'You're quite right,' he answered.

I brought a small painting, carefully packed, which was called *The Girl of Figueras*. He looked at it for at least fifteen minutes, and made no comment whatever. After which we went up to the next storey, where for two hours Picasso showed me quantities of paintings. He kept going back and forth, dragging out great canvases which he placed against the easel. Then he went to fetch others amongst an infinity of canvases stacked in rows against the wall. I could see that he was going to enormous trouble. At each new canvas he cast me a glance filled with a vivacity and an intelligence so violent that it made me tremble. I left without in turn having made the slightest comment. At the end, on the landing of the stairs, just as I was about to leave we exchanged a glance which meant exactly, 'You get the idea?' 'I get it!'[33]

Dalí never forgot this visit: Picasso was his hero, and to be taken seriously by him, a sort of rite of passage. After a few hectic days in Paris the party moved on to Brussels and the Flemish painters.

Buñuel, left behind, was more than ever in limbo. The diplomatic career would clearly never materialize; the possibility of making a living in films seemed equally to be fading. A Catalan friend, Juan Castanyer, had recently opened a restaurant in the Rue des Grands Augustins; and in 1927 another friend from the Spanish circle, Juan Vicens, suggested that he and Buñuel might do something similar. Why not open a cabaret? Vicens had some money, but more was needed. It was agreed that Luis would go back to Spain for a few weeks to try and persuade his mother to put in some capital. At the same time he arranged to bring with him some avant-garde films, which he would show in Madrid. He was known there as a film buff: he had been doing a little film criticism for *Cahiers d'Art* and also for the Madrid publication *La Gaceta Literaria*. The manager of the Studio des Ursulines, one of his regular haunts, helped him choose a programme, and Pepín Bello, a friend from the Residencia, arranged a projector.

Financially his visit was a failure: his mother would have nothing to do with the proposed cabaret. On the other hand, the Madrid occasion was a tremendous success. The delight and enthusiasm with which his programme was received reminded him (had he been in any danger of forgetting) that Madrid was a backwater, and that he, by contrast, lived at the centre of the artistic universe. As far as the Madrileños were concerned, the mere fact of living in Paris endowed him with tremendous cultural cachet. The distinguished philosopher José Ortega y Gasset confided that he would have liked to work in movies had he been a little younger (he had by then attained the ripe age of forty). Ramón Gómez de la Serna, a well-known writer, also expressed his enthusiasm. Buñuel, who had always been attracted to his work, suggested they might make a film together. Gómez de la Serna agreed, and proposed a story based on a newspaper, *El Mundo por diez Centimos* (*The World for Ten Cents*). A man buys a paper, and as he reads each story the film dramatizes it, with the headline for introduction. They worked together on the outline for two days. Then Buñuel returned once more to Paris.

*

To Buñuel's disappointment, neither Lorca nor Dalí had been in Madrid to hear his talk. In fact they were in Cadaqués. Lorca's play *Mariana Pineda*, which he had been trying to get performed for years, had finally been taken up by the Catalan actress Margarita Xirgu, and was to be premièred in Barcelona that June with sets by Dalí. They had been corresponding voluminously and affectionately, but it was a year since they had actually met. Lorca was as enchanted as ever with every aspect of Dalí; but there were already signs that Dalí was perhaps less willing to commit himself. Lorca's lyrical voice, with its troubadourish echoes, troubled his ultra-modern sensibilities:

> Here is what I think. No previous era has ever known such perfection as ours. Until the invention of the machine there were not perfect things, and mankind had never seen anything so *beautiful* or *poetic* as a nickel-plated engine. The machine has changed everything. Our epoch, compared to others, is MORE different than the Greece of the Parthenon from Gothic. You've only got to think of the badly made highly ugly objects produced before mechanisation. We are surrounded by a new, perfect beauty, productive of new poetic states.

308

We read Petrarch and we can see that he is the product of his period – mandolines, trees full of birds, antique curtains. He has recourse to the materials of his time. I read your 'orange and lemon' and can't sense the painted mouths of shop-window dummies. I read Petrarch and yes, I can sense those full breasts cushioned in lace.

I look at Fernand Léger, Picasso, Miró, etc., and I know that there are machines and new discoveries in Natural History.

Your poems are Granada without trams, with no aeroplanes yet; an antique Granada with natural elements, far removed from today, purely traditional and *constant*. Constant of course!, I know you'll say, but the constant, or eternal as you all call it, takes on in each period a flavour which is the flavour preferred by those of us who draw on those same constants, but in a new way.[34]

Dalí spent so much of his life constructing an elaborate and repellent front for public consumption that it has become hard to imagine why so many brilliant men and women found him (as they did) so extremely attractive. But perhaps letters such as this provide part of the answer. Behind his extraordinary talent lay a mind so questing, quirky, thoughtful and truly original that his company, when he relaxed sufficiently to stop play-acting, was a constant delight. This was the Dalí for whom Buñuel fought Lorca, the Dalí who enchanted André Breton, who would become Surrealism's last, best hope. 'He was so delightful at that time,' Buñuel remembered nostalgically, fifty years later.[35]

Unsurprisingly, when *Mariana Pineda* opened, Dalí's starkly modern sets and costumes, though generally admired, were felt by at least one critic to sit awkwardly with the play itself. However, it was a great success, and so was its author. Lorca returned from Barcelona triumphant, to the prospect of a happy few weeks by the sea in Cadaqués.

In the morning, the house was very active. Hardly – as García Lorca liked to put it – had the dawn lit up the coral in the Virgin's hand, than the notes of [the guitarist Regino] Sáinz de la Maza's guitar filled the air ... In his studio, Salvador had already begun to capture the light, and Lorca worked passionately on his *Sacrifice of Iphigenia.*

Our house was reflected in the crystal morning water. The fishermen spread their nets on the beach. As I laid out breakfast on the terrace, we would talk ...[36]

Dalí painted at least two important pictures during this time, *Honey is Sweeter than Blood* and *Gadget and Hand*. It seems likely that both of these relate to his sexual problems. *Gadget and Hand* features the guilty red hand of the masturbator. *Honey is Sweeter than Blood* shows, among other things, Lorca's severed head lying near Dalí's own and, on the other side of the picture, a mummified body that might belong to Buñuel. Dalí, as Ian Gibson points out, refers in his *Secret Life* to 'that familiar solitary pleasure, sweeter than honey', while blood was part of his and Lorca's habitual image of heterosexual intercourse (Lorca's metaphor for this being 'the jungle of blood').[37] So if honey is sweeter than blood, masturbation is sweetest of all. But if this was true for Dalí, it was not enough for Lorca. Twice in their relationship, according to Dalí, Lorca attempted to sodomize him, but without success. He, Dalí, explained, was not a 'pederast', and, furthermore, 'it hurt'.

But I was very flattered from the point of view of my personal prestige. Deep down I said to myself that he was a very great poet and that I owed him a little bit of the Divine Dalí's ar—![38]

The first of these attempts probably took place in 1925, and the solution they then arrived at was that Lorca should enact his desires vicariously – via a woman. The chosen vehicle was Margarita Manso, a young woman of exceptionally liberated sexual habits who frequented the Residencia and the Real Academia de Bellas Artes de San Fernando where Dalí was then still a student. Not only was she willing: she also had exceptionally small breasts, which was essential, since Lorca detested women's breasts. At the appointed time 'the girl without breasts was summoned to the sacrifice, which took place in front of Dalí himself. "It excited Federico to know I was watching . . . He transferred his passion to the girl." . . . Dalí insisted that this was the only time Lorca ever had sexual contact with a woman.'[39]

Did Lorca renew the assault during these weeks of excitement and enjoyment at Cadaqués? It seems possible. Certainly he remained as much in love with Dalí as ever. In a wistful letter written on the way back to Granada at the end of July, he wrote:

> Your pictorial blood, and in general the whole tactile concept of your physiological aesthetic, has such a concrete, well-balanced air, such a logical and true quality of pure poetry that it attains the category of *that which we need absolutely in order to live* . . .
>
> Now I realise how much I am losing by leaving you . . .
>
> I behaved towards you like an indecent ass, you who are the best thing I've got. With every minute I see it more clearly and I'm dreadfully sorry. But it only increases my affection for you and my identification with your ideas and your human integrity.[40]

But despite, or because of, the pleasures of that summer, Dalí was beginning to distance himself from Lorca both aesthetically and physically. Perhaps (as Ian Gibson speculates) he felt both his masculinity and his independence threatened by Lorca's homosexual attractions.

Buñuel, on holiday in far-off Brittany, knew nothing of all this. What he did know was that, having heard of his unexpected success in Madrid, Dalí and Lorca had written him a wounding letter from Cadaqués. Lorca was presumably eager to mark his closeness to Dalí – all the more so as he felt him slipping out of reach – while Dalí always enjoyed making malicious mischief. And if they desired to wound they certainly succeeded – not surprisingly, considering the combined talents of the writers and their intimate acquaintance with the recipient. At the end of July and the beginning of August Buñuel wrote plaintively on the subject to their mutual friend Pepín Bello. 'I have received a disgusting (*asqueroso*) letter from Federico and his acolyte Dalí. He's got him completely enslaved.' Evidently hurt, he returned to the subject in his next letter, a play on words hingeing on the coincidence between the adjective and the name of a village – Asquerosa – where the García Lorca family owned some property:

> Dalí is writing me disgusting letters.
> He's disgusting.
> With Federico that makes two of them, both disgusting.
> One because he's from Asquerosa, the other because
> he's disgusting. (*es asqueroso*)[41]

The subject continued to prey on his mind, for a month later he was still writing about it:

> Federico sticks in my craw incredibly. I thought that the
> boyfriend [Dalí] was putrescent, but now I see that the
> other is even worse. It's his awful aestheticism that has
> distanced him from us. His extreme narcissism was already
> enough to make a pure friendship with him impossible. It's
> his look-out. The trouble is that his work may suffer as a
> result.
> Dalí is deeply influenced by him. He believes himself to

be a genius, thanks to the love Federico professes for him
. . . How I'd love to see him arrive here and renew himself
far from the dire influence of García! Because Dalí is a real
male and very talented.[42]

Lorca's personality, which he had found so irresistible,
now annoyed him more and more. Where he had been happy
to listen, now he focused upon the poet's inordinate egotism.
He told the story of a conversation they had had once in
Toledo. 'Federico, I absolutely have to tell you the truth about
yourself,' began Buñuel. Lorca let him speak for some time.
'Finished?' 'Yes.' 'Fine, now it's my turn. I'm going to tell you
what I think of you. For instance, you say I'm lazy . . . But
really I'm not lazy at all. I'm . . .'[43]

Despite all the fine words, Buñuel's film career remained
exiguous. Epstein had promised him he could be 'assistant
assistant' on *The Fall of the House of Usher*, but that was not
yet quite financed. Ramón Gómez de la Serna continued to
temporize regarding *El Mundo por diez Centimos*. He had also
been offered the editorship of the cinema pages of *Cahiers
d'Art* in Paris and *La Gaceta Literaria* in Madrid. Giménez
Caballero, the *Gaceta*'s editor, introduced him as 'chief of the
cinema page which we shall periodically present to our readers
. . . He has accomplished what none of our *cinéastes* has
managed: to lodge himself in High Studies of Cinema.' He
mentioned the Gómez de la Serna project and Buñuel's 'first
work as a technician, seen this spring . . . in the context of
films of the avant-garde'. Buñuel, he added, was in Paris
'preparing . . . Preparing what? That is the question.'[44]

It was indeed. The *Gaceta*'s cinema pages appeared only
sporadically; and although Buñuel, in letters to Pepín Bello,
touted *Cahiers d'Art* as 'the best modern art magazine in Paris'
and his job on it as 'open[ing] every door in Paris to me', the
reality was rather different. *Cahiers d'Art* was run, not by a

Parisian but a Greek, Christian Zervos, and most of its cinema criticism was written not by Buñuel but by Jacques Brunius. But of course Buñuel's Madrid friends knew nothing of this; and for Dalí, at least, Buñuel's new connections made him extremely interesting.

Dalí was now writing as well as painting. He had recently published a long piece, 'Saint Sebastian', in the Catalan magazine *L'Amic des Arts*, expounding his current aesthetic of objectivity and asepsis, and the avoidance of sentimentality and 'putrescence' (a concept to which we shall return). But the Catalan audience is necessarily limited. Buñuel's new contacts offered the possibility of a much wider readership. He began to distance himself from Lorca, and to transfer his loyalties to Buñuel.

The new state of affairs became evident during a short visit Buñuel made to Madrid in November 1927. At Dalí's insistence the three friends met to hear Federico read his play *The Love of Don Perlimplín for Belisa in his Garden*, a May–December fable about an impotent husband who magically rediscovers his manhood. The three met in the cellar bar of the Hotel Nacional, which was divided into separate wooden booths. It was 'a magnificent play', Dalí told Buñuel; 'I absolutely had to hear it immediately.'

> Lorca was a superb reader, but something in the story about the old man and the young girl who find themselves together in a canopied bed at the end of Act One struck me as hopelessly contrived. As if that weren't enough, an elf then emerges from the prompter's box and addresses the audience.
>
> 'Well, eminent spectators,' he says. 'Here are Don Perlimplín and Belisa . . .'
>
> 'That's enough, Federico,' I interrupted, banging on the table. 'It's a piece of shit.'
>
> Lorca blanched, closed the manuscript and looked at Dalí.

'Buñuel's right,' Dalí said in his deep voice. *'Es una mierda.'*

Lorca, appalled, left the bar. The other two, embarrassed, followed him at a distance. They watched as he entered a church and, ignoring them, knelt before the altar and spread his arms wide like a penitent. They watched for a moment then went to a bar. Next day, Buñuel asked Dalí what had happened when he went back to the room he was sharing with Lorca. Dalí said, 'It's all right. He tried to make love to me, but couldn't.'[45]

The campaign continued with the appearance of Lorca's *Romancero Gitano* (*Gypsy Ballads*) in 1928. This was an immediate and enormous success, establishing Lorca in the public eye as a poet of the first order. But once again he was denied the applause he most desired. 'Naturally I can't share the opinions of those putrefying pigs the critics,' Dalí wrote. '... But you may be interested in my opinions ... Your poetry as it stands is entirely *traditional* ... absolutely tied to the ancient poetic norms, incapable of exciting us now or of satisfying our present desires...'[46] As for Buñuel, 'I saw Federico in Madrid, we got to know each other again; so you will know I'm really telling the truth when I say that his book of romances seems very bad to me, and anyone else who doesn't actually live in Seville,' he informed Pepín Bello.[47]

*

Buñuel and Dalí were both intensely attracted to Surrealism. Buñuel, from Paris, sent Dalí all the latest publications. They were eagerly received. Dalí took particular pleasure in the Surrealist practice of making violent and unprovoked attacks upon traditional tastes and respected artists. He and Buñuel decided to try it out for themselves. The possible candidates included Manuel de Falla and the Nobel prize-winning Andalusian poet

Juan Ramón Jiménez.[48] Jiménez was the author of a famous book about a boy and his donkey, *Platero y Yo*. He had been a particular supporter of their group at the Residencia. Imagine his feelings when he read the following missive:

> Our Distinguished Friend,
>
> We believe it is our duty to inform you in a totally disinterested way that your work is deeply repugnant to us because of its immoral, hysterical and arbitrary quality.
>
> In particular SHIT! for your facile and ill-intentioned *Platero y Yo*, the least donkeyish and the most odious donkey that we have ever encountered.
>
> SHIT. Sincerely

'When we arrived in Madrid, all the friends of Ramón refused to talk to us,' Buñuel remembered. 'We learned later that Ramón, who was a solitary, had been sick for three days because of our letter.'[49]

But satisfying though such exploits might be, they were no substitute for a career. Would Dalí, Buñuel wondered, be interested in collaborating on a Surrealist film?

Whatever he had in mind, it does not seem to have been the film that became *Un Chien andalou*. Denise Batcheff, whose husband Pierre would take the leading role, remembered her husband coming home one day from the shooting of a Josephine Baker vehicle, *La Sirène des Tropiques*, to tell her excitedly about a young Spanish assistant who 'had in his head a film that would revolutionize the world'.[50] But she gives no clue as to its contents. In fact Buñuel was still at this point (late 1928) thinking of the Gómez de la Serna scenario, hardly world-shaking. Perhaps he could persuade his mother to finance it? He returned to Zaragoza to try his luck once more. She had never approved of his cinematic ambitions (most unsuitable). On the other hand, his sisters had each been promised a dowry of 50,000 pesetas. Perhaps on grounds of equity, perhaps simply as a relatively cheap way to cure him of the film bug once and for all, the notary finally persuaded her to open her purse. Luis could have 25,000 pesetas. 'For the first and only time,' he said, 'I was my own producer.' In January 1929, he set off for Figueras and Dalí.

Dalí at once scornfully rejected the Gómez de la Serna project. Instead, he himself had just produced a very short scenario 'which had the touch of genius, and which was completely counter to the contemporary cinema'.[51]

It sounds plausible: Dalí's ultra-modern sensibility was at this point far in advance of Buñuel's, even though Buñuel was the one whose future career would be most affected by the direction they now took. Buñuel, however, says nothing of this scenario, remembering simply that 'One morning we told each other our dreams and I decided that they might be the basis for the film we wanted to make.'[52]

We needed to find a plot. Dalí said, 'Last night I dreamed that my hands were swarming with ants.' I said, 'And I dreamed that I cut someone's eye in half.' 'There's our film, let's do it.' We wrote the screenplay in six days. Our minds worked so identically that there was no argument at all. The way we wrote was to take the first thoughts that came into our heads, rejecting all those that seemed tainted by culture or upbringing. They had to be images that surprised us, and that both of us accepted without question. That's all. For example: the woman grabs a tennis racquet to defend herself from the man who wants to attack her. So then he looks round for something with which to counter-attack, and (here I'm talking with Dalí) 'What d'you see?' 'A flying toad.' 'Bad!' 'A bottle of brandy.' 'No good!' 'Well, I see two ropes.' 'Right, but what comes after the ropes?' 'He's pulling them, and he falls down, because it's something very heavy.' 'Yes, the fall's good.' 'With the ropes come two big dry pumpkins.' 'What else?' 'Two Marist brothers.' 'That's it, two Marists!' 'What else?' 'A cannon.' 'Bad! It should be a luxurious armchair.' 'No, a grand piano.' 'Very good, and on the grand piano, a donkey ... no, two rotting donkeys.' 'Wonderful!'[53]

Every afternoon Buñuel, who knew how to type, would set himself up with a packet of Lucky Strikes and a bottle of whisky, and settle down to write a scene embodying the morning's ideas. When he was satisfied he would sit back, light up, and drink a little whisky. He would call Dalí to comment on what he had just written, they would discuss it for a while, Buñuel would smoke another cigarette to let the discussion sink in, and start writing again.[54]

The film, of course, would become *Un Chien andalou*. It acquired its name, Buñuel said, because that was the title he had given to a collection of poems. He and Dalí had originally planned to call their film *Dangerous to Lean In*, a play on the familiar warning displayed on all train windows. But then they thought this too literary, and agreed that Buñuel's title was better. Lorca, however, put a darker gloss on the affair. In the Residencia, southerners were often referred to as *perros andaluces* (Andalusian dogs), and to Lorca, depressed at Dalí's defection and jealous of his supplanter, this could only be a reference to himself. When in 1930 he visited New York he told a friend, who later passed it on to Buñuel himself, that 'Buñuel has made a shitty little thing called An Andalusian Dog, and the Andalusian dog is me.'[55]

The question of who deserves credit for what in the two films Dalí and Buñuel made together, *Un Chien andalou* and *L'Âge d'or*, has led to an ongoing argument between partisans of the two. This argument, especially as it touched *L'Âge d'or*, would sour relations between them for ever. Dalinians assert that these two films are unlike anything else Buñuel ever produced, that he showed no such impetus before collaborating with Dalí, and that the imagery which pervades them –

insects, rotting donkeys, Marists, archbishops, perverse sex and the rest – is to be found throughout Dalí's work and echoes his obsessions.

So it is and so it does. But the same could equally be said of Buñuel. These images, so extraordinary, new and shocking to the non-Spanish eye, were part of the vocabulary of the whole Residencia group to which both Dalí and Buñuel belonged. For all of them in that harsh land, death pervaded life as it pervades the bloody icons of Spanish Catholicism. 'The two bases of my childhood', Buñuel said, 'were a deep eroticism, which was sublimated at first in a great religious faith, and a permanent awareness of death.'[56]

Within this general awareness, however, both Dalí and Lorca identified with death in very specific ways. Each had a brother who had died in infancy – in Dalí's case a year before he was born, in Lorca's when he was four – and with whom he morbidly identified. For Dalí the identification was doubly strengthened by the fact that the dead child was also called Salvador. There were, he liked to say, three Salvadors all sucking the life from him: his dead brother, his father (also Salvador) and Christ the Saviour.[57] 'All my childhood I was terrified by the thought that I was my brother and that I was really dead.'[58]

Lorca, too, was obsessed by the thought of his own death. He dealt with this fear by constantly acting it out.

He talked about death all the time ... for instance, every night it was impossible for Lorca to sleep before each of his friends came to his room. I remember one morning Lorca played dead. He said, 'This is the second day of my death,' and described 'my coffin coming in the streets of Granada', and the 'Ballet of the Death inside the Coffin'. Everybody came and everybody is completely anguished about this mimic representation – and Lorca laughed because of the look of terror in the face of the people and became relaxed, and very happy, and slept very well. This was necessary every night to make a representation of his death.[59]

And where there is death, there is also (especially in the Spanish consciousness) putrefaction. Several members of the group claimed the famous rotting donkeys as images from their childhood. Buñuel said, 'I was walking with my father in an olive-grove one day when I smelt a sweet, repellent stench wafting on the breeze. A hundred metres away a dead donkey, horribly swollen, was providing a banquet for a dozen vultures ... The peasants didn't bury dead animals because they thought it was good for the soil to let them decompose ... My father took my hand and led me away from there.'[60] In another version of this story the animal is an ox. Dalí, too, recounted tales of childhood encounters with rotting animals – in his case a dead hedgehog seething with maggots, significantly encountered on the day of his early erotic encounter with Julia Pichot, the 'Dulita' of the contentious *Rêverie*.

It was Pepín Bello who named these apparitions. He christened them *carnuzos*, and the word rapidly passed into common currency, a frequent term of abuse among the group (as their correspondence testifies). One of the members, the painter Santiago Ontañon, defined it as 'any form or apparition of something disagreeable, solid, fleshy and repellently dead. So that dead donkey which appears on a piano in *Un Chien andalou* ... [as] any member of the group ... knows perfectly well, is no more than one of Pepín Bello's *carnuzos* ... though of course it's Dalí's original idea.'[61] Buñuel disputed this: 'An idea of mine,' he said, 'which I'd had in my head since 1923.' He also claimed that the term *carnuzo* originated in his own childhood.[62] But the important point is not who was first, but the fact that these images were common currency. They pervade both Dalí's work and Buñuel's. *Both* are canons of sexual guilt, death, rottenness, insects, deformity and the subconscious. Both men continued throughout their lives to develop the shared themes of their youth. Dalí's great gift to Buñuel was the realization that there was no need to look any further for a subject than the recesses of his own mind.

Their collaboration consisted of variations upon this common pool of obsessions. And it was at once clear that the result was something out of the ordinary. By February 1929, Buñuel was back in Paris. 'You're right, we should have written from Figueras, but there was too much to say,' he wrote to Pepín Bello. 'We didn't send anyone so much as a postcard ... We've been working in close collaboration on a fantastic screenplay unlike anything in the history of film. It's something really big. You're going to love it. We're going to start filming in March.'[63]

He returned to Paris, where he changed his mother's money into francs, and at once blew half on treating his friends in cabarets and restaurants. Then ('because I'm a responsible fellow and I didn't want to disappoint my mother'),[64] he turned his attention to the film. Fortunately the rate of exchange was still favourable.

Buñuel rented a studio at Billancourt, and hired Epstein's cameraman, Albert Duverger, and the young actor Pierre Batcheff, whom he had met filming *La Sirène des Tropiques* and to whom he had confided his mysterious and revolutionary film idea. Batcheff was so keen to work on *Un Chien andalou* that he broke another contract in order to do so, at considerable financial loss. Unfortunately he was a drug addict who, according to Dalí, 'smelled continually of ether'.[65] Not long after *Chien andalou* was finished he committed suicide at the age of twenty-four.

The filming took just fifteen days. Buñuel was always famous for the speed of his filming. His screenplays were extremely detailed, he shot few retakes, and editing was largely a case of simply stringing the shots together (in the case of *Un*

Chien andalou, there was so little money for laboratory work that he did all the dissolves and fades by winding back the film and irising down the image). This was a silent film: the actors had no lines to learn and did not see the script. Buñuel shot mainly in sequence. He would say, 'Now look out of the window. There's an army passing.' Or, 'Two drunks are having a fight.'

The opening scene is of course one of the most notorious sequences in the history of cinema:

6 Medium square shot of man left-profile against French windows. He examines the strop and razor, then opens doors to go outside.
7 Longer square shot of balcony on to which man has just emerged, seen from opposite. He looks around him, and out across the balcony, continuing to test razor on thumb before stopping with hands on parapet.
8 Head-and-shoulders, three-quarter, right-profile of man as he raises head to look upwards.
9 Long shot of darkened sky with moon distant left, approached by slivers of horizontal cloud from right.
10 Similar to end of 8.
11 Square close-up of the female protagonist's face, other character's (man's) body half-glimpsed to her left (screen right), using left hand to open her left eye. When he does so, his right hand enters frame with razor and he goes to draw razor across eye. The man is now wearing a striped tie.
12 Similar to 9, but moon now sliced by cloud.
13 Close-up of eye, held open by fingers, slit by razor, exuding jelly.[66]

The eye was a (dead) calf's, shaved and made up; the man with the razor, Buñuel himself. Even though the calf was dead, he could barely bring himself to go through with the scene: after shooting it he felt sick for a week.

The question of provenance hovers particularly persistently over this scene, and it is worth examining in detail as an example of the claims and counter-claims that fly back and forth. Buñuel said, 'I put it in because I'd dreamed it, and I knew it would revolt people.'[67] And a poem he wrote, 'Palacio de hielo' ('Palace of Ice'), seems to support this:

When Napoleon's soldiers entered Zaragoza, VILE ZARA-GOZA, all they found was the wind in the deserted streets. Only in one puddle did they come across the croaking eyes of Luis Buñuel. Napoleon's soldiers finished them off with their bayonets.

He insisted that he wrote this in 1927, though it was not published until May 1929, after *Chien andalou* was finished. Also in 1927, Dalí had written a prose, *My Girlfriend on the Beach*, which included the phrase 'My girlfriend likes the sleepy delicacies of lavatories, and the softness of extremely fine scalpel cuts on the curved pupil which is dilated for the extraction of a cataract.' Both of them, moreover, would have seen Benjamin Péret's poem 'Les Arômes de l'amour', published in 1928 in *Le Grand Jeu*, a magazine they both avidly read: 'What greater pleasure/than to make love/the body wrapped in cries/the eyes shut by razors'.[68]

Who, then, originated the famous image? Perhaps, as so often happens, it was in the air; it can be traced to *all* these sources. But in none of them did it possess the shocking force of the film. If *Un Chien andalou* demonstrated anything, it was the unrivalled possibilities of film as a Surrealist medium.

Dalí arrived in Paris a few days before the end of shooting. He was supposed to be bringing some ants for the scene in which they swarm out of a hole in Pierre Batcheff's hand. Buñuel, a keen entomologist, had a particular fat, red-headed variety in mind and sent precise instructions for their capture and welfare ('I'm relying on you to make sure we don't have to put caterpillars or flies or rabbits in the hole . . .').[69] In the event Dalí failed in this mission and the ants were provided by a more reliable friend. He arrived to be met by Buñuel, Jeanne and her sister Georgette. Jeanne was deputed to take care of him, help him across the street and over other necessary hurdles. She had emerged from purdah to take part in the film: in the cause of art, all hands were pressed into service. Jeanne brought the money from the bank to pay the actors and was an extra in the film alongside Dalí (who also played one of the Marists). She also sewed Pierre Batcheff's jacket, but this proved too much for Buñuel, who caught Batcheff eyeing up his fiancée. After that, when Batcheff was around Jeanne was locked into another room, 'so they won't distract you'.[70] Dalí also helped with the preparation of the rotten donkeys. He improved on nature by enlarging their eye sockets and mouths with scissors, adding extra jaws, and applying quantities of runny glue to give the impression of blood.

At the end of filming Buñuel left for Madrid, where he had promised to present a programme of new American comedies for the film society. Jeanne was left in care of Salvador, who was Spanish and therefore trustworthy. Out walking one day, he tried to engage her in metaphysical experiment. Did she, he asked, believe in life after death? 'Probably.' 'Probably's not enough, it's necessary TO KNOW.' To this end, he proposed that he should kill her. If there were an afterlife, she could then prove it by appearing to him. Jeanne declined, and suggested that *she* kill *him*. The experiment was conveniently forgotten.[71]

*

Dalí had not come to Paris merely to take part in a film. He had more serious business in mind. He had for some time been in contact with the Catalan painter Joan Miró. Miró, who was ten years older than Dalí, lived and worked in Paris, where he was associated with the Surrealists. He admired Dalí's work, and as a fellow-Catalan felt to some extent responsible for him. In 1927 he had visited Dalí in Figueras and introduced him to his dealer, Pierre Loeb, who had been impressed. He now proposed to show Dalí around town and give him some useful hints and introductions.

In the early years, Dada and especially Surrealism had been dominated by writers and poets. Of course a number of visual artists – Picabia, Arp, Max Ernst, Man Ray – had always been associated with them, while the friendly but detached spirits of Duchamp and Picasso hovered in the background. But the theoretical running had been made by writers. Now, however, the balance was changing. Since the mid-1920s a number of painters had joined the Surrealist ranks, notably René Magritte, André Masson, Yves Tanguy and Joan Miró, and in 1928 Breton had marked their increasing importance by publishing his essay on 'Surrealism and Painting'. Not all the artists he discussed were practising Surrealists – for example, the section on Picabia concluded that 'only his perfect incomprehension of Surrealism and his likely refusal to subscribe to some of the ideas I express prevent me from considering him at length *as I should like to do*'.[72] And not all the artists welcomed what he had to say: he was particularly dismissive of Chirico's current *oeuvre*, a sad descent from his extraordinary and influential beginnings. (It was Chirico's *The Child's Brain*, seen from a bus, which had first attracted Breton to modern art in 1913: exactly the same epiphany, including the bus, had occurred with Tanguy, then a merchant seaman, some years later. 'He jumped off the bus and spent the rest of the afternoon staring at the painting, finally saying to himself, "This is opening paths for me. I want to become a painter and to enter such a world as this."')[73] But Miró's case presented none of these problems. He was producing fine work, of undoubted Surrealist pedigree.

In Breton's words, 'No-one comes near to him in associating the inassociable, or in calmly breaking what we'd never hoped to see broken.'[74]

For Breton, then, Miró embodied some of the essential Surrealist qualities. However, the overview he now offered Dalí was as far as could be imagined from Breton's austere notion of the Surrealist life. Miró had no time for the approved mixture of café evenings and distaste for vile success. He proposed, on the contrary, a swift lesson in social climbing. Art is a luxury product, and artists rely for their living on rich patrons. These therefore have to be cultivated. It was a lesson Dalí never forgot, and a dilemma the Surrealists never solved. Even the severe Breton had been glad to accept support from such a decadent figure as the couturier Jacques Doucet.

Over dinner, an otherwise silent meal, the businesslike Miró asked only if Dalí possessed a dinner jacket, and on hearing he did not, said, 'You must get yourself one. We'll have to go out in society.' Dalí ordered a dinner jacket next day. When it was ready Miró took him to dinner at the Duchess of Dato's, where the guests included the Countess Cuevas de Vera, later to become a friend. Miró (though not Dalí, who babbled) remained as impenetrably silent as ever. They went on to the Bateau Ivre, where they drank a bottle of champagne. Dalí envied Miró the ease with which he paid the bill. Walking home, Miró said, 'It's going to be hard for you, but don't get discouraged. Don't talk too much' (Dalí 'then understood that perhaps his silence was a tactic') 'and try to do some physical culture. I have a boxing instructor and I train every evening.' Between sentences, says Dalí, 'he would contract his mouth into an expression full of energy'.[75] Miró also took him to see Tzara and Pierre Loeb, and, most importantly, his neighbour Camille Goemans, a Belgian art dealer and close friend of René Magritte, who had followed him to Paris. Goemans had recently set up his own gallery, the Galerie

Goemans, in the Rue de Seine, opening with an exhibition of collages by Picasso, Arp and Magritte. Goemans liked Dalí's work, and gave him a contract stipulating that between 15 May and 15 November 1929, he would handle all Dalí's production. Dalí would receive 1,000 francs a month from the date of the contract; Goemans would organize a show of his work during the 1929–30 season. Goemans promised to visit him in Cadaqués later that summer. He also introduced Magritte, and took Dalí to the Bal Tabarin where he pointed out Paul Eluard: 'He's very important, and what's more he buys paintings. His wife is in Switzerland and the woman with him is a girlfriend of his.'[76] So the chain of introductions might have continued indefinitely, but 'The *Chien andalou*', said Dalí, 'distracted me from the society career to which Joan Miró would have liked to initiate me.'[77]

Soon after this Buñuel and Dalí began to show their film to distributors while waiting to see if the censors would clear it. Two were interested: Tallier, who owned the Studio des Ursulines, and a young avant-gardiste, Jean Mauclaire, who had opened a new art cinema, Studio 28, in Montmartre. Meanwhile Buñuel set about trying to arrange private screenings, to prepare the ground for the day when *Chien andalou* would be released. This was how he made his first contact with the Surrealists, in the shape of Aragon and Man Ray. The meeting, which Buñuel described several times in slightly different forms, took place in one of the Montparnasse cafés – the Dôme, or possibly the Coupole. Perhaps Léger introduced him to Man Ray, who took him to meet Aragon; perhaps Zervos introduced them. Man Ray had himself just made a film, *Le Mystère du Château de Dé*. He and Aragon saw *Un Chien andalou* the following day, liked it, and arranged for it to be screened at the première of Man Ray's own film at the Ursulines.

Buñuel was of course terrified. He liked to tell the story of how he stood with the gramophone behind the screen, his pockets filled with stones which he intended to hurl at the audience in true Surrealist style if they booed. ('He dreamed it,' said Aragon. 'He didn't have stones in his pockets and he wasn't behind the screen. Of course he was worried about what we'd think. But he needn't have been, because we all thought it was wonderful.')[78] Jeanne remembered sitting with Dalí at the back of the hall, clutching each other's hands for comfort.

In the event, the film was greeted with wild applause. Buñuel 'was stupefied and confused. I actually believed it was a joke.'[79] But it was not. Overnight, Luis Buñuel had become the hottest new talent in Paris. *La Revue du Cinéma* wanted to publish the script, to which Buñuel happily agreed. And the *Chien andalou*'s theatrical rights were at once bought by a distributor, Pierre Braunberger, whose company Studio-Film specialized in experimental work and had good contacts in the censorship office. By 1 July it had its certificate, despite the opening scene (which, Buñuel liked to boast, had caused twelve miscarriages during the private screenings alone).[80]

Breton, however, was not yet won round. On the contrary, he was if anything ill-disposed towards the newcomers. He had not yet seen this film which, to his indignation, 'everyone' was calling Surrealist, a name to which (from his point of view) it had no evident right whatever. Braunberger proposed to open it at Studio 28. One day Breton announced to the assembled Surrealists, over the regulation mandarin curaçao at their new venue, the Café Radio, 'There's a film at Studio 28 by two people called Buñuel and Dalí that we've never heard of. We must all go along this week and sabotage the showing.'[81]

This was a dangerous moment. Breton was expert at this kind of disruption, and particularly severe towards unauthorized 'Surrealists'. Some time earlier he had succeeded in ejecting a so-called 'Surrealist ballet' from the Champs Elysées; and when Germaine Dulac's *Le Coquille et le clergyman* opened at the Ursulines he engineered a riot following which Tallier, the proprietor, had refrained from calling the police: a circumstance which placed Breton in his debt, since Chiappe, the bullying police chief, would certainly have enjoyed this opportunity to stamp on the Surrealists. Now he proposed to mete out the same treatment to *Un Chien andalou.* At the last moment, however, he decided to take a look at the film before he destroyed it. A private viewing was arranged by Tallier. Breton emerged full of enthusiasm. As how should he not! It must have seemed (it still seems) as though Surrealism was made for the cinema, and the cinema for Surrealism. *Un Chien andalou* takes place entirely in the world of dreams and the subconscious. As Cyril Connolly put it, 'the Id had spoken'.[82] (In fact the film's dreamlike effects had more to do with Buñuel's unease at handling actors than conscious intention. They arose largely from his habit of giving his actors quite neutral directions so that their expressions did not necessarily reflect the action.)

Buñuel and Dalí were invited forthwith to Café Radio. '[Buñuel] was a little shy,' Georges Sadoul remembered, 'but he didn't need to say much before we realised that he was one of us ... He belonged to our group body and soul before he had even met us. That same day, or perhaps the day after, we met another shy Spaniard, as modest as his modest moustache. Salvador Dalí.'[83] Dalí, however, was eager to get away from Paris and devote himself to painting for his forthcoming exhibition. He left for Figueras, while Buñuel remained to take his place among their new friends.

Almost at once, it became clear that life among the Surrealists was a complicated affair. The first difficulty concerned the permission which had been granted *La Revue du Cinéma* to publish the screenplay. The Belgian magazine *Variétés* was about to publish a Surrealist number. Could they publish the screenplay? Regretfully, Buñuel explained that they could not. But couldn't he withdraw it from the *Revue du Cinéma*? ' "Impossible, I've given my word." They said, "Your word doesn't mean anything." I thought that was unfair. "Fairness doesn't exist," said Breton. "You must choose: are you with the police or with us?" ' Could he accept this? 'Absolutely. I'd abandoned all my hopes and my work to the Surrealists. That was a very serious moment for me.'[84] It was decided he must go to the printworks and destroy the letterpress of the screenplay. Nervously he agreed, but it was too late: the magazine had already been printed. A compromise was arrived at. Buñuel must write to twenty Paris periodicals protesting that Gallimard (who owned the magazine) had abused his trust. And the screenplay would be printed in *Révolution surréaliste*, with a note stating that this was the only authorized publication.

The first hurdle was surmounted, but others sprang up. Breton, despite his hatred of all things bourgeois, was a stickler for etiquette and formal manners, both of which demanded that any person arriving at the daily Surrealist gatherings must shake hands with all present. But the café was often crowded, and it was not always easy to reach Breton, deep in his corner. In those circumstances Buñuel would shake hands with whomever he could reach and wave to the rest. 'Does Buñuel have something against me?' demanded Breton.[85] More serious was a difficulty which arose when *Un Chien andalou* was four months into its run at Studio 28, where it was enjoying considerable commercial success. Breton summoned Buñuel to Rue Fontaine. He arrived to find himself confronted by a sort of tribunal. 'I was told, "It's a scandal. Your film is successful. Much too successful. The bourgeois all admire you. And you accept it. It's very simple, you've got to decide now, whose side are you on?" It sounds like a joke now. But it was TRAGIC. For the next few days I seriously thought of suicide.'[86]

The Surrealist bind seemed as impossible as ever. How was one to live while at the same time shunning both bourgeois society and commercial success? Breton himself suffered as much as anyone from these stern prohibitions. He was almost always terribly poor. He did not enjoy this: on the brief occasions when he found himself in possession of some money, he became 'high-spirited and changed'.[87] But compromise in the cause of mere happiness was not permitted.

In extremis, society was more acceptable than success. The market demanded more compromises than a sympathetic patron. Thus, Breton and Aragon had been supported by Doucet; Pierre Reverdy, Breton's ascetic early father figure, became the lover of Coco Chanel, sharing her Riviera villa, La Pausa; Nancy Cunard supported, as we have seen, Louis Aragon; while rich and artistic Americans such as Peggy Guggenheim and Caresse Crosby were permitted to open their purses and their houses to artistic talent. So the great stock market crash, which occurred in October 1929, put Breton in a highly embarrassing situation. On the one hand, he welcomed it: it furthered the cause of the revolution and hastened the end of bourgeois society. On the other hand, it wiped out many of those who kept artists – including Surrealist artists – afloat.

Not all, however. Among the most important of these generous and discerning millionaires were Charles and Marie-Laure de Noailles. He was the scion of an ancient family, she doubly qualified for the role of Surrealist Maecenas, being on one side moneyed – the daughter of the rich Jewish banker Bischoffsheim – and on the other impeccably descended from the Marquis de Sade. They owned a sumptuous mansion on the Place des Etats-Unis, and a modern villa near Hyères, where they liked to entertain their friends. They were among the most important and discriminating collectors of modern art. And the crash had made no impact upon their vast fortune.

Every year, as a birthday present for his wife, Charles de Noailles liked to commission a film from one of their friends. The previous year's had been Man Ray's *Mystère du Château de Dé*. Of course the Noailles had been among the audience at its première, and immediately realized that *Un Chien andalou* was a far better film. At Marie-Laure's instigation, Noailles sought out Buñuel to ask him to dinner. Buñuel, uncertain about this collision of worlds (if mere success was suspect to the Surrealists, were not aristocrats even more so?), warily asked Breton if he should go. He was assured that there would be no problem.[88]

With its liveried servants and full-length Goya portraits at the head of the staircase, the Noailles mansion must have felt as dreamlike as any scene from his film. When the meal had ended Noailles said, 'We would like to make a film with you . . . two reels, just like *Un Chien andalou*.'[89]

Without further ado, Buñuel took his leave and set off for Cadaqués and Dalí. He had no very clear idea in mind, simply a collection of visual gags – a cart driving through the middle of a salon, a gamekeeper who kills his son because he feels like it, a bishop thrown out of a window. Dalí had others, such as a man walking through a park with a stone on his head. For a few days they discussed these and other possibilities. But the urgent electricity which had fuelled the *Chien andalou* discussions was no longer there. For Dalí's attention was elsewhere, and 'it had become impossible to work with him'.[90]

*

Dalí had not stayed in Paris for the *Chien andalou*'s commercial opening, but had hurried off to Cadaqués to paint and meet the guests he had invited for the summer. The Goemans and Magrittes were already there when he arrived, to be followed some days later by Paul and Gala Eluard and their daughter Cécile.

If his account is to be believed, the prospect of all these celebrated and important people arriving to see him in Cadaqués reduced Dalí to a state of hysteria. Every time anyone spoke to him he burst into fits of uncontrollable laughter, which made conversation almost impossible. He spent hours on his appearance, shaving meticulously, sporting knife-creased white trousers, silk shirts of his own design with low necks and full sleeves, a necklace of imitation pearls, a bracelet of metallic ribbon, flattening his hair with pomade.

His first sight of Gala Eluard was not propitious. The Eluards had driven from Switzerland, they were tired, and Gala was in a bad mood. A drink later that evening, when everyone had had a chance to recover from the journey, went off a little better. They arranged to meet on the beach in front of the Dalí house at eleven the next morning. The tale of Dalí's demented preparation for this meeting is legendary.

> I took my finest shirt and cut it irregularly at the bottom, making it so short that it did not quite reach my navel. After which, putting it on me, I began to tear it artfully: one hole, baring my left shoulder, another, the black hairs on my chest, and a large square tear on the left side exposing my nipple that was nearly black.
>
> Once I had torn the shirt in all the appropriate places the great problem that confronted me was that of the collar ... should I leave it open or closed? ... I buttoned the top button, but cut off the collar entirely with a pair of scissors ... I now shaved the hairs under my arms. But failing to achieve the ideal bluish effect I had observed for the first time on the elegant ladies of Madrid, I went and got some laundry bluing, mixed it with some powder, and dyed my armpits with this ... Immediately my sweat caused the

makeup to run, leaving bluish streaks that ran down my sides . . . I took my gillette and began to shave again, pressing harder so as to make myself bleed. In a few seconds my armpits were all bloody. I now had only to let the blood coagulate, and I daintily began putting some everywhere, especially on the knees . . . I should have liked some kind of perfume . . . I had often smelled [goat manure] after dark in damp weather, when the smell became stronger. It pleased me very much but it was not complete. Back in my studio, I threw a handful of this manure, and then another, into the dissolved glue. With a large brush I stirred and stirred it until it formed a homogenous paste . . . I let the whole thing jell, and when it was cold I took a fragment of the paste that I had made and rubbed my whole body with it.[91]

Thus bedizened, he awaited the magic hour of eleven o'clock. Glancing out of the window, however, he saw that Gala had already arrived. And the sight of her body, its contours clearly visible under her swimsuit, overwhelmed him – especially 'her very delicate buttocks which the exaggerated slenderness of her waist enhanced and rendered greatly more desirable'. Suddenly appalled by all he had done, he undressed, washed off as much as he could of his various pungent pastes and cosmetics, put on his favourite pearl necklace and a red geranium, and ran out to meet his fate.

*

Dalí and Gala did not at once fall into each other's arms and declare undying love. For one thing – but this was the least of it – she was married, and her husband and child were present. More to the point, Dalí's state of nerves precluded any ease of communication. The laughing fits had taken uncontrollable hold of him: he was incapable of conversation. When Buñuel arrived hotfoot from the Noailles' he was greeted by a dis-tracted Dalí, babbling unstoppably. 'Oh, boy, you can't imagine, she's wonderful. Beautiful. Unimaginably intelligent . . . the most phenomenal woman you've ever met.'[92]

Dalí records that while the rest of the party were 'resigned' to this, Buñuel was 'terribly disappointed' because he wanted to get on with the new scenario.[93] It would certainly be surprising if this were not so. But there was more to it than that. Buñuel had no sexual interest in Dalí, but the emotional ties between them were very strong, and he had already fought off one rival for his friend's affection. He accused Gala of jealousy – 'She couldn't bear our intimate friendship,'[94] but of course he was jealous too. He and Gala were adversaries, in nothing less than a fight for Dalí's soul. Gala would change Dalí for ever, and those who had loved him as he was – most of all Buñuel and his sister Ana Maria – hated her for it.

Buñuel soon made his dislike apparent. 'We all had a drink together . . . and the French party decided to walk back to Dalí's house. Gala was walking next to me, and on our way we talked of various trivial things. I found myself saying that what repelled me more than anything else in the female anatomy was when a woman had a large space between her thighs. The next day we all went swimming, and, to my embarrassment, I saw that Gala had just this unfortunate physical attribute . . .'[95]

'Found myself saying' indeed! A few days later, Buñuel went even further and actually 'found himself' trying to strangle Gala, while her daughter Cécile rushed away to hide behind some rocks and Dalí, on his knees, pleaded for her life. ('All I wanted was to see the tip of her tongue between her teeth.')[96]

Dalí at this time was painting *Le Jeu lugubre* (*The Dismal Sport* – the title was suggested by Paul Eluard), a 'veritable anthology', as his biographer Ian Gibson puts it, of his current sexual and para-sexual preoccupations, including shit, castration, masturbation (the giant hand again), swarming ants, a vulva, a figure resembling Dalí's father, and innumerable other details.[97] It is a deeply disturbing picture, and Dalí relates how Gala, before she committed herself to a relationship, questioned him about it. Did it refer to his own life? If so, 'we can have nothing in common, because that sort of thing appears loathsome to me, and hostile to my kind of life'. If, on the other hand, it was simply propaganda, he should beware of reducing his paintings to 'mere psychopathological documents'.

Dalí, who had been absorbed for some days in the delicate painting and repainting of a pair of shit-stained underpants, immediately suspected that this was what Gala was referring to. 'I was suddenly tempted to answer her with a lie. If I admitted to her that I was coprophagic, it would make me even more interesting and phenomenal [a favourite expression] in everybody's eyes.' But he resisted this temptation, and said instead, 'I swear to you that I am not "coprophagic". I consciously loathe that type of aberration as much as you can possibly loathe it. But I consider scatology as a terrorizing element, just as I do blood, or my phobia for grasshoppers.' Following this she took his hand for the first time, and said, 'My little boy! We shall never leave each other.'[98] And they never did. From then on Gala joined Dalí's galaxy of obsessions; became, indeed, his chief obsession of all. A few days later Buñuel, the Belgians and Eluard returned to Paris, leaving Gala and the unfortunate Cécile with Dalí in Cadaqués.

No one reading this story can fail to be struck by the extraordinary complaisance of Gala's then husband, Paul Eluard. In fact until Gala left him for Dalí the two had achieved that rarity, often invoked but elusive as the unicorn: a truly open marriage. 'He was an extraordinarily human person, Paul,' said his great friend Roland Penrose. '. . . And of course his love for women was quite exceptional because he managed to love so many women, without making them jealous of each other.'[99] And, he might have added, without being jealous himself.

Paul and Gala had met in 1912, in a Swiss tuberculosis sanatorium. He was then seventeen, she, eighteen. He was Parisian, she (her name was Helena Diakonova), Russian, from the provincial city of Kazan. They fell in love; they returned to their respective homes. In 1914, Eluard was mobilized, first (because of his health) in the auxiliaries, then, in 1916, in a field hospital near the front line. Finally, in December 1916, he was moved, at his own request, to an infantry regiment. But before this, in September, Gala had arrived in France from Russia. In February 1917, they married.

They were (or so Eluard always told his daughter) both virgins at that point. And indeed, since Gala, having nowhere else to go, had to lodge in Paris with Eluard's upright and disapproving mother, this is easy to believe. But in the letters she wrote him at this time the passionate and unbridled woman is already present: 'I bless your life, I'm terribly grateful that you exist. I adore your thought, your mind, your body, your ways, everything, everything everything about you for ever.'[100]

In 1917 this idyll was interrupted by the unwelcome arrival of a child; but the marriage continued after the war, with Paul working in his father's construction business while also, of course, spending increasing amounts of time with Breton and his group.

By 1921, it seems both Paul and Gala had recognized that they required more variety than any conventional marriage could offer. It will be remembered that that summer, at the end of *Dada en plein air* at Tarrenz-bei-Imst, Breton and Simone went on to beard Freud in Vienna while Eluard and Gala left for Cologne, where they were to visit Max Ernst. Ernst himself had not yet been to Paris – quite apart from anything else, Germans were not welcome in France so soon

after the war. But his work was known there – Breton, Simone
and Aragon had organized an exhibition of it earlier that year
– and Eluard felt a particular affinity with the magical and
delicate paintings of this man whom he had so recently faced
across the barbed wire of no man's land. ('Max and I were at
Verdun together and used to shoot at each other,' he liked to
say.)[101] He looked forward to meeting him in person; and to
that end the tall, seraphically smiling Ernst (who very much
resembled his own creation Lop-lop King of the Birds)
arranged for the Eluards to take an apartment across the
landing from where he himself lived with his wife Lou and
little son Jimmy.

The Ernst marriage was already in some trouble, and the
new arrivals did nothing to help it. Max started spending more
and more time in the Eluards' apartment, and finally moved
across the landing altogether. Lou Ernst described Gala as
'That Russian female . . . that slithering, glittering creature with
dark, falling hair, vaguely oriental and luminous black eyes
and small delicate bones, who had to remind one of a panther.
This almost silent, avaricious woman, who, having failed to
entice her husband into an affair with me in order to get Max,
finally decided to keep both men, with Eluard's loving con-
sent.' All Lou's worst fears were realized one rainy day when
they were sitting together in the living room. 'Max was working with Gala on the translation of one of his books and in his
arguments about some nuance of language became very sharp
and insulting. Meaning to tease her amicably, I remarked,
"Why do you allow him to scream at you like this? That is
something he never dared with me." Max looked up briefly
and replied, "Yes, I also never loved you as passionately as I
do her." '[102]

The following summer, after the second Dada holiday at
Tarrenz, Ernst decided to follow the Eluards to Paris. 'You are
twenty-eight years old,' he told Lou with the cavalier certainty

338

of one who is about to do exactly what he pleases. 'You know all about love, you have a son ... What more do you want? Your life with the child will be a happy one.'[103] He smuggled himself into France and moved in with the Eluards at Eaubonne, just north of Paris. This *ménage à trois* seems to have worked well, at least for a time. Soon all the walls of the house were covered with Ernst's fantastic frescoes: one in the dining room showed a naked woman with all her entrails picked out in vivid colours, which Cécile found very frightening.

In 1923, Gala, Ernst and Eluard went to Rome to meet Giorgio di Chirico. Gala was to be the bait which would lure him into the Surrealist camp. They invited him to join them in bed, which he did, though (as he later confessed) he was not enraptured by the idea of four in a bed. In the end he got bored with their constant presence and threw them out, though he briefly thought of inviting Gala to stay. He decided against it after realizing that she could (or would) neither cook nor clean the house. However, he gave her two pictures, which she continued to cherish.[104]

Paul, however, evidently found all this harder to cope with than he would admit. In March 1924, with no warning, he took off for the South Seas. He left a note telling his father not to institute a police search, and advising him to spread the story of a sudden haemorrhage having necessitated a swift departure for Switzerland. But, it was not long before he was writing to Gala from Tahiti. 'Darling, I hope you'll come soon. I'm bored.'[105] Gala and Max joined him, and the Eluards returned to France while Max, by then tiring of Gala and her incessant demands, made a more leisurely journey back via the Far East. After this, relations with Max were uneasy. In 1927, when Gala was on a visit to Russia, Ernst ('The Pig'), urged on by his then wife Marie-Berthe, punched Eluard in the eye. She was jealous of Gala and had said some unforgivable things. 'That's it between us, for ever,' Eluard declared.[106]

It was sheer chance that brought the Eluards to Cadaqués that fateful August of 1929. In July, their itinerary was still not settled. 'Where are we going to go with Cécile?' Eluard wrote. He had recently returned to Paris from Berlin and Belgium, where he had spent some time with a girlfriend, Alice Apfel, familiarly known as La Pomme ('these journeys ... weren't disagreeable, but your ghost followed us everywhere, because you are the truth'). In June, Pomme was still with Eluard, Gala in Switzerland with a lover ('Why don't you go to Arosa now? But for how long!! For the moment I'm not alone. Perhaps you should make the most of it.')[107] By July, however, the summer holidays loomed. 'Breton is in Brittany. Goemans is going to Cadaqués, in Spain, with some Spaniards who've made a terrific film. We need to find somewhere very cheap ... Perhaps we should go to Evian first. It's excellent for the stomach. And to Lac Léman. What do you think? Then perhaps on to Spain after that. Or to the seaside.'[108] Meanwhile he had found them a wonderful new apartment in Rue Becquerel, near the Sacré Coeur. The move would cost them 'some fetishes and a large Chirico. It's worth it. We'll get more pleasure out of it.'[109] (It will be remembered that Eluard, who had an excellent eye and, of course, unrivalled contacts, made an occasional living as an art dealer.) Finally all was arranged, and it was time to set out with Cécile for Evian, where they were to meet. 'I adore you, you know that. I'm ill at the thought of seeing you, of having you again. I kiss you everywhere, everywhere.'[110]

Gala's sexual voracity is apparent from this correspondence, as is Eluard's: both enjoyed many partners. In his dreams,[111] and when possible in the flesh, Paul liked to share her with other men – 'Understand, and make him understand, that I'd like us both to have you together sometimes, as we arranged.'[112] In this sexual freedom they were perfectly suited. Such physical details had never interfered with the love that existed between them – 'I love you, I love only you, the most beautiful, and in all women I find only you: the whole of Woman, the whole of my love, so great, so simple.'[113] The affair with Dalí, then, at first bothered Eluard not at all. There had been so many affairs, and none had threatened their marriage.

Least of all this one! For Gala was sex personified, while Dalí...? All his pictures were witness to his obsession with sex – but (as Gala herself had wondered) *what* sex, exactly? Not, at any rate, what usually goes on between men and women. 'Salvador was a virgin,' Buñuel said.[114] In the view of Edward James, who was for a while his lover, 'His real interests were instinctively far more homosexual than hetero-sexual; Gala tried to believe that she had cured him of his homosexuality, but she knew in her heart that she had not really at all.'[115] In fact his 'real interests' were probably more narcissistic than anything else, consisting almost entirely of masturbation. He also enjoyed voyeurism – he tells how, on first arriving in Paris, he had a taxi-driver take him straight to a brothel where, when he stated his preferences, they led him straight to the voyeurs' peepholes.

Did Dalí and Gala ever in fact make love? He hints that they did – eventually. 'Gala was beginning to make repeated allusions to "something" which would have to happen "inevit-ably" between us ... But could she depend on me in my present overwrought state which, far from growing more normal, on the contrary bedecked itself with all the showiest tinsel of madness...?'[116] By now it was September; everyone else had gone home. They took endless walks among the olive trees while Gala waited for Dalí to calm down. They set a day. He kissed her. And then – who knows? He said (or *says* he said), 'Now tell me what you want me to do to you! But tell me slowly, looking me in the eye, with the crudest, the most ferociously erotic words that can make most of us feel the greatest shame.' He was, of course, expecting some 'ardent erotic proposal'. Instead, however, Gala replied, 'I want you to kill me.' 'I was suddenly afraid of destroying the faith Gala had had until then in my potentialities of moral courage and madness. Again I seized her in my arms, and in the most solemn manner of which I was capable I answered, "YES!" And I kissed her again, hard, on the mouth, while I repeated deep within myself, "No! I shall not kill her!" ... Gala thus weaned me from my crime, and cured my madness. Thank you! I was to marry her.'[117]

Certainly Buñuel assumed he had finally done the deed. 'I can't tell you what a letter he wrote me when he finally went to bed with Gala. What a eulogy to coitus! As though it was something that had only ever happened to him.'[118] But if it did happen, it did not happen often. Sex was not the foundation of their relationship, as it was of the relationship between Gala and Eluard. According to Edward James, Gala 'had managed to keep [Dalí's homosexuality] "sublimated" (if you can call it that) by channelling it into erotic drawings and some obscene pictures which are owned by private collectors who buy pornography ... As for Dalí's sex life with his wife, far from being jealous of her sexual infidelities, he actually facilitated them; one day he confessed to me: *"Je laisse Gala prendre des amants quand elle veut. Actuellement, je l'encourage et je l'aide, parce que cela m'excite."*'[119]

Prominent among these lovers was Eluard. Gala's departure left him terribly sad, despite the fact that he had recently met Nusch, the woman who would become his second wife. 'My only pleasure is in constantly looking at your nude photographs,' he wrote in April 1930,[120] and six months later, 'Nusch's presence at the time we finally decided to get divorced stopped me realising how lonely I was going to be. I don't think I could ever live with anyone, Nusch or anyone else. I've loved you too long, Gala, I've lived with you too long, and whatever you may think, I've shaped myself entirely according to your desires, to your dreams, to *your nature*.'[121] Nusch's views on Eluard's continuing passion for Gala are not known. Eluard had picked her off the street: she was a failed actress and, at the time he met her, so desperate that she was ready to take a client to keep warm and have a roof over her head. Perhaps she felt silence was advisable. David Gascoyne, then a young British Surrealist in Paris, remembers being at the Dalís' apartment when Eluard came to lunch there with Cécile. 'In the middle of lunch Eluard said: "Do you know the best love poem I've ever written?" And he read *Nuits partagées* (*Shared Nights*) out loud in the middle of lunch – while Dalí fiddled around with a long, long baguette and pretended not to notice.'[122] This reading must have taken some time. 'Nuits partagées' is a long, sensuous prose poem, very similar in tone to many of Eluard's letters to Gala, about the durability of love even in absence, and of fidelity even in the midst of infidelity.

Eluard, Dalí, Ernst, Chirico, Man Ray … The roll-call of Gala's lovers is impressive. Like Alma Mahler, she was a genius-hunter. Her relationship with Dalí can be viewed cynically, and often is: she wanted to be rich, and saw in him her best chance of achieving this. For what else did he offer? 'I could not understand why anyone would prefer this small, almost skeletal apparition with big intense eye-pupils in a chalk-white face, and the pencil mustache that would have gone well with the caricature of a gigolo, to Eluard or Max,' wrote Jimmy Ernst, Max's son.[123] True, he could be enchanting company. But under Gala's spell this side of him retreated, masked and eventually swamped by the persona he cultivated along with his famous moustache. Eventually, both would achieve grotesque proportions.

But if Gala had, in the sexual sense, been the perfect woman for Eluard, in another mode she was equally perfect for Dalí.

He was no fool. When he said that Gala 'cured his madness', he may, for once, have told no more than the truth. She may not have converted him to the pleasures of heterosexual love, but she enabled him to establish an equilibrium which would allow him to live and work. Left to himself, he might simply have imploded. Ana Maria Dalí, who hated Gala and all she stood for, sneered that he 'grabbed hold of Surrealism as if it would lead him to the solution of all his problems'.[124] But maybe it did. In that sense, Gala saved him; and for this he was eternally grateful. 'She had him hexed,' Buñuel said.[125] And that, too, was the truth. Both Dalí and Eluard remained completely under her spell, in Dalí's case for life, in Eluard's for years after his remarriage. His burning letters cool only as war approaches and their meetings become less frequent; as painfully, slowly, his life acquires a shape separate from Gala's.

Witches, however, are not generally loved by those outside the enchanted circle, and Gala was no exception to this rule. She was loathed by most women, and also by some men. Buñuel (who was of course not neutral in this matter) spoke of her as 'the woman I most hate ... She turns the milk sour.'[126] Not only was she a witch – she was a whore. 'It's not that I'm prejudiced,' he said, perhaps even believing this, 'but a woman who had been to bed with Chirico, Max Ernst, Man Ray, and who was married to Eluard...'[127] There was yet another side to this coin: Buñuel had always been attracted to whores. In his autobiography, he recounts how, 'fifty years later ... I suddenly dreamed of Gala. She was sitting in a box at the theatre with her back to me. I called her softly, she turned around, stood up, and kissed me lovingly on the lips. I can still smell her perfume and feel the incredible softness of her skin.'[128] He was more surprised by this dream, he says, than by any other he ever dreamt.

*

By November the cast had reassembled, this time in Paris. Gala and Dalí had returned to prepare for Dalí's show at the Galerie Goemans. Eluard had also requested some pictures for his own dealing business, including *Le Jeu lugubre*, which was soon after acquired by the Noailles. Buñuel had moved to the Terrass Hotel, which provided occasional refuge, too, for Eluard (Dalí and Gala had taken possession of the Rue Becquerel apartment) and Breton, who between Simone and Suzanne had been temporarily forced out of the Rue Fontaine.

Dalí was concentrating on his forthcoming exhibition. It was clearly going to be a great success: despite negative notices, not to speak of the great stock market crash which had taken place on 24 October, most of the pictures sold for between 6,000 and 12,000 francs. Fortified by this happy news, Dalí and Gala left Paris before the opening, bound for Spain on a 'voyage of love'. Buñuel, meanwhile, had had more discussions with the Noailles about the new film. A few days later, in Christian Zervos' office, the details were finalized. It would be more expensive than the first had been, because where *Un Chien andalou* had been silent, this one would have a sound-track. Buñuel always liked to boast that Noailles had offered him a million francs, and that he had come in under budget and returned the extra money. In fact he was offered 12,000 francs a month during shooting, 6,000 a month during editing and an advance of 9,000 francs, aiming at a final cost 'in the neighbourhood of 350,000 francs'. Only as it lengthened from two reels to seven did the film's budget begin to approach the million.[129] Committed now, Buñuel left Paris for Spain. On 15 December, he arrived in Figueras, where he and Dalí (who was now alone, Gala having returned to Paris) had agreed to spend a week working on their scenario.

An extraordinary scene greeted him on his arrival at the Dalí apartment. 'At first, all I could hear were angry shouts; then suddenly the door flew open and, purple with rage, Dalí's father threw his son out, calling him every name in the book. Dalí screamed back while his father pointed to him and swore that he hoped never to see that pig in his house again.'[130]

The respectable Dalí family had of course been outraged by Salvador's recent behaviour. The Surrealists, they felt, had perverted their son: 'The sunlight on the sea, the silver olive-leaves, everything trembled with fright when these strange persons ... turned their reddened eyes upon them.'[131] His involvement with a married woman (and what a woman!) was bad enough. But now he had committed an even more unforgivable sin – a pen-and-ink drawing of the Sacred Heart of Jesus emblazoned with the legend 'Sometimes I spit for pleasure on the portrait of my mother'. That was too much. Dalí and Buñuel moved into the Cadaqués beach house. Photographs of each other from this week survive. Dalí, visibly unnerved, has shaved off all his hair in a penitent's gesture; on top of his head is balanced something that looks like a sea urchin, but may be the front view of a Mohican hairdo. Buñuel, unshaven and slouching, looks like a bandit. They spent their week working together, though the atmosphere can hardly have been ideal for prolonged concentration, then returned to Paris and did a little more. On 10 January, Buñuel left for the Noailles' country place near Hyères, the Abbaye Saint Bernard, a mediaeval ruin to which they had added a modern house designed by the fashionable architect Robert Mallet Stevens. He was to report on progress and continue with his screenplay.

Buñuel spent ten days there. He was, by the sound of it, almost as shocked as the Dalí family might have been by the decadent habits of his new friends. His fellow-guests included Stravinsky, Jean Cocteau and the painter Christian Bérard. 'They were all opium addicts. There were some rooms where there was such a smell you couldn't even go in there,' he told

Max Aub.[132] He recounted to another friend how, standing with Stravinsky and a young orchestral conductor, the conductor said, 'You realise they're all inverts except us.' 'I hadn't realised,' Buñuel replied. 'What does it matter?' That night, naked as usual in bed with all the windows open (he had not lost his health-fiend habits), he saw his door slowly open. In slipped the young conductor, whose intentions were unmistakable. Buñuel, indignant, threw him out. He realized that the racket must have wakened all his fellow-guests, and was afraid they would take him for a Spanish savage. Next day, when a convenient silence fell, he announced: 'I owe you all an explanation. I didn't throw that person out of my room for the reasons you think, but for something much more serious: *because he was a liar.*'[133] He worked steadily at his scenario, reading each day's work to his hosts. To his relief they liked it – 'they found everything "exquisite" and "delicious"'.[134] The film ends in a Sadeian orgy; when the Duc de Blangis and his guests finally stagger over the bridge and away from their castle, one of them is transformed into Christ. To Buñuel's amusement, Charles de Noailles excused himself from the late-night reading of this scene, saying he had to be up early next day for Mass.

Dalí and Gala were also now in the south of France: they were to spend the next two months closeted in the Hotel du Château at Carry-le-Rouet near Marseille. Eluard's letters, which had been cheerful and loving the previous September – 'Do whatever you like, my beautiful darling. All I want is your happiness, all I want is your freedom'[135] – now became increasingly fevered and depressed. 'I can't talk, I keep thinking about our life, our love, our greatness. I'm sleeping badly: I dream so much about you, and you're there too when I awake, taller, more delicate, more full of life than ever – but desperately inaccessible.'[136] The fact that Gala was not coming back to him had finally sunk in. They would often meet again, they would often make love again, but never again would they share each other's lives.

*

L'Âge d'or was shot with Buñuel's habitual speed and efficiency. The interiors, at Billancourt, took three weeks, the sound shoot two days, and the unit moved to Spain for the exteriors on 3 April. As usual the cast, apart from the principals, consisted largely of family and friends: Max Ernst was one of the bandits, Pierre Prévert (brother of Jacques) was another; King Victor Emmanuel of Italy, or someone very like him, was played by Josep Artigas, a small Catalan friend with a large moustache. Eluard did a voice-over for Gaston Modot, an actor whom Buñuel knew from Montparnasse – 'very Hispanophile'.[137]

Dalí was not present in Cadaqués for the filming. Gala had been ill, and they decided to take up a friend's offer of a cottage in Torremolinos, where they received intermittent news from the outside world via passing friends. 'This was how in a matter of a few hours we found out that Buñuel – probably under the influence of his Marxist friends – had started shooting *L'Âge d'or* without waiting for me to be there, suggesting betrayal with the worst kind of banalities, and that the Galerie Goemans had gone broke. I was morally and materially ruined.'[138]

If this sounds a surprisingly jaundiced view of events given the two friends' recent close collaboration, this is because, between the filming of *L'Âge d'or* and its first screenings some months later, the relationship between Dalí and Buñuel broke down. For if there is some controversy about who originated *Un Chien andalou*, there is far more about *L'Âge d'or*. Buñuel, throughout his life, refused to credit Dalí with anything more than the most tangential contribution to it. In his autobiography he said, 'Dalí sent me several ideas, and one at least found its way into the film: A man with a rock on his head is walking in a public garden. He passes a statue. The statue also has a rock on its head!'[139] Elsewhere he said he left Cadaqués with only thirty images, and that Dalí later sent him 'a postcard with a few more ideas'.[140] When the film was shown, Dalí's name was omitted from the credits: indeed, no credits appeared at all – simply the legend *'Film de Luis Buñuel'*. Dalí protested; Buñuel replied that he had no time for the usual interminable list of credits. He was trying to break free of tradition, and this was all part of the effort.

Unsurprisingly, this did nothing to assuage Dalí's fury. 'If you saw the film announced as *L'Âge d'or, film de Dalí*, I'm sure you wouldn't feel so cheerful,' he retorted, dismissing, in any case, the notion that a film might have an 'author'. 'Why don't you go *a little further* since it doesn't cost you anything (*ni un centimito*) and put that I shared in the *scenario*, which is *true*? You know *I care very much* and besides, if for no other reason, there exists a friendship which would seem to justify it, since as you know in a *Surrealist film* the scenario, the plot, are more *important* than in other films . . .'[141] But Buñuel remained intransigent.

Why? And was he justified? Buñuel blamed Gala for the breakdown of the wonderful working partnership which had existed previously: 'With *L'Âge d'or* everything was different. It didn't work. We didn't get on. He didn't like any of my suggestions and I hated his. I said to myself, "That's Gala."'[142]

But it was more than just Gala. Between *Un Chien andalou* and *L'Âge d'or* Buñuel, too, had had an epiphany. One momentous evening, Robert Desnos and Roland Tual had introduced him to the works of the Marquis de Sade. Tual lent him 'the only copy in France' of the *120 Days of Sodom*. It had previously passed through the hands of Proust and Gide; now it overturned Buñuel's world.

The discovery of Sade was an extraordinary thing for me. It didn't have anything to do with erotology, but with atheist thought. I realised that until that moment freedom had simply been hidden from me, that I had been totally deceived about religion and its effects, and above all about morals. I was an atheist, I had lost my faith, but I'd replaced it with liberalism, with anarchism, with a feeling of man's inner goodness, at bottom I was convinced that it was simply capitalism and the way the world was organised that minimised the human predisposition towards goodness. Suddenly I found that that all meant nothing, . . . that the only important thing was total liberty of thought and that there was no such thing as good or bad . . . At that moment, in 1929, I realised what lay behind my absolute affinity with Surrealism. Sade more than anyone was the great influence, not only on me, but on the Surrealists and Surrealism.[143]

Unfocused anticlericalism had always been an unsatisfactory substitute for the rigorous discipline of Spanish Catholicism. Now, in Sade's merciless freethinking, the void was finally and satisfactorily filled. Sade provided a framework for Buñuel's revolutionary fervour. This, he realized, more than any other, was the foundation of his affinity with Surrealism. And *L'Âge d'or* reflected this. *Un Chien andalou* had been to a very large extent a succession of what Buñuel called 'gags', more or less arbitrary. Meaning might be attached to them, but it was by no means integral. *L'Âge d'or*, by contrast, though retaining the 'gags' and the dreamlike atmosphere, has a definite theme. It is 'an attack on what might be called bourgeois ideals: family, patriotism and religion'.[144] This is of course the theme behind all Buñuel's subsequent work. It is also present in Dalí's, but only in a far more narrowly personal sense. His work is obsessively inturned, a commentary on his own life, a quasi-therapeutic working through of his own problems.

Where the revolutionary's thoughts are concerned with society, Dalí never had energy to spare for such extraneous details. He was always far too busy concentrating upon himself. In this important sense, *L'Âge d'or* is very much Luis Buñuel's film.

Not entirely, however. Dalí's correspondence with Buñuel – peppered with his detailed drawings – shows that even though he was not present during the film's shooting he continued to take a close and detailed interest in its progress, and also that he was familiar with the storyline, which must therefore have been largely concocted while they were together.

> Dear Luis –
> I'm sending you the drawing of a dream, it's very good, you can use it in the *Documental de Roma* ... and another thing: are you going to go to Cadaqués to film the bandits? [The opening scenes with the bandits and archbishops were indeed filmed there, among the rocks of Cap Creus so familiar from Dalí's paintings.] ... In the love scene, he could kiss the tips of her fingers and tear out a nail with his teeth, you could use a dummy hand to show the horrible gash ... here she could give a short sharp scream, spinechilling, and then everything goes on as before ... turn the page, I've suddenly seen how to realise your dream of putting a cunt on the screen ... [this was an elaborate succession of images involving lips and ostrich feathers] ... someone could have their fly-buttons slightly *undone* (very slightly!) so that you can see the shirt, but so little that people will believe that it's *inadvertent* and not done on purpose to annoy; you should see the person *quite a lot* including a close-up ... During the love-scene we should hear a bed creaking if possible, obviously that's a very slight detail and perhaps excessive. I LIKE OUR FILM BETTER EVERY DAY ...[145]

Buñuel used a number of these details. He adopted all Dalí's suggestions for sound effects, and also the open fly-button. Other Dalí suggestions included Gaston Modot's bloodied face during the love scene (*'muy bueno'*). And on 11 May Buñuel informed Pepín Bello that he had just finished 'a spectacular film more than an hour long . . . I did the plot with Dalí, like *Chien andalou*.'[146]

A film is of course far more than the sum of its details, or even of its screenplay. Buñuel's subsequent work is proof, were it needed, that these are great films largely if not entirely because he was a great film director. But his stand was clearly unreasonable in the highest degree. As Dalí himself pointed out,[147] films are the work of many hands, and this may be acknowledged (and almost always is) without in any way detracting from the director's own credit. Given the part Dalí had played in the film's genesis, not to speak of his status as Buñuel's closest friend, the latter's refusal to budge on this matter remains a mystery. It is not as though they had quarrelled. The bad blood that arose between them was a result rather than a cause of Buñuel's intransigence on this matter. The cooling can be traced in Dalí's letters. In May he is begging his 'dear Luis' to come and spend a few days in Cadaqués, signing off with 'love from your DALI'. A little later, he is justifiably furious with his 'Amigo Buñuel', having just seen *Chien andalou* and failed to see any mention of his own name. '*I shall fight this to the very end*. Regards, DALI.' And the next letter, addressing in detail Buñuel's 'pretty colossal' intention '*to deny our collaboration*' is addressed only to 'Dear Buñuel', and the signature a mere 'DALI': even the regards are omitted.[148]

As soon as the new film was ready, the Noailles put on a series of private screenings. The first, for a few friends and Dalí, was, said Buñuel, 'a triumph. Dalí said, "I like it a lot. It's like a Hollywood film." '[149] There were other showings for

352

various friends, including one for the Surrealists, at which the Noailles were not present. (The soundtrack included the famous opening bars of Beethoven's Fifth Symphony: the tone-deaf Breton, seated next to André Thirion, leaned across and hissed, 'Who wrote that? It's very beautiful.')[150] Afterwards Tzara and Thirion, to show their contempt for aristocrats, went on a bottle- and glass-breaking binge in the sumptuous bar of the Noailles mansion. Their hosts, gentlemen to the tips of their toes, never so much as mentioned this vandalism. Finally, on 22 October, there was a showing for 'le tout-Paris' at the Panthéon cinema, to be followed by a reception.

What had the Noailles expected? Spending all their time among artists, they had evidently overlooked the fact that *L'Âge d'or* was a sustained attack upon precisely such people as their guests, and everything they stood for. It was the Surrealist dilemma, but seen from the other side. In order to support their art, the Surrealists had to swallow their principles and cultivate the bourgeois society they scorned. In the same way the Noailles, if they wanted to mix with artists, had to overlook the fact that many of these same artists ardently wished for the overthrow of everything they stood for. In the pleasure of lion-hunting they were happy to overlook the fact that carnivores make dangerous company. But their guests were less tolerant.

Dalí had written a programme note for the film, setting his stamp upon it: this was his opportunity to stake his claim to the credits. His outline of the screenplay made its subversive nature all too unmissably clear. The viewers might not have guessed that the castle scenes at the end of the film act out a Sadeian scenario, nor that one of the most enthusiastic sinners represents Christ, but Dalí's note told them so. 'I could have avoided insisting on certain scenes in the film,' Dalí explained to Noailles, '. . . but this would have created a serious problem since the programme notes are not aimed only at the spectators but at a great number of people who will never see the film. If I had suppressed the reference to Christ I would have betrayed, clearly, Buñuel's idea . . .'[151] As a final insult, a considerable number of the guests themselves appeared on screen, for the society party which takes place in the film was an actual party, thrown by the Noailles and filmed by Buñuel. Unfortunately, after editing it turned out not to have been quite as they remembered it. Many walked out before the end, which was greeted in stony silence. The Noailles stood at the door: their guests filed past without so much as an acknowledgement. Charles de Noailles, who was president of the fashionable Jockey Club, was forced to resign. Otherwise the club would disband, since most members would not associate with him. Marie-Laure's Jewish ancestry was much remarked on. There was even talk of excommunication – rumour had it that Charles's mother-in-law, the Princesse de Poix, had to intervene personally with the Pope to prevent it.[152]

In spite of all this, the public opening of *L'Âge d'or* went ahead as planned. The censors had granted a certificate without seeing it, having read a synopsis which presented the film as the story of a madman. It opened on 28 November, in Studio 28. Dalí, continuing his campaign of appropriation, wrote a programme-leaflet for the occasion. It began with the words, 'My general idea when I wrote the script of *L'Âge d'or* . . .' At the last moment Breton added the words 'with Buñuel'. The foyer of the cinema was devoted to a Surrealist exhibition, including paintings by Dalí, Miró, Ernst, Arp, Picasso, Picabia, Man Ray and Tanguy. A noise-organ, the original bruitist instrument built in 1921 by the Italian Futurist Russolo, was also on display.

For six days all went well. Then, on 3 December, all hell broke loose. The cinema was attacked by a commando group of the Anti-Jewish League and the League of Patriots. They threw ink at the screen, set off smoke bombs, and broke up the exhibition in the foyer, destroying most of the artworks (and the organ).

The press, almost unanimously, applauded the attack. *L'Ami du Peuple* thought the film a product of 'misbegotten thinkers, dissolute mystics, throw-outs from their own countries who legitimise with their newly-acquired French nationality works rejected with disgust by the entire world'. 'If the Jews keep quiet, we'll keep quiet,' cried the *Petit Oranais*, outraged by this example of 'judeobolshevist cinema'. And Gaëtan Sanvoisin in the *Figaro*, furious at this 'essay in a very particular variety of bolshevism ... aimed at corrupting us all' finished with a plea to the chief of police, Chiappe: 'Sweep them away, M. Chiappe! You can and you must.'[153]

Mauclaire, the owner of Studio 28, had already cut the scenes featuring the archbishops on the beach; on 8 December the Prefecture of Paris requested that he also remove 'the passage about Christ'. On being told there was no such scene, the Prefect agreed to make do with the deletion of Dalí's remark in the programme note that 'the Duc de Blangis is obviously Christ'. But the bandwagon was rolling now. De Launay, the Provost of the Municipal Council, wrote directly to Chiappe: 'We are in greater and greater numbers committed to react against the systematic poisoning of our society and of French youth.' The next day, Chiappe banned the film and ordered all copies seized and burned. Fortunately Noailles was able to rescue the negatives and hide them with Jeanne at the Spanish Bookshop. Buñuel never forgave Chiappe: his film *Le Journal d'une femme de chambre* (*Diary of a Chambermaid*) ends with the cry '*Vive Chiappe!*' shouted by the anti-Semitic and sadistic murderer of a young girl. ('A coincidence,' he insisted later.)[154]

Breton was delighted with the scandal: Surrealism's latest recruits had fulfilled all his fondest hopes. He and Eluard prepared a pamphlet on the events of 3 December, including photographs of the slashed Dalís and vandalized screen, captioned '*A Christian Alphabet*'. Noailles was less delighted. He wrote a panic-stricken letter to Buñuel: 'Your personality (and your name as well, as you will see from the clippings) is more and more marginalised in favour of those of the [Surrealist] group and our name since they provoke more scandal . . . We are obliged to avoid all scandal in future. *We must be forgotten.* I see from the papers that Mauclaire is being prosecuted but I don't think it's very important. Will you please ask him *not to mention my name any more!*' He also wrote to Dalí: he would not be buying any more of his paintings for the moment.[155]

*

Buñuel was not present at the *Âge d'or* riot. Soon after the first Noailles screening MGM invited both the film's director and its leading lady, the luscious Lya Lys, to Hollywood. Lya Lys was almost certainly the main attraction: Marlene Dietrich had created a market for European *femmes fatales*, and many arrived with a lover in tow – Greta Garbo with Mauritz Stiller, Hedy Lamarr with Gustav Machaty, Dietrich with both her husband Rudolf Sieber and her lover Josef von Sternberg. Unlike these legendary names, Lya Lys was soon destined to fade into obscurity, undone, like so many stars of the silent screen, by the coming of sound. But for the moment she twinkled brightly, and Buñuel was (they assumed) a necessary part of the package.

Buñuel, however, thought the studio was interested in his talents as a director. He was so excited, Jeanne remembered, that 'he'd already left even before the trip started'.[156] But it soon became clear that, for Buñuel as for so many bright talents, the Hollywood dream would be nothing but a mirage. No one had the slightest idea who he was nor what to do with him. After a few aimless (though salaried) months he returned to Europe, intent on making some sort of career in the Spanish film industry. Together with some Surrealist friends – Elie Lotar and Pierre Unik – he shot the terrifying documentary *Las Hurdes* (*Land Without Bread*), about the bestial lives of the very poor in rural Spain.

By now (after eight years' engagement) he and Jeanne were married with a son, Juan Luis. They lived for a while in Madrid, then, when war broke out, moved back to France, where Luis worked for the Loyalist embassy in Paris. It became clear that the war was lost. Spain was closed to him; France, which had its own troubles, offered a cool welcome to left-wing foreigners. In 1937, he decided to try Hollywood again. And the old quarrel with Dalí came back to haunt him.

Only seven years earlier Buñuel had been the great new name in film. Now he had returned to virtual anonymity in a market glutted with celebrated European refugees. Without contacts you were lost. And he had only one contact of any relevance – his one-time friend and collaborator, Salvador Dalí.

For as Buñuel sank into obscurity in America, Dalí rose to fame there. By the end of 1936 he had even appeared on the cover of *Time*. In January 1937, he and Gala travelled to Hollywood, where they stayed luxuriously at the Garden of Allah and met some of Dalí's California fans, including Harpo Marx, for whom he wrote a screenplay, *The Surrealist Woman* (never performed). He was also introduced to Cecil B. De Mille by an old Paris friend, the composer George Antheil. 'Ah, Mr De Mille,' Dalí cried, seizing the great man's hand and kissing it. 'I have met you at last, you, the greatest Surrealist on earth.'

Surrealist? What, De Mille wanted to know, was a Surrealist? Antheil explained; De Mille, intrigued, asked to hear more. It was suggested he might like to see *Un Chien andalou* – a wonderful, beautiful film, Antheil assured him. A showing was arranged forthwith. It felled the audience like a virus. 'One of the biggest producers on the lot got violently ill,' Antheil remembered. 'He had to leave very suddenly. The rest were nailed to their seats as if hypnotized by a king cobra ... Cecil B. De Mille, King of the Surrealists (American branch), was a pale green when the lights went up. He got up and left without a word. So did the others, when they recovered.'[157] Even so, Dalí was too hot a property to abandon. Antheil was asked to bring him in to Paramount to discuss a contract as a design consultant. But he refused, insisting he wanted to work as a screenwriter, not a designer, and swept back to New York.

Meanwhile the *Chien andalou*'s director lived from hand to mouth. Buñuel had none of the arrogance and pushiness essential for survival in Hollywood. For two years he and Jeanne existed from one unsatisfactory crumb of work to another. Antheil met him at this time. 'Inasmuch as [Buñuel], his wife and his little boy seemed to be such absolutely normal, solid persons, as totally un-Surrealist in the Dalí tradition as one could possibly imagine, I asked him whether Dalí "puts it on".' Buñuel assured him that indeed he did: 'It's good business.'[158]

By 1939, finally and completely penniless, despairing of finding a job, he swallowed his pride and wrote to Dalí – not, at first, mentioning money. In return he received a letter that, though patronizing, was tolerably friendly:

You already know that I don't believe there'll be a world war. Although we're experiencing some moments of 'objective danger', I'm convinced that before two months are up there'll be a sudden change (already prepared and decided). France and Italy will patch things up and once the 'axis' is broken Stalin will arrange things with Hitler ... In two weeks I have to leave here for Montecarlo to see my show, which will be put on in the Paris Opera in June, and then London. In principle I'm still interested in Hollywood but since my financial situation is improving each day, and

there's no need for me to go there, *the cleverest thing for me to do* is to wait and to refuse all projects until the moment (inevitable, given the acceleration of my *prestige and popularity*) when they ask me to go as *dictator* – with as *many dollars* for my film as I *fucking want* . . . Good day, write to me and if you come to New York let's see each other immediately,
Dalí.[159]

Heartened, Buñuel wrote again, this time mentioning his current financial straits. Could Dalí lend him some money? The reply is an exercise in sadism and revenge:

Dear Luis:
    I can't send you anything at all, and it's a decision taken after great hesitations and much reflection, which I'm now going to explain to you. This is the reason for my delay in answering you, since normally I hate making people wait for replies having to do with money . . .
    All the predictions and experiences I've had recently counsel me not to lend you money – Before I got your letter its arrival had been foretold to me in various different ways, particularly by a female Swiss medium, one of the most important in New York at the moment, who guides me a lot (although it's I who decide whether I'm convinced or not). My present situation is as follows: the overcoming of my William Tell complex, that is to say, the end of hostilities with my father, the reconstruction of the ideal of The Family, sublimated in racial and biological factors, etc. etc. etc. As a result of this, I send everything I can to Cadaqués (everything I am able to do in this sense will contribute to my own triumphant self-construction). At the same time it's been predicted that I'll be assailed by all the myths of family inconformity, represented by my old friends . . .
    To recapitulate – my life must now be *orientated towards Spain* and The Family. *Systematic destruction* of the

infantile past represented by my Madrid friends, images which have no *real consistence*. Gala the *unique reality* because she's incorporated in a *constructive* sense of my libido. It would be impossible for me to talk to you more FRANKLY.

Long live the *individuality* of the sharks (Marquis de Sade) who eat the weak – NIETSCHE [sic] – and the Empordà, realist-Surrealist.

What shit Marxism is, the last survival of Christian shit – Catholicism I respect *a lot*, it's SOLID.

Ask Noailles for money, he won't refuse you (Dalí guarantees it) and it'll be within tradition: 'STELLAR configuration' . . .

Here I'm designing a Surrealist pavilion for the World's Fair with genuine explosive giraffes.

Good day from your friend DALI – 1929.[160]

Ian Gibson speculates as to whether this slip – 1929 for 1939 – was deliberate, a possibility he considers strengthened by an afterthought added in the letter's margin: 'In the past our collaboration was bad for me. Remember that I had to make great efforts to have my name on *Un Chien andalou.*' Indeed, it was just ten years since they had made that momentous film: ten years in which Dalí had assiduously nursed his grudge. Now, at leisure, he took his revenge. Buñuel, who for years carried this letter in his wallet, never forgave him.

Leaving Jeanne and Juan Luis with a friend (she was by now pregnant once more), Buñuel set out for New York to see what or whom (not including Dalí) he could find there to support them. But here, too, jobs in the arts were notable only for their scarcity. Should he take a job as a hotel dance-partner? With every day his expectations sank. He had just contacted a fellow-Spaniard with connections in the hotel-workers' union, with a view to dish-washing, when he ran into George Antheil, who introduced him to Iris Barry of the

Museum of Modern Art film library and conservation department. Here at last was someone who knew his name: in 1933 she had arranged a showing of *L'Âge d'or* in New York. Now she took Buñuel under her wing, putting him up in her own house while he looked for work, and introducing him to the sculptor Alexander Calder, who loved children. Calder generously offered the Buñuels part of his large apartment, whose lease they later took over.

Since the demise of the Madrid film industry (while that in Berlin was so very much alive), the fight was on for Hispanic hearts and minds. Iris Barry had persuaded Nelson Rockefeller, Co-ordinator of Inter-American Affairs and MOMA's richest patron, to allocate some funds to cultivating this area. It might, she hinted, be useful politically. Her efforts paid off. In January 1941, Buñuel (having evaded the question 'Are you a Communist?' with the reply 'I am a Republican') was offered a job as chief editor and head of the writers' department at the Museum, to collate and dub suitable films and arrange for their shipment to Latin America. Anticipating that this job would eventually come under Federal control, he applied for American citizenship, and settled back into family life.

But once more security eluded him. Hollywood, feeling the loss of its European markets, was eager to get its hands on the South American film operation. They had their sights set on Buñuel, and Barry, who had powerful enemies of her own, was increasingly unable to hold out against them. The campaign was spearheaded by the trade paper, the *Motion Picture Herald*, which ran headlines such as 'Senate Unit to Weed out Meddlers in U.S. Films'.

Late in 1942, Dalí published *The Secret Life of Salvador Dalí*, his heavily revised and fantasticated autobiography. In it he set out his new line on *L'Âge d'or*. Once he had indignantly protested Buñuel's hogging of the credit for this coruscating film. But Franco's victory had (as his letter to Buñuel hinted) converted him to the virtues of right-wing Catholicism. The alternative, expulsion from Cadaqués, was unthinkable – the equivalent of an amputation. Cadaqués was worth a mass. *L'Âge d'or*, he asserted now, was 'no more than a caricature of my ideas' full of Buñuel's extreme anti-clericalism 'without the biological poetry I had wanted'. Buñuel had changed the most extreme passages 'with the goal of adapting it to Marxist ideology ... The scandal of *L'Âge d'or* remained suspended over my head like a sword of Damocles ... I accepted the responsibility of the sacrilegious scandal, though it was not what I had wanted.'[161] In short, Buñuel, not Dalí, had been responsible for the blameworthy aspects of the films they had made together, while any artistic credit was Dalí's.

All this was just what Hollywood had been looking for. The passages were pointed out to the Catholic authorities, and the powerful *Catholic Herald* added its weight to the fight. Buñuel was an irreligious Commie foreigner, and he had to go. In June 1943, amid mounting pressure, he resigned from MOMA.

Had he remained there, he might never have made another film. The obvious progression would have been to an academic post; and the assurance of a steady income, after the hardships and uncertainties he had already endured, would have been difficult to resist. Instead he found himself once more on the rough road that would lead eventually to Mexico and the films which the world knows.

Was it, as legend likes to insist, Dalí who brought the relevant passages to the attention of those who might know how best to use them? There is no way of knowing. The witch-hunters needed little help when it came to rooting out the evidence they required. Dalí, at any rate, seems to have felt remorseful. More than once, as the years went on, he held out an olive branch to Buñuel: always to be rebuffed. 'I'd very much like to see Buñuel again,' he told Max Aub, 'but I know he doesn't want to and I don't want to push it.'[162] Not until 1979 did Buñuel admit that he might like to drink a glass of champagne with Dalí before he died. To which Dalí replied, 'I'd like that too, but unfortunately I don't drink.'[163]

In 1982,[164] Dalí made one last try to re-establish relations. On 6 November that year he sent his old friend a telegram:

> Dear Buñuel
> Every ten years I send you a letter with which you disagree but I insist, tonight I've thought up a film which we could make in ten days not about the demon of philosophy but about our own 'little demon'. If you wish, come and see me in Pubol. I embrace you.
> Dalí.

And this time, finally, Buñuel replied.

> Great idea for film little demon but I withdrew from the cinema five years ago and never go out now. A pity. Embraces.[165]

It was the last contact between them. Buñuel died a few months later, in July 1983, and in January 1989, Dalí followed him.

*

Buñuel's career followed a strange path, bouts of fame punctuated by long stretches of blank frustration. For years at a time, during his twenties and again between his mid-thirties and late forties – years when his friends were forging ahead – he seemed doomed to failure, yet another instance of brilliant promise unfulfilled. How nearly he was sunk by Dalí's vengeance! Those bleak and prolonged years in the wilderness explain only too clearly his later cynicism when finally, in his fifties and sixties, the world decided to recognize his talents.

Only a chance encounter in Hollywood with his old friend Denise Tual set him back on the road to film directing. It was not until *Los olvidados* (*The Young and the Damned*) in 1950 (by which time he too was fifty) that it seemed possible his promise might finally be fulfilled, and that *Chien andalou* and *L'Âge d'or* would count as his early, not his only, work. Even then he had to rely on potboilers for his bread and butter. It would be many years before he could afford the luxury of directing only what he wanted, and on his own terms. But gradually (and especially in France) his fame grew; and by the time he died such films as *Belle de jour* (1967), *Le Charme discret de la bourgeoisie* (*The Discreet Charm of the Bourgeoisie*) (1972) and *Cet obscur objet du désir* (*That Obscure Object of Desire*) (1977) had made him a player on the world stage.

By then it had become clear that Buñuel, almost alone of working artists, had carried Surrealism from its inter-war niche into the modern age. For everyone else it was a youthful, if pervasive, memory: Breton lived on, but in the sidelines. For Buñuel, however, Surrealism remained a living creed, a uniquely fruitful way of seeing and rendering the world. 'I am more Surrealist than ever,' he told Max Aub towards the end of his life.

Indeed, it could be argued that Buñuel alone fully realized Surrealism's artistic possibilities. His films achieve real greatness: it is hard to think of many other Surrealist productions of which as much could be said. Breton's talent was for thinking and leading – a function of that lucidity he deplored but also incomparably deployed. And his rigid stance (as with Aragon) stifled rather than enhanced other writers' inspiration. Everyone agreed that Eluard's poetry, though exquisite, was never really Surrealist. The Surrealist painters – Ernst, Magritte, Miró, Tanguy – produced fine works, but had none of Picasso's power. Dalí, who might have achieved greatness, opted instead for popularity.

The Spaniards possessed one great quality unique among Surrealists: their work was filled with passion. Nothing – not even Breton – could edge them into bloodlessness. Their fault lay rather in the other direction. Endowed with a cultural excess of turmoil, thunder and repressed emotion, Surrealism showed them how this might be accessed, controlled, and sublimated into art. In Dalí's case this often bordered on the psycho-therapeutic – a fact, as we shall see, that he both recognized and exploited.

Buñuel, too, incorporated his obsessions into his work – his leg and foot fetishes, his preoccupation with priests and Catholicism, his taste for dwarves and deformities, echo through his films. The effect, however, is not that of psycho-therapy made flesh. Doubtless this is partly because Buñuel's psychic problems were less disabling. His thoughts might be extreme, but they did not dominate the way he lived. And this passionate tension – the dichotomy between his subversive imaginings and his correct Spanish patriarch's life – informed his films: was, indeed, their subject. Beneath those stiff exteriors – the bourgeois dinner party of *El ángel exterminador* (*The Exterminating Angel*) and *Le Charme discret de la bourgeoisie*, the fashionable *mondaine* of *Belle de jour*, the respectable elderly gentleman of *Tristana* – anything may happen, and (in the films) does. 'You're a Communist, but totally bourgeois,' Max Aub remarked, to which Buñuel replied, 'Yes, and I'm a sadist, but a completely normal man.'[166] We immediately think of the mutilated heroine of *Tristana*, the buzzing box in *Belle de jour*. But they are simply part of a dreamlike whole. We watch and accept, as we accept the equally logic-free movie that unreels every night inside our head. Breton wanted to turn the subconscious into art: Buñuel did so. Film, his chosen medium, is perhaps the most perfect of Surrealist forms: the most oneiric, the most immediate. Buñuel often transposed his dreams onto the screen, and would incorporate a happy chance, as when the last supper scene in *Viridiana* suddenly fell into the form of Leonardo's *Last Supper*.[167] That could not often happen: Buñuel is the most closely-prepared of directors, and film the least impromptu of media. But at the same time it is the least distanced, the least intellectual, in its effect: *the* twentieth-century medium, accessible to all, accessed by all. In Buñuel, Surrealism became the working tool of a modern master.

All this was still far in the future, and, perhaps fortunately, the future is something we cannot see, however hard we may try. Breton certainly tried. As the 30s progressed he became increasingly preoccupied with the paraphernalia of clairvoyance – the Tarot, mediums, astrology; he marshalled the forces of magic, he *would not* be rational. Painstakingly he cast horoscopes, working at them six or seven hours a day, much longer if the subject was a friend. He cast Buñuel's: it ran to a hundred and eight pages. He predicted that Buñuel would die in a distant sea, or as a result of a medical mix-up – that instead of a purge he would take arsenic.[168]

But, as chance would have it, he was wrong.

CHAPTER EIGHT

ART AND
POWER

In the summer of 1935, the AEAR – the Association of Revolutionary Writers and Artists – decided it would hold an international congress in Paris. This was the organization first mooted by Breton, only to be lifted from under his nose by the Party. Since then he had lost no opportunity to criticize it, and was branded a counter-revolutionary for his pains. Nevertheless, he was determined to speak at this congress.

It was on the face of it an unrealistic ambition, since the principal organizer was the review *Commune* edited by (among others) Aragon, now Breton's sworn enemy. However, Breton was supported by another member of the editorial board, René Crevel. It was agreed that though the Surrealists would not figure on the official programme they would be allowed one speech with no restrictions as to content. Breton was designated the Surrealist spokesman.

Crevel was particularly close to the Eluards; he, too, was tubercular, and like them constantly in and out of Swiss sanatoria. He was also a constant drug-user, addicted to opium. Every so often he would retire to Switzerland for a detox; then, 'We'd see him pop up in Paris, overflowing with life like a joyful child, dressed like a superior gigolo, dazzling, with a super permanent wave, and already in the throes of an optimism that unfolded freely in acts of revolutionary generosity.'[1] And then the opium would take over again, until he was tired and broken, and off to Switzerland once more.

Through the Eluards he had also become close to Dalí. He wrote a philosophical study of him (*Dalí ou l'anti-oscurantisme*), and spent long weeks at the Dalís' house at Port Lligat 'stark naked in the olive grove, face to face with the harshest, most lapis-lazulian sky in the whole of the Mediterranean, the most meridionally extremist of skies in a Spain that was already dying of extremism'.[2] But these were peaceful interludes in a difficult life. 'A solution? Yes,' he had replied to the famous question 'Is suicide a solution?' – not such a surprising reply, perhaps, given that he had already made the attempt once (albeit in a state of somnambulistic unconsciousness). It ran in the family: his father, a song-publisher, hanged himself when René was fourteen (he was born in 1900). His mother forced the boy to confront the body while she insulted it hysterically. He loathed her ever afterwards. He had spent some years in analysis, and liked to say he had not an Oedipus but an Orestes complex: he hated his mother and loved and constantly sought his father. He was handsome (he had, said his friend Dalí, 'the sullen, deaf, Beethovenesque, bad-angel face of a fern shoot'),[3] brilliant, surrounded by friends. But he was also homosexual, a Communist, and devoted to André Breton: a fatal combination.

What was Crevel to do? To break with Breton was out of the question. He knew too well – having seen it so often in others – what one sufferer called 'the bitterness and despair which are the lot of the excommunicated'.[4] 'Breton', wrote another, 'was the only man in whom I ever had absolute confidence. When that confidence went, everything went. Inspiration folded its wings.'[5] It was a cruel test, and Crevel knew that his shaky equilibrium would never stand it. So he did his best to pretend, sometimes even to himself, that he was not *really* homosexual. But he did not succeed. It remained the great unspoken fact, constantly present. In this way Crevel and Breton could continue as friends. But any such friendship must be fraught with difficulties. And then there were the political problems. Crevel was a Communist – devoted and committed to the Party. And in the summer of 1933, André Breton was formally expelled from the Communist Party.

During the dispute with Aragon, Crevel had supported Breton wholeheartedly, rejecting what he called Aragon's 'path of intellectual mediocrity'.[6] Communist he might be, but not to the point of supporting Socialist Realism and relinquishing his intellect to the Party cadres. When they expelled Breton he went so far as to rough out a letter to a high Communist official in which he pointed out Breton's unique credentials as a revolutionary writer and thinker. But the letter was never sent. Crevel was already retreating from Breton's brand of Surrealist orthodoxy, and the riots of February 1934, which saw pitched battles in Paris between Communists and Fascists, with the police taking a particularly brutal anti-Communist line, confirmed him in this. The Party, as the anti-Fascist front line, must claim his first allegiance. By 1935 he no longer took part in Surrealist activities. The AEAR congress gave him a chance to demonstrate his continuing loyalty to his friend.

All his good work, however, was ruined by a chance encounter. Shortly before the opening of the congress, Breton, his (second) wife Jacqueline Lamba and Péret spent the evening with two Czechoslovak friends, Nezval and Toyen, members of the Czech Surrealist group and also of the Party, in town for the congress. Walking towards the Closerie des Lilas, Toyen pointed out Ilya Ehrenburg, who had just left the café and was about to cross the road.

Breton had never met Ehrenburg, though he was well-known in Paris. But he had a bone to pick with him. The previous year Ehrenburg had published a pamphlet on contemporary French letters, *Vus par un écrivain de l'U.R.S.S. (Seen by a writer of the USSR)*, in which he bitterly attacked the Surrealists in terms particularly hurtful to Breton – not so much lies as half-truths which could not entirely be denied:

> These young 'revolutionists' will have nothing to do with work. They go in for Hegel and Marx and the revolution, but work is something to which they are not adapted. They are too busy studying pederasty and dreams ... Their time

is taken up with spending their inheritances or their wives' dowries; and they have, moreover, a devoted following of rich American idlers and hangers-on ... In the face of all this, they have the nerve to call the rag they publish *Surrealism At the Service of the Revolution*.[7]

Now Breton said, 'Where is he? I've never seen him.' Ehrenburg was pointed out. Breton approached him and said, 'I've got a score to settle with you, Monsieur.'

> 'And who are you, Monsieur?' Ehrenburg enquired.
> 'I am André Breton.'
> 'Who?'
> André Breton repeated his name several times, each time with one of the epithets with which Ehrenburg had honoured him in his lying pamphlet ... Each of these introductions was accompanied with a slap. Then it was Péret's turn. Ehrenburg didn't try to defend himself. He just stood there, protecting his face with his hand. 'You'll be sorry for that,' was all he said ...[8]

Leaving Breton seething, Ehrenburg immediately went to the congress committee (of which he was a member) and demanded that the Surrealists be stripped of their right to speak. Otherwise the entire Soviet delegation would walk out. It was a potent threat: what was an international Communist congress without Soviet participation? Nezval protested to one of Ehrenburg's Russian colleagues, Mikhail Kolcov, who replied with a masterly show of logic: 'If Breton had slapped Ehrenburg for these personal insults a year ago, then that would have been their private affair. But now Ehrenburg is the official correspondent of *Izvestia,* and an official Soviet delegate, so that when Breton slapped him he insulted the official representative of the Soviet Union.'[9]

Throughout the weekend Crevel worked frantically behind the scenes to get the ban lifted. Dalí remembered how he 'ran back and forth between the Communists and the Surrealists, seeking exhausting and desperate reconciliations . . . The most terrible crisis was the irreparable breach with Breton. Crevel, in tears, came to tell me about it.'[10] All his careful scheming had been brought to nought. Breton would be furious: he would never trust Crevel again. The situation might still be resolved if Breton were to make some kind of conciliatory gesture, but that, as everyone knew, was out of the question. As for Ehrenburg, all he would say was, 'Breton acted like a cop.'[11] In the end it was agreed that Eluard should be allowed to present Breton's speech. He was given notice to be ready for mid-afternoon, but was finally called at twenty past midnight. The hall was due to close in ten minutes; the lights were turned off even as he spoke. The contentious words echoed round an almost-empty hall. Next day, Aragon launched a direct attack on his one-time friends. 'Who has shouted the loudest for freedom of expression? Marinetti. And look where it has led him: to fascism. We have nothing to hide, and that is why we welcome as a joyful expression the new slogan of Soviet literature, Soviet realism. Culture is no longer something for just a handful of people.'[12] Breton heard him out with what was described as a 'frankly amused' smile.

Dalí knew he should telephone Crevel, who needed reassurance. When finally he got around to doing so, 'a strange voice answered at the other end with Olympian disdain: "If you are any friend of Crevel's . . . take a taxi and come at once. He is dying. He has tried to kill himself." '[13]

David Gascoyne, who was translating an essay for the catalogue of a Dalí exhibition in New York, had been coming to the apartment every morning for a week. That morning he arrived as usual to find a desperate-looking Dalí rushing out the door. Gala said, 'For God's sake don't try to touch him!'[14]

Dalí arrived at Crevel's to find a fire engine parked outside

the house. His friend's room was full of firemen. At the end
of the congress, at which Breton had not spoken, Crevel had
gone home, swallowed some sleeping pills and turned on the
gas. 'With the gluttony of an infant, René was sucking oxygen.
I have never seen anybody so attached to existence.'[15] He did
not, however, succeed in hanging on to it, but died in the
Boucicaut hospital that evening, 18 June 1935. A label, tied
firmly to his wrist, read: 'RENE CREVEL. PLEASE
CREMATE ME. DISGUST.'[16]

At this point a Catholic friend of Crevel's, Marcel Jouhandeau, published an article in the *Nouvelle Revue Française*
virtually accusing Breton of causing Crevel's death. He had
died, said Jouhandeau, of a 'dangerous admiration', of 'having
believed in someone too much'. Crevel had told Jouhandeau,
'When I have no more belief in anything, in myself or in
anyone, I shall still believe in Breton.' Perhaps the Surrealists
had even played some more active part in this death. They had
been hanging around Crevel's house and the hospital where he
had died – the sign of a guilty conscience, drawing them back
to the scene of the crime.[17]

Breton reacted with understandable fury. He cited the
probable causes of Crevel's death – a sudden deterioration in
his health (he had recently heard that all the sanatoria had not
succeeded in saving even part of his lungs), overstretched
nerves, Party conflicts – 'who knows what other torments,'
Breton added: a form of words referring, perhaps, to the
homosexuality he had never allowed Crevel to reveal. As for
the veiled – or not-so-veiled – accusation, it was treated with
the contempt it deserved. (The Surrealists *had* been hanging
about, but this was in order to make sure Crevel got the
cremation he had desired, not the Christian burial his Catholic
family had wanted to impose.)

Nevertheless, Breton must have recognized that other factors had probably also played their part. Crevel's suicide was not a one-off in the history of Surrealism, and this was no coincidence. 'Suicide should be a vocation,' wrote Jacques Rigaut, whose only vocation it had turned out to be, '... the most absurd of acts, a brilliant burst of fantasy, the ultimate unconstraint ...'[18]

Hardly the words for poor René Crevel, who had simply decided to end the unequal struggle. Surrealist approbation only enhanced his own long-standing inclination: this suicide was no flamboyant gesture but a long-desired release. Nevertheless, in the eyes of the world Rigaut expressed what Breton thought.

And what he thought mattered. Dalí said many years later, 'The [Surrealist] group was a coterie of pederasts all in love with André Breton. They all adored him and he enjoyed exercising his implacable power over them.'[19] A travesty, perhaps; but as so often with Dalí, the travesty contained (and especially with regard to René Crevel) an undeniable kernel of truth.

*

Dalí was deeply shocked by Crevel's death. Years later he mused upon the strange and tragic circumstances surrounding it.

> Congresses are strange monsters surrounded in essence by corridors through which float people who are psychologically appropriate to this movement. Now whatever you may think of Breton, he is above all a man of integrity and as rigid as a St Andrew's Cross. In any corridors, in any backstage manipulations, and especially in those of a congress, he quickly becomes the most obstructive and the least assimilable of all foreign bodies. He can neither flow nor stick to the walls.[20]

But as the 1930s progressed it became increasingly clear that such qualities were desirable, if not essential for survival. And Dalí wished above all to survive. Unlike Breton or Crevel, he would always flow or stick if survival demanded it. Dalí and Breton, the ungraspable and the immovable. Who would prevail? For this was a fight. Dalí's aim was to become the leader of Surrealism and he made no secret of the fact.

When Buñuel and Dalí had burst onto the Surrealist scene, Breton was at a very low ebb. Aragon, his oldest and dearest friend, was slipping inexorably away from him; Desnos had joined the ranks of the enemy; his adored Suzanne Muzard 'was not there any more, nor was it likely that she would ever be there again ... I had to resign myself to knowing nothing any longer about what had become of her, what she would become; it was atrocious, it was insane.'[21] Breton needed a new hero, someone to provide a fresh and intoxicating intellectual adventure. And by 1931 it had become clear that this person was going to be Salvador Dalí.

Not unnaturally, Dalí did not immediately take in the complexities of the Paris scene. Miró, his first guide, was by 1929, when he showed Dalí the ropes, comparatively distant from Breton and much closer to Georges Bataille and Robert Desnos. Only poverty prevented Desnos from buying Dalí's painting *The First Days of Spring*, and Bataille's review, *Documents*, was, in September 1929, the first Paris review to reproduce his paintings. For his December issue Bataille wanted another: the *Jeu lugubre*. But by then Dalí had become aware of the divisions between Surrealists and ex-Surrealists, and, not wanting to antagonize Breton, refused.

Breton at once saw both the possibilities and drawbacks of the new recruit. 'We seem to see him hesitating (but the future will show that he did not hesitate at all) between talent and genius, as in another age one might have said between vice and virtue,' began his catalogue introduction to Dalí's show at the Galerie Goemans.

> On the one hand there's the moth which infests his clothes and won't even leave him when he goes outside; the moth in question tells him that Spain and even Catalonia are fine, that it's wonderful that a person should paint such small things so well (and that it's even better when he makes them bigger) ... that it's about time that the streets of our dear country and its dilapidated capital swarmed with vermin ... On the other hand we have a certain hope: the hope that in the end everything will not fall apart ... For the first time, perhaps, Dalí opens wide the windows of the mind, and we feel ourselves sliding towards the trapdoor of the wild sky.[22]

And what could be seen through this trapdoor? Nothing less, it appeared, than a development of the very core of Surrealist thinking.

Surrealism's fundamental method, as set out in the first Surrealist manifesto, was 'pure psychic automatism'. But this, as no one knew better than Breton, had its limitations. It was hard to achieve the necessary state of passivity, which meant the abdication of all self-editing – any artist's habitual reflex. And even if this could be achieved it rarely gave rise to anything really interesting. The negation of personality seemed to lead to a sort of primordial, depersonalized language – literary in the worst sense of that word.

In 1930, Breton and Eluard explored a development of this automatism. For some time they had been interested in the extraordinary quality of images sometimes to be found in the art of the insane. They were able to study such images at first hand in the Saint-Anne hospital through a young psychiatrist, Jacques Lacan, who had close connections with the Surrealists – his wife was one of three sisters: the other two were married to André Masson, a faithful Surrealist, and Georges Bataille, a pugnacious expellee. This connexion to the enemy did not, however, affect Breton's relations with Lacan – relations as productive for Lacan as for his Surrealist friends: they had led him to write *De la psychose paranoïaque dans ses rapports avec la personnalité* (*Paranoic Psychosis and its Connections with Personality*), which made his name. Would the simulation of paranoiac states produce comparable imagery? In their book *The Immaculate Conception*, for which Dalí provided the illustrations, Breton and Eluard had set themselves to find out.

Breton's and Eluard's method was still essentially passive. After having assumed (they hoped) the right state of mind, they noted down the images in the received automatic manner. Now Dalí proposed a new method. He wanted to move away from passivity towards the active harnessing of this paranoiac creative power. In a seminal text, *The Rotten Donkey*, dedicated to Gala (who had edited his random jottings of the past several years into a coherent sequence), he outlined his 'Paranoiac-critical method': 'I believe the moment is at hand when, by a paranoiac and active advance of the mind, it will be possible (simultaneously with automatism and other passive states) to systematize confusion and thus to help discredit completely the world of reality.'[23] As to exactly how his method was to be implemented, he gave (and would give) no detailed instructions. Forty years later he said, 'I don't know exactly what it consists of but . . . it works very well!'[24]

However, he offered a few clues. To judge by his description, the paranoiac he had in mind was himself:

Doctors agree that the mental processes of paranoiacs are often inconceivably swift and subtle, and that, availing themselves of associations and facts so refined as to escape normal people, paranoiacs often reach conclusions which cannot be contradicted or rejected and in any case nearly always defying psychological analysis.

378

The work produced by the process also resembled Dalí's. He lays particular emphasis upon the double and triple images preoccupying him at that time:

> The image of a horse which is at the same time the image of a woman may be extended, continuing the paranoiac advance, and then the presence of another dominant idea is enough to make a third image appear (for example, the image of a lion) and so on, until there is a number of images limited only by the mind's degree of paranoiac capacity.[25]

If this sounds like a form of therapy, that was exactly how Dalí saw it. During his first trip to America he explained to a surprised interviewer, who had assumed that his work must be the result of hallucinatory drugs, that, on the contrary, he neither drank nor smoked: he painted his obsessions in order to stay sane, and was careful never to risk anything that might destroy his 'privileged faculty'.[26] He trod a dangerous tightrope, and this sense of danger pervaded his art – it was, as Breton noted, 'genuinely menacing'.[27] To be able to paint in this way was Dalí's salvation: truly, for him, a matter of life and death. It was on this trip that he first formulated the phrase which was to become his signature-tune: 'the only difference between me and a madman is that I am not mad'.

Dalí's method was given added psychiatric credibility by Lacan. In the first number of a new Surrealist review, *Minotaure*, his piece, 'Le Problème du style et la conception psychiatrique des formes paranoïaques de l'expérience', was placed next to Dalí's paranoiac-critical interpretation of Millet's *Angelus*, in which he analyses the latent content of this 'sublime image of symbolic hypocrisy' to try and discover why it should fascinate him so much. (He discovers that it is an essentially oedipal image in which the rather slight man/son's hat, held in front of his penis, is covering an erection, the mark of his desire for the much stouter woman/mother, while the fork stuck in the ground beside them symbolizes intercourse.) Lacan, for his part, is concerned with using paranoiac experience to construct a theory of style, something 'of imperative importance for artists'.

Lacan became a figure of great significance for Dalí: 'In Lacan', he later declared, 'we find Freud's ultimate consequences.'[28] The first actual meeting between the two was marked, however, by a certain absurdity. Dalí was working on a portrait of Marie-Laure de Noailles (it was by then 1933, the *Âge d'or* scandal had receded and the Noailles were once more in the market for Dalís). This was painted on burnished copper whose reflections made it impossible for Dalí to see his drawing. He found that the difficulty could be overcome if he stuck a piece of white paper on the end of his nose: the drawing showed up in the reflection of the paper. At this point Lacan arrived, and they at once plunged into a technical discussion of psychoanalytic theory. Dalí noticed that Lacan peered at him from time to time with an odd smile. 'Was he intently studying the convulsive effects upon my facial morphology of the ideas that stirred my soul?' Only after Lacan left did Dalí discover that he had forgotten to remove the piece of paper from his nose.[29]

But though he might have moments of endearing absentmindedness (and was he really unaware of the piece of paper on his nose?), Dalí was already an unnerving figure:

His hair was jet-black, very straight, stuck down with a copious dose of brilliantine. The face, its skin as tightly stretched as that of a drum, as brilliant as enamelled porcelain, was brown and looked as if it had just been attended to by the make-up man in a theatre or film studio. A tiny moustache – the finest line, imperceptible at first glance, as if traced by a surgeon's knife – protected the upper lip. In that waxen child's face, hard, inexpressive and stiff, there shone, with extraordinary intensity, two minuscule, febrile, terrible, menacing eyes. Terrifying eyes, the eyes of a madman.

The tone of his voice was rough and hoarse. Indeed, you would have thought he suffered from chronic hoarseness. He was loquacious in the extreme. The words gushed from a mouth which, when it smiled its sinister smile – Dalí never laughed outright, loudly – revealed little teeth sharp as cutting implements. He had an abrupt, nervous way of speaking, but *what* he said was incontrovertibly logical. Everything he said was articulate, coherent, and to the point. He gave you the sensation that, having laboriously solved a series of moral and aesthetic problems, he had managed to secure certain crystal-clear ideas regarding the divine and the human, and now he was explaining them with absolute clarity ... What may be stated without fear of contradiction is that in him irony reached the level of incredible cruelty. A cold, dauntless, terrible quiet cruelty. Everything he said and did revealed a total absence of heart. He had, on the other hand, a privileged and devastatingly lucid intelligence.[30]

Breton's latest hero, in other words, was dynamite – always exciting, never less than dangerous, and liable to blow you apart when you least expected it.

*

It is generally agreed that this period, when Dalí formed part of the Surrealist circle in Paris, was the most creative of his life. His reputation both as a painter and as a theorist was growing steadily, he was full of original ideas, and he could not get over his extraordinary luck at having met Gala. He still retained the charm that had marked his student days. A friend of that time observed that 'He was young and gay and full of interest and curiosity ... he hadn't yet developed fake madness, that came later when he built up his personality ... There is no doubt that he was a genius. He had conceptions of the greatest originality.'[31]

He and Gala were nevertheless still very poor. Eluard was prepared to help, but the crash had undermined his family finances: his letters at this time are full of worries over how to find the money for end-of-month bills; as often as not it was Gala who helped him. Since Gala and Dalí had appropriated the Rue Becquerel apartment he took a studio at 42 Rue Fontaine, in the same building as Breton. It was cheap, but it meant that he was now responsible for two Paris apartments as well as the house at Eaubonne where they had lived with Ernst. He hoped at one time that his mother might buy the house, but she, too, was short of cash. Now that they were divorced he urged Gala to marry Dalí. 'Think, my little girl, if Dalí should die [he added: 'or went mad' – then crossed it out] you would get nothing ... All *your* pictures (and therefore *mine*) would belong to [his father] ... The father might have disinherited the son, but the son can't disinherit the father, nor the sister. It's extremely serious. It certainly wouldn't be right if the half of all our pictures which belongs to me should become the property of Dalí's father – nor your half either.'[32]

It had been clear from the start that Gala would have to take Dalí's finances in hand. His absolute incapacity in that area had been made apparent early in their relationship. When, in Malaga, they had received the bad news regarding Goemans' closure, Dalí had written to ask Noailles for enough money to buy a shack in Port Lligat, on the next cove to Cadaqués. The ever-supportive Noailles obliged with a cheque for 29,000 francs, in return for which he was to choose a picture. However, when it came to cashing the cheque, Dalí demurred.

At the bank I was surprised that the gentleman in the cashier's window deferentially called me by my name. I was not aware of my already great popularity in Barcelona, and this familiarity of the bank employee, instead of flattering

me, filled me with suspicion. I said to Gala, 'He knows me
but I don't know him!'

Gala was furious at such survivals of childishness and
told me I would always remain a Catalonian peasant. I signed
my name on the back of the check, but when the employee
was about to take it I refused to give it to him.

'I should say not!' I said to Gala. 'I'll let him have my
check when he brings me the money.'

'But what do you expect him to do with your check?'
said Gala, trying to convince me.

'He might eat it,' I answered.

'But why would he eat it?'

'If I were in his place I would certainly eat it!'[33]

Truth or fiction? In the life Gala and Dalí constructed
together, the question became irrelevant. That life was as much
an artwork as anything Dalí ever painted. But Gala, around
whom it revolved, remains cloaked in mystery: a conundrum.
Who was she? In the world's eyes, a nymphomaniacal harpy.
References to her are almost unremittingly hostile. Yet she
entranced three men of undoubted genius – Dalí, Ernst and
Eluard – of whom two, Dalí and Eluard, remained devoted to
her throughout their lives. How could this be?

If we consider the real nature of Gala's crime, however,
the mystery becomes explicable. It was, of course, to overstep
– and by how many miles! – the boundaries of what the
Surrealists (and not only them!) found acceptable in a woman.

Women occupied a very particular place in the Surrealist
world-view. Although later there were a few Surrealist women
painters and sculptors – Meret Oppenheim, Toyen, Leonor
Fini, Leonora Carrington, Eileen Agar – women attended
Surrealist gatherings mostly as companions. They were there
to facilitate the lives of (male) artists. This help might take a
material form, as with Nancy Cunard and Louis Aragon,
Caresse Crosby and Salvador Dalí, Peggy Guggenheim and

Max Ernst. Living with a rich woman was one way around the problem of work, or rather, of no work. But, more importantly, woman was an icon, the incarnation of *amour fou*, mad love, the nearest man could approach to the wonderful – that ultimate goal.

> O woman, you take the place of every solid thing ... When you walk in the sky I am steeped in shadow. Following you into the night, I passionately abandon all memory of day. Bewitching substitute, you are the essence of the wonderful world, of the natural world, and you are reborn whenever I close my eyes. You are the wall and its foundation. You are horizon and being. The ladder and the iron bars. Total eclipse.[34]

Such a creature demanded nothing less than total adoration: and this the Surrealists were happy to vouchsafe her. But this allotted role of inspiration, of iconic embodiment, made it very hard for women to become active Surrealists. Where should they find *their* inspiration? How would *they* embody the marvellous? From the (male) Surrealist standpoint, the question did not arise. Women were there to enchant, not to create. The compositions of Man Ray, quasi-official image-maker to the group, dramatically reflect this aspect of the Surrealist vision. The female torso was a subject to which he continually returned – idealized, erotic, and as often as not headless. 'But you are speaking!' said Man Ray, surprised, to Meret Oppenheim when they met after the war. 'Why do you say that?' she wondered. 'You never said a word formerly,' he explained.[35]

In 1936, Oppenheim, then a very young girl, had created one of the most famous of all Surrealist objects – the furry teacup and saucer now in the New York Museum of Modern Art. Breton immediately named it *Déjeuner en fourrure*, echoing Manet's *Déjeuner sur l'herbe* and Sacher-Masoch's *Vénus en fourrures* – two of his favourite works, and both concerned with essentially masculine fantasies. *Déjeuner en fourrure* might have been made by a woman, but it was immediately claimed for the male psyche.

Such an act smacks of usurpation: but such a thought would never have crossed Breton's mind, a region innocent of any notion of female autonomy. For what could be less autonomous than inspiration? It exists only as a function of *someone else's* mind. Breton makes this quite clear in his book *Nadja*. Nadja's mental troubles are used by him as a path to his own unconscious; he uses her visionary powers for his own ends.[36] When finally she succumbs to mental illness, he does not visit her. She has played her part in his life, and now that part is over. As a separate person she is of no interest to him. In the same way Simone Breton, highly intelligent and culti-vated, never contributed to either *Littérature* or *La Révolution surréaliste*. Her assigned role was that of helper and amanu-ensis. When the Bureau de Recherches Surréalistes opened up shop in 1924, Simone was on the duty-roster for the boring business of standing around while nothing much happened. When Desnos had his sleeping-fits, it was Simone at the typewriter who noted down what he said. Later, when Breton met his second wife, Jacqueline Lamba, he would '. . . have no other goal than to reinvent you. I shall reinvent you for me, since I desire to see poetry and life re-created perpetually.'[37] But when Jacqueline took up her own artistic life, he could only respond with sarcasm and fury: 'Oh la la! We're "work-ing", we're "making a living", . . . we're even living alone . . .'[38]

Even the notion of female sexual autonomy was alien to Breton:

PÉRET: I always follow the woman's preference [in lovemaking]. I always ask what she prefers.

BRETON: Queneau?

QUENEAU:	I agree with Péret . . .
BRETON:	Morise?
MORISE:	It is a matter of whatever is mutually agreeable.
PÉRET:	Unik?
UNIK:	Like Péret, I always ask the woman what she prefers.
BRETON:	I find that absolutely extraordinary, quite phenomenal! Talk about complications! . . .
UNIK:	Why does Breton find it extraordinary to ask the woman's opinion?
BRETON:	Because it is quite out of place.[39]

It is notable that only four of the twelve Surrealist inquiries into sex actually included women. Marcel Duhamel remembered Breton going round his friends' wives, after some of these sessions, during which the question of female orgasm had been discussed, asking whether they really had orgasms at all – 'bent on proving that 90 percent of women only pretend to enjoy sex'.[40] He and Simone had an open marriage, but its conditions were notably lopsided. Breton obeyed the Surrealist diktat and followed his fancy. But when Simone revealed that she, too, had been having an affair (with Max Morise) he berated her for betraying his trust. He argued, not entirely unreasonably, that where he had always been open, she had deceived him. Even so, one can't help feeling this was a convenient excuse for less admissible indignations. 'I have the *duty* to say I don't love you any more,' he concluded coldly, signing himself 'André Breton'.[41] He yearned to be modern in these matters, for instance lauding 'sexual cynicism' as one of every Surrealist's active duties,[42] but this remained an unattainable ideal; and just as his earnestness precluded cynicism, so his attitude towards women remained one of the utmost chauvinist conventionality.

Why should the Surrealists, so dedicated in all other respects to the destruction of convention, have chosen to uphold it in this one area? For their 'headless' view of women merely echoed that of the political establishment they despised. French policy at this time – aimed at replacing the generation lost in World War I and directing scarce jobs towards men – was to encourage large families, echoing Hitler's Germany, where *Kinder, Kirche, Küche* were promoted as women's lot for similar reasons. Reproduction machine or love goddess? From the woman's point of view it amounts to much the same thing – a denial of autonomy. Women would not get the vote in France for another half century.[43]

Julia Kristeva compares the Surrealist cult of *amour fou* to the convention of courtly love. She sees it as a development of that quasi-esoteric obsession with the feminine, especially Salome the bloody woman and her counterpart the despairing man, which characterized the decomposing Catholicism of the late nineteenth-century decadents – Huysmans, Péladan, Gustave Moreau.[44] To these names we may add that of Oscar Wilde, who not only shared their obsessions but wrote his *Salome* in French. In short it is a product of Latin Catholic culture – a culture notoriously unsympathetic to assertive women. And it is noticeable that Hans Arp, Max Ernst and Hugo Ball, who came from a different cultural tradition, did not see women in this way. Their women were partners in every sense of the word. Emmy Hennings played a vital role in the Cabaret Voltaire; Arp considered his wife Sophie Taeuber his equal in every way; while the relations between Max Ernst and the two painters he lived with, Leonora Carrington and (later and finally) Dorothea Tanning, were also those of equals.

The 'Surrealist Woman' has predictably engendered a good deal of *post hoc* indignation among academic feminists. But, for whatever reason, this does not seem to have led to a corresponding rehabilitation of Gala. Yet she despised Breton's views as heartily as any, and spectacularly failed all tests of feminine acceptability. Married to a Frenchman, she rejected the maternal role and refused to be bound by its responsibilities; wife to two Surrealists, she lived life entirely on her own terms. Why not? Gala was not bound by French preconceptions or habits of thought. For she, too, came from a different cultural tradition.

In this she was not alone in Surrealist circles. One instantly thinks of that other supremely determined Russian, Elsa Triolet, in both origins and trajectory so extraordinarily similar. Both were of Jewish ancestry; both had independence forced upon them by the revolution, were flung into the world by events. Both became cult-objects for Surrealist men of genius, demanding nothing less than total enslavement – and obtaining it. And both (despite such obvious contributing factors as Breton's impossible demands, or the personal foibles of Dalí and Aragon) were made scapegoats for their lovers' defection from the Surrealist cause. Aragon's desertion of Surrealism and espousal of Stalinism was laid at Elsa's door ('She demanded and got everything she wanted'). And the pathological and single-minded pursuit of wealth which marked Dalí's life after 1939 was blamed upon Gala's insatiable greed.

Had they been men, or rich, they might have made a buccaneering career in business or the arts. They possessed the entrepreneur's ruthlessness, always more easily accepted in men than women. But, being women, and poor, they were forced to achieve their ends indirectly, socially, through men. Such manoeuvrings are rarely admirable. They neither improve the character nor earn the world's approval. But Gala and Elsa cared nothing for that. How else could they have done what they did? They had no choice but to assert themselves. All they needed for that was the courage to take the first step.

And the habit soon became addictive. It was easier and more effective than they could possibly have imagined.

Yet for their chosen men Gala and Elsa were no harpies. They remained, on the contrary, agelessly enchanting, extravagantly hymned reasons for living. It was as though, along with fearsome determination and bottomless appetites, their Russian baggage included Puck's magic drops of Love-in-Idleness. Aragon's devotion even extended to the endorsement of his wife's writings, so that she became part of the French literary firmament in her own right – 'not', as her friend André Thirion patronizingly remarked, 'that her stuff was any worse than the writings of a few other successful women authors'.[45] She demanded – and got – 'love, ego gratifications, money, remedies for boredom'.[46]

Gala demanded the same, but in larger, ever larger quantities. Only quantities so enormous as to be almost inconceivable were enough for her. She allowed neither marriage nor motherhood to stand between her and the freebooting life she desired. And Eluard, her first husband, for whom at the age of twenty she had traversed Russia and war-torn Europe, was far from being shocked by this, though sometimes saddened on their daughter's behalf. On the contrary, he loved her brave and independent spirit and embraced the freedom it allowed them both. In 1934, four years after she had left him for Dalí, he was still writing of 'the nervous, pure and pathetic girl that you have always been for me'.[47] And a few months later, 'We lived well, we lived *courageously*.'[48] As for Dalí, he and Gala were ideally matched. In Gala, uniquely, he met someone as clear-eyed, as steely, as himself.

And what did she see in him? She craved, above all, excitement. In Dalí she recognized the possibility of new and greater adventures, to a degree that outweighed even his sexual disadvantages. Sex is available everywhere, but Dalí, as she instantly understood, was unique. The terms of their partnership were implicitly – or explicitly – set out during those electric walks among the olives in Cadaqués. She, the most supremely confident of women, would put that confidence at his disposal. It would enable him to live, work, take his place in the world. In return, sexually and financially, their life would be organized on Gala's terms.

*

By 1933 the Dalís had moved their Paris headquarters from Rue Becquerel to an apartment in the Villa Seurat, a block of artists' studios where Henry Miller, Anaïs Nin and Chaim Soutine also lived. It became a meeting-place for those Surrealists who, while not wishing to leave the movement, felt (for one reason or another) out of step with Breton. The group consisted of some students from the Surrealist fringes upon whom Gala had fixed her predatory eye, plus Roger Caillois, René Char, René Crevel, Eluard and Tzara. These were close friends, all now Party members and irritated by Breton's on-off manoeuvrings vis-à-vis the Communist Party. Dalí, with Gala as his partner, was consolidating his position, constructing the power base from which he would take Surrealism over. 'For Gala,' noted Henri Pastoureau (one of the students), 'it wasn't a question any more of gambling on her intuition to draw a lucky card, as she had with Eluard in 1913 and with Dalí in 1929. She was building the future, as Dalí moved along the road to fame and fortune.'

But these were not Gala's only gatherings. 'You must come to our Wednesdays,' she told Pastoureau, seeing him off after his first visit.

Gala's Wednesdays were sexual investigation sessions, presumably modelled on the Surrealist sessions chaired by Breton, which she never attended (though Eluard sometimes did). But Gala's gatherings were very different from the sobersided (if exhaustive) social inquiries Breton oversaw. They seem to have been more a form of verbal orgy. A recent hysterectomy had left her temporarily incapable of the sexual exertions she preferred; instead, she held the floor before her audience of young men, describing 'in the crudest details, her wildest debaucheries'.[49] Gala resisted all attempts to invite other women. Perhaps she did not yet feel fit enough to take part should the evening pass from discussion to experimentation; perhaps, simply, she had no desire for competition.

Dalí remained silent on these occasions, except when the conversation took a scatological turn. 'Then he waxed lyrical. He was extremely interested in ... snot and blackheads, but above all "genuine and authentic shit".'[50] In this fascination with body fluids and solids he was not alone. In his preface to Cabanne's *Dialogues with Marcel Duchamp*, who once painted a picture using sperm, Dalí recounts a railway journey during which Duchamp 'spoke to me ... of a new interest in the preparation of shit, of which the small excretions from the navel are the "de luxe" editions. To this I replied that I wished to have genuine shit, from the navel of Raphael...'[51] Dalí, however, was less catholic in his tastes than Duchamp. Sperm held no interest for him, nor, for that matter, urine, blood or tears. The anus, and everything relating to it, was the grand theme of these evenings. Coprophagy was the subject of heated debates: in *La Femme visible* (the document in which he had first outlined his paranoiac-critical theory) Dalí had announced that he adored eating Gala's shit. 'It didn't repel her at all,' Pastoureau remembered.[52] But although she tolerated his coprophilia, recognizing that it must be accepted if he was to free himself from shame and devote his energies to work, she was far from sharing it. Later, when he became rich and famous, he could always find models willing to act out his fantasies and provide him with his 'erotic masses'. But Gala never took part on these occasions.[53]

She and Eluard (as his letters make clear) still maintained sexual relations. Pastoureau recalled an evening at Breton's apartment at which both the Dalís and Eluard were present. Breton and Dalí were engaged in intellectual discussion; Gala and Eluard, leaving them to it, retired to a divan in a shadowy corner and made uninhibited love. Breton averted his eyes. 'She was trying to provoke Breton, whom she detested.'[54]

Of course she did: and her detestation was heartily returned. How could it have been otherwise? Each represented what the other abhorred. Gala might be Eluard's muse, not to say Dalí's, but she was as far as could be imagined from Breton's vision of woman-as-muse. The Surrealist Woman inspired her man, but she did not dominate him. And to say that Breton was unlikely to appeal to Gala is to understate the case. Breton, prudish Breton, who thought that even recourse to 'artificial methods' in order to achieve simultaneous orgasm smacked of 'libertinism'[55] and denied love?

This was not the only respect in which Breton embodied Gala's nightmares. He was by now approaching forty; and – inevitably, given his wholly anti-practical views – his life was as uncertain as ever. His second wife, Jacqueline, whom he married in 1934, spoke about 'the years spent with no money, surrounded by a priceless collection. When collecting reaches that degree, it's a pathological phenomenon.'[56] Declining to sell his one remaining Picasso collage to Roland Penrose at a time of exceptional poverty, Breton said: 'If I parted with it, I'd feel poorer than ever.'[57] Amidst deathless art and compulsive collector's flotsam, he lived without life's most basic necessities:

Between [two windows] on a wooden panel, face to face, are two *death masks*, one of Breton, the other, Eluard. To the left of the door . . . the complete works of Hegel and Lenin;

on the side wall a hanging bookshelf full of old bindings . . . Facing us hang Dalí's *William Tell*, quite an old Miró and Jindrich Styrsky's *Scissors-root* which he'd been given in Prague. In a little gilded frame the drawing for *Nadja* called 'Dawn', a surrealist object by Valentine Hugo with a rubber glove, some dice and . . . the great key of the Château de Sade, hung on a hook . . . Facing [this] study is a little room filled with pictures which can't be hung because there's no room . . . My attention was drawn to a table covered with a strange collection: little bottles, fragments of everyday objects . . . all coloured green. André Breton collects them – green is his colour . . . I saw a green oil lamp whose shabbiness had the special charm of a 'found object'. But André Breton showed me the cut ends of the electric wires, and with a sad smile added that for months now he had unfortunately had to make do with nothing more than the light of that lamp . . .[58]

Was this – could it be – the acme of the Surrealist dream? For Gala, Breton's prohibitions, both sexual and financial, were ludicrous. 'Gala was the first to warn me that among the Surrealists I would suffer the same vetos as elsewhere and that they were all ultimately bourgeois,' said Dalí. '. . . I entered the group armed with a Jesuitical good faith, but determined to become its leader as soon as possible. Why should I burden myself with Christian scruples concerning my new father, André Breton, when I had none for the one who had brought me into the world?'[59]

*

During these years political questions were becoming daily less theoretical and more a matter of actual battle. Fighting in the streets, especially between students and police, was now a common occurrence in Paris. In Germany and Italy, Fascist regimes were in power; in Spain, the Right had won the 1933 elections, the Fascists were regrouping, and it was only a matter of time before the young Republic would be openly threatened.

It was at this point that Dalí adopted a new enthusiasm: Adolf Hitler. 'His plump back, especially when he appeared in uniform with his leather belt and cross-belt biting into his flesh gave me a delicious gustatory *frisson* originating in the mouth and culminating in a Wagnerian extasy. I often dreamed of Hitler as a woman. His flesh, which I imagined whiter than white, ravished me.'[60] Worse: he often conflated Hitler with Breton's hero Lenin. They 'excited me tremendously – Hitler even more than Lenin'.[61]

These preoccupations were reflected both in Dalí's painting and in his writing. In the enormous picture *The Enigma of William Tell*, the villainous Tell, one of Dalí's favourite subjects at this time (reflecting the father-son conflict in which he was then engaged), is portrayed as a smiling Lenin whose enormously elongated buttock is propped up by a crutch. (Breton loathed this picture, and it is not the *William Tell* noted in the description of his apartment: Dalí painted several variations on this theme.) As for Hitler, Dalí had written to Breton in July 1933 urging that Hitler be 'considered from the Surrealist point of view' because the Surrealists were 'the only ones who could say anything really good' on this subject.

Could he really mean it? Breton, always uncertain where humour was concerned, felt reluctant to condemn out of hand even such a sally as this. It worried him 'moderately', but perhaps it was just a particularly outrageous way of pointing up certain bizarre modes of thought with which Surrealists were not entirely unfamiliar?[62] (Doubtless Breton was referring to the Stalin-worship enjoined on all good Communists.) The trouble was that with Dalí one could never tell. Was he serious or joking? Sane or mad? It was never possible to be entirely sure – and this, of course, is what makes Dalí such a worrying figure.

Not everyone was so tolerant. Aragon, for whom as we have seen politics and laughter now sat in two quite separate compartments, though recognizing Dalí's skill as a painter, never found his jokes in any degree funny. An early *casus belli* concerned an incident in which some Macedonian anarchists planted a bomb in the first-class carriage of the Orient Express. Dalí declared: 'If I wanted to put a bomb in a train I wouldn't put it where the rich people are, I'd put it in third class, because that would make more of a scandal.' 'I never spoke to him again,' Aragon said.[63] The incident with the glasses of milk was a continuation of this feud, and the Dulita affair merely confirmed Aragon's judgement.

Breton could not dismiss Dalí in this way. He admired his brilliance as a painter and capacity for scandal, and recognized their potential importance for Surrealism – always, for him, the overriding consideration even had he not personally liked Dalí; which, to start with, he most certainly did. Of course Dalí's reaction to the train bomb shocked him, as it had been intended to. How, even in the name of scandal, could he think such a thing? Dalí had his reply ready. Switching the focus, as was his habit, from the general to the particular – himself – he declared that quite apart from any question of scandal, the pleasure he would take in blowing up the poor rather than the rich was a form of sexual perversion particular to himself, resulting in 'erection, irresistible masturbatory desires, [and] splendid wet dreams'.

As usual, his argument was unanswerable but disturbing. If this *was* a sexual perversion, did not Surrealism support the principle of total sexual freedom? Besides, Dalí's bomb was not real but imaginary: and did not Surrealism insist, along with its mentor Sade, that nothing should be unthinkable? As

Buñuel put it, replying to an interviewer who questioned his devotion to Sade on the grounds that his hero provided *a priori* justification for Nazism and the concentration camps: 'But those are quite different things. Sade only committed his crimes in his imagination. It was a way of freeing himself from criminal desires. The imagination can allow itself every sort of liberty . . . The imagination is free, man is not.'[64] Dalí, characteristically, took his argument even further. If witnessing other people's pain was a source of pleasure to him, would not this pleasure be much diminished in its psychological significance if the sufferers were to be nothing more than hated enemies? The suffering of *friends*, as Sade would surely have recognized, created an altogether more interesting psychosexual situation.[65]

One might accept such an argument, but one could not like having to do so. This was, after all, the real world, and Hitler a dreadful presence in it. Dalí had never pretended to be other than absolutely contemptuous of political involvement. But if Surrealism was (as Breton constantly asserted) a revolutionary movement of the Left, how – even if only to provoke – could such utterances any longer be tolerated within it? And supposing they were not mere provocation? Supposing this enthusiasm for Hitler as sexual object and artistic fetish masked some element of genuine admiration? But one of the difficulties of debating with Dalí lay in the impossibility of pinning him down. The argument was never conducted on the real issues. He always slid away into some delirious fantasy of his own, whether sexual or gustatory – unsettling and unanswerable in equal measures.

The situation came to a head early in 1934. Dalí had been exhibiting with a dealer named Pierre Colle, but his gallery had shut down. Dalí (or Gala) therefore decided to put the recently completed *Enigma of William Tell* (the picture Breton hated) on show at their own apartment, thus violating not only taste but the Surrealist ukase against courting the market. This was too much. On 23 January, Breton sent Dalí a stern letter.

Breton's discomfort in this letter is clear. How should he approach Dalí? At what point does a joke become intolerable? Was it possible to take Dalí's 'sexual perversion' defence any more seriously than (at the opposite extreme) Aragon's absurd stand about the 'wasteful' glasses of milk? At any rate, joke or no joke, things had now passed the point where they could be dismissed as a laughing matter, or circumvented by sophistry. Not only was Dalí lauding Hitler to the skies, he was now taking a stance *against* modern art and *for* academicism – this at a time when modern art was under attack both from Fascist Germany and Communist Russia. There could be no more beating about the bush; the position of Dalí's tongue, in or out of his cheek, was no longer germane; this was quite simply reactionary. *The Enigma of William Tell* was academic, systematic and ultra-conscious. What, if anything, could it have to do with Surrealism? It was essential that Dalí sign a text protesting against German Fascism, and disclaiming some of his recent 'paranoiac-critical' pronouncements. They could hardly continue, otherwise, to appear side by side. Breton wanted answers, written answers, and he wanted them now.

Dalí replied with a long letter full of the very jokes and sophistry Breton deplored. As regarded the theoretically bombed third-class carriage, he continued to repose his defence in Sade. As regarded modern art, he pronounced himself *for* Surrealist art but *against* the miserable intellectualizations of other 'modern' artists – exception made for Gris, Braque, and, obviously, Picasso. An academic technique happened to be the one most suited to what he wanted to say at present. Why should this exclude automatically-inspired images? And how about Breton's own enthusiasm for Manet? As for his alleged Hitlerism ('and I'm so delighted with your utterly mediaeval letter') – Dalí's own books – *The Visible Woman, Love and*

Memory – would be the first into the Nazi flames should they ever fall into Hitler's hands. He had made a study of German racism showing that Hitler was a wetnurse with four testicles and four foreskins. How, then, could he be called a Hitlerite? On the other hand, a phenomenon like Hitler needed an exegesis somewhat more sophisticated than that provided by the Communists' simplistic methods . . . He thought himself, all things considered, an exemplary Surrealist. (As for his picture, what difference was there between exhibiting it at Colle's place or in his own studio? It represented his father who wished to eat him; the buttock meat represented the paternal balls. But 'I only make things worse when I try and explain them.')[66]

Breton remained unconvinced. The final straw came when Dalí exhibited *The Enigma of William Tell* at the Salon des Indépendants, which the Surrealists had agreed to boycott. On 2 February, Breton led a party to attack it: unfortunately (or fortunately) it was hung out of reach of his cane. His response was to summon Dalí to appear before a Surrealist tribunal, which would consider his exclusion for repeated counter-revolutionary acts tending to the glorification of Hitlerian Fascism. Poor Breton! Once again principle seemed poised to come between him and a man he loved and admired. The summons to the tribunal was sent on 3 February; Breton, always the politician, had timed the meeting to coincide with the absence of Eluard, Tzara, Crevel and René Char – all members of the Dalí faction – in Nice. They were invited to make their views known by post.

> *Cher ami,*
> We are counting on your presence at the meeting to be held on Monday 5 February, at 9 o'clock precisely, at Breton's apartment, 42 rue Fontaine.
> Agenda. – Dalí having repeatedly committed counter-

revolutionary acts, tending to the glorification of Hitlerian fascism, the undersigned propose, despite his declaration of 23 January 1934, to exclude him from Surrealism as a fascist element and to fight him using all available means . . .

A sad little note was enclosed with Dalí's copy of this missive. He should be in no doubt as to Breton's personal affection and admiration for him. But that could not be set above the necessity of maintaining Surrealism's revolutionary orientation.

Eluard's unshakable loyalty to Gala meant that he had to support Dalí; indeed, all the Nice party did so. But, as he told Gala in a number of letters, they did not do so entirely happily.

> We expressed our regret at the violence of the attacks on Dalí and said we didn't see how Surrealist activity could go on without him . . . But one can't ignore the hopeless difficulties if Dalí goes on with these Hitlerite-paranoiac attitudes. He *absolutely must* find another fetish. It's essential, for him as well as us, that we maintain contact. And praising Hitler, even or especially as Dalí likes to do it, is unacceptable and will lead to the ruin of Surrealism and to our separation . . . If he leaves Hitler out of it, quite a lot of us will support everything he does.[67]

Eluard, Crevel and Tzara requested that their letters be read to the meeting. This irritated Breton so much that he demanded the exclusion of Eluard as well as Dalí. Eluard was never told of this decision, but (inevitably) found out. After that his relations with Breton never regained their old warmth.

The only person unconvinced of the gravity of the situation was Dalí himself. At the appointed hour he arrived with Gala, to find Breton's studio already crowded:

> . . . some on a divan, the rest here and there, on chairs or on the floor. The plaster masks of Breton and Eluard still face

each other in the reveal of the small window . . . On the left Dalí's 'Gradiva' still reigns . . .

Dalí makes a spectacular entry, dressed in a huge camel coat. He stumbles along in shoes without laces. He is preceded by Gala, with her hunted rat's expression, who can't see why her genius of a husband is being tormented, nor her protégé attacked. She immediately seats herself comfortably on the already crowded divan.

The lost, aggressive face of Dalí emerges from the collar of his overcoat. His moustache might have been drawn by a Japanese watercolourist. His lips grip something that might be a pencil. He takes it out, consults it, replaces it, and explains that it's a thermometer . . . He will keep [it] under his tongue during the entire meeting, checking his temperature at each stage of the discussion . . .[68]

The proceedings between Breton and Dalí echoed, as might be expected, their correspondence. Breton made detailed accusations – Dalí countered them with delirious fugues and fantasies. He made particular play of Hitler's gastronomic qualities, 'the succulence of [his] breast pierced by a safety-pin symbolising childhood memories, the exquisiteness of Hitler's soft flesh and his moustache, his photograph torn up in a dish of eggs . . .' All this, Dalí claimed, proved that Hitler should be considered as a Surrealist phenomenon.[69]

Perhaps for the first time Breton had met someone who took Surrealism to its ultimate, unanswerable conclusion. There was no countering Dalí in his own terms: the situation must be taken in hand. But how? Dalí droned unstoppably on in his singsong Catalan accent, developing his fantasy, presenting the company with a Hitler who 'becomes a sort of grand metteur-en-scene of abominations, a Cecil B. De Mille of massacre'. Consulting his thermometer, he declared that his fever was rising and stripped off his topcoat to reveal many layers of sweaters beneath. Breton could find nothing to say.

He continued to urge Dalí to renounce his Hitlerian fantasies on pain of exclusion. Dalí removed another sweater, then another. Soon he was surrounded by discarded sweaters. Finally, stripped to the waist, barefooted, he went down on one knee in front of Breton. Assuring Breton of his unconditional Surrealism – 'My dear Breton, if I dream of you tonight, if I dream I'm fucking you in some erotic position, I shan't hesitate to paint the scene tomorrow morning in whatever colours I have to hand' – he tried to kiss his master's hand: hurriedly, Breton removed it. 'I don't advise it, my friend,' was all he could find to say. Arp observed later that 'It was like Columbus discovering America.'[70]

It was a farce: and the temptation is to dismiss both protagonists, Breton as a solemn, self-important fool (which was of course what Dalí intended), Dalí as a brilliant maniac (which was how he presented himself). But one would be wrong, on both counts.

Breton's case is the more obvious. Its urgency was underlined the very next day, when a large Communist demonstration was attacked by Fascists, who cut the legs of the police horses with razors. The rioting was so severe that the order was given to fire on the crowd. A few days later another Communist demonstration was pitilessly suppressed. That night Aragon and Breton met on a barricade at the Gare de l'Est: they did not speak.[71]

That Dalí may have had a valid point is harder to accept. His object of enthusiasm, his behaviour, his style of argument – all are outrageous. They go too far. Going too far was Dalí's trademark: perhaps he was incapable of doing anything else. Nevertheless, with his usual unnerving accuracy, he had identified Surrealism's central weaknesses.

The first of these was the point Breton found so unanswerable. Dalí went too far: but was not Surrealism predicated upon exactly this? What he said was outrageous. But did not the Surrealists deal in outrage? He was simply applying their own rules – against themselves. Was this not a perfectly Surrealist act – possibly the most perfectly Surrealist act of all? Dalí was right when he told André Parinaud that 'there was a censorship determined by reason, aesthetics, morality, of Breton's taste, or by whim' and concluded that 'there is a contradiction to the very fundamental of pure automatism in setting up immediate taboos'.[72] Was Breton now arguing that Surrealists must only overstep *approved* frontiers of taste?

The central question in the tussle between Breton and Dalí boils down to this: were they talking about politics, or were they talking about art? And what should be the relationship between the two? It was the inescapable question, the question that had already split Breton and Aragon. For this was the age of dictators, and dictators of every stripe wish to control hearts and minds. The new, the strange, the experimental, are anathema to them. Therefore, as Breton had pointed out, modern art was under attack from both Communists and Fascists. In Russia the glories of Agitprop and Constructivism had been replaced by the agricultural tableaux of Socialist Realism; in Germany Klee, Kokoschka and Kandinsky languished in the proscribed ranks of Decadent Art while Arno Breker, Hitler's favourite sculptor, produced clean-limbed stone youths *a-go-go*. An exception might perhaps be made for the Futurists, whose machine visions were warmly embraced by Mussolini. (But when Marinetti was invited on an official visit to Germany, to his embarrassment he found that all his friends were proscribed decadents. Kurt Schwitters agreed to accompany him to a Nazi banquet, at which they were seated between the head of the National Socialist Organization for Folk Culture and the leader of the Strength through Joy movement.

The more Schwitters drank, the more fondly he regarded his neighbour.

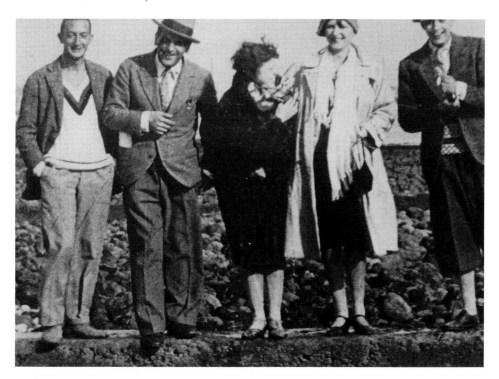

Dalí, Buñuel, Simone Mareuil, Jeanne Rucar, Pierre Batcheff, during the filming of *Un Chien andalou*

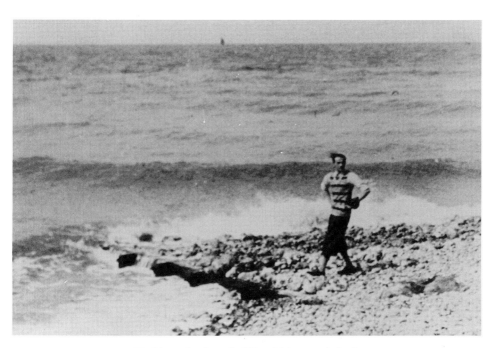

Dalí on the beach (*Un Chien andalou*)

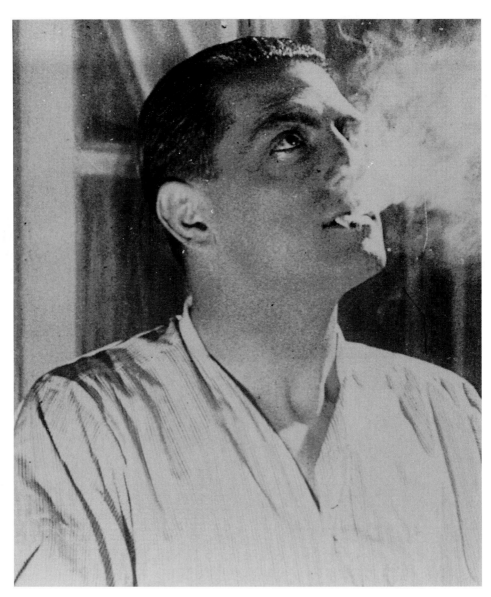

Buñuel (*Un Chien andalou*)

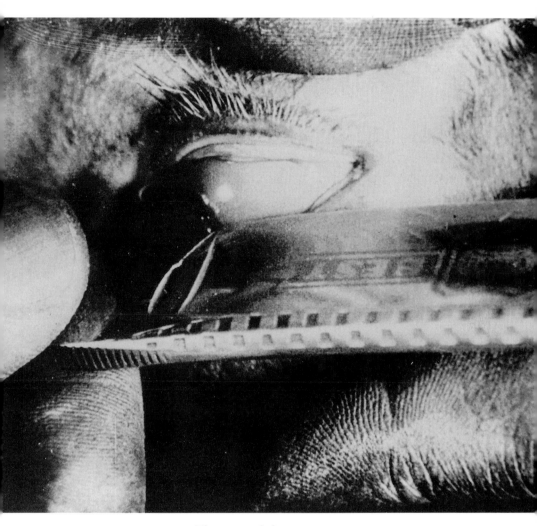

The eye and the razor

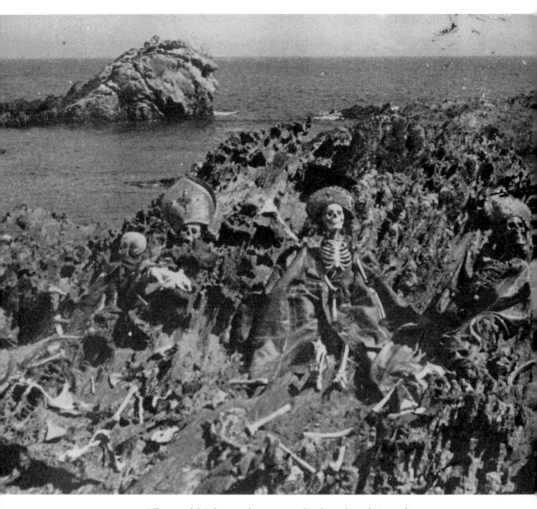

The archbishops decay on the beach – *l'Age d'or*

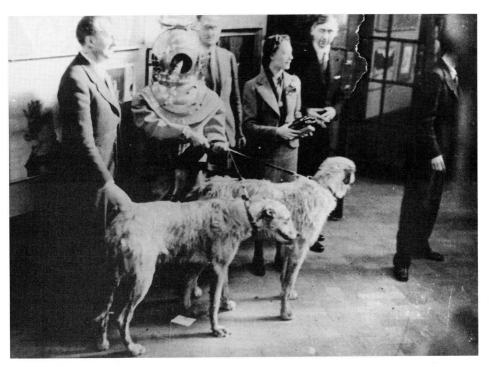

First international Surrealist exhibition, London, 1936. L. to r: Paul Eluard,
Dalí (in diving suit), unknown, Gala, Herbert Read

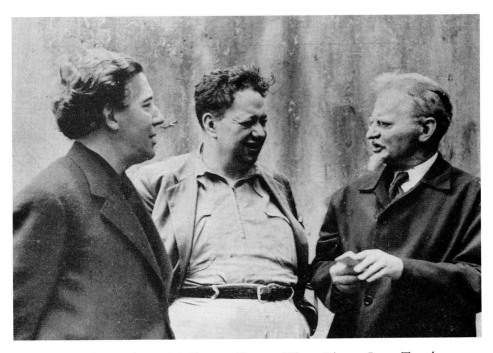

Breton in Mexico, 1938. L. to r.: Breton, Diego Rivera, Leon Trotsky

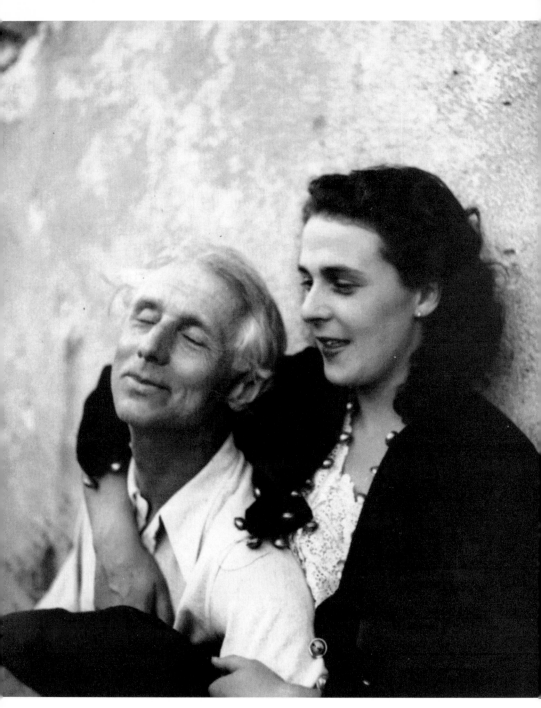

Max Ernst and Leonora Carrington, St Martin d'Ardèche, 1939

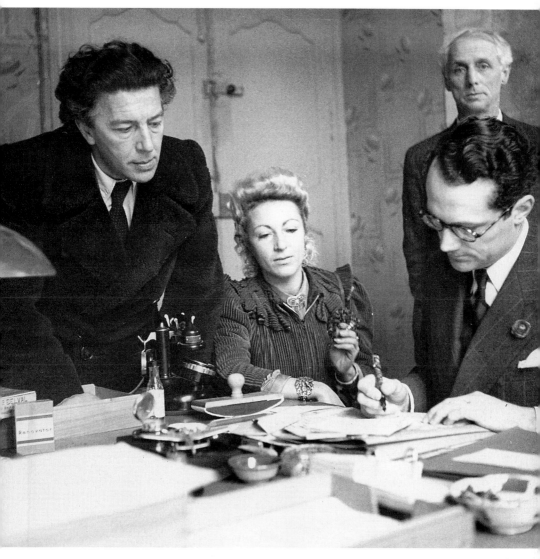

Breton, Jacqueline Breton, Max Ernst and Varian Fry in the offices of the Centre américain de secours, Marseille, 1941

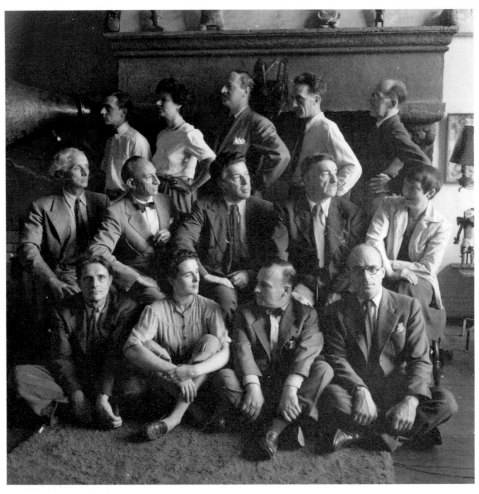

Artists in exile, New York, 1942. Left to right, front row: Stanley
William Hayter, Leonora Carrington, Frederick Kiesler, Kurt Seligmann;
second row: Max Ernst, Amédée Ozenfant, André Breton, Fernand Léger,
Berenice Abbott; third row: Jimmy Ernst, Peggy Guggenheim,
John Ferren, Marcel Duchamp, Piet Mondrian

'I love you, Cultural Folk and Joy,' he said. 'Honestly, I love you. You think I'm not worthy of sharing your chamber, your art chamber for strength and folk, ha? I'm an idiot too, and I can prove it ... You think I'm a Dadaist, don't you? ... That's where you're wrong. I'm MERZ.' He thumped his wrinkled dress shirt near his heart. 'I'm Aryan – the great Aryan MERZ. I can think Aryan, paint Aryan, spit Aryan ... Oh joyful babyface,' he muttered, tears running down his cheeks. 'You will not prohibit me from MERZing my MERZ art?'

The word 'prohibit' had finally penetrated the foggy brain of the 'Strength through Joy' man.

'Prohibited is prohibited,' he said with great firmness and a heavy tongue. 'and when the Führer says *Ja* he says *Ja* and when the Führer says *Nein* he says *Nein. Heil Hitler!*')[73]

Breton, more than anyone, knew that the springs of art are obscure, that art cannot be created at a dictator's whim. But what was he doing, if not dictating? He, too, wanted to control hearts and minds. Dealing with artists, he behaved like a despot. Surrealism was the search for a revolution of the mind – the essential underpinning of any real political revolution. Would Breton's revolution alone, in this age of revolutions, achieve the feat of avoiding dictatorship? Breton was at once subversive and repressive, insubordinate and dictatorial. It was the contradiction at the heart of both Breton and Surrealism, the central paradox of a supremely paradoxical man.

*

Following the inconclusive pseudo-trial Dalí and Gala returned to Port Lligat, where Breton sent them an oddly conciliatory letter. He asked for photographs of Dalí's current work, and hoped their friendship could continue unimpaired: 'Do please write, and please both forget our recent difficulties, as I have – it was just a momentary thing.' [74]

Gala, however, was not so sure. Slowly but surely, she was transforming Dalí. As his confidence grew, she encouraged him to indulge his natural eccentricity. Until they met he had made some effort to hold it in check, afraid that otherwise it might run out of control. But now he was able to give a free rein to his exhibitionist needs, safe in the certainty that Gala would moderate them when necessary. Meanwhile she turned her attention to money matters. She assiduously courted the *beau monde* which constituted the market for Dalí's works in Paris, and they were happy to amuse themselves with this titillatingly dangerous new player. For a while Dalispeak became the fashionable argot: 'My dear, I have a phenomenal desire to cretinise you . . . for two days, I haven't been able to localise my libido . . . how was Stravinsky's concert? It was beautiful, it was gluey! It was *ignominious*!'[75] But most potential customers already owned at least one Dalí. Pastures new were needed, and it was clear where they were to be found. 'America! I wanted to go over there and see what it was like, to bring my bread, place my bread over there; say to the Americans, "What does that mean, eh?" '[76]

Dalí's name was already known in New York. In 1931, his dealer Pierre Colle had introduced him to a young man called Julien Levy, who had just opened a gallery there. Levy was much impressed with the canvases Colle showed him, but afraid that the person who produced them might be somewhat 'slick or pandering'. However, when he met Dalí (who wore 'a black shirt and crimson tie, a tightwaisted black pinstripe suit, and orange shoes'), it was at once clear that this was not the case.

> He was disquieting to me. He has never ceased to be so, not because of ambiguity but rather because of his singleminded intensity and frankness. He fixed his piercing black eyes on me, he crowded against me, his restless hands alternately

picking at my sleeve or suit lapel or fluttering emphatically as he described his very newest, his most revolutionary of all Dalinian theories ... He bombarded me with staccato mispronunciations of the French language that would seem untranslatable and incomprehensible, except that their intensity propelled them directly from his conception to my reception – as if the words were not conveyors but merely an accompaniment of background noise. '*Les comédons authentiques, les brais comédons scubdur supériorre, d'anderiorr, brotté combissiffmong.*' To me, in English, it roughly meant 'authentic meteorites, true meteorites, superior sculpture of the interior, rubbed convulsively...' they were, actually, I was to learn, in Dalí's tortured vocabulary, small bits of snot. (Much later, I found the exact translation of *comédons* was blackheads.)[77]

If Dalí was disquieting, this was still in part a reflection of the barely-suppressed panic which still pervaded his life. He flourished his complexes 'exuberantly', Breton remembered; 'leaving my apartment to meet our friends in the café at place Blanche (no more than a hundred metres) he would always hail a taxi, and once we'd arrived he'd throw a hundred-franc note at the driver and rush off so as not to have to deal with the change'. Breton also remarked on Dalí's habit of scattering over his compulsively groomed self a few perfectly constructed artificial flies.[78]

Levy was taking a risk with Dalí, and was grateful for the unconditional help offered by Pierre Colle. But he need not have worried. The show was a wild success: it sold out completely. Levy offered to put on another, as soon as possible.

Dalí spent the summer of 1934 painting in Port Lligat. In the autumn they would travel back to Paris via Barcelona, where he had agreed to give a lecture. This was fixed for 5 October. On 1 October, however, a reshuffle of the Spanish cabinet gave the right-wing Catholic Party three important ministries: Agriculture, Labour and Justice. With the example of Hitler's meteoric rise to power the previous year fresh in their memories, the Left, terrified that this heralded a Fascist takeover, called a revolutionary general strike on 4 October. In Barcelona the shutters came down; on 6 October, a 'Catalan Republic within the Spanish Federal Republic' was declared. Dalí and Gala, terrified, fled by taxi to the frontier, convinced that civil war was about to break out. The 'Catalan Republic' in fact lasted only a few hours, but this did not reassure them. America, where the new Dalí exhibition was about to open at Julien Levy's, seemed more inviting than ever. Could he and Gala not make the desired crossing along with his pictures?

Unfortunately they had no money. Dalí had no regular gallery to provide him with an income, he had spent all his money on the Port Lligat house, and Eluard, who might otherwise have helped, was also broke. However, a means to attain his goal now presented itself in the alluring shape of Caresse Crosby. The rich and energetic Caresse, expatriate, socialite, literary dilettante and inventor of the brassière, had met the Dalís through René Crevel. She lived outside Paris at Ermenonville, where her converted mill-house offered a luxurious welcome to mixed parties of artists and society stalwarts. (She remembered Breton fishing gravely from the bridge 'where no fish were' in his dark double-breasted suit, high black button shoes, stiff collar and flowing tie.)[79] On 7 November she was to embark on the *Champlain* for her thirtieth Atlantic crossing. If the Dalís would take tickets for the same voyage, she would look after them. Urged on by Caresse, Picasso offered help with the fares.

Dalí was terrified. He insisted on arriving at the station three hours early so as not to miss the train:

> In a third-class compartment next to the engine he sat like a hunter in covert, peering out from behind the canvases that

were stacked around, above, below and in front of him. To each picture he had attached a string. These strings were tied either to his clothing or his fingers. He was very pale and very nervous. 'I am next to the engine,' he said, 'so that I'll get there quicker.' He refused to eat lunch on the way for fear someone would pickpocket a soft watch or two.[80]

This terror lasted for the entire Atlantic crossing. It was the first time Dalí had sailed out of sight of land: if we are to believe his account he spent the entire voyage reading on his bunk with his lifebelt strapped on, leaving the cabin only to attend life-saving drills, about which he was fanatical.

As the ship approached New York he remained closeted in his cabin. He had been packed and ready since the third day out. His privacy, however, was soon invaded. The press had been tipped off by Julien Levy; Mrs Crosby gave them the number of Dalí's cabin, and offered to interpret. 'These are the gentlemen of the Press and they can take or leave you,' she hissed at him in French, but he needed no encouragement: on the contrary, he was dying to meet the fabled New York reporters. 'Everyone spoke of these reporters with horror and contempt. "Those awful uneducated people," they said, "who never stop chewing their gum while they ask you endless questions." ... But beneath this puerile hypocrisy, it was very easy to see that everyone desired and thought of only one thing – the opportunity to be interviewed.'[81]

His own interview, stage-managed by Caresse Crosby, was all he could have hoped. She encouraged him to show his pictures, and as the paper wrappings were stripped off, she explained about Dalí and Surrealism. 'When they asked Dalí which was his favourite picture he answered, "The portrait of my wife." "Yes," I agreed, "you see he has painted her with lamb chops on her shoulder." "Lamb chops?" they roared. That did it! The pencils began to move, the cameras to click.'[82]

That very evening the *New York Evening Journal* published a piece entitled 'Painter Here With "Chop" On Shoulder'. A photograph of Dalí and Gala was captioned, 'From Lamb Chops To Art.' 'I may have done Dalí a good turn but I am not so sure,' Mrs Crosby mused. Dalí himself was in no doubt. 'These reporters were unquestionably far superior to European reporters,' he said. 'What Piranesi invented the ornamental rites of your Roxy Theater? And what Gustave Moreau apoplectic with Prometheus lighted the venomous colours that flutter at the summit of the Chrysler Building?'[83] Clearly New York was made for Dalí, and he for it.

The opening of the show at Julien Levy's gallery was a triumph. Dalí had brought one of his Surrealist objects, this time an aphrodisiac dinner jacket with hundreds of small glasses containing crème-de-menthe straws and dead flies (a variation on the glasses of milk which had so outraged Aragon). He had also composed a short Surrealist manifesto, written phonetically, to read aloud:

> Aye av ei horror uv joks
> Surrealism is not ei jok
> Surrealism is ei strangue poizun
> Surrealism is zi most vaiolent and daingeros
> toxin for dsi imaigineichon zad has so far
> bin invented in dsi domein ouve art
> Surrealism is irrezisteible and terifai-ingli
> conteichios
> Biuer! Ai bring ou Surrealism
> Aulredi meni pipoul in Nui York jave bin infectid
> bai zi laifquiving and marvelos sors of Surrealism.[84]

Breton, writing in December, was extremely excited about this new platform for the Surrealist message. It had been too long confined: he looked forward to its triumph in America. The various recent hiccups had led to a falling-off in numbers, and he hoped for new recruits and a fresh access of Surrealist energy.[85]

Dalí, however, had his mind on higher – or lower – things. New York was working its magic on him. Like Duchamp and Picabia before him, he was the lionized centre of attention, and adoring it. He lectured, he partied, and he was rich. Twelve of his paintings had been sold at high prices: he had 5,000 dollars to take back to Europe. On 18 February 1935, the day before he and Gala were to embark on their return voyage, Caresse Crosby and Julien Levy's wife Joella organized a Dream Ball (or Bal Onirique). The dinner-jacketed waiters wore horn-rimmed spectacles and paste tiaras. The barmen had white coats and ties of either blond or auburn hair. In the entrance was a hundred-pound block of ice done up in red satin ribbon. A dead cow in a white wedding veil sat at one end of the room. Dalí himself appeared as a corpse, in a tailcoat with a bandage round his head. Set into his shirt-front was a square opening lit from inside, illuminating a pair of tiny breasts encased in a brassière – a touching homage to Mrs Crosby. But it was Gala's costume which hogged the headlines. She wore a black headdress in the middle of which was a baby doll. In the middle of its forehead was a wound filled with painted ants; its skull was in the grip of a lobster and a pair of gloves acted as wings on either side. It was (or was read as) a clear reference to the Lindbergh baby, recently kidnapped and murdered.

The press went mad: the story of Gala's dead baby head-dress made headlines throughout the world, including even Russia. Julien Levy was horrified. This was just the kind of publicity to stop Dalí's sales dead. He made Dalí deny any reference to the Lindbergh tragedy. But nothing could erase the headlines. 'Mad Dream Betrayal of New York Society at the Astounding Party to its Newest Idol,' they shrieked. Once and for all, Surrealism had found its American image. 'I was no longer master of my legend,' Dalí wrote, 'and henceforth Surrealism was to be more and more identified with me, and with me only.'[86]

*

New York had begun a process which was to continue for the rest of Dalí's life: the creation of an impenetrable and gleaming persona, clown, soothsayer, gold-plated violator of norms, immune from affect: 'I . . . began to look around me, and from then on I regarded most of the people I met solely and exclusively as creatures I could use as porters on my voyages of ambition.'[87] Breton would unforgettably name this person: *Avida Dollars*.

Dollars' approach to the world was one of simple self-interest. Principle played even less part in his thinking than it had in Dalí's: in any situation he took the path that led to his own advancement. In his autobiographical writings, Dalí does his best to convince both the world and himself that he and Avida were always one and the same person. But this was not the case: the transition was gradual, though the potential was always there – visible from the start in Dalí's readiness to discard his friends when their usefulness was outrun, in his blank refusal to discriminate between appropriate and inappropriate subjects for outrage.

At what point did Dalí vanish and the appalling Dollars take over entirely? For a long time Breton could not make up his mind. Throughout the 30s he and Dalí performed an elaborate quadrille, drawing nearer, retreating, approaching each other once more. Letting go was not so easy, on either side. For Breton, Dalí provided an endless supply of sparks, new ideas, possibilities, publicity; in Dalí resided the only real hope of new Surrealist directions. It is a refrain that echoes through their correspondence: Breton constantly hopes that on Dalí's return from his current excursion they will get together at leisure and map out a new plan of action. As for Dalí, the constraints Breton imposed, forcing him constantly to rethink and justify his position, formed a framework within which he produced his strongest and most original work. Indeed, as his later work so abundantly proved, only Breton stood between him and the ever-present temptations of self-indulgence and facile repetition.

But Dalí's growing fame, although it spread the Surrealist word, also had (from Breton's point of view) its downside. It continually posed the question: who embodied Surrealism? For the Surrealists themselves, the question answered itself: obviously, Breton. But for the rest of the world (and, especially, America), the answer was equally obvious: Dalí. Who had ever heard of André Breton? And who had *not* heard of Salvador Dalí?

Dalí, for example, was the undoubted star of the great Surrealist exhibition mounted in London in June 1936, by Herbert Read and Roland Penrose. His appearance at the show was sensational. His talk was entitled 'Authentic Paranoid Fantasies', and concerned the benefits of immersion in the subconscious. He therefore decided to dress appropriately in a diving suit (topped by a car radiator, with plasticine hands on the bodice and a dagger in a belt round his waist), through which he spoke in his idiosyncratic French, through loud-speakers. Unfortunately, although the diving suit company had supplied a special helmet for the trip, he soon began to suffocate, since in the absence of water no one had thought to attach a supply of air. It was only after some while that anyone realized something was wrong. David Gascoyne was dispatched to find a spanner (no easy matter, as he liked to point out, in the middle of Bond Street). The *Star* reported that in the event the spanner 'was no use, but [a nearby] billiard-cue came in handy as a can-opener. Now and again the lanternist put the slides in sideways or upside down but nobody knew or minded. "Surrealism is like that". But if anybody thinks this crazy business is funny ... pause: people buy these daft pictures. Who laughs last?'[88] Undoubtedly, Dalí. And two years later, at another international Surrealist exhibition, this time in Paris at the Galerie Beaux Arts, it was Dalí who once again caught everybody's eye with his *Rainy Taxi* in which a mannequin sits drenched by intermittent internal rainstorms amid greenery swarming with live snails.

That year, 1938, he pulled off yet another coup, one which can only have increased Breton's ambivalence towards him: a meeting with his idol and Breton's, Sigmund Freud. By then Freud was in London, a tired old man forced out of his home by the Nazis, and suffering from cancer of the mouth. Not surprisingly he saw few visitors, but agreed to meet Dalí at the special request of his friend Stefan Zweig. 'You know how carefully I have always refrained from introducing people to you,' Zweig wrote.

> Tomorrow, however, there will be an important exception. Salvador Dalí, in my opinion (strange as many of his works may appear) is the only painter of genius of our epoch, and the only one who will survive, a fanatic in his conviction, and the most faithful and most grateful disciple of your ideas among the artists. For years it has been the desire of this real genius to meet you ... As a kind of legitimation, we are going to show you his last picture in the possession of Mr Edward James ... The picture is called 'Narcissus' and may have been painted under your influence.[89]

This bizarre and extraordinary meeting cannot have been much helped by the fact that Dalí spoke no German and little English. However, it seems he said very little, spending most of the time sketching Freud, whose cranium he rendered as a snailshell. Most of the talking seems to have been done by Edward James, who was tremendously excited by the whole event. He thought Freud 'adorable', though a little thrown by his recent deafness. Dalí's eyes blazed with such excitement that Freud was moved to whisper, 'That boy looks like a fanatic. Small wonder they have civil war in Spain if they look like that.'[90]

Freud, too, was pleased by the visit. The following day he wrote to Zweig:

> I have to thank you indeed for the introduction of our
> visitor of yesterday. Until now I was inclined to regard the
> Surrealists – who seem to have adopted me for their patron
> saint – as 100 per cent fools (or let's rather say, as with
> alcohol, 95 per cent). This young Spaniard, with his
> ingenuous fanatical eyes, and his undoubtedly technically
> perfect mastership, has suggested to me a different estimate.
> In fact, it would be very interesting to explore analytically
> the growth of a picture like this . . .[91]

Zweig told Dalí what Freud had written: Dalí was particularly delighted with the comment on his 'fanaticism', to which he frequently referred thereafter. Of course he told Breton all about this visit: 'He remarked (I showed him one of my pictures) that "in the paintings of the Old Masters one immediately tends to look for the unconscious whereas, when one looks at a Surrealist painting, one immediately has the urge to look for the conscious".'[92]

What can Breton have felt? All his attempts to approach Freud had been unsatisfactory. Eleven years after the bathetic encounter in Vienna, in 1921, Breton had sent Freud a copy of *Les Vases communicants*, in which he analyses several of his own dreams. Presumably he was hoping for the Master's comments on these attempts. A short correspondence did indeed follow, but almost totally unsatisfactory from Breton's point of view, since Freud's side of it was chiefly concerned with a bibliographic reference omitted from the French edition of *The Interpretation of Dreams*. He only made one reference to Surrealism:

> And now a confession, which you will have to accept with tolerance! Although I have received many testimonies of the interest that you and your friends show for my research, I am not able to clarify for myself what Surrealism is and what it wants. Perhaps I am not destined to understand it, I who am so distant from art.[93]

Whatever he may have felt, however, Breton was not about to encourage Dalinian triumphalism by admitting any chagrin of his own. Addressing him distantly as '*Mon cher Salvador Dalí*' he looked forward, not very hopefully, to hearing what conclusions Dalí had drawn from the visit. He sent his regards to Gala – 'if she's in a mood to receive them'.[94]

By now the Spanish Civil War had ended, and with it any scruples still remaining to Dalí. Without a backward glance he threw in his lot with Franco and the Fascists. A more complete volte-face could not have been imagined. His friend, patron and sometime lover Edward James remembered that in 1936, when the Spanish Civil War finally broke out, Dalí and Gala, then his guests in London, had daily cheered the news of Communist and Anarchist victories in Barcelona. A fellow house-guest, the very Catholic, very conservative Marquesa de Casa Fuerte, declined to join the applause. Dalí's reaction had been that the only reason she couldn't agree that Franco was 'a scoundrel and a bandit' was because she was a Marquesa. Shortly afterwards Dalí introduced James to Buñuel, then in Paris working for the Spanish government. Dalí suggested James might fund the purchase of aeroplanes from Czechoslovakia, against the security of some El Grecos then being exhibited in London to raise money for the Republicans.[95]

James took all this to mean that Dalí was committed to the

Left, and one can hardly blame him for thinking so. As he observed, 'All your old associates had been of the Leftist intelligentsia.'

Of course that did not in itself imply commitment. One needs commitment to swim against the stream, not with it. If all Dalí's friends, even his father, supported the Left, might not that simply have seemed the natural road to take – especially if at the time it had seemed that the Left might win? And if as an added bonus this allowed him to outrage the establishment (in the persona of the Marquesa de Casa Fuerte), so much the better. It was no more than they expected from him: all part of the Dalí package.

But real commitment, as he now knew, was another matter. It was dangerous. It had begun to pick off his friends. First René Crevel had killed himself because he cared too much. And the following year Lorca, the friend and lover of his youth, was assassinated by the Fascists in Granada.

The news reached Paris in September 1936. How did it affect Dalí? He wrote nothing about it until 1941, in the *Secret Life*, whose project was to recreate Dalí's life in terms of Avida Dollars'. There he insists that Lorca's death was more a matter of envy than politics:

At the very outbreak of the revolution my great friend, the poet of *la mala muerte*, Federico García Lorca, died before a firing squad in Granada, occupied by the Fascists. His death was exploited for propaganda purposes. This was ignoble, for they knew as well as I did that Lorca was by essence the most a-political person on earth. Lorca did not die as a symbol of one or another political ideology, he died as a propitiatory victim of that total and integral phenomenon that was the revolutionary confusion in which the civil war unfolded. For that matter, in the Civil War people killed one another not even for ideas, but for 'personal reasons', for reasons of personality; and like myself Lorca had personality and to spare, and with it a better right than most Spaniards to be shot by Spaniards.[96]

In fact this was far from the whole truth. Although personal scores did play some part in Lorca's death, so, too, did politics: Lorca was vocal and vehement in his support for the Republic, and had written particularly venomously about the local Fascists. But by the time Dalí (or Dollars) wrote his words the poet had been dead five years, and the first terrible impact of the news had worn off. That there was not such an impact is inconceivable. Not only had Lorca been Dalí's friend and lover, but Dalí had witnessed countless rehearsals for this very death – the death which haunted Lorca throughout his life.

The effect of such news on the timorous Dalí was only too predictable. As the war thundered on and Franco's victory drew ever nearer, it became clear that from the point of view of self-preservation, changing sides was no more than prudence dictated. As Dalí himself had observed, one must 'flow, or stick to the walls'.

Edward James mapped his change of heart. When it became clear that Franco would probably win, Dalí began to change sides. First he refused to donate any pictures or drawings to fund-raising efforts for Republican refugees. Later, while Picasso was painting his *Guernica* for the Spanish Pavilion at the World's Fair, Dalí procrastinated, finally justifying his refusal by saying he had found the Republican deputed to request his participation personally unattractive and somewhat '*arriviste*'. He added that he found the representatives of both sides equally 'oripillant'.[97]

But such an outcome was almost inevitable. For by now two new factors had arisen. One concerned the old question: what sacrifices should art make to politics? Had Dalí maintained his original leftist stance, he would, like so many other

Spaniards – for example, Luis Buñuel – have found himself unable to return home. And that was unthinkable. Perhaps more than any other artist he needed his native soil, the mineral shoreline of Cap Creus which was the constant setting for his pictures, the inspiration for his thoughts. That alone necessitated an accommodation with Franco.

But there was more. In 1939, when the Civil War finally ended, Dalí picked his way across the bomb-blasted landscape of his youth and looked for his house and his family. What he found, he wrote in a letter to Buñuel.

> The Reds imprisoned my sister in Barcelona for twenty days! They tortured her, she went mad, she's in Cadaqués, they have to force-feed her, she shits in her bed, imagine the tragedy of my father from whom they sold everything, he has to live in a boarding house in Figueres, naturally I'm sending him dollars, he's turned into a fanatical worshipper of Franco, he considers him a demi-god, the 'glorious Caudillo' as he calls him in each of his delirious letters (they managed to keep all my things in the house in Cadaqués safe). The revolutionary effort was such a disaster that everyone prefers Franco. On this subject I'm receiving tremendous information. Life-long Catalanists, federal Republicans, bitter anti-clericals – they're all writing to me enthusiastically about the new regime.[98]

In the same letter he advised Buñuel 'as a friend, as the Dalí of the Toledo days ... to disinfect yourself of all those Marxist points of view, since Marxism, philosophically and from every point of view, is the most imbecilic theory of our civilisation, it's totally false and Marx is probably the acme of abstraction and stupidity.'[99] As for his own position, 'Negrín [the Republic's last Prime Minister] was leading us in the direction of a nauseating Socialist mediocrity that has been totally surpassed by the "Falanges", by Spanish biological reality ...'¹⁰⁰ He who had criticized Lorca for his 'Granada without trams or aeroplanes', for his 'antique Granada with natural elements ... purely traditional and *constant*' now turned to 'the PAST ... consecrated hosts, melons, rosary beads ... the drums of Calanda, the *sardanas* danced on the beaches...'¹⁰¹ Truly the wheel had turned. The prophet of modernity, of sterility, was advocating the very things upon which he had urged his friends to turn their backs. 'The young group surrounding Falange is surely one of the most intelligent, the most inspired and the most original of our times,' he wrote Caresse Crosby. '... I prophesy that the spirit of this world will be saved by Spain, which only believes in realism.'¹⁰²

That was it. There were no more excuses to be made. Breton signalled the end of his dalliance with Dalí in an article entitled 'The Most Recent Tendencies in Surrealist Painting' published in what would turn out to be the last issue of *Minotaure*, the luscious magazine which took over from *Surréalisme au service de la révolution* as the Surrealists' showcase. 'Surrealist painting,' declared Breton now, '... is showing a marked return to *automatism*.' The most notable influence for the younger painters, he noted, was Yves Tanguy, Dalí's great rival and influence among Surrealist painters, whose 'idealism remains whole and intact, whose nature is alien to all compromise'. By contrast Dalí

is in rapid decline. It was inevitable, given his paroxystic desire to please, which forces him to push his contradictions to ever greater extremes. Dalí declared in February, 1939 – and I have this from his own lips, having made quite sure that there was no possible question of humour involved – that all the world's current troubles are *racial*, and that the solution is for the white races to unite in order to reduce the world's coloured peoples to slavery. I don't know what doors this declaration may open for him in Italy or the

United States, between which he now shuttles, but I know which ones it will shut.

After this, Breton concluded, it was no longer possible to consider Dalí seriously. 'Already his painting is marked by a deep and unmistakable monotony.'[103]

That was inevitable: it was no longer the work of a person but a marionette. As Dalí's politics moved to the Right, so the artificial construct wholly replaced the natural man. Dalí's hairline moustache developed into Dollars' elaborately waxed extravaganza; the shock of raw psychology was replaced by the height of repetitive artifice. What had once been panic reactions, odd eccentricities, orthographical or spoken tics resulting from the headlong impetus of ideas and slapdash immersion in too many languages at once, now ossified into a flamboyant shell resembling one of the painter's favourite exoskeletal sea-creatures – a sea urchin, perhaps, or a lobster. Edward James noticed that even though his thick Spanish accent when speaking French (pronouncing the French 'v' as if it were a 'b', adding 'e' before 'sp' and 'st' in French, as in 'estatues' and 'espectre') considerably lessened over the years, he would 'catch himself up pronouncing the word right and correct himself carefully to the wrong pronunciation ... remembering it had always made a hit from his earliest years in Paris to call a widow une "beuve" and his workroom an "estudio"'.[104] A chasm had opened between Dalí's self and what, for argument's sake, may be called the real world.

'The imagination is free, man is not,' said Buñuel of Sade. That philosophy, the basis of Dalí's victory in his duel with Breton over Hitler, had evolved through unending years of physical captivity, the triumph of mind over bars. The bitter irony was that only in a free country could such an argument as theirs possibly have taken place. In the five years since then the activities of Hitler and his fellow-dictators had turned much of the world into a prison fortress. In Germany, Russia, Italy, Spain, such an argument would now lead to imprisonment, possibly even death. What, in these circumstances, was Avida Dollars? He was a joke; and the joke was over.

CHAPTER NINE

MODERN ART COMES TO NEW YORK

THE ENEMY NOW was Fascism, personified by Hitler, Mussolini, Franco. That much was clear. Or was it? The Hitler–Stalin pact meant that, not for the last time, Party members found themselves in a quandary. 'Life really felt like a Kafka novel,' commented Breton.[1] He himself, in a further absurd twist, was posted as medical officer to a pilots' training-school in Poitiers. Medical officer! It was twenty years since he had thought about medicine. When he arrived at the café on leave, friends noticed medical textbooks sticking out of his uniform pockets. And then France fell, and Hitler invaded Russia, and a whole new set of choices had to be made. To stay or to leave? Where best to continue the fight – and what fight to continue?

For Aragon, Eluard and René Char, all long-standing Party members, the choice was clear-cut. They would stay and resist. Desnos, too, remained: he was to die in 1945, in Terezin. For others, however, flight was indicated.

Man Ray was so reluctant to believe in war that, as 1939 drew to a close, he assured his sister that 'all the newspaper talk is rot – no-one wants war here, and it's all a political game, like chess'.[2] And if it did happen he was American, and therefore neutral. But once France fell all that meant nothing beside the dangerous fact of his Jewish ancestry. Departure, however unwelcome, was unavoidable.

For Max Ernst, too, flight was the only option. Arrested as an enemy alien as soon as war was declared, he was imprisoned in a series of camps, and repeatedly escaped. Arriving back at his house in the Ardèche he discovered his one-time neighbours in occupation, and faced arrest once more. His final camp was an old brick-factory, where he was required to draw portraits of all the officers. As a reward, he was assigned a special task – to wheel the rubbish outside the camp gates. Naturally he escaped once more, and set out again for his house, to try and burgle back some of the pictures he had left there. He managed to remove a few of the smaller canvases from their stretchers and hurriedly departed, the paintings rolled in newspapers under his arm.

Breton decided that he, too, must leave. 'The important thing for intellectuals then was not to let this purely military defeat, which had nothing to do with them, bring down the life of the mind along with everything else.'[3] If he stayed, all thought would inevitably be dominated by the overwhelming reality of war and the evasion of arrest. For Surrealism's sake, he must get out.

Thus by the end of 1940 a good many Surrealists (including, at different times, Breton, Duchamp, Ernst, Masson, Péret and Tzara) found themselves in Marseille, waiting for exit visas. Breton, Jacqueline and their daughter Aube were given a room in a dusty villa, Chateau Air-Bel, rented by Eleanor Roosevelt's Emergency Rescue Committee, and here everyone tended to foregather.

Breton – a father? It seemed unthinkable. Dorothea Tanning put the Surrealist attitude to parenthood at its mildest: 'Procreation was considered sloppy even though a few of them had, albeit ruefully, become fathers and mothers.'[4] But Breton's own views had for a long time been far more violent. 'If it ever happened to me despite everything, I would make sure I never met the child. Public Welfare has its uses. The sad joke that began at my birth must end with my death,' he had declared in 1928.[5] By 1932, however, he had changed his mind, concluding rather bitterly that 'the systematic elimination of reproduction' was 'the kind of error that has definitively ruined my life'.[6] There was a rumour that he had insisted Simone have an abortion;[7] perhaps he now blamed that for the current emptiness of his emotional life. But this was before he met Jacqueline, a moment resounding with supremely Surrealist echoes of impulse, clairvoyance, coincidence and objective chance.

André Breton and Jacqueline Lamba met in May 1934. A short while before this meeting, Breton had been lunching in a bistro near his apartment when the proprietor called the pretty waitress: *'Ici, l'Ondine!'* ('Here, Ondine!') Breton was struck by the punning and apposite phrase – *Ici l'on dine* (One dines here). It was still running through his head when the Undine herself (for Jacqueline, it turned out, made her living as a swimmer in an underwater ballet) precipitated herself into his life:

The young woman who just entered appeared to be swathed in mist – clothed in fire? Everything seemed colorless and frozen next to this complexion imagined in perfect concord between rust and green ... This color, taking on a deeper hue from her face to her hands, played on a fascinating tonal relation between the extraordinary pale sun of her hair like a bouquet of honeysuckle ... She was very young, but her distinctive youth did not strike me at first sight, because of this illusion she gave of moving about, in broad daylight, within the gleam of a lamp. I had already seen her two or three times, her coming announced before I saw her each time by an undefinable quiver moving from one pair of shoulders to the next, from the door of this café toward me. For me this motion itself, which, as it is disturbing to a common assembly, quickly assumes a hostile character, has always, whether in art or in life, signalled the presence of the *beautiful*. And I can certainly say that here, on the twenty-ninth of May 1934, this woman was *scandalously* beautiful ...

This young woman who had just entered was writing – she had also been writing the evening before, and I had already agreeably supposed very quickly that she might have been writing to *me*, and found myself awaiting her letter.

Naturally, nothing. At seven-thirty, on May 29, she once again assumed the same attitude ... How near that moment seems! ... She tells me she has written me – this letter just now was destined for me – and was surprised no one had given it to me, and, as I was totally incapable of thinking then how to retain her, she rapidly said farewell to me, giving me a rendezvous for that same evening at midnight.[8]

The two spent a rapturous night walking together through Paris, a night (Breton now realized) perfectly described in a poem he had written eleven years earlier, 'Tournesol' ('Sunflower'). The poem was dedicated to Pierre Reverdy: the only other poem Breton had ever dedicated to him was entitled 'Clé de sol', or 'Key of G', 'transpos[ing] the emotion that I felt on the death of Jacques Vaché'.[9] Thus Vaché, too, could be said to authenticate this union. And so the chain of wonderful coincidences continued until, 'the following August 14, I married the all-powerful commander of the night of the sunflower'.[10] It was a union made as nearly as could be imagined in Surrealist heaven, satisfying Breton's deep and ever-increasing need to authenticate every detail of his life by the elaborate rule-book he had established.

For a while sexual bliss reigned. And then Jacqueline found she was pregnant. This time there was no abortion. The baby, Aube Solange, was born on 20 December 1935. Breton did not see her at once – he was suffering from flu. Finally, for the first time, he held her in his arms. 'I was finally able to see my little girl,' he wrote to a friend. 'However much my eyes have always been turned toward the marvellous, I was a long way from feeling up to the situation.'[11]

Breton was, it turned out, a devoted father. But his life was not designed to accommodate the demands of an infant, and Jacqueline was resentful of the constant attention Aube demanded. Her swimming had never been more than a means to an end – she had always wanted to paint. But Breton refused

426

to take her seriously. His view of women painters may be gleaned from his comments in 'Surrealism and Painting' on the Hungarian Judith Reigl: 'It seems so unlikely that the ship sweeping forward could be steered by a woman's hand that some quite exceptional force must be assumed to be helping to drive it along.'[12] Jacqueline's role in his life was the Surrealist one of muse and mistress: to these was now added that of nanny – no fun in the grinding poverty to which Breton's principles and his collector's mania condemned them.

Fun, indeed, seems to have played little part in their life together. She told Charles Duits, a young man who struck up acquaintance with the Bretons in New York, 'I once dyed my hair green. André was so furious when he saw it . . . He said, "You wash that out or I'm leaving you."'[13] Perhaps she had hoped to please, since green was his colour: he wore green suits, wrote in green ink, waiters knew to infuse his drink with a few drops of green colouring. But a green wife was more than he could take. Perhaps it was with this in mind that she used the adjective *glauque* to describe anything – a person, a book – which, for complex Surrealist reasons, Breton loved and she detested. In September 1936, Eluard reported to Gala that Jacqueline had left Breton, 'definitively, I think. She's found work in Algeria [actually in Ajaccio, Corsica]. Breton's all alone with the child. His parents have ceased all communication with him.'[14] She stayed away for thirty-five days, and although she eventually returned, the happy certainty of reciprocated love did not. For the moment, however, they remained together. 'Both Jacqueline and Aube followed Breton everywhere and the child was a pest in cafés,' Peggy Guggenheim acidly recalled. (She was at that time pursuing Yves Tanguy, who 'adored the whole Breton family', and resented this division of his loyalties.)[15]

A tense period now ensued during which they waited helplessly, playing endless games of cards and consequences, while the Committee's Marseille representative, Varian Fry, battled to obtain the necessary visas. His efforts were obstructed at every turn by the Vichy Government and the American consul-general in France, who felt Americans ought not to meddle in France's internal affairs. Eventually most (though not all: Tzara, forced to remain in France, went on to help run the Resistance in Toulouse) were successful, sliding away just ahead of the Vichy militia. Breton and Ernst were actually imprisoned for some days during an official visit by Marshal Pétain, only to be winkled out again by the indefatigable Fry.

This, for Ernst, was the final straw. He had no visa, but having already tasted the camps, he felt he could wait no longer. A friendly *préfet* constructed him an impressive piece of paper, with many rubber stamps. At the Spanish border, however, it was rejected. Max would have to return to Pau. At the last moment a customs-officer demanded to know what he had rolled up under his arm.

> So took place the exhibition of his life, with the unrolling of those wild and sumptuous canvases that in what seemed like a few minutes got tacked to peeling walls of the dreary little station. Travellers looked and marvelled.
>
> There before them were the forests and their glistening basilisks, the green eyes of rampant nature that stared down the officious customs inspector ... He gazes, walks away and back again. In the general commotion he has made a decision. He plants himself before Max and his voice must have trembled slightly: '*Monsieur, j'adore le talent. Vous avez un grand talent. Mais je dois vous envoyer à Pau. Voilà la direction pour Pau. Voilà à gauche le train pour Madrid. Voici votre passeport. Ne vous trompez pas de train. Adieu, Monsieur.*' ('Monsieur, I adore talent. You have a great talent. But I must send you back to Pau. There is the train for Pau. Here on the left is the train for Madrid. Here is your passport. *Don't take the wrong train.*')[16]

Once over the border, the next stop was Lisbon, where a number of Surrealists were already in residence. Here waiting was once again the order of the day – this time for a berth to America. Such was the demand that Man Ray had to make do with a space on the floor of the ship's library. The Dalís travelled first-class on the same boat; arriving at New York, Man Ray, furious to be there (and under such circumstances!), huffily refused to act as Dalí's interpreter for the press. Ernst was luckier: Peggy Guggenheim, who had fallen in love with him, bought him a seat on a Pan-Am Clipper. Unfortunately Pan-Am refused to take responsibility for admitting an enemy alien to American soil. On landing, Ernst was whisked away to Ellis Island, where he spent three days until his case could be heard and his final release secured. It took the combined efforts of Guggenheim, Ernst's son Jimmy and the gallery-owner Julien Levy to release him from this final trauma.

*

Breton in New York presents a figure of terrible loneliness. Weighed down with significance – 'the forest of Brocéliande in a three-piece suit',[17] his solitary state was the more marked because he had not arrived alone.

New York had fatally changed the balance of his relationship with Jacqueline. In Paris Breton had been a powerful figure, and Jacqueline in every way secondary. But in New York this no longer held true. He sulked, hating America, wishing himself back in Paris. She, however, blossomed. He refused to learn English: she made a point of doing so. 'We're speaking English as brilliantly as ever,' wrote Breton crossly to Péret; 'oh, la, la!' In the same letter he decried Jacqueline's plunge into an autonomous working life.[18] But she was not to be deflected by sarcasm, however magisterial. Encouraged by Peggy Guggenheim, she rented an attic in Little Italy, and there, joyfully disregarding domestic chores, she painted, while

André looked on with a mocking smile and resolutely refused to help in the house ('poets are no good at washing up').[19] Jacqueline took a lover, a young sculptor named David Hare who had been entrusted by Breton with the editorship of a new Surrealist magazine, *VVV*. Once he had loved to show off her naked body to his friends: he took them to see her swim, nude photographs of her were prominently displayed in their apartment. Now he watched sourly from the screen porch ('I'm perfectly all right here, thanks') while she and David ran naked along the beach.[20] It is a measure of Breton's ineptitude during these years that he actually allowed a book of his poems to be translated as *Young Cherry Trees Secured Against Hares*.

It was clear by the summer of 1942 that the marriage was doomed. 'Awful, terrible depression,' Breton wrote Péret. '*Everything* in life is very dark: as for Jacqueline, incomprehensible (moving further away, becoming lost)...'[21] Once again his hopes of sexual and emotional fulfilment had ended in tears.

Sexually as in so many other ways, Breton's Surrealist principles warred with his emotional inclinations. Extolling Sadeian perversity and the right to complete sexual freedom (except for homosexuals) his real desire was romantic: himself and one woman, a vision of eternal bliss. Even in erotic games he tended to chastity. Asked to improvise an erotic text he wrote simply: 'I love your knee.'[22] He 'flirted with daring but only in words ... These Surrealist men loved to kiss [a woman's] hand; they did not back her into a corner as a "sexual" fellow would have done and as some women might have liked.' Excess of imagination lessened the potency of actual life. They felt, thought Dorothea Tanning, 'rather little of the fire in their loins but much of the imaginative luster'. [23]

But women are often less romantic than men, and for Breton's women imaginative lustre had evidently not been enough. First Simone, then Suzanne, and now Jacqueline had left him. No wonder he felt depressed. Most painful of all was his distancing from Aube. 'All the injustice, all the harshness in the world had taken this child from me, had deprived me of her beautiful awakenings which were my joy, had made me lose my marvellous daily contact with her ... I would not have a hand in shaping her young mind, which had come toward me so sparkling, so open.'[24] Rigidly monumental, brimming with emotion, he faced the rigours of exile alone. 'He strode back and forth, his arms held tightly to his sides. Always very upright: when you saw him from behind, you were surprised by the rigidity of his nape. It seemed as though his entire being was concentrated there, an iron bar joining his head to his shoulders. The rather heavy, graceless body disappeared. In the room there floated an enormous face, pale and angry, the face of an old habitué of the abyss modelled in a block of lightning.'[25]

Breton's almost compulsive rejection of everything American was an expression, perhaps, of his misery. English was anathema to him: he 'was careful not to learn even three words of [it] for fear of dulling the edge of his own exquisite writing instrument ... It was simply preposterous, a doughty menace to his best possession. Wonderful it was to think of him tiptoeing around his precious language bed, administering antibiotics to keep the Americanisms at bay.'[26] But this anti-English stance only led to a spiral of increasing depression. Lack of communication put him in a bad mood, which in turn meant he was unable to work or write.

Instead he turned from the terrors of the unknown to the comfort of the familiar: the intellectual and emotional frameworks he had constructed for himself over the past twenty years. His Surrealist devotion to parlour games was particularly incomprehensible to onlookers. Such games (for example consequences, pictorial or verbal, which they called *Cadavre exquis* after the first phrase obtained in this way: *le cadavre –*

exquis – boira – le vin – nouveau) brought into play the whole gamut of automatism, non-selectivity, objective chance. But it was essential to take them seriously. Not to do so reduced the whole thing to the level of – a parlour game. The hostesses who opened their doors to the newcomers in search of amusement or a little artistic frisson remained mystified.

> We went to lots of parties at various houses, but the best ones were given by Mrs. Bernard Reis [wrote Peggy Guggenheim]. She was a wonderful hostess and served marvelous meals. She loved to fill her home with Surrealists and then give them a free hand to do what they liked. Of course Breton took advantage of this to make us all play his favorite game, *Le jeu de la vérité*. We sat around in a circle while Breton lorded it over us in true schoolmasterly spirit. The object of the game was to dig out people's most intimate sexual feelings and expose them. It was like a form of psychoanalysis done in public. The worse the things that we exposed, the happier everyone was . . . It was ridiculous and childish, but the funniest part was the seriousness with which Breton took it. He got mortally offended if anyone spoke a word out of turn; part of the game was to inflict punishment on those who did so. You had to pay a forfeit. Breton ruled us with an iron hand, screaming '*Gage!*' at every moment . . .[27]

Even Guggenheim – friend, collector and now Surrealist wife, having recently married the bird-like Max Ernst and set him to reign among her trophies – failed to get the point.

The accumulation of allies and casting-out of enemies was another time-honoured pastime that continued unabated. 'Around Breton,' observed Georges Ribemont-Dessaignes, 'there was always an aura of secret societies.'[28] This was as true of New York as it had been of Paris. He exhorted Roland Penrose to write: 'It's absolutely essential . . . that here and in London we do our best to express ourselves *collectively* as we've always done.'[29] But a collective demands members, and the ranks of reliable allies seemed each day more reduced.

A loss that particularly rankled had been that of Paul Eluard. As with other valued lieutenants – Aragon, Desnos, Dalí – this had not been a sudden break but rather a pulling-apart over years of aggravation. The abortive expulsion at the time of the Dalí/Hitler contretemps continued to rankle. After that Breton had criticized Eluard's collection *La Rose publique* for breaking various Surrealist prohibitions. Indeed, could such a poet as Eluard, lyrical, sensuous, devoid of outrage, really be considered a Surrealist? His critical success rendered him particularly suspect: '[He] was the only one of our group to receive unvarying critical acclaim. His few moments of violence were never held to his account, everyone said it was the crowd he mixed with, his funny friends. All anyone was interested in were his poems, which were absolutely lacking in aggression, their only criterion was aesthetic – unlike most Surrealist poems.'[30]

As with a dying marriage, the surface of friendship was stretched ever more tightly over widening chasms of discontent. 'I've *definitively* broken with Breton, after a relatively calm discussion at the café,' Eluard told Gala in April 1936. 'I can't bear the dreadful way he has of arguing when he's in front of other people. That's it, I shan't participate in any activities with him ever again. I've had enough ... of his puerilities and inconsequence and bad faith. I want to be able to criticise without Breton turning for support to people who'll say anything at all, like a flock of sheep.'[31] Only a few months later, however, he was helping Breton organize the great International Surrealist Exhibition in London. But in 1938 he finally made the long-heralded break and threw in his lot with Aragon and the Party, publishing a group of poems in *Commune*, a Stalinist review particularly hostile to Surrealism.

As always after he had broken with an old friend, misery made Breton particularly bitter. The columns of such magazines as Charles-Henri Ford's *View* and the New York Surrealist review *VVV* rang with attacks which much of the readership must have found both incomprehensible and extraordinary. Asked, in *View*, 'What is the present orientation of Surrealism?' Breton veered off on a wild tangent: '*That which is ending* is the illusion of independence, I will even say of the transcendence of the work of art ... We see today where this has led Eluard: collaboration in *La Nouvelle Revue Française* of Paris (a new series sponsored by the Germans) with a poem ... which would not be out of place in an old number of "Keepsake".'[32] The implication was that Eluard was a collaborator in more than just poetry. Breton even went so far, on one occasion, as to state this outright – at which Max Ernst threatened to walk out unless he retracted.[33] This was even more outrageous considering that Eluard had remained to fight on in France while Breton had fled to the safety of New York. Man Ray, writing from Hollywood where he had set up home for the duration (New York held no happy memories for him), complained to Roland Penrose about

> the New York crowd, whose activity I condemn very much ... Breton is still playing his little games of surrounding himself with flunkeys, and excommunicating all others. It is probably a form of optimism that flourishes in the present tragic situation, because he knows that there is no immediate comeback possible. When he criticized Paul for writing poems about birds and flowers, I pointed out that he was himself scouring the countryside of New York for unfamiliar specimens of flora and fauna. It is this sense of the monopoly of poetry as well as of good sense that brands Breton the coward he is. The only way he has been able to believe in himself is to be disillusioned about every friend he ever made. Or has he ever really had a friend?[34]

Such was the emotional carnage, it seemed that perhaps he had not. Breton seemed determined to alienate everyone within reach. Max Ernst was a case in point. A close friend of Eluard (old jealousies having long since receded), his relations with Breton had been troubled by their rupture. But when he finally made it out of Ellis Island Breton was the first person he sought out in New York. And on the Avida Dollars front he was irreproachable. Max, too, hated the lobster telephones, exploding giraffes and self-aggrandizement Dalí was purveying in the name of Surrealism. He and his son Jimmy, then working at MOMA (that refuge for lost transatlantic sheep), ran into Avida on the sidewalk, holding out a supplicating hand. Hissing 'ce chien couchant', Max ignored the hand and pulled Jimmy over to the opposite side of the street. 'She has become a parody of a woman,' he said, warning Jimmy off Gala, his one-time paramour, 'and he resembles those horrid jellies that Americans eat for dessert . . . Stay away from Spanish olives and Russian vodka.'[35]

Such an ally as Ernst, such a friend in the desert, was surely worth hanging on to? But Breton and Ernst seemed unable to get along in New York. Perhaps they had simply been too much in each other's company: the tense weeks of enforced cohabitation in Marseille had taken their toll. 'They got on each others' nerves,' observed Charles Duits. He remembered one occasion when Breton, uncharacteristically cheerful (he had just found his title for *Young Cherry Trees Secured Against Hares* in a horticulturist's catalogue), was altogether too effusive – unconvincingly so – in his praise for a just-finished Ernst picture, while Max 'somehow *wouldn't look at him*'.[36] On another occasion, in the middle of a party, a silence suddenly fell as Breton declared *'Je n'écrirai jamais plus un mot sur vous!'* ('I shall never write another word about you!') to which Max replied, *'Je m'en fous!'* ('I don't give a fuck!')

and Breton raised a hand in disbelief: '*Il s'en fout! Il s'en fout!*'[37]

Once again the old pattern repeated itself. The quarrels did not last, but each one left its mark. 'By the time we came to Paris, five years later, all was forgotten, at least on the surface,' wrote Dorothea Tanning, Max's companion on that occasion (and for the rest of his life).

> Yet, across the years, their homeric struggle deepened, with each time the spasm lasting a little longer until, one sudden day, there was nothing left to be banished from. Arp was gone, if he had ever been there; Aragon, Tzara, Eluard had long since fallen out of favor and into more dubious company involving cards. Tanguy and Duchamp were already American, thus remote if indulgent; Miró, in Spain, deeply locked in his own universe . . . Breton's answer to the truth-game question, 'Have you any friends?' was, '*Non, mon ami.*'[38]

The fact was that tact and kindness were qualities precluded by the stern demands of Surrealism, and these are qualities without which friendly relations are hard to maintain. Breton was not unfeeling – his outpourings of love (in *Libre union*, *L'Amour fou*, the lament for Aube in *Arcane 17*) are testimony to that. Was not Surrealism itself just such an outpouring, a continual homage to his greatest, most enduring love of all, for Jacques Vaché? But when it came to the demands of the movement mere emotion was ruthlessly suppressed, whatever suffering that might entail. Breton's gratuitous cruelty to those he cast out was noticeable and shocking, and his insistence upon the absolute precedence of principle over friendship scarcely less so. He had, observed Charles Duits, no sense that he might ever be in the wrong. 'He was absolutely, so to speak, on his own side.'[39] If he behaved in a particular way, then that was *ipso facto* the only possible way to behave.

Even with his idols Breton was unable (or unwilling) to avoid the prickly intrusions of principle. For example, in 1938 he visited Trotsky in Mexico. Ever since the revelation of the Lenin biography Trotsky had been an object of reverence for Breton, a reverence only increased by his hero's banishment and vilification at the hands of Stalin. Indeed, Trotsky's outcast position was perhaps an essential ingredient of Breton's unconditional admiration. Had Trotsky ever regained power, its inevitable compromises, together with Breton's compulsive inclination towards the outsider's role, could only have led to disillusion and disgust. But there was no danger of that; and their positions were (from Breton's standpoint) wonderfully similar. Both were Communist idealists rejected by the official Party, both brilliant intellectuals crucified by dolts. His aim was to obtain Trotsky's support for his old dream of a Federation of Revolutionary Artists – and they did in fact publish a joint manifesto to this effect.

Mexico was a revelation to Breton. He loved both the country – 'the surrealist place par excellence',[40] 'black humour's promised land'[41] – and the people he met there; above all Trotsky himself, who measured up in every respect to Breton's dreams. Yet this did not prevent him taking Trotsky gratuitously to task. Walking one day with the great man and his dog, he noticed that when Trotsky spoke of dogs,

> his speech became less precise, his thought less exacting . . .
> He went so far as to express love for the animal, lending it
> natural goodness, he even spoke, like everyone else, of
> animal devotion. I tried to point out to him that there was
> something arbitrary about endowing beasts with feelings . . .
> It became clear that he was vexed to follow me along this
> path: he clung to the idea . . . that the dog felt *friendship* for
> him, and in the full sense of the word.[42]

This nit-picking lecture must have seemed not just pedantic, but hurtful. Just before Breton's visit Trotsky's son had died; he had few enough consolations – why should he not find comfort in a faithful dog? Under some circumstances, even delusions are permissible. But such considerations never cut any ice with Breton. Yet he was devoted to Trotsky, and distraught when he heard of his assassination, to the point of sobbing out loud. After the fall of France Mexico offered him refuge – Tanguy and his wife Kay Sage engineered an invitation for a year's lecturing there. But he turned it down: the 'surrealist place' had withdrawn Trotsky's guards, leaving him at the mercy of Stalin's assassin. When it really mattered, Mexico had let the world down. Breton preferred to take his chances in New York.

A similar trivial and offensive point of principle arose with Peggy Guggenheim. Guggenheim had been a good friend to the Surrealists in general and Breton in particular. During the dangerous days before and just after the fall of France she had made it a point of honour to buy a painting a day from working artists, which was certainly good for the Guggenheim collection, but also saved the bacon of a great many painters. She had provided the money for Breton's transatlantic fare, and let him have 200 dollars a month until he could find work in New York. (He finally found a job broadcasting for the French language service of the Voice of America. It was 'a great burden', but he shouldered it as his contribution to the spirit of the Resistance.)[43]

For a while Guggenheim had intended to establish a Museum of Modern Art in London as a suitable setting for her unrivalled collection, 'the only [enterprise]', in Breton's view, 'capable of dissipating the confusion sown here by Dalí and some others'.[44] That project had foundered, a casualty of war, and now she proposed another: a lavish new gallery in Manhattan to be called 'Art of This Century', a project on which

Breton became her close advisor. Over dinner one evening a dispute blew up regarding a free advertisement for 'Art of This Century' in *VVV*. Max Ernst had promised Peggy the ad. He was keen to keep her happy, and gestures such as this were a painless way of doing so, a sop to his guilty conscience. For Max was always in love – with someone other than Peggy. First there was the beautiful Leonora Carrington, the talented painter with whom he had lived for some years before the war. She had since suffered a mental breakdown, and married someone else, but Max saw her in New York and even though 'he always protested and said he was no longer in love with [Leonora], and that I was the person he wanted to live and sleep with',[45] Peggy could not really believe him: 'Max was so insane about [her] that he really could not hide it.'[46] Poor Peggy suffered agonies of jealousy. She was constantly aware that although she might be Max's wife, she was not his intimate. 'He considered me a sort of lady whom he was slightly afraid of, and never addressed me as *tu* . . . Once, when I asked him to write something in the books he had given me, he merely wrote "For Peggy Guggenheim from Max Ernst." This was upsetting as I remembered what he had written for [Leonora].'[47] Then Leonora left for Mexico, and Peggy breathed a sigh of relief. But almost immediately another rival materialized in the shape of yet another young and beautiful painter, Dorothea Tanning. Max suggested to Peggy that she might let him take Dorothea to Arizona, after which he would return to New York and the marital fold. 'I nearly had a fit,' she said.[48] Soon Max would leave her: she knew it.

This was how things stood when the dispute over the advertisement arose. But Breton, ignoring the tension, insisted that she must pay. Peggy resisted: 'I wanted it [for free] on principle, as I felt I had done so much for the Surrealists. But Breton maintained that all his life he had sacrificed to truth, beauty and art, and he expected everyone else to do as much.'[49]

Peggy's daughter remarked on the Surrealists' penchant for quarrels, Breton took offence at being criticized by a child, Max took the opportunity to leave for Dorothea's, and the evening broke up in fury.

The one island of calm detachment in this seething morass of intrigue was Marcel Duchamp.

Duchamp had arrived in New York in 1942, after some time travelling around France in the guise of a cheese merchant. *Marchand du sel* (salt merchant) had long been one of his punning alter egos, and perhaps he felt there was not too much distance between that and *Marchand de fromages*. Unlike the other exiles he was instantly at home in New York, and free from money worries. There were still several Brancusis in his attic from the stock he had acquired with Roché many years earlier. 'I looked up Roché, offered him one, and he gave me quite a bit of money for it.'[50] Living was cheap: he paid forty dollars a month rent, and his other expenses were minimal. Detached, enigmatic, austere, he hovered on the sidelines, and, as always, everyone turned to him. Breton remembered his New York years as 'despairing', but lightened by 'short bursts of delight such as the occasional lunch ... with my admirable friend Marcel Duchamp'.[51]

Duchamp remained one of the few people Breton truly revered. '[Breton] was naturally central, just as Duchamp was naturally peripheral. But when the latter was present, Breton refused to take his place. Everyone looked at him, listened to him; but he looked to Duchamp.'[52] Why? It was the old question, and there were no more answers than there ever had been. 'Perhaps there are some men who simply cannot but be "known",' hazarded Charles Duits.

> ... Perhaps the connection we like to establish between a man's fame and the value of what he does is simply non-existent ... Duchamp's interventions made one think of the

fragments of grit which pearl farmers insert into oysters. Around each one grew an exegetical sphere of oriental lore . . . [His] suggestions were always the most original (or the only ones with any originality at all); maliciously unpleasant (I'm thinking of the ageing breast on the cover of the 1947 Surrealist exhibition) . . .[53]

His works were as occasional and as slight as ever. A cover intended for *Vogue*, of George Washington in the shape of the United States, his face replaced by an American flag of sagging sackcloth, was rejected as too scandalous (Breton bought it for 300 dollars). Then there were some covers for the magazine *VVV* and a few window displays for Surrealist publications. *View* published in facsimile a letter-form he had sent Breton from Paris in 1941; he helped Breton arrange a Surrealist exhibition in New York. Not much, by any standards. But notoriety, as always in New York, followed him regardless.

*

New York continued to be Duchamp's town; secretive, private, he preferred its network of individual apartments to the public declarations of the café terrace.

Breton's, by contrast, was a rhetorical life. Alone he was lost: he existed only within a group, as its leader. But America was not built for group life. He might summon his troops – he did so, repeatedly – but where should they gather? In what Charles Duits called the 'scattered palace' of New York Surrealism there were 'a thousand rooms, each in a different street, communicating by invisible corridors'.[54] But how to make contact between these rooms? In Paris one always knew where to find people: Breton in Place Blanche, Man Ray in Montparnasse, and so forth. That was how Jacqueline had met Breton. (For of course their meeting, so poetic and wonderful for him, had not really been fortuitous: she had set her sights on him, knew where he was to be found, and simply waited until he noticed her – not long, since she was so very noticeable.) But in New York, as Ernst observed, 'you [had] to phone and make an appointment in advance. And the pleasure of a meeting had worn off before it took place. As a result, in New York we had artists, but no art.' Art, for Ernst as for all the Surrealists, was essentially a group experience – a meeting of friends. It was no coincidence that his two group portraits of the Surrealists had been entitled *Au Rendezvous des amis*. 'Art', he concluded, 'is not produced by one artist but by several. It is to a great degree a product of their exchange of ideas with one another.'[55]

Where Surrealism had evolved, ideas were paramount. Before life and art could take on any kind of shape, a theoretical framework must be constructed for them. After that, to the best of your ability, you squeezed and disciplined your life to fit the prescribed parameters. If this was no longer possible you left the movement, or were expelled. But splitting hairs over points of principle was not the anglophone style. In America as in England, only results mattered. Nobody really cared how they had been arrived at.

This lack of interest in theoretical superstructure might well have proved fatal to Surrealism in its anglophone exile. Divorced from their intellectual context, it was all too easy to dismiss, ridicule or (as in the case of Aragon and his bathetic encounter with the glasses of milk) completely misread individual works. The kind of problems that might be encountered were epitomized in George Orwell's review of Dalí's *Secret Life*.

It was inevitable that Orwell, of all people, should loathe and distrust Dalí. Orwell was a veteran of the International Brigade: Dalí's political volte-face alone was enough to render him despicable. But there was more. Ever since his encounter with the dogma-driven schisms which had accompanied and

442

amplified the Left's defeat in the Spanish Civil War, the entire thrust of Orwell's work had been devoted to the discrediting of theoretical hypocrisy. Dogmas and theories, for Orwell, were malevolent mists to be dispelled; people must learn to trust instead the evidence of their own common sense.

Orwell was too honest and clear-sighted not to recognize that Dalí, whom he found 'as anti-social as a flea', nevertheless presented a complex case. It was clear that 'such people are undesirable, and a society in which they can flourish has something wrong with it'. On the other hand, Dalí was undeniably an artist, and this presented specific difficulties for an intellectual such as Orwell, always battling with the British penchant for comfortable philistinism. He found himself caught in a double bind. 'If you showed this book, with its illustrations . . . to any "sensible" art-hating English person – it is easy to imagine what kind of response you would get. They would flatly refuse to see any merit in Dalí whatever.' That was clearly wrong. On the other hand, could Dalí really be defended? Not in any way Orwell might approve of.

> If you talk to the kind of person who *can* see Dalí's merits, the response that you get is not as a rule very much better. If you say that Dalí, though a brilliant draughtsman, is a dirty little scoundrel, you are looked upon as a savage. If you say that you don't like rotting corpses, and that people who do like rotting corpses are mentally diseased, it is assumed that you lack the aesthetic sense . . . It will be seen that what the defenders of Dalí are claiming is a kind of *benefit of clergy*. The artist is to be exempt from the moral laws that are binding in ordinary people. Just pronounce the magic word 'art', and everything is OK.[56]

That indeed was the Surrealist view; for Orwell, deserving only the bitterest contempt. No leading left-wing intellectual in continental Europe could ever have written such a piece. It would have been inconceivable; as inconceivable as that *Rêverie*, or Dalí's exposition of the paranoiac-critical method, with its accompanying Lacanian exegesis, could ever have seen the light in an English review. (They were translated, for Edward Titus' review *This Quarter*, but that was another matter altogether – an exposition of French culture for monoglot enthusiasts.) It was a fundamental difference of temperament. Perhaps Breton's gloom was justified. Perhaps Surrealism – true Surrealism – was doomed to remain for ever inaccessible to the anglophone mind.

That this did not happen was, ironically, largely due to Dalí. Breton had arrived in New York to find it awash with Surrealism – of the Dalinian variety. Dalí, with his customary acuteness, had seen that to render himself acceptable to the American market he must scuff off all shackles of theory or principle. All that mattered was the product. And that product was, first of all, Dalí himself: a monstrous and outrageous joke which he called Surrealism. Everything he made and did was an extension of this. He was soon established as a sort of pet alien, from whom anything might be expected, to whom anything might be permitted; a person to whom life's normal boundaries and prohibitions did not apply. And by the mere act of purchase it was possible to join the elect: to become, as it were, a member of the alien classes! He became a sensation, so cataclysmic as almost to satisfy even himself.

From where Breton stood, this seemed wholly deplorable – cheap, meretricious, unprincipled. Dalí, he declared, was 'hunting sensational publicity to illustrate the pitiful rapport of a badly made woman's foot and a worn-out shoe, the beginning of his "classical period"'.[57] But for once Breton was wrong. Dalí's American success marked a breakthrough, and in more than just a personal sense.

In 1936, the Museum of Modern Art had staged a show entitled 'Fantastic Art, Dada, Surrealism', curated by Alfred

Barr. Man Ray, as an expatriate American, took a particular interest in its reception. When he had left in disgust and disillusion fifteen years earlier, much of the art America was producing had seemed second-rate, its patrons backward-looking, its attitudes philistine. Marius de Zayas was claiming in *291* that 'America has the same complex mentality as the true modern artist', but the small group around Stieglitz had seemed alone in sensing this connection. New life, new thought – true modernity – emanated from Europe, and Man Ray had followed it to its source.

As a result the work he produced during the 1920s was largely unknown in America, though it had appeared in many of the little magazines such as *Broom* and *transition* that maintained a transatlantic dialogue in the arts. But the 1929 crash, and the Depression that followed it, had depleted their numbers, and it was clear that in Europe freedom of speech was increasingly threatened. If art's future lay anywhere now, it was surely in New York. For Man Ray, Alfred Barr's show would indicate how far things had progressed on the American art scene. He wanted it to do well, and tried to persuade Barr to resist Breton and Eluard when they insisted that it should be a political Surrealist manifestation. In his view, 'America [was] different.'

In the event the show's reception was disappointing. Surrealism was allowed to be intriguing (especially Meret Oppenheim's fur-lined cup and saucer), but it could not be taken seriously. Man Ray wrote an indignant, if disingenuous, letter of complaint to the *New York Herald Tribune*. 'President Roosevelt and Surrealism have much in common – both have been called Communist for attempting something new. What's wrong with fur on cups? What difference is there between putting furs on inanimate objects or on women?' he demanded.

As late as 1936, then, America had still not been ready for the Surrealist message. And then the big breakthrough occurred: Dalí's second trip to America, in 1936–7. His first sortie had made a distinct if eccentric impression: but by 1936 he was an altogether less erratic figure, 'no longer the half-timid, half-malicious foreigner, but . . . expensive and elegant and quite formidable'.[58]

Julien Levy (whose view this was) had arranged for Dalí to dress Bonwit Teller's Fifth Avenue windows as a publicity stunt to coincide with the opening of his third exhibition at Levy's gallery. Dalí was enchanted at the prospect of working in three dimensions. 'I used a [mannequin] whose head was made of red roses and who had fingernails of ermine fur. On a table, a telephone transformed into a lobster; hanging on a chair, my famous "aphrodisiac coat".'[59] The mannequin, fully clothed, was to lie in an old-fashioned white bathtub. The management, however, more interested in the mannequin's clothes than Dalí's tableau, decided overnight to lift her out of her tub into full view. Passing by his window next morning Dalí registered the alteration. Overcome with fury, he plunged in to rescue his creation. Such was the force of his attack that bathtub, mannequin and Dalí flew together through the plate glass and onto the sidewalk. Several passers-by narrowly missed serious injury and Dalí himself was almost beheaded by flying glass. As publicity – for Dalí – it was out of this world. Bonwit's sued, insisting that there could be nothing accidental about such a coup. Gala indignantly reminded the court that her husband had narrowly missed fatal injury. 'He would not have been interested in his own death,' she argued. But Dalí admitted to Julien Levy that he had fallen into a rage. ' "Rage for the absolute," he asserted.'[60]

Whatever the reality of the matter, it ensured a sell-out show and coast-to-coast sensation. This was when Dalí appeared on the cover of *Time*, in a photo by Man Ray, backed by a soft piano, an archbishop and a blazing pine tree falling from a window – a reference to *l'Âge d'or*, doubtless lost on

Time's readers. What was not lost on them, however, was the association of the words 'Dalí' and 'Surrealism'.

Avida Dollars was King of New York. He divided his time between the city and Caresse Crosby's newly refurbished Virginia estate, where Pathé News was able to report that a heifer occupied the hearthrug in the library and a grand piano had been hung from a tree.

> In no time at all, there it hung. We had a truck on the place with a great steel cable, used for pulling farm machinery out of waterholes, or station wagons out of ditches. Shep and Len and four of the younger generation of 'hands' made light weight of bearing the grand piano from the front room to the front lawn, a coil of cable hurled over a sturdy upper limb was belted round the instrument's waist, then the cable attached to the truck which, in lowest speed, majestically advanced swinging the mahogany music box into the magnolia branches . . .[61]

Dalí's witty and sensational version of Surrealism took a firm hold on the popular imagination. It struck a chord with Americans, where de Zayas, Stieglitz and New York Dada had failed twenty years earlier. Dalí thus performed the universal service of opening up the public imagination to modern art in general and Surrealism in particular. But Breton could hardly be expected to rejoice, since at the same time he appeared to have fulfilled his long-standing ambition of taking Surrealism over – at least in the public eye. And to Dalí the public eye was all that mattered – precisely one of the Dalinian aspects Breton most deplored.

It was the final round of the old fight, the fight they had waged throughout the previous decade. And Dalí seemed to hold all the trump cards. Not the least was that he worked chiefly in visual images. Anyone could look at a Dalí; even if no effort was made to understand it the visual impact remained. At the most superficial level a soft watch is an intriguing visual idea, and as such has continued to pervade advertising to this day. The visual image is always more memorable than the verbal. The names most commonly associated with Surrealism now are those of painters and photographers – Magritte, Dalí, Duchamp, Picabia, Ernst, Arp, Man Ray.

By contrast with Dalí's popular picturings, Breton's Surrealism remained essentially verbal. Although (as with Apollinaire) painting and painters were an essential part of his life, words always came first with him. 'Surrealism and Painting', his first serious consideration of the visual arts, was not published until 1928; his earliest confederates in what would become Surrealism – Vaché, Aragon, Soupault, Eluard – all worked in words. Surrealism is a philosophy: although Magritte's paintings (for example) *are* Surrealist, it would not be possible to explain Surrealism purely by looking at them. As Robert Motherwell put it, 'to approach Surrealism through its visual works would be like trying to understand Marxism through *its* visual works, which is obviously the *least* effective way of understanding what Karl Marx actually thought'.[62]

This did not bode well for Breton's attempts to counter the Dalinian influence in America. Anyone could appreciate Dalí's jokes. But what Breton had to say demanded an effort that only a few were prepared to make. His resolute refusal to learn English did not help matters, since it naturally limited his interaction with the natives. But even had he done so, would they have been any the wiser? Breton was the man who wrote (in a passage full of resonance for anyone who has wrestled with his dense and difficult prose), 'A monstrous aberration makes people believe that language was born to facilitate their mutual relations.'[63]

Motherwell, then a young painter, was one of the few prepared to make the necessary effort. For him, Surrealism meant Breton. 'In my very first meetings with Surrealists,' he said, 'I used to ask Max Ernst to define Surrealism a bit for me, and Max would point to André Breton and say point-blank "Breton *is* Surrealism," in the same way that one might point to Karl Marx and say he *is* Marxism.'[64] But even for such a willing pupil as Motherwell, Breton's teachings were by no means easy.

New York's junk shops provided the setting for many of these lessons in Surrealism. In Paris one of the favourite Surrealist pastimes had been to wander around the flea markets in search of found objects, whose interest arose not on account of any intrinsic beauty but because the Surrealist gaze invested them with a wholly personal significance quite divorced from any earlier function. 'Only on the level of analogy have I ever experienced intellectual pleasure,' Breton remarked. 'For me the only *manifest truth* in the world is governed by the spontaneous, clairvoyant, insolent connection established under certain conditions between two things whose conjunction would not be permitted by common sense.'[65]

Now, in New York, he and Ernst took to haunting the junk shops of Third Avenue. Ernst, freed from money worries for the first time in his life by his marriage to Peggy Guggenheim, delighted in native American art – kachina dolls, totem carvings, *art sauvage* of the sort the Surrealists had always prized – and bought it up wholesale. Breton, hard-up as ever, could not emulate these spending sprees even had he wanted to. Instead he used the expeditions to explain Surrealist messages and techniques. Most importantly, and hardest of all for visual artists, the notion of art as aesthetics, inculcated from childhood, had painfully to be *un*learned.

> In a sense Surrealism was trying to make expressions that were identical with reality itself, as in more primitive times religious things must have seemed so to the communicants

449

[wrote Motherwell]. I learned the lesson myself when Breton would take the Surrealist group into the junk shops and second-hand stores of Third Avenue of the early 1940s and force us to decide which objects were Surrealist and which were not. I had always looked at such shops before aesthetically and I still remember vividly how one's mind felt twisted in the effort to overcome one's aesthetic conditioning – my mother's passion was antique-collecting, of which she was a master, and in accompanying her I had learned to look aesthetically or as a connoisseur. From a Surrealist standpoint that was to be a dilettante, a *castrato*, a blasphemy.[66]

These experiences permanently altered Motherwell's approach to beauty. Ever after, he could not bear to see 'voodoo objects from Haiti or African spirit masks in a Mies van der Rohe or Edwardian living room'.[67] But absolute non-aestheticism was difficult for anyone – most of all an artist – to take on board. Duchamp, scourge of the 'retinal', deplored the fact that readymades like the bottle-rack, the bicycle-wheel, the urinal, originally intended as anti-art gestures, were increasingly objects of admiration for *aesthetic* reasons. People looked for beauty in them, and found it. Even Motherwell failed this purity test. 'It is evident, thirty-five years later,' he wrote, 'that the bottle-rack [Duchamp] chose has a more beautiful form than almost anything made, in 1914, as sculpture.'[68]

Notwithstanding, he understood Breton's message and was entranced by it. He saw that Surrealism was a quite different thing from the product purveyed by Dalí. But how was this Surrealism to be conveyed to Americans? Not only was what Breton had to say difficult and idiosyncratic (inevitably so, considering that Surrealist theory was in large part a generalization from his own psyche); there was also the problem of his approach. Breton, like all dictators, had no time for half measures. Either you swallowed the whole dish, or none.

There could be no question of picking and mixing. But this was not the American way. Many young American painters were beginning to get interested in Breton's message. None, however, wished to swallow it whole. As Louise Nevelson put it, 'I don't want to get anyone angry, but I'd just as soon wait to see if some of his pronouncements make it across the ocean in the bottom of a ship. And once they get here they might not have any meaning for me.'[69]

The message was clear. In New York, undiluted Breton was unacceptable. If he was to have any influence, it would have to be mediated. Motherwell would be one important such mediating influence. Others were Arshile Gorky and a young Chilean Surrealist, Matta Echaurren.

Gorky's aim was to work through an external starting point to an inner vision, until the latter had arrived at something quite separate from the former – 'the first painter to whom this secret has been fully revealed,' enthused Breton.[70] Breton prompted Julien Levy to give Gorky his first important exhibition: Gorky illustrated Breton's book *Young Cherry Trees Secured Against Hares*.

It was Matta, however, who was the main vehicle for the Surrealist word in America. Robert Motherwell thought him a

> ... hypnotic proselytizer ... I went to Mexico with him, and it was the turning point in my own development. It was his desire to make a 'palace revolution' inside Surrealism that made contacts between myself and Baziotes with Pollock, de Kooning, Kamrowski, Busa and Hofmann. About 1943, he shifted Gorky from copying *Cahiers d'art* to a full blown development of his own (as well as running off with his wife).[71]

Motherwell also pointed out that, unlike Breton, Masson, Tanguy or Ernst, Matta 'spoke English quite well, and therefore had much more connectedness with the American scene'.[72]

451

Small, dark and intense, his swirling paintings and drawings extended the biomorphic world of such painters as Tanguy and Masson. He made friends with the young New York artists, who liked the abstraction of his paintings, unaware (not that they would have cared) that this nonfigurative work was considered something of a deviation by some of the Surrealists. Matta was quite prepared to advise about painting technique without reference to philosophy – though clearly the abstract expressionists' use of imagery arrived at by manual gesture alone had much in common with such Surrealist techniques as automatism.

So began (in Julien Levy's words) an 'acute struggle between the . . . Surrealists . . . and the rising tide of independence asserted by the artists who were to become the New York school' – Louise Nevelson, Peter Busa, William and Ethel Baziotes, Willem de Kooning, Jackson Pollock: the group who would become the most important painters of the post-war years.

In the end Surrealism left two quite distinct legacies in America. One was Dalí's – what the critic Leslie Fiedler called

> the transformation of Surrealist gallows humour into commercial entertainment . . . an extraordinary process which begins for literature in the columns of the *New Yorker* and for art in the cartoons of the same magazine, as well as in certain shop-windows decorated by Salvador Dalí . . . The avant-garde images of twenty-five years ago . . . have become now the common property of gifte shoppes and greeting-card racks, fall as stereotypes from the mouths of twelve-year-olds.[73]

The other, almost in spite of himself, was Breton's. New York's young men and women – by way of Motherwell and Matta – became also Breton's young men and women. If Dalí made his indelible mark upon the public imagination, Breton –

as was only appropriate – lived on in the factory lofts of SoHo, where young artists camped illegally in industrial premises, stealing electricity from the mains and joyfully sharing food, wine and love *au rendezvous des amis*. In the Breton/Dalí fight, neither side won in the sense of finally obliterating the other. It may rather be said to have ended in a draw.

In order to move Surrealism forward, it had been necessary to leave Paris – so much Breton had recognized. New York was by contrast an accident, the place where the fortunes of war happened to have washed him ashore. For him, New York remained a hiatus. Nevertheless, his instinct had been correct, and his landing fortunate. For the second war, draining Europe as it energized America, achieved what the preceding one had not: the arena of new artistic thought moved, definitively, to the other side of the Atlantic. This was something Duchamp and Dalí knew by instinct. But Breton could never accept it.

After Breton, the New York school; after Dalí, a thousand commercials. What striving, what ambition, that sentence represents! But Surrealism had one last, great joke to play. For its largest artistic legacy turned out to lie in the most unexpected quarter. In the hall of infinitely self-referential mirrors that is late twentieth-century art, no one is more constantly reflected than Marcel Duchamp, scourge of the retinal, the man of no ambition at all who proclaimed the end of painting, declined every fight and turned his back on influence. Hoping to draw a line under art, he turned out merely to have started it on another tack. The bicycle-wheel, the bottle-rack and R. Mutt's *Fountain* take their place as the Great Ancestors, constantly rediscovered. In Dorothea Tanning's words, 'After the war they went back to where they came from, leaving the key in the door. Many others have used it since, but no one has brought in any new furniture.'[74]

*

On the day of the German surrender, Breton, Duchamp and Man Ray walked through New York looking for a restaurant.

> We went from restaurant to restaurant, everything was jammed, people were celebrating – we finally ended up at the old German restaurant, Lüchows, on 14th Street. This, too, was crowded – with Germans subdued and weeping. The pianist played German tunes, all stood up reverently, but we had a table and remained seated. We managed to get served with Breton railing against the cooking – he always railed at any cooking but French.[75]

Soon, though, he would be able to go back to France. And what then? Breton had been lonely in New York. But what would he find in Paris? Grey-haired now, stocky, a figure of tremendous authority, Breton, approaching fifty, faced what Vaché had avoided: middle age and obsolescence.

At least he would not face this prospect alone. 'Against all my expectations I found happiness in America,' Breton said. He was referring to Elisa Bindhoff, his third wife. They met during one of those lunches with Duchamp that Breton so enjoyed. She stared at him so insistently from a nearby table that he (always open to a chance encounter) went over and introduced himself. By the following month he was declaring to Péret '[she is] the person I love, the only person I adore'.[76] She, like Breton, was in a depressed state: her teenage daughter had drowned off New England the previous year. Together they helped each other to recover. On 30 July 1945, Breton divorced Jacqueline in Reno, Nevada, and later the same day he and Elisa were married. Once again, as with Jacqueline, the shade of Vaché appeared to bless the union. Travelling through the Nevada desert after the wedding they came upon

> a bar standing among ruins . . . tended by a man surrounded by an astounding array of bottles and a whole set of girlie pinups . . . The hammock he used for sleeping hung from the

ceiling. He contended that he had been sick when he had first arrived there and that he had cured and 'preserved' himself ... by taking large doses of living ants, a glassful of which sparkled enticingly on the next table. No matter: even though he said that at that moment as at any other time he was alone, everything seemed ready, all the circumstances were right for Jacques Vaché to enter, coming from *inside*, from the back rooms, rather than from outside. He would not have changed since 1918.[77]

Everything else, though, had.

Breton, Elisa and Aube reached Le Havre on 25 May 1946, and immediately made their way to Paris. The apartment at Rue Fontaine had been deserted for five years, though the rental payments had been kept up by Breton's father. What would they find there? After such an absence one could never be sure, even with family and friends to keep an eye on things. Cécile Eluard, for example, had sold off some of the Dalís left in her safekeeping in order to eat: a lapse for which Gala never forgave her. But Breton's pictures were still on the walls, the masks and fetishes on the shelves. The only really valuable objects missing were some Sade manuscripts, a dreadful loss that argued discriminating thieves. But even that could be survived. And although the place was a mess – windows broken, no heat, no telephone, walls damaged by damp – time and hard work would put it right.

The intellectual climate, however, was another matter. As Breton wrote in *Arcane 17*: 'A bridge was soon thrown up between the Paris of early 1940 and the Paris of 1944, but it would be simplistic to imagine that these two Parises are the same.'[78]

There had, in New York, been hints of what he might expect. Albert Camus and Jean-Paul Sartre, leaders of the rising generation, had both visited America as journalists and had long talks with Breton. What he had seen of Camus's articles had led Breton to hope for the best: 'Suddenly, the air seemed breathable again.'[79] But in conversation the young men painted a less optimistic picture. Sartre 'emphasised ... the "reign of terror" exercised by the Stalinists in the literary world. According to him, it would have been extremely unwise publicly to criticise Aragon's *Crève-coeur* [his latest collection of poems]: you risked not waking up next morning.'[80]

The reality was less melodramatic. But in essence Sartre was right. The Communists had been the only truly organized group in the Resistance. Now they emerged, uniquely uncompromised, to take over the key positions in publishing, newspapers, radio – in short, the literary-artistic establishment. And who were they? Aragon, Eluard, Char, Tzara – the very people who had once been Breton's closest friends, and were now his bitterest enemies. In the edgy world of liberated France, with its pervasive climate of blame and recrimination, old grudges flourished. The kind of thing Breton had to endure may be glimpsed in Eluard's letters to Gala in New York. They abound with hate-filled references to 'M. Breton'. He was spreading lies about Dalí, saying that he had painted the portrait of Franco's Ambassador (this was in fact the truth).[81] 'M. Breton, whom I have not met (glimpsed) since his return, maintains a historical position, very much the exile – always and everywhere.'[82] (Eluard nevertheless requested copies of *VVV* and *Arcane 17*, well wrapped and in mint condition: 'I'm still a bibliophile.') Even Tzara, who would have left France if he could, and whom Breton had supported in his efforts to obtain an exit visa, shunned him. Breton had sold out: he had left the sinking ship. Now that it was refloated those who had remained would do nothing for him.

Still Breton gathered his disciples around him, a new generation of young men who fell under his spell; still he tried with all his might to push forward the frontiers of Surrealism.

But the world was no longer interested. It had moved on, the centre was elsewhere.

Sartre, the man of the moment, dismissed his predecessors with a cruel phrase. 'Some killed themselves, others are in exile; those who have returned are exiled among us. They were the proclaimers of catastrophe in the time of the fat cows; in the time of the lean cows they have nothing more to say.'[83]

So (it might be retorted) the experience of the latest war blots out the one before. Had not Breton's generation been through its own horrors? Was it possible to imagine anything more appalling than the trenches?

But that hell, however ghastly, was not deliberately designed. The universal enemy then had been war itself, and the crass and callous stupidity of the generals and politicians who promoted and prolonged it. From that arose the howl of fury that became Dada, and hence Surrealism. Received opinion had supported the war: received opinion, in all its forms, was the source of evil and must be confounded.

World War II was different. This time the enemy was specific, and deliberately wicked. The death camps opened up entirely new vistas of evil, which had to be fought and defeated. And – another great difference – the victims were overwhelmingly civilian. The front line was everywhere: everyone – whether through bombing or occupation – faced daily and extreme danger.

All this demanded a different level of response, artistic and intellectual. The question was no longer one of inciting mutiny but of individual responsibility.

A week did not go by that we did not ask ourselves: 'Suppose I were tortured, what would I do?' And this question alone carried us to the very frontier of ourselves and of the human ... Those who had immediately preceded us in the world ... practised modest virtues and remained in the moderate regions ... Because of this, their writers gave them a literature of *average situations*. But we could no longer find it *natural* to be men when our best friends, if they were taken, could choose only between abjection and heroism ...[84]

Time has borne Sartre out. Fifty years on, Sartre and Camus, *Huis clos, L'Etranger, La Peste*, still speak to us all. And who (apart from a few scholars) reads *Nadja*?

Yet Breton's influence remains pervasive. His achievement is subtler and more universal. The world is a surreal place: everyone knows it, just as everyone knows the disjunctions, the bizarre concatenations, the dreamlike illogic, that the adjective implies. Presumably it has always been so. But until Breton named it, there was no word for this state of things – one that, perhaps more than any other, defines our time. So the force of intellect that was André Breton, the obstinacy, the rigidity, the rigour, have been transmuted into the rarest kind of immortality. Along with his hero Freud, he is one of that select group who defined for our century a new way of looking at the world.

ENDNOTES

1: A BAS GUILLAUME

1 Jacques Vaché to Theodore Fraenkel, 16 June 1917.
2 Programme note to *Parade*, 18 May 1917.
3 Preface to *Les Mamelles de Tirésias*, 24 June 1917.
4 Quoted Roger Shattuck, *The Banquet Years*, p. 243.
5 *SIC*, June 1917.
6 André Breton, *Second Manifeste du surréalisme*, 1929.
7 Max Jacob to Tristan Tzara, 26 February 1916; Michel Sanouillet, *Dada à Paris*, p. 605.
8 Guillaume Apollinaire, *Journal intime*, 1907.
9 Georges Ribemont-Dessaignes, *Déja Jadis*, p. 25.
10 Quoted Calvin Tomkins, *Duchamp*, p. 104.
11 Gabrielle Buffet-Picabia, *Rencontre avec Apollinaire*, Le Point, autumn 1937.
12 André Billy, *Avec Apollinaire*, p. 10.
13 Guillaume Apollinaire, *Le Bestiaire*.
14 Guillaume Apollinaire Correspondence, *Oeuvres complètes* vol. 4, pp. 873–6.
15 André Breton and André Parinaud, *Entretiens 1913–1952*, pp. 16–17.
16 Adrienne Monnier, A*ndré Breton*, quoted Sanouillet, *Dada à Paris*, p. 82.
17 Germaine Everling, *l'Anneau de Saturne*, p. 95.
18 Ibid.
19 Adrienne Monnier, *Rue de l'Odéon*, quoted Henri Béhar, *André Breton*, p. 37.
20 Ibid.
21 Arthur Rimbaud to Paul Demeny, 15 May 1871.

22 Jean-Paul Sartre, *What Is Literature?*, pp. 124–5.
23 Georges Ribemont-Dessaignes, 'André Breton ou l'intégrité noire', in *Nouvelle Revue Française*.
24 André Breton to Theodore Fraenkel, 22 April 1915, quoted Marguerite Bonnet, *André Breton: Naissance de l'aventure surréaliste*, p. 70.
25 Guillaume Apollinaire to Serge Férat, quoted Shattuck, *The Banquet Years*, p. 207.
26 Guillaume Apollinaire, *Tendre comme le souvenir*, Oeuvres complètes vol. 4.
27 Buffet-Picabia, *Rencontre avec Apollinaire*.
28 Guillaume Apollinaire to 'Lou', 5 September 1914, quoted Shattuck, *The Banquet Years*, p. 203.
29 Guillaume Apollinaire to Paul Léautaud, quoted Shattuck, *The Banquet Years*, p. 205.
30 Guillaume Apollinaire to Lou, 9 April 1915, *Lettres à Lou*, p. 271.
31 Guillaume Apollinaire to Jane Mortier, 26 April 1915, *Oeuvres complètes* vol. 4.
32 André Breton to André Paris, quoted Mark Polizzotti, *Revolution of the Mind: The life of André Breton*, p. 46.
33 Guillaume Apollinaire, *Tendre comme le souvenir*, Oeuvres complètes vol. 4.
34 Guillaume Apollinaire to Jacques Doucet, *Oeuvres complètes* vol. 4, p. 893.
35 Guillaume Apollinaire to André Breton, 2 April 1917.
36 André Breton, 'La Confession dédaigneuse', in *Les Pas perdus*.
37 Ibid.
38 José Pierre ed., *Investigating Sex: Surrealist discussions 1928–1932*, tr. Ian Imrie, p. 27.
39 André Breton, 'Jacques Vaché', in *Les Pas perdus*.
40 André Breton, 'Trente ans après', in *La Clé des champs*.
41 Jacques Vaché to André Breton, 20 April 1917.
42 Jacques Vaché to André Breton, 11 October 1916.
43 Breton and Parinaud, *Entretiens 1913–1952*, p. 28.
44 Jacques Vaché to André Breton, 29 April 1917.
45 Ibid.

46 Ibid.

47 André Breton, introduction to *Anthologie de l'humour noir*, 1940.

48 André Breton, 'Guillaume Apollinaire', in *Les Pas perdus*.

49 Breton and Parinaud, *Entretiens 1913–1952*, p. 25.

50 Philippe Soupault, 'Si mes souvenirs son exacts', in *Les Lettres Françaises*, 6–12 October 1966.

51 Breton, 'Trente ans après', in *La Clé des champs*.

52 Philippe Soupault, *Mémoires de l'oubli*, p. 39.

53 Ibid.

54 André Breton to Simone Kahn, 6 August 1920, quoted Bonnet, *André Breton: Naissance de l'aventure surréaliste*, p. 119.

55 Louis Aragon, 'Lautréamont et nous', in *Les Lettres Françaises*, 6 June 1967.

56 Guillaume Apollinaire to André Breton, *Oeuvres complètes* vol. 4, p. 937.

57 Monnier, *Rue de l'Odéon*, p. 102.

58 Guillaume Apollinaire to Philippe Soupault, *Oeuvres complètes* vol. 4, p. 894.

59 Guillaume Apollinaire, *Oeuvres complètes* vol. 3, p. 397.

60 Jacques Vaché to André Breton, 18 August 1917.

61 Breton, 'Guillaume Apollinaire', in *Les Pas perdus*.

62 Breton and Parinaud, *Entretiens 1913–1952*, p. 23.

63 Louise Faure-Favier, quoted Francis Steegmuller, *Poet Among the Painters*, p. 328.

64 Louis Aragon, 'André Breton', in *Les Lettres Françaises*, 6–12 October 1966.

65 Jacques Vaché to Louis Aragon, November 1918.

66 Jacques Vaché, *Les Lettres de guerre*, appendix.

67 Jacques Vaché to André Breton, 5 July 1916.

68 Marc-Adolphe Guégan, *La Ligne de coeur*, quoted Breton, 1940.

69 Jacques Vaché to André Breton, 14 November 1918.

70 André Breton, 'Jacques Vaché' in *Les Pas perdus*.

71 In *La Révolution surréaliste* no. 2.

72 See for example his letter to Lou, 28 January 1914. 'The harder I whip the more your bum moves, higher and higher,

revealing your sex all wet and swollen. Next time you must move them further apart so that I can wallop that shady crack . . .'

73 Shattuck, *The Banquet Years*, p. 235, where this point is discussed at length.

74 Louis Aragon, 'André Gide' in his *Projet d'histoire littéraire contemporaine*, ed. Marc Dachy, p. 36.

75 Letter from Jacques Vaché to André Breton, 16 June 1917.

2: THE DEATH OF ART

1 Ribemont-Dessaignes, *Déja Jadis*.

2 Tomkins, *Duchamp*, p. 175.

3 Pierre Cabanne, *Dialogues with Marcel Duchamp*, p. 17.

4 Ibid., p. 35.

5 Ibid., pp. 81–3.

6 Raymond Roussel, *Comment j'ai écrit certains de mes livres*.

7 Cabanne, *Dialogues with Marcel Duchamp*, pp. 33–4.

8 Ibid., p. 37.

9 Hans Richter, *Dada: Art and anti-art*, p. 71.

10 Gabrielle Buffet-Picabia, 'Some Memories of Pre-Dada' (1949), in *The Dada Painters and Poets*, ed. Motherwell.

11 Cabanne, *Dialogues with Marcel Duchamp*, p. 37.

12 Ribemont-Dessaignes, *Déja Jadis*, p. 44.

13 Cabanne, *Dialogues with Marcel Duchamp*, p. 32.

14 Hugo Ball, *Flight out of Time*, tr. Elderfield, p. 8.

15 Interview with John Russell, *Sunday Times*, 9 June 1968, quoted Tomkins, *Duchamp*, p. 93.

16 Interview with Jennifer Gough-Cooper and Jacques Caumont, quoted Tomkins, *Duchamp*, pp. 111–12.

17 So he told Calvin Tomkins. Tomkins, *Duchamp*, p. 113.

18 Quoted Michel Sanouillet and Elmer Peterson, *Duchamp du signe*, p. 174.

19 William Carlos Williams, *Autobiography*, p. 138.

20 Gabrielle Buffet-Picabia, *Aires abstraites*, p. 33.

21 Marcel Duchamp to Jean Schuster, quoted Octavio Paz, *Marcel Duchamp: Appearance stripped bare*, tr. Rachel Phillips, p. 62.
22 Quoted Ron Padgett, 'Duchamp and Roussel', unpublished lecture given at the Museum of Modern Art, New York, July 1974.
23 Sanouillet and Peterson, *Duchamp du signe*, p. 174.
24 Paz, *Marcel Duchamp: Appearance stripped bare*, p. 60.
25 *This Quarter*, 1932, tr. J. Bronowski.
26 Ibid.
27 Paz, *Marcel Duchamp: Appearance stripped bare*.
28 Marcel Duchamp to Walter Pach, 19 January 1915, quoted Tomkins, *Duchamp*, p. 140.
29 Interview in *New York Tribune*, 24 October 1915.
30 Tomkins, *Duchamp*, p. 140.
31 Marcel Duchamp to Walter Pach, 27 April 1914, quoted Tomkins, *Duchamp*, pp. 141–2.
32 Cabanne, *Dialogues with Marcel Duchamp*, p. 45.
33 Beatrice Wood, *I Shock Myself*, p. 24.
34 Quoted Tomkins, *Duchamp*, p. 155.
35 Cabanne, *Dialogues with Marcel Duchamp*, p. 49.
36 Ibid., p. 58.
37 Wood, *I Shock Myself*, p. 22.
38 Ibid., p. 24.
39 Ibid., p. 46.
40 Williams, *Autobiography*, p. 136.
41 Ibid.
42 Poem: '391' by Francis Picabia, in *391* no. XVII, p. 4.
43 Buffet-Picabia, 'Some Memories of Pre-Dada', in Motherwell, *The Dada Painters and Poets*.
44 Ibid.
45 Ibid.
46 Ibid.
47 Quoted Tomkins, *Duchamp*, p. 174.
48 Mina Loy, 'Colossus', in Kuenzli ed., *New York Dada*.
49 Williams, *Autobiography*, pp. 140–1.
50 Loy, 'Colossus', in Kuenzli ed., *New York Dada*.
51 Cabanne, *Dialogues with Marcel Duchamp*, p. 55.

52 In *The Blind Man*.

53 Cabanne, *Dialogues with Marcel Duchamp*, p. 47.

54 Ibid.

55 Samuel Taylor Coleridge, *Biographia Literaria* – cited by Roger Shattuck in 'Marcel Duchamp, Alfred Jarry and Pataphysics' – unpublished lecture given at the Museum of Modern Art, New York, 10 January 1974.

56 Quoted Sanouillet, *Francis Picabia et 391*, vol. II, p. 46.

57 'Magic City', in *391* no. IV.

58 For a full discussion of all these possibilities, see Maria Lluisa Borràs, *Cravan: Une stratégie de scandale*.

59 André Salmon, quoted Borràs, *Cravan: Une stratégie de scandale*.

60 Nina Hamnett, quoted Willard Bohn, 'Chasing Butterflies with Arthur Cravan', in *New York Dada*, ed. Kuenzli, p. 120.

61 *Maintenant* no. 3, October–November 1913.

62 *Maintenant* no. 2.

63 Amiot-Dumont, *Gide Vivant*, 1952.

64 Quoted Tomkins, *Duchamp*, p. 187.

65 Quoted Borràs, *Cravan: Une stratégie de scandale*, p. 185.

66 *391* no. V, p. 8 June 1917.

67 Williams, *Autobiography*, p. 141.

68 Mina Loy to Julien Levy in his *Memoirs of an Art Gallery*, pp. 42–3.

69 Juliette Roche, *Demi cercle*, Paris, 1920.

70 Man Ray, *Self-Portrait*, p. 59.

71 Letter from Marcel Duchamp to Alfred Stieglitz, Sanouillet, *Dada à Paris*, p. 244

72 Man Ray to Katherine Dreier, quoted Neil Baldwin, *Man Ray: American artist*, p. 77.

73 Ray, *Self-Portrait*, p. 82.

74 Ibid., p. 68.

75 Ibid., p. 91.

76 Quoted Baldwin, *Man Ray: American Artist*, p. 72.

77 Ray, *Self-Portrait*, p. 89.

78 Quoted Tomkins, *Duchamp*, p. 224.

79 Ibid., p. 225.

464

80 Ray, *Self-Portrait*, p. 100.
81 Ibid., p. 101.
82 Quoted Baldwin, *Man Ray: American Artist*, p. 73.
83 *New York Times*, 24 October 1915.
84 In 1922, for instance, Edmund Wilson warned: 'Do not try to make pets of the machines! Be careful that the elephants do not crush you! . . . The buildings are flattening us out; the machines are tearing us to pieces . . . The electric signs in Times Square make the Dadaists look timid; it is the masterpiece of Dadaism, produced naturally by our race, and without premeditation that makes your own horrors self-conscious.' in 'The Artistic Upheaval in France', in *Vanity Fair*, February 1922.

3: THE CELESTIAL ADVENTURE OF M. TRISTAN TZARA

1 Richard Huelsenbeck, 'En Avant Dada', in Motherwell, *The Dada Painters and Poets*, p. 26.
2 Guillaume Apollinaire to Tristan Tzara, 6 February 1918.
3 Quoted Annabelle Melzer, *Dada and Surrealist Drama*, p. 24.
4 Ibid., p. 28.
5 Ball, *Flight out of Time*, p. 126.
6 Richter, *Dada: Art and Anti-Art*, p. 13.
7 Ball, *Flight out of Time*, p. 117, 7 June 1917.
8 Lenin's interlocutor was a young Rumanian, Marcu. See Motherwell, *The Dada Painters and Poets*, p. xviii.
9 Hugo Ball, *Cabaret Voltaire*, 15 May 1916.
10 Ball, *Flight out of Time*, p. 50, 2 February 1916.
11 Ibid., p. 50, 5 February 1916.
12 Matthew Josephson, *Life Among the Surrealists*, p. 102.
13 Richter, *Dada: Art and Anti-Art*, p. 19.
14 Ibid., p. 27.
15 Tristan Tzara, 'Zurich Chronicle (1915–1919)', in Motherwell, *The Dada Painters and Poets*, p. 235.
16 From *Dada Manifesto on Feeble Love and Bitter Love*, tr. Barbara Wright.

17 Tzara, 'Zurich Chronicle (1915–1919)', in Motherwell, *The Dada Painters and Poets*, p. 235.
18 Ball, *Flight out of Time*, p. 64, 24 May 1916.
19 Richter, *Dada: Art and Anti-Art*, p. 45.
20 Ball, *Flight out of Time*, p. 57, 15 March 1915.
21 Ibid., p. 63, 18 April 1916.
22 Richter, *Dada: Art and Anti-Art*, p. 32.
23 Huelsenbeck, 'Dada Lives!', in Motherwell, *The Dada Painters and Poets*, p. 280.
24 Ibid.
25 Ball, *Flight out of Time*, pp. 63–4, 24 May 1916.
26 Tristan Tzara, *Dada Manifesto, 1918*, tr. Barbara Wright. Read in Zurich (Salle Meiser), 23 March 1918. Published in *Dada 3*.
27 Ball, *Flight out of Time*, p. 19, 15 June 1915.
28 Richter, *Dada: Art and Anti-Art*, p. 49.
29 Ball, *Flight out of Time*, *Dada Manifesto*, pp. 220–1.
30 Ibid., p. 73, 6 August 1916.
31 Ibid., p. 71, 1 August 1916.
32 Ibid., p. 156, 12 July 1918.
33 Ibid., p. 79, 22 September 1916.
34 Ibid., p. 69, 20 June 1916.
35 Huelsenbeck, 'En Avant Dada', in Motherwell, *The Dada Painters and Poets*, pp. 28–9.
36 Ibid., p. 26.
37 Huelsenbeck, 'Dada Lives!', in Motherwell, *The Dada Painters and Poets*, p. 281.
38 Richard Huelsenbeck, *The End of the World* (1916).
39 George Grosz, *Das Kunstblatt*, February 1924, quoted Beth Irwin Lewis, *George Grosz*, p. 53.
40 Huelsenbeck, 'En Avant Dada', in Motherwell, *The Dada Painters and Poets*, p. 26.
41 Herzfelde, quoted Helena Lewis, *The Politics of Surrealism*, p. 4.
42 Ibid., p. 39.
43 Richter, *Dada: Art and Anti-Art*, p. 34.
44 Huelsenbeck, 'En Avant Dada', in Motherwell, *The Dada Painters and Poets*, p. 39.

45 Ibid.
46 Quoted Josephson, *Life Among the Surrealists*, p. 198.
47 Ibid., p. 41.
48 Quoted Lewis, *The Politics of Surrealism*, p. 11.
49 George Grosz, *Moja Zhizn* (My Life), 1928, quoted Lewis, *The Politics of Surrealism*, p. 66.
50 Huelsenbeck, 'En Avant Dada', in Motherwell, *The Dada Painters and Poets*, p. 27.
51 Quoted Lewis, *The Politics of Surrealism*, p. 67.
52 Huelsenbeck, 'En Avant Dada', in Motherwell, *The Dada Painters and Poets*, p. 26.
53 Richter, *Dada: Art and Anti-Art*, p. 33.
54 From *Dada Manifesto on Feeble Love and Bitter Love*, tr. Barbara Wright.
55 Huelsenbeck, 'En Avant Dada', in Motherwell, *The Dada Painters and Poets*, p. 26.
56 Quoted Tomkins, *Duchamp*, pp. 192–3.
57 Tristan Tzara to Francis Picabia, 21 August 1918, Sanouillet, p. 489.
58 Everling, *l'Anneau de Saturne*, pp. 20–1.
59 Tristan Tzara to Francis Picabia, 26 September 1918, Sanouillet, p. 493.
60 Francis Picabia to Tristan Tzara, 7 January 1919, Sanouillet, *Dada à Paris*, p. 500.
61 Francis Picabia to Tristan Tzara, 11 January 1919, Sanouillet, p. 503.
62 Richter, *Dada: Art and Anti-Art*, p. 64.
63 Buffet-Picabia, 'Some Memories of Pre-Dada', in Motherwell, *The Dada Painters and Poets*.
64 Arp, quoted William A. Camfield, *Francis Picabia – His art, life and times*, p. 119.
65 Read at the 8th Soirée Dada in Zurich (Salle Kaufleuten), 8 April 1919.
66 Richter, *Dada: Art and Anti-Art*, p. 54.
67 Tzara, *Dada Manifesto, 1918*, tr. Barbara Wright.
68 Richter, *Dada: Art and Anti-Art*, p. 72.
69 Francis Picabia to Tristan Tzara, 9 February 1919, Sanouillet, pp. 504–5.

70 Francis Picabia to Tristan Tzara, 25 February 1919, Sanouillet, p. 509.
71 This, at any rate, was what he told Louis Aragon. Aragon, 'Tristan Tzara arrive à Paris', in Dachy, ed., *Projet d'histoire littéraire contemporaine*, p. 59.
72 Francis Picabia to Tristan Tzara, 30 December 1919, Sanouillet, p. 527.
73 Everling, *l'Anneau de Saturne*, p. 94.
74 Francis Picabia to André Breton, January 1920, Sanouillet, p. 540.
75 Everling, *l'Anneau de Saturne*, pp. 96–7.
76 Ibid., p. 98.
77 Tristan Tzara to Francis Picabia, beginning of February 1920. Sanouillet, p. 529.

4: DADA COMES TO PARIS

1 Aragon, 'Lautréamont et nous', in *Les Lettres Françaises*, p. 8.
2 André Breton to Tristan Tzara, 22 January 1919, Sanouillet, p. 456.
3 André Breton to Tristan Tzara, 18 February 1919, Sanouillet, p. 458.
4 Tristan Tzara to André Breton, 21 September 1919, Sanouillet, p. 467.
5 André Breton to Tristan Tzara, 8 November 1919, Sanouillet, p. 471.
6 André Breton to Tristan Tzara, 20 April 1919, Sanouillet, p. 462.
7 André Breton to Tristan Tzara, 29 July 1919, Sanouillet, p. 464.
8 André Breton to Francis Picabia, 4 January 1920, Sanouillet, p. 539.
9 Aragon, 'Tristan Tzara arrive à Paris', in Dachy, ed., *Projet d'histoire littéraire contemporaine*, pp. 56–7.
10 Soupault, *Mémoires de l'oubli*, pp. 109–11.
11 Ibid., p. 119.
12 Aragon, 'Tristan Tzara arrive à Paris', in Dachy, ed., *Projet d'histoire littéraire contemporaine*, p. 56.

13 Ibid.

14 Ibid.

15 Ibid.

16 Ribemont-Dessaignes, *Déja Jadis*, p. 67.

17 Aragon, 'Tristan Tzara arrive à Paris', in Dachy, ed., *Projet d'histoire littéraire contemporaine*.

18 Soupault, *Mémoires de l'oubli*, p. 88.

19 André Breton to Tristan Tzara, 26 December 1919, Sanouillet, p. 473.

20 Tristan Tzara, 'Memoirs of Dadaism', in Edmund Wilson, *Axel's Castle*, p. 239.

21 Louis Aragon, 'Premier vendredi de Littérature', in Dachy, *Projet d'histoire littéraire contemporaine*, p. 74.

22 Ibid., p. 75.

23 Quoted Sanouillet, p. 160.

24 Tzara, 'Memoirs of Dadaism', in Wilson, *Axel's Castle*, p. 240.

25 Ibid.

26 Ribemont-Dessaignes, *Déja Jadis*, p. 67.

27 Ibid., p. 71.

28 Tzara, 'Memoirs of Dadaism', in Wilson, *Axel's Castle*.

29 Soupault, *Mémoires de l'oubli*, p. 141.

30 Ribemont-Dessaignes, *Déja Jadis*, p. 68.

31 Jean Cocteau to Francis Picabia, 29 March 1920, Sanouillet, pp. 584–5.

32 Quoted Dachy in his preface to *Projet d'histoire littéraire contemporaine*.

33 Breton and Parinaud, *Entretiens 1913–1952*, p. 58.

34 Breton is referring to the celebrated riot which followed the first night of Victor Hugo's *Hernani* in 1830, which led to the fall of Charles X and the beginning of the Romantic movement.

35 Breton and Parinaud, *Entretiens 1913–1952*, p. 58.

36 Ibid., pp. 64–5.

37 Louis Aragon, 'L'homme coupé en deux' in *Les Lettres Françaises*, 8 May 1968, p. 8.

38 Quoted Sanouillet, p. 203.

39 Ibid., p. 187.

40 Tristan Tzara to Francis Picabia, 11 July and 28 July 1920, Sanouillet, pp. 531, 534.

41 Breton and Parinaud, *Entretiens 1913–1952*, p. 59.

42 Soupault, *Mémoires de l'oubli*, p. 70.

43 Ribemont-Dessaignes, *Déja Jadis*, p. 89.

44 Jean Cocteau to Francis Picabia, 29 March 1920, Sanouillet, p. 584.

45 Louis Aragon, *Le Paysan de Paris*, p. 91.

46 Ibid., p. 94.

47 André Breton to Francis Picabia, 19 June 1920, Sanouillet, p. 544.

48 Francis Picabia to Tristan Tzara, 3 July 1920, Sanouillet, p. 530.

49 André Breton to Simone Kahn, 31 August 1920, cited Bonnet, *André Breton: Naissance de l'aventure surréaliste*, p. 235.

50 Louis Aragon, 'Vernissage Picabia chez Povolozky', in Dachy, *Projet d'histoire littéraire contemporaine*.

51 Soupault, *Mémoires de l'oubli*, p. 144.

52 André Breton, *Les 'Enfers artificiels': Ouverture de la 'Saison dada 1921'*, in *Oeuvres complètes* vol. 1, p. 626.

53 Bonnet, *André Breton: Naissance de l'aventure surréaliste*, p. 29.

54 Soupault, *Mémoires de l'oubli*, pp. 150–1.

55 Breton and Parinaud, *Entretiens 1913–1952*, p. 68.

56 Francis Picabia, 'Francis Picabia et Dada', in *l'Esprit nouveau* no. 9, June 1921, quoted Camfield, *Francis Picabia – His art, life and times*.

57 Simone Kahn to her cousin Denise Lévy, 31 July 1920, quoted Bonnet, *André Breton: Naissance de l'aventure surréaliste*, p. 232.

58 Ibid., p. 231.

59 Ibid., pp. 231–2.

60 Louis Aragon, 'Débuts de Littérature', in Dachy, ed., *Projet d'histoire littéraire contemporaine*, pp. 46–7.

61 Soupault, *Mémoires de l'oubli*, p. 75.

62 Ibid., p. 72.

63 Breton, *Carnet*, in *Oeuvres complètes* vol. 1, p. 620.

64 Ibid.

65 Breton, 'Entrée des médiums', in *Littérature*, November 1922.

66 Breton, *Carnet*, in *Oeuvres complètes* vol. 1.

67 Aragon, 'L'homme coupé en deux', in *Les Lettres Françaises*, 8 May 1968.

68 Breton and Parinaud, *Entretiens 1913–1952*, p. 56.

69 Soupault, *Mémoires de l'oubli*.

70 Aragon, quoted Roger Garaudy, *l'Itinéraire d'Aragon*, p. 72.

71 Aragon, 'L'homme coupé en deux', in *Les Lettres Françaises*, 8 May 1968.

72 Ibid.

73 Breton, 'Entrée des médiums', in *Littérature*, November 1922.

74 'Of course both Arp and Tzara were already creating poems at this time using superficially similar techniques – random dictionary findings, words drawn out of a hat. But these were explorations of chance, rather than deliberate journeys into the subconscious.'

75 Soupault, *Mémoires de l'oubli*, p. 151.

76 Quoted Sanouillet, p. 299.

77 Polizzotti, *Revolution of the Mind: The life of André Breton*, p. 161.

78 André Breton to Theodore Fraenkel, quoted Polizzotti, *Revolution of the Mind: The life of André Breton*, p. 162.

79 Breton, 'Interview du Professeur Freud à Vienne', in *Littérature*, March 1922.

80 Ibid.

81 'Tristan Tzara va cultiver ses vices', interview with R. Vitrac, *Le Journal du Peuple*, 14 April 1923, quoted Sanouillet, p. 335.

82 Breton, 'Lâchez tout', in *Les Pas perdus*.

83 Breton in 'La Confession dédaigneuse', in *Les Pas perdus*, quoted Sanouillet, p. 334.

84 Picabia in *Comoedia*, 19 January 1922, quoted Sanouillet, p. 340.

85 Quoted Sanouillet, p. 341.

86 Josephson, *Life Among the Surrealists*, p. 149.

87 André Breton to Francis Picabia, 15 February 1922, Sanouillet, pp. 553–4.

88 Breton, 'Lâchez tout', in *Les Pas perdus*.

89 Ibid.

90 This is clear from Aragon's 'Soirée du Coeur à barbe', in Dachy, ed., *Projet d'histoire littéraire contemporaine*, from which this account is largely drawn.

91 Ibid.

92 Ibid.

93 Breton, *Nadja*, original edition, p. 21.

94 Sanouillet, p. 397.

5: A SEA OF DREAMS

1 *391* no. XII.

2 Arturo Schwartz, 'Rrose Sélavy alias Marchand du Sel alias Belle Haleine', unpublished lecture given at the Museum of Modern Art, New York, 13 January 1974.

3 Julien Levy, *Memoirs of an Art Gallery*, pp. 26–7.

4 André Breton, 'Marcel Duchamp', in *Les Pas perdus*.

5 In his introduction to Maupassant's *What is art?*

6 Cabanne, *Dialogues with Marcel Duchamp*, p. 62.

7 Breton, 'Marcel Duchamp', in *Les Pas perdus*.

8 André Breton to Jacques Doucet, 12 August 1922, quoted Tomkins, *Duchamp*, p. 253.

9 Breton, 'Marcel Duchamp'.

10 Quoted Tomkins, *Duchamp*, p. 251.

11 Cabanne, *Dialogues with Marcel Duchamp*, p. 64.

12 As enumerated by Calvin Tomkins, *Duchamp*.

13 Peggy Guggenheim, *Out of This Century*, p. 250.

14 Cabanne, *Dialogues with Marcel Duchamp*, p. 81.

15 Josephson, *Life Among the Surrealists*, p. 151.

16 Ibid., p. 119.

17 Ibid., pp. 110–11.

18 Marcel Duchamp to Man Ray, July 1921, quoted in 'Man Ray, Paris' by Billy Klüver and Julie Martin, in *Perpetual Motif*, ed. Foresta.

19 Ray, *Self-Portrait*, p. 108.

20 Ibid., p. 109.

21 Soupault, *Mémoires de l'oubli*, p. 146.

22 Breton, *Manifeste du surréalisme*, in *Oeuvres complètes* vol. 1, p. 344.

23 Soupault, *Mémoires de l'oubli*, p. 202.

24 Man Ray to Ferdinand Howald, 18 August 1921, quoted Klüver and Martin, in Foresta, *Perpetual Motif*, p. 94.

25 Ray, *Self-Portrait*.

26 Josephson, *Life Among the Surrealists*, p. 109.

27 Ray, *Self-Portrait*, p. 115.

28 Ibid.

29 Baldwin, *Man Ray: American Artist*, p. 90.

30 Man Ray to Katherine Dreier, 20 February 1921, Société Anonyme archive, Beinecke Library, Yale University.

31 Ray, *Self-Portrait*, pp. 128–9.

32 Which was in fact a result of Lee Miller, then Man Ray's assistant, feeling a mouse run over her foot while in the darkroom and accidentally exposing the negatives to light for a second.

33 1928, quoted Dickran Tashjian, *A Boatload of Madmen – Surrealism and the American avante-garde 1920–1950*, p. 102.

34 Klüver and Martin, in Foresta, *Perpetual Motif*, p. 139.

35 Quoted Foresta, *Perpetual Motif*, p. 33.

36 On 28 May 1922.

37 Ray, *Self-Portrait*, p. 209.

38 Ibid., p. 210.

39 *l'Européen*, 25 August 1929.

40 Ray, *Self-Portrait*, p. 143.

41 Alice Prin, *Kiki's Memoirs*, tr. Samuel Putnam, p. 42.

42 Ray, *Self-Portrait*, p. 149.

43 Antony Penrose, *The Lives of Lee Miller*, p. 38.

44 Ray, *Self-Portrait*, p. 151.

45 Ibid., p. 156.

46 Prin, *Kiki's Memoirs*, tr. Samuel Putnam, p. 43.

47 Ibid.

48 Josephson, *Life Among the Surrealists*, p. 117.

49 Ibid., p. 219.

50 Ibid., pp. 141–2.

51 Ibid., p. 326.
52 Octavio Paz, 'La Recherche du commencement', in *Nouvelle Revue Française*, 1966.
53 Marcel Duchamp in conversation with André Parinaud, *Arts*, 5–11 October 1966.
54 Robert Desnos, *Les Nouvelles Hébrides*, p. 297.
55 André Breton, *Clairement.*
56 Desnos, *Les Nouvelles Hébrides*, p. 300.
57 Ibid., pp. 303–5.
58 Josephson, *Life Among the Surrealists*, p. 216.
59 *Littérature*, October 1922.
60 Breton, 'Entrée des médiums', in *Littérature*, November 1922.
61 René Crevel, 'The Period of Sleeping-fits', in *This Quarter*, 1932, tr. J. Bronowski.
62 Breton, 'Entrée des médiums', in *Littérature*, November 1922.
63 Louis Aragon, *Une Vague de rêves*, pp. 21–2
64 Crevel, 'The Period of Sleeping-fits', in *This Quarter*, 1932, tr. J. Bronowski.
65 Ibid.
66 Aragon, *Une Vague de rêves*, p. 22.
67 Breton, *Robert Desnos*, in *Oeuvres complètes* vol. 1, p. 473.
68 André Breton, 'Les Mots sans rides', in *Littérature*, December 1922.
69 Breton, 'Marcel Duchamp', in *Littérature*, October 1922.
70 Breton, 'Les Mots sans rides', in *Littérature*, December 1922.
71 Ibid.
72 Breton, *Nadja*, 1945 facsimile edition, pp. 36–7.
73 Breton, 'Les Mots sans rides', in *Littérature*, December 1922.
74 André Breton from Marcel Duchamp, 25 November 1922, *Oeuvres complètes* vol. 1, p. 1315.
75 Josephson, *Life Among the Surrealists*, p. 214.
76 Marcel Janco to Tristan Tzara, quoted Sanouillet, p. 388.
77 Breton and Parinaud, *Entretiens 1913–1952*, pp. 90–91.
78 Ibid., p. 90.
79 Aragon, *Une Vague de rêves*, p. 23.
80 Ibid.
81 Ibid., p. 15.

82 Robert Desnos to André Breton, 7 April 1923, *Oeuvres complètes* vol. 1, p. 1440.

83 Breton, *Manifeste du surréalisme*, in *Oeuvres complètes* vol. 1, p. 331.

84 Breton, *Second Manifeste du surréalisme*, p. 812.

85 Breton, 'La Confession dédaigneuse', in *Les Pas perdus*.

86 'André Breton n'écrira plus', in *Le Journal du Peuple*, 7 April 1923, quoted Sanouillet, p. 389.

87 Josephson, *Life Among the Surrealists*, pp. 135–7.

88 Germaine Everling, quoted Polizzotti, *Revolution of the Mind: The life of André Breton*, p. 185.

89 William Carlos Williams, in *Imaginations*, prologue to *Kora in Hell*, p. 8.

90 Marcel Duchamp to J. J. Sweeney, in Sanouillet and Peterson, *Duchamp du signe*, p. 172.

91 Desnos, *Les Nouvelles Hébrides*, p. 308.

92 See Tomkins, *Duchamp*, pp. 270–1.

93 Breton, *Second Manifeste du surréalisme*, p. 782.

94 André Breton, *Poisson soluble* no. 25, in *Oeuvres complètes* vol. 1, p. 382.

95 Josephson, *Life Among the Surrealists*, p. 179.

96 Ibid.

97 Paul Eluard, *Nudité de la vérité*.

98 Simone Breton to Denise Lévy, quoted Pierre Daix, *Aragon*, p. 177.

99 Quoted Pierre Daix, *Aragon*, p. 187.

100 André Breton to Simone Breton, 11 March 1924, *Oeuvres complètes* vol. 1, p. 1335.

101 Louis Aragon to Marc Dachy, quoted in Dachy's introduction, *Project d'histoire littéraire contemporaine*, p. viii

102 Aragon, *Une Vague de rêves*, p. 20.

103 André Breton, 'Pour Dada', in *Les Pas perdus*.

104 Breton, 'Entrée des médiums', in *Littérature*, November 1922.

105 R. J., 'Chez Francis Picabia', *Paris-Journal*, 9 May 1924, quoted Camfield, *Francis Picabia – His art, life and times*, p. 204.

106 Notice in 'Petites Nouvelles', *Le Journal du Peuple*, 3 May 1924, quoted Camfield, *Francis Picabia – His art, life and times*, p. 204.

107 *391* no. XVII, p. 4.

108 André Breton to Simone Breton, 17 June 1924, *Oeuvres complètes* vol. 1, p. 1337.

109 Aragon, *Une Vague de rêves*, p. 17.

110 Ibid., p. 38.

111 Breton, *Manifeste du surréalisme*, in *Oeuvres complètes* vol. 1, p. 319.

112 Aragon, *Une Vague de rêves*, p. 28.

113 Breton, *Manifeste du surréalisme*, in *Oeuvres complètes* vol. 1, p. 329.

114 Ibid., pp. 328–9.

115 Breton, *Oeuvres complètes* vol. 1, p. 473.

116 Breton, *Manifeste du surréalisme*, in *Oeuvres complètes* vol. 1, p. 331.

117 Ibid., p. 319.

118 Breton, *Nadja*, p. 107, 1945 facsimile edition.

119 Breton, *Lettre aix voyantes*, in *Oeuvres complètes* vol. 1, p. 910.

120 Roger Caillois, 'Divergences et complicités', in *Nouvelle Revue Française*, 1966.

121 Breton, 'Marvelous versus Mystery', in *La Clé des champs*.

6: DREAMS AND COMMISSARS

1 André Breton to Louis Aragon, 13 November 1918, in *Oeuvres complètes* vol. 1, p. 1346.

2 Breton, *Manifeste du surréalisme*, in *Oeuvres complètes* vol. 1, pp. 313–14.

3 Louis Aragon to Jacques Doucet, August 1922, quoted in Edouard Ruiz, introduction to Aragon, *La Défense de l'infini*, 1986.

4 Louis Aragon to Jacques Doucet, April 1923, quoted Ruiz.

5 Louis Aragon, foreword to *Oeuvres croisés*, p. 35.

6 Louis Aragon, *Le Con d'Irène*, p. 43.

7 Louis Aragon, 1964 introduction to *Le Libertinage*.

8 Louis Aragon, preface to *La Nuit des temps*, quoted Garaudy, *l'Itinéraire d'Aragon*, p. 156.

9 Louis Aragon, 'Révélations sensationnelles', in *Littérature* no. 13, p. 22.
10 Breton, 'Les Mots sans rides', in *Les Pas perdus*.
11 Aragon, *Le Libertinage*, preface.
12 Louis Aragon, *Anicet*, pp. 93–5.
13 Breton and Parinaud, *Entretiens 1913–1952*, p. 40.
14 André Breton, 'Leon Trotsky: Lénine', in *Oeuvres complètes* vol. 1, p. 913.
15 Breton and Parinaud, *Entretiens 1913–1952*, p. 95.
16 Daix, *Aragon*, p. 184.
17 Jean Bernier, 'Un Cadavre', in *Clarté*, 15 November 1924.
18 Breton and Parinaud, *Entretiens 1913–1952*, p. 118.
19 Quoted Daix, *Aragon*, p. 193.
20 Aragon, *Le Libertinage*, p. 16.
21 Quoted Daix, *Aragon*, pp. 195–6.
22 *Nouvelle Revue Française*, 1 August 1925.
23 *Nouvelle Revue Française*, 1 September 1925.
24 Breton, *Oeuvres complètes* vol. 1, p. 1698.
25 Breton, 'Leon Trotsky: Lénine', in *Oeuvres complètes* vol. 1, pp. 911–14.
26 Aragon, *Le Paysan de Paris*, pp. 244–5.
27 Pierre ed., *Investigating Sex: Surrealist discussions 1928–1932*, p. 40.
28 Jacques Baron quoted Daix, in *Aragon: Lettres à Denise*, p. 71.
29 Louis Aragon, in *Nouvelle Revue Française*, 1 September 1925.
30 Aragon, *Lettres à Denise*, p. 76.
31 Drieu La Rochelle, *Journals*, quoted Daix, *Aragon*, pp. 221–2.
32 Louis Aragon, *Je n'ai jamais appris à écrire ou les Incipit*, p. 56.
33 Ibid., pp. 38–9.
34 Quoted Daix, *Aragon*, p. 238.
35 Ibid., p. 57.
36 Aragon, *Le Paysan de Paris*, p. 128.
37 Daix, *Aragon*, p. 227.
38 Pierre ed., *Investigating Sex: Surrealist discussions 1928–1932*, p. 48.
39 Max Aub, *Conversaciones con Buñuel*, p. 72.

40 André Thirion, *Révolutionnaires sans révolution*, tr. Neugroschel, p. 140.

41 Aragon, *Le Paysan de Paris*, p. 243.

42 Pierre ed., *Investigating Sex: Surrealist discussions 1928–1932*, p. 47.

43 Ibid., p. 45.

44 Ibid., p. 29.

45 Anne Chisholm, *Nancy Cunard*, p. 149.

46 'Voyages'. From *La Grande Gaîté*, quoted Daix, *Aragon*, p. 234.

47 Jacques Baron, quoted Daix, *Aragon*, p. 240.

48 André Breton, *Légitime Défense*.

49 This account is taken from *Archives du surréalisme, 3. Adhérer au parti communiste?*, Gallimard, 1992, pp. 26–7, quoted Daix, *Aragon*, pp. 254–5.

50 Quoted Polizzotti, *Revolution of the Mind: The life of André Breton*, p. 273.

51 Quoted Lewis, *The Politics of Surrealism*, p. 64.

52 Victor Crastre, quoted Lewis, *The Politics of Surrealism*, p. 64.

53 Breton and Parinaud, *Entretiens 1913–1952*, p. 142.

54 Quoted Polizzotti, *Revolution of the Mind: The life of André Breton*, p. 282.

55 Breton, *Oeuvres complètes* vol. 1, p. 1503.

56 Louis Aragon, *Oeuvres poétiques* vol. IV, p. 281, quoted Daix, *Aragon*, p. 265.

57 Louis Aragon, *Théâtre/Roman*, quoted Daix, *Aragon*, p. 266.

58 Daix, *Aragon*, p. 266.

59 Ibid., p. 269.

60 André Breton to Simone Breton, 9 August 1927, *Oeuvres complètes* vol. 1, p. 1504.

61 See, for example, Julia Kristeva, *Sens et non-sens de la révolte*.

62 Ibid.

63 Quoted Polizzotti, *Revolution of the Mind: The life of André Breton*, p. 364.

64 Daix, *Aragon*, p. 271.

65 Polizzotti, *Revolution of the Mind: The life of André Breton*, p. 288.

66 Thirion, *Révolutionnaires sans révolution*, p. 148.

67 Ibid., p. 144.

68 Ibid., p. 143.

69 Ibid., p. 142.

70 Ibid., p. 151.

71 Ibid., p. 146.

72 Ibid. pp. 149–50.

73 Breton and Parinaud, *Entretiens 1913–1952*, p. 127.

74 Breton, *Second Manifeste du surréalisme*, p. 796.

75 Maxime Alexandre, quoted Lewis, *The Politics of Surrealism*, p. 84.

76 Polizzotti, *Revolution of the Mind: The life of André Breton*, p. 309.

77 André Breton to Paul Eluard, May 1928, December 1928, *Oeuvres complètes* vol. 1, p. 1584.

78 Thirion, *Révolutionnaires sans révolution*, pp. 176–7.

79 André Breton, *A suivre: petite contribution en dossier de certains intellectuels à tendances révolutionaires*, in *Oeuvres complètes* vol. 1, pp. 988–9.

80 Polizzotti, *Revolution of the Mind: The life of André Breton*, p. 318.

81 Breton, *Second Manifeste du surréalisme*, pp. 782–3.

82 Ibid., p. 783.

83 Ribemont-Dessaignes, *Déja Jadis*, p. 143.

84 Breton, *Second Manifest du surrealisme*, p. 821.

85 See my book *The Spiritualists*, pp. 139–47.

86 Denise Tual, *Le Temps dévoré*, p. 113.

87 Paul Eluard, *Lettres à Gala (1924–1948)*, p. 97.

88 Breton and Parinaud, *Entretiens 1913–1952*, p. 149.

89 André Breton, 'The Ship of Love founders on the Current of Life', in *Oeuvres complètes* vol. 2, pp. 310–18.

90 Thirion, *Révolutionnaires sans révolution*, p. 286.

91 Breton and Parinaud, *Entretiens 1913–1952*, p. 163.

92 Thirion, *Révolutionnaires sans révolution*, p. 295.

93 Daix, quoted Lewis, *The Politics of Surrealism*, p. 105.

94 Daix, *Aragon*, p. 306.

95 Ibid., p. 306.

96 Quoted Lewis, *The Politics of Surrealism*, p. 104.
97 René Char *et al.*, *Paillasse*, quoted Lewis, *The Politics of Surrealism*, p. 104.
98 Breton and Parinaud, *Entretiens 1913–1952*, p. 164.
99 Paul Eluard, *Certificat* in *Tracts* vol. 1.
100 Quoted Irwin Lewis, *The Politics of Surrealism*, pp. 106–7.
101 Louis Aragon to Dominique Arban, quoted Daix, *Aragon*, p. 313.
102 Louis Aragon, *Henri Matisse, a novel*, quoted Daix, *Aragon*, p. 314.
103 Breton, *Oeuvres complètes* vol. 2, p. 1294.
104 Ibid., p. 1296.
105 Aragon, *Oeuvres poétiques* vol. V, p. 141.
106 Breton, *Oeuvres complètes* vol. 2, p. 1297.
107 André Breton, *Misère de la poésie*, in *Oeuvres complètes* vol. 2, p. 20.
108 Breton, *Oeuvres complètes* vol. 2, p. 39.
109 Breton and Parinaud, *Entretiens 1913–1952*, p. 167.
110 Maxime Alexandre's word: *Mémoires d'un surréaliste*, p. 109.
111 Breton and Parinaud, *Entretiens 1913–1952*, p. 166.
112 Ibid., p. 168.
113 Quoted Polizzotti, *Revolution of the Mind: The life of André Breton*, p. 374.
114 Breton and Parinaud, *Entretiens 1913–1952*, p. 168.
115 Paul Eluard to Gala Eluard, 15 March 1932, *Lettres à Gala (1924–1948)*, p. 164.
116 Louis Aragon, *Pour un réalisme socialiste*.
117 Eluard, *Certificat* in *Tracts* vol. 1.
118 Aub, *Conversaciones con Buñuel*, p. 72.
119 Jacques Rigaut, *Papiers posthumes*, in Breton, *Anthologie de l'humour noir, Oeuvres complètes* vol. 2, p. 1142.
120 Kristeva, *Sens et non-sens de la révolte*, p. 308.
121 See Ian Gibson, *The Shameful Life of Salvador Dalí*, pp. 122–3.
122 Josephson, *Life Among the Surrealists*, p. 342.
123 Polizzotti, *Revolution of the Mind: The life of André Breton*, p. 375.

124 Eluard, *Certificat* in *Tracts* vol. 1.
125 Breton and Parinaud, *Entretiens 1913–1952*, p. 217.
126 Aub, *Conversaciones con Buñuel*, p. 363.
127 Aragon, 'Lautréamont et nous', in *Les Lettres Françaises*, 6 June 1967.

7: ANDALUSIAN DOGS

1 Luis Buñuel, *My Last Breath*, p. 229.
2 Salvador Dalí, *The Secret Life of Salvador Dalí*, quoted Gibson, *The Shameful Life of Salvador Dalí*, p. 116.
3 Aub, *Conversaciones con Buñuel*, p. 142.
4 Buñuel, *My Last Breath*, p. 15.
5 Salvador Dalí, *Diccionario privado de Salvador Dalí*, p. 32.
6 Buñuel, *My Last Breath*, p. 57.
7 Ana Maria Dalí, *Salvador Dalí vu par sa soeur*, p. 127.
8 Buñuel, *My Last Breath*, p. 158.
9 Ibid., p. 64.
10 Dalí, *The Secret Life of Salvador Dalí*, pp. 175–6.
11 Ibid., p. 176.
12 Antonia Rodrigo, *Lorca-Dalí: Una amistad traicionada*.
13 Buñuel, *My Last Breath*, p. 62.
14 José de la Colina and Tomás Pérez Turrent, *Luis Buñuel: Prohibido asomarse al interior*, p. 28.
15 Notably in the biography *Dalí* by Meredith Etherington-Smith.
16 Dalí, *The Secret Life of Salvador Dalí*, quoted Gibson, *The Shameful Life of Salvador Dalí*, p. 116.
17 Ibid., p. 203.
18 Ibid., p. 127.
19 Agustín Sanchez Vidal, *Buñuel, Lorca, Dalí: El enigma sin fín*, p. 95.
20 Buñuel, *My Last Breath*, p. 87.
21 Ibid.
22 Ibid., p. 88.
23 Luis Buñuel to León Sánchez Cuesta, 10 February 1926, quoted Sanchez Vidal, *Buñuel, Lorca, Dalí: El enigma sin fín*.

24 Buñuel, *My Last Breath*, p. 89.

25 Ibid., pp. 89–90.

26 Ibid., p. 57.

27 Jeanne Rucar de Buñuel, *Memorias de una mujer sin piano*, p. 36.

28 Aub, *Conversaciones con Buñuel*, p. 56.

29 Jeanne Rucar de Buñuel, *Memorias de una mujer sin piano*, p. 39.

30 Ibid., p. 38.

31 Tual, *Le Temps dévoré*, p. 60.

32 De la Colina and Pérez Turrent, *Luis Buñuel: Prohibido asomarse al interior*, p. 28.

33 Dalí, *The Secret Life of Salvador Dalí*, p. 206.

34 Quoted Gibson, *The Shameful Life of Salvador Dalí*, p. 153.

35 De la Colina and Pérez Turrent, *Luis Buñuel: Prohibido asomarse al interior*, p. 28.

36 Ana Maria Dalí, *Salvador Dalí vu par sa soeur*, p. 164.

37 See Gibson, *The Shameful Life of Salvador Dalí*, pp. 164–5.

38 Salvador Dalí to Alain Bosquet, 1955.

39 Dalí interviewed by Gibson, quoted Sanchez Vidal, *Buñuel, Lorca, Dalí: El enigma sin fin*.

40 Quoted Gibson, *The Shameful Life of Salvador Dalí*, p. 164.

41 Quoted John Baxter, *Buñuel*, p. 59.

42 Quoted Ian Gibson, *Federico García Lorca: A life*.

43 Buñuel, *My Last Breath*.

44 Quoted Baxter, *Buñuel*, p. 64.

45 Buñuel, *My Last Breath*, pp. 101–2.

46 Salvador Dalí to Federico García Lorca, July 1928, Sanchez Vidal, *Buñuel, Lorca, Dalí: El enigma sin fin*.

47 Luis Buñuel to Pepín Bello, 14 September 1928, in Sanchez Vidal, *Buñuel, Lorca, Dalí: El enigma sin fin*.

48 Buñuel, quoted Sanchez Vidal, *Buñuel, Lorca, Dalí: El enigma sin fin*.

49 Baxter, *Buñuel*, p. 68.

50 Ibid., p. 60.

51 Dalí, *The Secret Life of Salvador Dalí*, quoted Gibson, *The Shameful Life of Salvador Dalí*, p. 192.

52 Aub, *Conversaciones con Buñuel*, p. 60.

53 De la Colina and Pérez Turrent, *Luis Buñuel: Prohibido asomarse al interior*, pp. 22–3.

54 Ana Maria Dalí, in Rodrigo, *Lorca-Dalí: Una amistad traicionada*, p. 215.

55 De la Colina and Pérez Turrent, *Luis Buñuel: Prohibido asomarse al interior*, p. 21.

56 Sanchez Vidal, *Buñuel, Lorca, Dalí: El enigma sin fin*, p. 19.

57 Ibid., p. 25.

58 Dalí, *Diccionario privado de Salvador Dalí*, p. 37.

59 Dalí quoted Gibson, *The Shameful Life of Salvador Dalí*, pp. 140–1.

60 Sanchez Vidal, *Buñuel, Lorca, Dalí; El enigma sin fin*, p. 28.

61 Santiago Ontañon, quoted Sanchez Vidal, *Buñuel, Lorca, Dalí: El enigma sin fin*, p. 28.

62 Aub, *Conversaciones con Buñuel*, p. 41.

63 Sanchez Vidal, *Buñuel, Lorca, Dalí: El enigma sin fin*, p. 189.

64 De la Colina and Pérez Turrent, *Luis Buñuel: Prohibido asomarse al interior*, p. 24.

65 Dalí, *The Secret Life of Salvador Dalí*, p. 212.

66 *Un Chien andalou*, Luis Buñuel and Salvador Dalí, tr. Philip Drummond.

67 De la Colina and Pérez Turrent, *Luis Buñuel: Prohibido asomarse al interior*, p. 23.

68 See the discussion in Agustín Sanchez Vidal, 'The Andalusian Beasts', in *Salvador Dalí, The early years*, p. 194.

69 Luis Buñuel to Salvador Dalí, March 1929, Sanchez Vidal, *Buñuel, Lorca, Dalí: El enigma sin fin*, p. 205.

70 Rucar de Buñuel, *Memorias de una mujer sin piano*, p. 40.

71 Ibid., p. 41.

72 André Breton, *Le Surréalisme et la peinture*, p. 21.

73 Levy, *Memoirs of an Art Gallery*, p. 12.

74 Ibid., p. 40.

75 Dalí, *The Secret Life of Salvador Dalí*, p. 209.

76 Ibid., p. 217.

77 Ibid., p. 213.

78 Aub, *Conversaciones con Buñuel*, p. 361.

79 Baxter, *Buñuel*, p. 87.

80 Tual, *Le Temps dévoré*, p. 66.
81 Georges Sadoul, *Rencontres, chroniques et entretiens*, p. 166.
82 Quoted Baxter, *Buñuel*, p. 93.
83 Sadoul, *Rencontres, chroniques et entretiens*, p. 46.
84 De la Colina and Pérez Turrent, *Luis Buñuel: Prohibido asomarse al interior*, pp. 25–6.
85 Baxter, *Buñuel*, p. 99.
86 Sadoul, *Rencontres, chroniques et entretiens*, p. 167.
87 Valentine Hugo, quoted Polizzotti, *Revolution of the Mind: The life of André Breton*, p. 362.
88 Aub, *Conversaciones con Buñuel*, p. 62.
89 Baxter, *Buñuel*, p. 88.
90 Aub, *Conversaciones con Buñuel*, p. 64.
91 Dalí, *The Secret Life of Salvador Dalí.*
92 Aub, *Conversaciones con Buñuel*, pp. 55, 63.
93 Ibid., p. 230.
94 Ibid., p. 64.
95 Buñuel, *My Last Breath*, p. 96.
96 Ibid., p. 97.
97 For an explication of this picture see Gibson, *The Shameful Life of Salvador Dalí*, pp. 216–17.
98 Dalí, *The Secret Life of Salvador Dalí*, pp. 231–3.
99 Roland Penrose, radio interview, Penrose Archive, Sussex.
100 Gala Eluard to Paul Eluard, 26 November 1916.
101 Josephson, *Life Among the Surrealists*, p. 177.
102 Lou Straus-Ernst, quoted Jimmy Ernst, *A Not-So-Still Life*, p. 20.
103 Ibid., p. 12.
104 Meredith Etherington-Smith, *Dalí*, p. 34.
105 Eluard, *Lettres à Gala (1924–1948)*, p. 17.
106 Ibid., letters 3 and 5.
107 Ibid., letter 52.
108 Ibid., letter 54.
109 Ibid., letter 59.
110 Ibid.
111 For instance letter 14.
112 Ibid., letter 50, p. 72.

113 Ibid., letter 14.
114 Aub, *Conversaciones con Buñuel*, p. 63.
115 Etherington-Smith, *Dalí*, p. 260.
116 Dalí, *The Secret Life of Salvador Dalí*, p. 241.
117 Ibid., pp. 243–6.
118 Aub, *Conversaciones con Buñuel*, p. 64.
119 Etherington-Smith, *Dalí*, p. 260.
120 Eluard, *Lettres à Gala (1924–1948)*, letter 75, April 1930.
121 Ibid., letter 91, 21 October 1930.
122 Conversation with David Gascoyne, May 1996.
123 Jimmy Ernst, *A Not-So-Still Life*, p. 37.
124 Ana Maria Dalí, *Salvador Dalí va par sa soeur*, p. 178.
125 Aub, *Conversaciones con Buñuel*, p. 64.
126 Ibid., pp. 55–6.
127 Ibid., p. 63.
128 Buñuel, *My Last Breath*, p. 97.
129 Ibid., p. 91.
130 Ibid., p. 115.
131 Ana Maria Dalí, *Salvador Dalí vu par sa soeur*, p. 178.
132 Aub, *Conversaciones con Buñuel*, p. 65.
133 Sanchez Vidal, *Buñuel, Lorca, Dalí: El enigma sin fin*, p. 129.
134 Buñuel, *My Last Breath*, p. 164.
135 Eluard, *Lettres à Gala (1924–1948)*, letter 64, p. 89.
136 Ibid., letter 67, p. 93.
137 Ibid., p. 31.
138 Salvador Dalí, *The Unspeakable Confessions of Salvador Dalí*, p. 106.
139 Buñuel, *My Last Breath*, p. 116.
140 Quoted Baxter, *Buñuel*, p. 96.
141 Salvador Dalí to Luis Buñuel, quoted Sanchez Vidal, *Buñuel, Lorca, Dalí: El enigma sin fin*, p. 249.
142 Aub, *Conversaciones con Buñuel*, p. 64.
143 Ibid., p. 68.
144 De la Colina and Pérez Turrent, *Luis Buñuel: Prohibido asomarse al interior*, p. 30.
145 Sanchez Vidal, *Buñuel, Lorca, Dalí: El enigma sin fin*, pp. 237–43.

146 Ibid., p. 246.
147 Ibid., p. 249.
148 Ibid., pp. 246–9.
149 Aub, *Conversaciones con Buñuel*, p. 65.
150 Thirion, *Révolutionnaires sans révolution*, p. 283.
151 Gibson, *The Shameful Life of Salvador Dalí*, p. 271.
152 Aub, *Conversaciones con Buñuel*, p. 65.
153 Sadoul, *Rencontres, chroniques et entretiens*, p. 51.
154 De la Colina and Pérez Turrent, *Luis Buñuel: Prohibido asomarse al interior*, p. 31.
155 Baxter, *Buñuel*, pp. 120–1.
156 Rucar de Buñuel, *Memorias de una mujer sin piano*, p. 45.
157 Antheil, quoted Baxter, *Buñuel*, p. 170.
158 Baxter, *Buñuel*, p. 172.
159 Quoted Gibson, *The Shameful Life of Salvador Dalí*, p. 393.
160 Ibid., p. 395.
161 Dalí, *The Secret Life of Salvador Dalí*, pp. 303–4.
162 Aub, *Conversaciones con Buñuel*, pp. 553–4.
163 Sanchez Vidal, *Buñuel, Lorca, Dalí: El enigma sin fin*, p. 302.
164 Ian Gibson puts this exchange a year later, in November 1983, but by then Buñuel was dead – he died in July 1983.
165 Gibson, *The Shameful Life of Salvador Dalí*, pp. 596–7.
166 Aub, *Conversaciones con Buñuel*, p. 149.
167 Ibid., p. 67.
168 Ibid., p. 53.

8: ART AND POWER

1 Aub, *Conversaciones con Buñuel*.
2 Salvador Dalí, foreword to René Crevel's *Un Mort difficile*.
3 Ibid.
4 Roger Vailland, *Un Jeune Homme seul*.
5 Charles Duits, *André Breton a-t-il dit passe*, p. 151.
6 Dalí, *The Secret Life of Salvador Dalí*, p. 339.
7 Quoted Polizzotti, *Revolution of the Mind: The life of André Breton*, p. 418.

8 Vitezslav Nezval, *Rue Gît-le-coeur*, p. 21.

9 Ibid., p. 97.

10 Salvador Dalí, *Diary of a Genius*, p. 77.

11 Polizzotti, *Revolution of the Mind: The life of André Breton*, p. 419.

12 Ibid., p. 423.

13 Dalí, *Diary of a Genius*, p. 80.

14 Conversation with David Gascoyne, May 1996.

15 Dalí, *Diary of a Genius*, p. 80.

16 Polizzotti, *Revolution of the Mind: The life of André Breton*, p. 419.

17 André Breton, *Sur la Mort de René Crevel*, in *Oeuvres complètes* vol. II, p. 555.

18 Breton, *Anthologie de l'humour noir*, p. 1142.

19 Dalí, *Diccionario privado de Salvador Dalí*, p. 16.

20 Dalí, *Diary of a Genius*, p. 77.

21 André Breton, *Communicating Vessels*, tr. Mary Ann Caws and Geoffrey T. Harris, p. 26.

22 André Breton, *Première Exposition Dalí*, in *Oeuvres complètes* vol. II, pp. 307–8.

23 Dalí, 'The Rotten Donkey', in *This Quarter*, 1932, tr. J. Bronowski.

24 Quoted Gibson, *The Shameful Life of Salvador Dalí*, p. 255.

25 Dalí, 'The Rotten Donkey', in *This Quarter*, 1932, tr. J. Bronowski.

26 Gibson, *The Shameful Life of Salvador Dalí*, pp. 339–41.

27 Ibid., p. 309.

28 Dalí, *Diccionario privado de Salvador Dalí*, p. 55.

29 Dalí, *The Secret Life of Salvador Dalí*, pp. 16–17.

30 Quoted Gibson, *The Shameful Life of Salvador Dalí*, pp. 146–7.

31 Prince Jean-Louis de Faucigny-Lucinge, quoted Etherington-Smith, *Dalí*, pp. 174–5.

32 Eluard, *Lettres à Gala (1924–1948)*, letter 160, p. 191.

33 Dalí, *The Secret Life of Salvador Dalí*.

34 Aragon, *Le Paysan de Paris*.

35 Helena Lewis, *Dada Turns Red: The politics of surrealism*, p. 72.

36 See Rudolf E. Kuenzli, 'Surrealism and Misogyny', in Mary Ann Caws, Rudolf Kuenzli and Gwen Raaberg eds., *Surrealism and Women*, p. 19.

37 André Breton, *Mad Love*, pp. 84–5.

38 Polizzotti, *Revolution of the Mind: The life of André Breton*, p. 512.

39 Pierre ed., *Investigating Sex: Surrealist discussions 1928–1932*, p. 9.

40 Thirion, *Révolutionnaires sans révolution*, p. 294.

41 Quoted Polizzotti, *Revolution of the Mind: The life of André Breton*, p. 309.

42 Breton, *Second Manifeste du surréalisme*, p. 785.

43 See Robert Belton, 'Speaking with Forked tongues: "Male" discourse in "Female" Surrealism?', in Caws, Kuenzli and Raaberg, *Surrealism and Women*, p. 52.

44 Kristeva, *Sens et non-sens de la révolte*, p. 257.

45 Thirion, *Révolutionnaires sans révolution*, p. 156.

46 Ibid.

47 Eluard, *Lettres à Gala (1924–1948)*, letter 197, p. 243.

48 Ibid., letter 205, p. 251.

49 Henri Pastoureau, *Ma Vie surréaliste*, pp. 148–53.

50 Ibid.

51 Cabanne, *Dialogues with Marcel Duchamp*, p. 13.

52 Pastoureau, *Ma Vie surréaliste*, p. 153.

53 Tim McGirk, *Wicked Lady: Salvador Dalí's muse*, p. 76.

54 Pastoureau, *Ma Vie surréaliste*, p. 150.

55 Pierre ed., *Investigating Sex: Surrealist discussions 1928–1932*, p. 22.

56 Quoted Polizzotti, *Revolution of the Mind: The life of André Breton*, p. 415.

57 André Breton to Roland Penrose, 6 July 1936, Scottish National Gallery of Modern Art.

58 Nezval, *Rue Gît-le-coeur*, pp. 25–8.

59 Dalí, *Diary of a Genius*, pp. 22–3.

60 Salvador Dalí, *Comment on devient Dalí*, p. 153.

61 Ibid.

62 André Breton to Salvador Dalí, 23 January 1934, Scottish National Gallery of Modern Art.

63 Sanchez Vidal, *Buñuel, Lorca, Dalí: El enigma sin fin*, p. 334.

64 De la Colina and Pérez Turrent, *Luis Buñuel*, p. 33.

65 Salvador Dalí to André Breton, January 1934, Scottish National Gallery of Modern Art.

66 Letters at Scottish National Gallery of Modern Art.

67 Eluard, *Lettres à Gala (1924–1948)*, letter 185, p. 230.

68 Georges Hugnet, *Pleins et Déliés*, pp. 25–7.

69 Ibid.

70 Ibid.

71 Ibid.

72 Dalí, *The Unspeakable Confessions of Salvador Dalí*, quoted Etherington-Smith, *Dalí*, p. 283.

73 Sybil Moholy-Nagy, quoted Motherwell, *The Dada Painters and Poets*, pp. xxiii–xxiv.

74 André Breton to Salvador Dalí, 8 March 1934, Scottish National Gallery of Modern Art.

75 Etherington-Smith, *Dalí*, p. 185.

76 Dalí, *The Secret Life of Salvador Dalí*, p. 322.

77 Levy, *Memoirs of an Art Gallery*, p. 72.

78 Breton and Parinaud, *Entretiens 1913–1952*, p. 160.

79 Caresse Crosby, *The Passionate Years*, p. 292.

80 Ibid., p. 329.

81 Dalí, *The Secret Life of Salvador Dalí*, pp. 329–30.

82 Crosby, *The Passionate Years*, p. 331.

83 Dalí, *The Secret Life of Salvador Dalí*, pp. 330–3.

84 Quoted Etherington-Smith, *Dalí*, p. 220.

85 André Breton to Salvador Dalí, 28 December 1934, Scottish National Gallery of Modern Art.

86 Dalí, *The Secret Life of Salvador Dalí*, p. 338.

87 Ibid., p. 260.

88 Quoted Gibson, *The Shameful Life of Salvador Dalí*, p. 360.

89 Quoted Etherington-Smith, *Dalí*, p. 278.

90 Quoted Gibson, *The Shameful Life of Salvador Dalí*, p. 383.

91 Ibid., p. 382.

92 Fonds Breton, Bibliothèque littéraire Jacques Doucet, quoted Gibson, *The Shameful Life of Salvador Dalí*, p. 382.

93 Sigmund Freud to André Breton, 26 December 1932, quoted in Breton, *Communicating Vessels*, p. 151.

94 André Breton to Salvador Dalí, 6 January 1939, Scottish National Gallery of Modern Art.

95 Edward James to Salvador Dalí, 1939, quoted Etherington-Smith, *Dalí*, pp. 249–50.

96 Dalí, *The Secret Life of Salvador Dalí*, p. 361.

97 Quoted Etherington-Smith, *Dalí*, p. 250.

98 Luis Buñuel Archive, Ministry of Culture, Madrid, quoted Gibson, *The Shameful Life of Salvador Dalí*, p. 394.

99 Ibid., p. 393.

100 Ibid., p. 395.

101 Ibid., p. 395.

102 Etherington-Smith, *Dalí*, p. 305.

103 André Breton, 'Des tendances les plus récentes de la peinture surréaliste', in *Minotaure* no. 13, May 1939.

104 James was writing in 1944. James Thrall Soby papers, Museum of Modern Art, New York.

9: MODERN ART COMES TO NEW YORK

1 Breton and Parinaud, *Entretiens 1913–1952*, p. 194.

2 Baldwin, *Man Ray: American artist*, p. 222.

3 Breton and Parinaud, *Entretiens 1913–1952*, p. 194.

4 Dorothea Tanning, *Birthday*, p. 22.

5 Pierre ed., *Investigating Sex: Surrealist discussions 1928–1932*, p. 61.

6 Ibid., twelfth session, p. 152.

7 Cited by Pastoureau, *Ma Vie surréaliste*, p. 237.

8 Breton, *Mad Love*, pp. 41–3.

9 Ibid., p. 66.

10 Ibid., p. 67.

11 André Breton to Rose Adler, quoted Polizzotti, *Revolution of the Mind: The life of André Breton*, p. 429.

12 Breton, *Le Surréalisme et la peinture*, quoted Caws, Kuenzli and Raaberg, *Surrealism and Women*.

13 Duits, *André Breton a-t-il dit passe*, p. 115.

14 Eluard, *Lettres à Gala (1924–1948)*, letter 223, p. 270.

15 Guggenheim, *Out of This Century*, p. 218.

16 Tanning, *Birthday*, p. 54.

17 Duits, *André Breton a-t-il dit passe*, p. 70.

18 Polizzotti, *Revolution of the Mind: The life of André Breton*, p. 512.

19 Duits, *André Breton a-t-il dit passe*, p. 127.

20 Ibid.

21 André Breton to Benjamin Péret, 27 August 1942, quoted Polizzotti, *Revolution of the Mind: The life of André Breton*, p. 512.

22 Duits, *André Breton a-t-il dit passe*, p. 70.

23 Tanning, *Birthday*, p. 22.

24 André Breton, *Arcane 17*.

25 Duits, *André Breton a-t-il dit passe*, p. 80.

26 Tanning, *Birthday*, p. 20.

27 Guggenheim, *Out of This Century*, pp. 309–10.

28 Ribemont-Dessaignes, *Déja Jadis*, p. 80.

29 André Breton to Roland Penrose, 7 November 1941, Lee Miller Archive.

30 Breton and Parinaud, *Entretiens 1913–1952*, p. 192.

31 Eluard, *Lettres à Gala (1924–1948)*, letter 216, p. 263.

32 *View*, October–November 1941.

33 Ernst, *A Not-So-Still Life*, p. 217.

34 Man Ray to Roland Penrose, 24 September 1942, Lee Miller Archive.

35 Ernst, *A Not-So-Still Life*, pp. 154, 217.

36 Duits, *André Breton a-t-il dit passe*, pp. 95–6.

37 Tanning, *Birthday*, p. 21.

38 Ibid., pp. 21–2.

39 Duits, *André Breton a-t-il dit passe*, p. 67.

40 Polizzotti, *Revolution of the Mind: The life of André Breton*, p. 485.

41 'Souvenir de la Mexique', in *Minotaure* no. 10, winter 1937.

42 André Breton, 'Prolegomena to a Third Manifesto of Surrealism or Else', in *VVV*, June 1942.

43 Breton and Parinaud, *Entretiens 1913–1952*, p. 197.

44 André Breton to Roland Penrose, 7 November 1941, Lee Miller Archive.

45 Guggenheim, *Out of This Century*, p. 309.

46 Ibid.

47 Ibid., p. 308.

48 Ibid., p. 327.

49 Ibid.

50 Cabanne, *Dialogues with Marcel Duchamp*, p. 83.

51 Breton and Parinaud, *Entretiens 1913–1952*, p. 196.

52 Ibid., p. 108.

53 Duits, *André Breton a-t-il dit passe*, pp. 109–10.

54 Ibid., p. 90.

55 Max Ernst interviewed for the Museum of Modern Art *Bulletin* vol. 13 nos. 4–5, 'Eleven Europeans in America'.

56 George Orwell, 'Benefit of Clergy: Some notes on Salvador Dalí', in *Collected Essays*, June 1944.

57 Interviewed in *View*, October–November 1941.

58 Levy, *Memoirs of an Art Gallery*, p. 173.

59 Dalí, *The Secret Life of Salvador Dalí*.

60 Levy, *Memoirs of an Art Gallery*, p. 199.

61 Crosby, *The Passionate Years*, p. 344.

62 Robert Motherwell, 'Two Letters on Surrealism', in *Collected Writings*.

63 Motherwell ed., *The Dada Painters and Poets*, p. xxxiii.

64 Motherwell, 'Two Letters on Surrealism', in *Collected Writings*.

65 André Breton, 'Ascendant Sign', in *La Clé des champs*, p. 104.

66 Motherwell, 'Two Letters on Surrealism', in *Collected Writings*.

67 Ibid.

68 Motherwell ed., *The Dada Painters and Poets*, p. xxiii.

69 Ernst, *A Not-So-Still Life*, p. 186.

70 Breton, *Surrealism and Painting*, pp. 199–200.

71 Motherwell, 'Two Letters on Surrealism', in *Collected Writings*.

72 Ibid.

73 Leslie Fiedler, 'Development and Frustration', in B. Siegel ed., *Critical Essays on Nathanael West*.

74 Tanning, *Birthday*, p. 23.

75 Ray, *Self-Portrait*, pp. 192–3.

76 Polizzotti, *Revolution of the Mind: The life of André Breton*, p. 520.

77 Breton, 'Trente ans après', in *La Clé des champs*, p. 123.
78 Breton, *Arcane 17*, pp. 113–14.
79 Breton and Parinaud, *Entretiens 1913–1952*, p. 203.
80 Ibid., p. 205.
81 Eluard, *Lettres à Gala (1924–1948)*, letter 263, p. 309.
82 Ibid., letter 267, p. 316.
83 Sartre, *What is Literature?*, p. 146.
84 Ibid., pp. 162–3.

SELECT BIBLIOGRAPHY

Adam, Villiers de l'Isle. 'l'Etonnant couple Montonnet', in *Chez les passants* (Paris, 1890)

Adéma, Marcel. *Apollinaire*, tr. Denise Folliot (London, 1954)

Ades, Dawn. *Dali* (London, 1982)

    Dada and Surrrealism Reviewed, Arts Council of Great Britain (London, 1978)

Agar, Eileen, with Andrew Lambirth. *A Look at My Life* (London, 1988)

Apollinaire, Guillaume. *Apollinaire on Art: Essays and reviews 1902–1918* (London, 1972)

    Le flâneur des deux rives (Paris, 1928)

    Il y a (Paris, 1925)

    Lettres à Lou, ed. Michel Decaudin (Paris, 1993)

    Les Onze mille verges (Paris, 1907)

    l'Hérésiarque et cie (Paris, 1910)

    l'Enchanteur pourrissant (Paris, 1921)

    Tendre comme le souvenir (Paris, 1952)

    Les Mamelles de Tirésias (Paris, 1946)

Aragon, Louis. *Le Paysan de Paris* (Paris, 1928)

    Anicet ou le Panorama, roman (Paris, 1921)

    Le Libertinage (Paris, 1924)

    La Défense de l'infini, New augmented edition by Lionel Follet (Paris, 1997)

    Entretiens avec Francis Crémieux (Paris, 1964)

    Projet d'histoire littéraire contemporaine (outlined in *Littérature* series 2 no. 4, September 1922), text ed. Marc Dachy (Paris, 1994)

Persécuté persécuteur (Paris, 1931)

Une Vague de rêves (Paris, 1924)

Je n'ai jamais appris à écrire, ou les Incipit (Geneva, 1969)

'Lautréamont et nous', in *Les Lettres Françaises*, 1 June 1967, 8 June 1967. Reprinted Toulaise: Sables, 1992

'l'Homme coupé en deux', in *Les Lettres Françaises*, 8 May 1968

Aranda, Francisco. *Luis Buñuel: A critical biography* (London, 1975)

Arp, Jean. *Arp on Arp: Poems, Essays, Memories*, ed. Marcel Jean, tr. Joachim Neugroschel, (New York, 1972)

Artaud, A, and R. Vitrac. *Le Théâtre Alfred Jarry et l'hostilité publique* (Paris, 1930)

Aub, Max. *Conversaciones con Buñuel* (Barcelona, 1985)

Balakian, Anna. *André Breton, Magus of Surrealism* (Oxford, 1971)

Baldwin, Neil. *Man Ray: American artist* (New York, 1988)

Ball, Hugo. *Flight out of Time* [Flucht aus der Zeit], translated from the German and edited by John Elderfield (Berkeley, 1996)

Baxter, John. *Buñuel* (London, 1994)

Béhar, Henri. *André Breton* (Paris, 1990)

Billy, André. *La Terrasse du Luxembourg* (Paris, 1948)

Avec Apollinaire (Paris, 1966)

Blumenkranz, Noémie. 'Lettres à un ami d'enfance', in *Les Lettres Françaises*, 13 December 1951

Bohn, W. *Apollinaire and Breton: Journal of aesthetics and art criticism 2* (New York & Baltimore, 1977)

Bonnet, Marguerite. *André Breton: Naissance de l'aventure surréaliste* (Paris, 1975)

Borràs, Maria Lluisa. *Cravan: Une stratégie du scandale* (Paris, 1995)

Bosquet, Alain. *Conversations with Dalí* (New York, 1969)

Brassai. *The Artists of My Life* (New York, 1982)

Breton, André. *Oeuvres complètes* vol. 1 (Paris, 1988)

Oeuvres complètes vol. 2 (Paris, 1992)

Manifestos of Surrealism, tr. Richard Seaver and Helen R. Lane (Ann Arbor, 1969)

Free Rein [La Clé des Champs], translated from the French by Michel Parmentier (Nebraska, 1997)

Le Surréalisme et la peinture (Paris, 1965)

Breton, André, and André Parinaud, *Entretiens 1913–1952* (Paris,

1952) Published in English by Marlowe and Company New York 1993 as *Conversations: The Autobiography of Surrealism With André Parinaud and others*. Tr. and with an introduction by Mark Polizzotti

Breton, André, and Paul Eluard, *Dictionnaire abrégé du surréalisme*

Buffet-Picabia, Gabrielle. *Aires abstraites* (Geneva, 1957)
  'Arthur Cravan and American Dada', in Robert Motherwell (ed.), *The Dada Painters and Poets*
  Rencontres (Paris, 1977)
  'Un peu d'histoire', in *Paris-New York*, eds. du Centre Pompidou (Paris, 1977)

Buñuel, Luis, *My Last Breath*, tr. Abigail Israel (London, 1985)
  Obra Literaria, ed. A. Sanchez Vidal (Zaragoza, 1982)
  L'Âge d'or correspondance, eds. Bouhours and Schoeller (Paris, 1993)

Buot, François. *René Crevel* (Paris, 1991)

Burke, Carolyn. *Becoming Modern: The life of Mina Loy* (New York, 1996)

Cabanne, Pierre. *Dialogues with Marcel Duchamp*, tr. Ron Padgett (London, 1971)

Camfield, William A. *Francis Picabia – His art, life and times* (Princeton, 1979)

Carassou, Michel. *Jacques Vaché et le groupe de Nantes* (Nantes, 1986)

Caws, Mary Ann, Rudolf Kuenzli and Gwen Raaberg (eds.), *Surrealism and Women* (Cambridge, Mass., 1991)

Chapon, François. *Mystère et splendeurs de Jacques Doucet* (Paris, 1984)

Cowles, Fleur. *The Case of Salvador Dalí* (London, 1959)

Crastre, Victor. 'Trois héros surréalistes: Vaché, Rigaut, Crevel', Nantes-réalités no. 33, May–June 1970

Cravan, Arthur. (Fabian Lloyd), *Maintenant* (revue scandaleuse), Paris 1913–15

Crevel, René. *Les Pieds dans le plat* (Paris, 1974)
  Dalí, ou l'antioscurantisme (Rome, 1978)

Dachy, Marc. *Dada & les dadaïsmes: Rapport sur l'anéantissement de l'ancienne beauté* (Paris, 1994)

Dalí, Ana Maria. *Salvador Dalí visto por su hermana* (Barcelona, 1949)

Dali, Salvador. *Dalí, oui: méthode paranoiaque-critique et autres textes* (Paris, 1971)
The Secret Life of Salvador Dali, tr. Haakon M. Chevalier (London, 1968)
The Unspeakable Confessions of Salvador Dali as told to André Parinaud, tr. Howard J. Salemson (London, 1976)
Diary of a Genius (London, 1966)
Continuation of Book no. 6 of my Impressions and Private Memoirs, privately printed by the Stratford Press for the Morse Foundation (Ohio, 1962)
Diccionario privado de Salvador Dalí, recopilado y ordenado por Mario Merlino (1980)
Comment on devient Dalí (Paris, 1973)
Dalí by Dalí, tr. E. Mestie (New York, 1970)

De Chirico, Giorgio. *The Memoirs of Giorgio de Chirico*, tr. Margaret Crosland (London, 1971)

De la Colina, José, and Tomás Pérez Turrent. *Luis Buñuel: Prohibido asomarse al interior* (Mexico City, 1986)

Descharnes, Robert. *Salvador Dali* (London, 1985)
The World of Salvador Dali (London, 1972)
Dalí de Gala (Lausanne, 1962)

Desnos, Robert. *Les Nouvelles Hébrides* (Paris, 1978)

De Zayas, Marius. *How, When, and Why Modern Art Came to New York* (Cambridge, Mass., 1996)

Dreier, Katherine. *Five Months in the Argentine: From a woman's point of view 1918–1919* (New York, 1920)

Duchamp, Marcel. *Notes*, arr. and tr. Paul Matisse (Boston, 1983)
Letters to Walter and Louise Arensberg 1917–21, ed. and tr. Francis M. Naumann
'Eleven Europeans in America', in the Museum of Modern Art *Bulletin* vol. 13, nos. 4–5

Duhamel, Marcel. *Raconte pas ta vie* (Paris, 1972)

Duits, Charles. *Andre Bréton a-t-il dit passe* (Paris, 1991)

Dumas, Marie-Claire. *Robert Desnos ou l'exploration des limites* (Paris, 1980)

Eluard, Paul. *Lettres à Gala (1924–1948)* (Paris, 1984)
   Lettres de jeunesse (Paris, 1962)
   Au Rendez-Vous Allemand (Paris, 1945)
Eluard, Paul, with Man Ray. *Facile* (Paris, 1935)
Ernst, Jimmy. *A Not-So-Still Life* (New York, 1984)
Ernst, Max. *Beyond Painting* (New York, 1948)
Etherington-Smith, Meredith. *Dalí* (London, 1992)
Everling, Germaine. *l'Anneau de Saturne* (Paris, 1970)
   C'était hier: Dada (Paris, 1955)
Flanner, Janet. *Darlinghissima: Letters to a friend* (New York, 1988)
Ford, Hugh. *The Left Bank Revisited: Selections from the Paris Tribune* (Pennsylvania, 1972)
Foresta, Merry (ed.). *Perpetual Motif* (Washington, D.C., 1989)
Fraenkel, Theodore. *Carnets* (Paris, 1990)
Fry, Varian. *Surrender on Demand* (New York, 1945)
Garaudy, Roger. *l'Itinéraire d'Aragon* (Paris, 1961)
García Lorca, Federico. *Selected Letters*, ed. and tr. David Gershator (London, 1984)
Gibson, Ian. *Federico García Lorca: A life* (London, 1989)
Gleizes, Juliette Roche. *La Minéralisation de Dudley Craving Macadam* (Paris, 1924)
Goemans, Camille. *Oeuvre, 1922–57* (Brussels, 1970)
Gold, Mary-Jayne. *Crossroads* (Marseille, 1940)
Gomez de la Serna, Ramón. *Dalí* (London, 1984)
Gough-Cooper, Jennifer, and Jacques Caumont. *Ephemerides on and about Marcel Duchamp and Rrose Sélavy 1887–1968* (Milan, 1993)
Green, Julien. *Journal (1926–34) Les Années faciles* (Paris, 1970)
   Personal Record: 1928–1939 (London, 1940)
Guggenheim, Peggy. *Out of This Century* (New York, 1946)
   Confessions of an Art Addict (London, 1980)
Halicka, Alice. *Apollinaire Familier* (Paris, 1962)
Huelsenbeck, Richard. *Memoirs of a Dada Drummer* ed. Hans J. Kleinschmidt and tr. Joachim Neugroschel (New York, 1974)
Hugnet. *Pleins et Déliés* (Paris, 1972)

James, Edward. *Swans Reflecting Elephants: My early years*, ed. George Melly (London, 1982)

Jarry, Alfred. *Dr Faustroll* (Paris, 1923)
  Ubu-Roi (Paris, 1896)

Josephson, Matthew. *Life Among the Surrealists* (New York, 1962)

Klüver, Billy, and Julie Martin. *Kiki's Paris* (New York, 1989)

Krauss, Rosalind. *l'Amour fou: Photography and surrealism* (Washington, D.C., 1985)

Krauss, Rosalind, and Jane Livingston. *Photography and Surrealism* (New York, 1985)

Kristeva, Julia. *Sens et non-sens de la révolte* (Paris, 1996)

Kuenzli, Rudolf (ed.). *New York Dada* (New York, 1986)

Kuenzli, Rudolf M., and Francis M. Naumann (eds.). *Marcel Duchamp, Artist of the century* (Cambridge, Mass., 1987)

Lacan, Jacques. *De la psychose paranoïaque dans ses rapports avec la personnalité* (Paris, 1955)

Lake, Carlton, and Linda Ashton. *H. P. Roché: An introduction* (Austin, Texas, 1991)

Lear, Amanda. *My Life with Dali* (London, 1985)

Lebel, Robert. *Marcel Duchamp*, tr. George Heard Hamilton (London, 1959)

Leiris, Michel. *Mots sans mémoire* (Paris, 1969)
  Manhood, a Journey from Childhood into the Fierce Order of Virility, tr. Richard Howard (New York, 1963)
  Breton le patron

Lewis, Helena. *Dada Turns Red: The politics of surrealism* (Edinburgh, 1990)

Levy, Julien. *Memoirs of an Art Gallery* (New York, 1977)

Loy, Mina. 'Colossus', in Kuenzli ed., *New York Dada*

Macniven, Ian (ed.). *The Durrell-Miller Letters 1935–80* (London, 1988)

Marquis, Alice Goldfarb. *Marcel Duchamp: Eros, c'est la vie* (New York, 1981)

Mauriac, Claude. *André Breton* (Paris, 1949)

McAlmon, Robert. *Being Geniuses Together* (New York, 1968)

McGirk, Tim. *Wicked Lady: Salvador Dalí's muse* (London, 1998)

Melzer, Annabelle. *Dada and Surrealist Performance* (Ann Arbor, Mich., 1980)

Motherwell, Robert (ed.). *The Dada Painters and Poets* (New York, 1951)

Collected Writings, ed. Stephanie Terenzio (New York, 1992)

'The New York School', *Art International* (Summer 1967)

Nadeau, Maurice. *History of Surrealism*, tr. Richard Howard (New York, 1965)

Documents surréalistes (Paris, 1968)

Naville, Pierre. *Le Temps du surréel* (Paris, 1977)

Nin, Anais. *The Diary of Anais Nin* (London, 1970)

Olivier, Fernande. *Mémoires* (Paris, 1933)

Orwell, George. 'Benefit of Clergy: Some notes on Salvador Dalí', in *Collected Essays* (London, 1944)

Pach, Walter. *Queer Thing, Painting* (New York, 1938)

Padgett, Ron. 'Duchamp and Roussel'. Unpublished lecture given at the Museum of Modern Art, New York, 7 February 1974

Pastoureau, Henri. *Ma Vie surréaliste* (Paris, 1992)

Paz, Octavio. *Alternating Current* (New York, 1973)

Marcel Duchamp: Appearance stripped bare, tr. Rachel Phillips (New York, 1978)

Penrose, Antony. *The Lives of Lee Miller* (London, 1985)

Perloff, Marjorie. *The Futurist Movement: Avant-Garde, avant-guerre, and the language of rupture* (University of Chicago Press, 1987)

Pierre, José (ed.). *Investigating Sex: Surrealist discussions 1928–1932*, tr. Malcolm Imrie (London, 1992)

Polizzotti, Mark. *Revolution of the Mind: The life of André Breton* (London, 1995)

Prin, Alice. *Kiki's Memoirs*, tr. Samuel Putnam (Paris, 1930)

Raeburn, Michael (ed.). *Salvador Dalí: The early years* (London, 1994)

Ray, Man. *Self-Portrait* (Boston, 1963)

Photographs by Man Ray 1920 Paris 1934 (New York, 1979)

Ribemont-Dessaignes, Georges. *Déja Jadis* (Paris, 1958)

Richter, Hans. *Dada: Art and anti-art* (London, 1966)

Roché, Henri-Pierre. *Carnets: Première partie 1920–1* (Marseille, 1990)

Victor (Paris, Centre Pompidou, 1977)

Rodrigo, Antonia. *Lorca-Dalí: Una amistad traicionada* (Madrid, 1981)

Rosemont, Franklin (ed.). *What is Surrealism?* (London, 1978)

Roussel, Raymond. *Comment j'ai écrit certains de mes livres* (Paris, 1964)

Locus Solus (Paris, 1963)

Impressions d'Afrique

Rouveyre, André. *Souvenirs d'un commerce* (Paris, 1921)

Rucar de Buñuel, Jeanne. *Memorias de una mujer sin piano* (Mexico City, 1993)

Sadoul, Georges, *Rencontres, chroniques et entretiens* (Paris, 1984)

Samaltanos, Katia. *Apollinaire: Catalyst for Primitivism, Picabia and Duchamp* (Ann Arbor, 1984)

Sanchez Vidal, Agustín. *Buñuel, Lorca, Dalí: El enigma sin fin* (Madrid, 1988)

'The Andalusian Beasts', in *Salvador Dalí: The early years* (London, 1994)

Sanouillet, Michel. *Dada à Paris*, revised edition (Paris, 1993)

Francis Picabia et 391 (Paris, 1966)

Sanouillet, Michel, and Elmer Peterson (eds.). *Duchamp du signe* (Paris, 1975)

Santos Toroëlla, Rafael. *La Miel es más Dulce que la Sangre* (Barcelona, 1981)

Salvador Dalí: Lettere a Federico (Milan, 1987)

Sartre, Jean-Paul. *What Is Literature?*, tr. Bernard Frechtman (London, 1950)

Schwartz, Arturo. *Man Ray* (London, 1977)

'Rrose Sélavy alias Marchand du Sel alias Belle Haleine'. Unpublished lecture given at the Museum of Modern Art, New York, 13 January 1974

Breton and Trotsky

New York Dada

Secrest, Meryle. *Salvador Dali, Surrealist Jester* (London, 1986)

502

Sélavy, Rrose. *'Men before the Mirror' Photographs by Man Ray* (Paris, 1934)

Shattuck, Roger. *The Banquet Years* (London, 1959)
'Marcel Duchamp, Alfred Jarry and Pataphysics'. Unpublished lecture given at the Museum of Modern Art, New York, 10 January 1974

Siegel, B. (ed.). *Critical Essays on Nathanael West* (New York, 1994)

Soupault, Philippe. *Mémoires de l'oubli* (Paris, 1981)
Le vrai André Breton
Profils perdus (Paris, 1963)
'Guillaume Apollinaire', *Revue européenne*, 1 June 1926

Stein, Gertrude. *Everybody's Autobiography* (London, 1938)
Didn't Nelly and Lilly Love You? (1922), Yale edition vol. 4

Tanning, Dorothea. *Birthday* (Santa Monica, 1986)

Tashjian, Dickran. *A Boatload of Madmen – Surrealism and the American avant-garde 1920–1950* (New York, 1995)

Thirion, André. *Révolutionnaires sans révolution* (Paris, 1972)

Tual, Denise. *Le Temps dévoré* (Paris, 1980)

Vaché, Jacques. *Les Lettres de guerre de Jacques Vaché, précédées de quatre préfaces d'André Breton* (Paris, 1949)

Vailland, Roger. *Le Surréalisme contre la révolution* (Paris, 1948)

Valette, Robert D. *Livre d'identité* (Paris, 1967)

Whitford, Frank. 'The Many Faces of George Grosz', *The Berlin of George Grosz* (London, 1997)

Wilson, Edmund. *Axel's Castle*, including Tristan Tzara's 'Memoirs of Dadaism' (New York, 1931)

Youki. *Confidences*

Young, Alan. *Dada and After: Extremist modernism and English literature* (Manchester, 1981)

INDEX

Cabaret Voltaire, 53, 97–106,
134–5; *Cabaret Voltaire*
magazine, 93; *Dada*, 94, 114;
Kandinsky's influence, 53, 94;
manifesto, 115; marriage, 95–6;
war experiences, 95–6
Ballets Russes, 17
Balzac, Honoré de, 157, 250
Bar du Château, 263–4, 266
Barbusse, Henri, 272, 277
Baron, Jacques: *Un Cadavre*,
266; conversation with
Aragon, 236; Dada
performances, 167; relationship
with Breton, 193–4, 195, 218,
263, 266; runaway, 193–4
Barr, Alfred, 444, 445
Barrès, Maurice, 152–4, 164,
197–8
Barry, Iris, 360–1
Bataille, Georges, 262–3, 265,
266, 376, 377–8
Batcheff, Denise, 316
Batcheff, Pierre, 316, 321, 323–4
Baudelaire, Charles, 27, 34, 243,
265
Baziotes, Ethel, 452
Baziotes, William, 451, 452
Beethoven, Ludwig van, 353
Bello, Pepín: *carnuzos*, 320–1;
education, 296; relationship
with Buñuel, 307, 312, 313,
315, 321, 352; relationship with
Dalí, 296
Bérard, Christian, 346
Berl, Emmanuel, 255, 261, 267
Bernhardt, Sarah, 49, 65, 168
Bernier, Jean, 232, 243, 244
Bernstorff, Count, 68
Berton, Germaine, 233
Billy, André, 13, 36

Blutige Ernst, Der, 112
Boeuf sur le Toit nightclub, 12,
178, 240
Boiffard, J. A., 218, 266
Bolshevism, 229
Bonwit Teller, 446
Borel, Petrus, 243
Brancusi, Constantin, 164, 188–9,
212, 256, 440
Braque, Georges, 35, 47, 64, 254,
397
Braunberger, Pierre, 328
Breker, Arno, 402
Breton, André: APPEARANCE:
in early life, 15–16; at twenty-
five, 183, 192–3; in New York,
431; CAREER: family
background, 13–14; education,
14, 156, 325; war experiences,
9, 13, 18, 30; meeting with
Valéry, 15; correspondence
with Apollinaire, 13–14;
meetings with Apollinaire,
22–4, 36–7; first experience of
Surrealism, 9, 11, 29; Vaché's
death, 37–42; *Littérature*
magazine, 41, 122, 134–6, 197;
Dada movement, 129, 136–9,
141–2, 144–6, 148–55, 163,
167–9, 180–1, 215, 229; arrival
of Tzara, 129–34; Palais des
Fêtes performance, 137–9;
Dada Manifesto reading, 141;
Théâtre de l'Oeuvre
performance, 142; Salle Gaveau
performance, 144–6, 155;
Barrès trial, 152–4; Ernst
exhibition, 338; Tarrenz-bei-
Imst holiday, 161–2, 337;
Freud visit, 162–3, 337, 413;
Congrès de Paris, 163–6;

Rif declaration (1925), 233–4
Rigaut, Jacques: death, 41, 283, 375; marriage, 211; relationship with Man Ray, 182; social life, 184, 197; *391* magazine, 216
Rimbaud, Arthur: influence on Ball, 105–6; influence on Breton, 24, 27, 32, 159, 180, 218; influence on Surrealism, 34, 218, 243, 265; letter in *Nouvelle Revue Française*, 16–17; religion, 234; renunciation of poetry, 15, 16, 40, 208, 253
Rivière, Jacques, 214–15
Robertson, Lila, 216
Roche, Juliette, 64, 80–1, 121
Roché, Henri-Pierre: friendship with Duchamp, 46, 69, 79; love affair, 65; picture collection, 212, 440; social life, 191; war experiences, 67; works, 46, 70
Rockefeller, Nelson, 361
Rodin, Auguste, 57
Rolland, Romain, 277–8
Romoff, Serge, 167
Roosevelt, Eleanor, 424
Roosevelt, Franklin D., 445
Rostand, Edmond, 49
Rousseau, Henri, 12
Roussel, Raymond, 45, 48–51, 59, 157, 218, 264
Routchine, Hania, 142
Rucar, Georgette, 304, 324
Rucar, Jeanne, *see* Buñuel
Russolo, Luigi, 354

Sacher-Masoch, Leopold von, 384–5
Sacco, Madame, 252
Sacco, Nicola, 247

Sade, Marquis de (Donatien-Alphonse-François, comte de Sade): descendants, 331; influence on Ball, 105; influence on Breton, 218, 455; influence on Buñuel, 349–50, 396; influence on *Clarté*, 232; influence on Dalí, 360, 397; influence on Surrealism, 3, 34, 265, 395–6; manuscripts, 455; moralism, 41
Sadoul, Georges: Communist Party interrogation, 279; Kharkov congress, 270–5; love affair, 255; relationship with Elsa, 257–8; social life, 255–6
Sage, Kay, 438
Saint-Julien-le-Pauvre churchyard, 152
Sáinz de la Maza, Regino, 310
Salle Gaveau, 144–6, 155
Salmon, André, 137–8, 139
Salon Dada, 183
Salon des Indépendants, 47–8, 77, 139, 398
Sanger, Margaret, 56
Sanvoisin, Gaëtan, 355
Sartre, Jean-Paul, 16–17, 455–8
Satie, Erik, 9, 167, 186, 216
Schwartz, Arturo, 60, 174
Schwitters, Kurt, 112, 402–3
Second World War, *see* World War II
Sélavy, Rrose, 178–9, 203–5, 216
Serner, Walter, 162, 216
Shakespeare, William, 162
Shattuck, Roger, 41–2
Shaw, George Bernard, 291
SIC (Sons, Idées Couleurs), 9
Six, les, 136
Social Realism, 402

ACKNOWLEDGEMENTS

The author and publishers would like to express their gratitude to the following who have very kindly given their permission for the use of copyright materials: M. Christophe Tzara for permission to quote *Poem-Recipe* by Tristan Tzara; Mme. Christine Soupault for permission to quote Philippe Soupault's *poèmes-portraits* of Louis Aragon and André Breton; the Fundació Gala-Salvador Dalí for permission to quote from Salvador Dalí's correspondence; Colonial S.A. for permission to quote from *The Secret Life of Salvador Dalí*. Extract from *Oda a Salvador Dalí* by Federico García Lorca from *Obras Completas*, Galaxía Gutenberg, 1996 edition © Herederos de Federico García Lorca. Translation by Ruth Brandon, © Ruth Brandon and Herederos de Federico García Lorca. All rights reserved. For information regarding rights and permissions for works by Federico García Lorca, please contact William Peter Kosmas, Esq., 8 Franklin Square, London W14 9UU, England. Every effort has been made to trace all copyright holders, but if any have inadvertently been overlooked, the author and publishers will be pleased to make the necessary arrangements at the first opportunity.

527